R.A. SALVATORE

FORGOTTEN

EXILE

R.A. Salvatore
WRITER

Andrew Dabb
SCRIPT

Tim Seeley
PENCILS

John Lowe, Marco Galli, Dennis Crisostomo
Rob Atkins, Cory Hamscher, Robert Grabes,
Serge LaPointe, Rebekah Isaacs, Johnny Timmons,
Shaun Beaudry, Alex McCaffrey
INKS

Blond
COLORS

Brian J. Crowley, Steve Seeley
LETTERS

Mark Powers
EDITOR

DEVIL'S DUE PUBLISHING

ash Blaylock RESIDENT	**Michael O'Sullivan** SENIOR EDITOR	**Evan Sult** ART DIRECTOR	**Caitlin McKay** WEBSTORE MANAGER
am Wells SSISTANT PUBLISHER	**Crank!** COMPUTER OPERATIONS	**Sean Dove** GRAPHIC DESIGNER	
usan Bishop P MARKETING	**Tim Seeley** STAFF ARTIST	**Brian J. Crowley** STAFF LETTERER	**Kunoichi Ad Sales** 773-321-8478

Licensed by:

 Hasbro Properties Group

 OFFICIAL LICENSED PRODUCT

 DDP

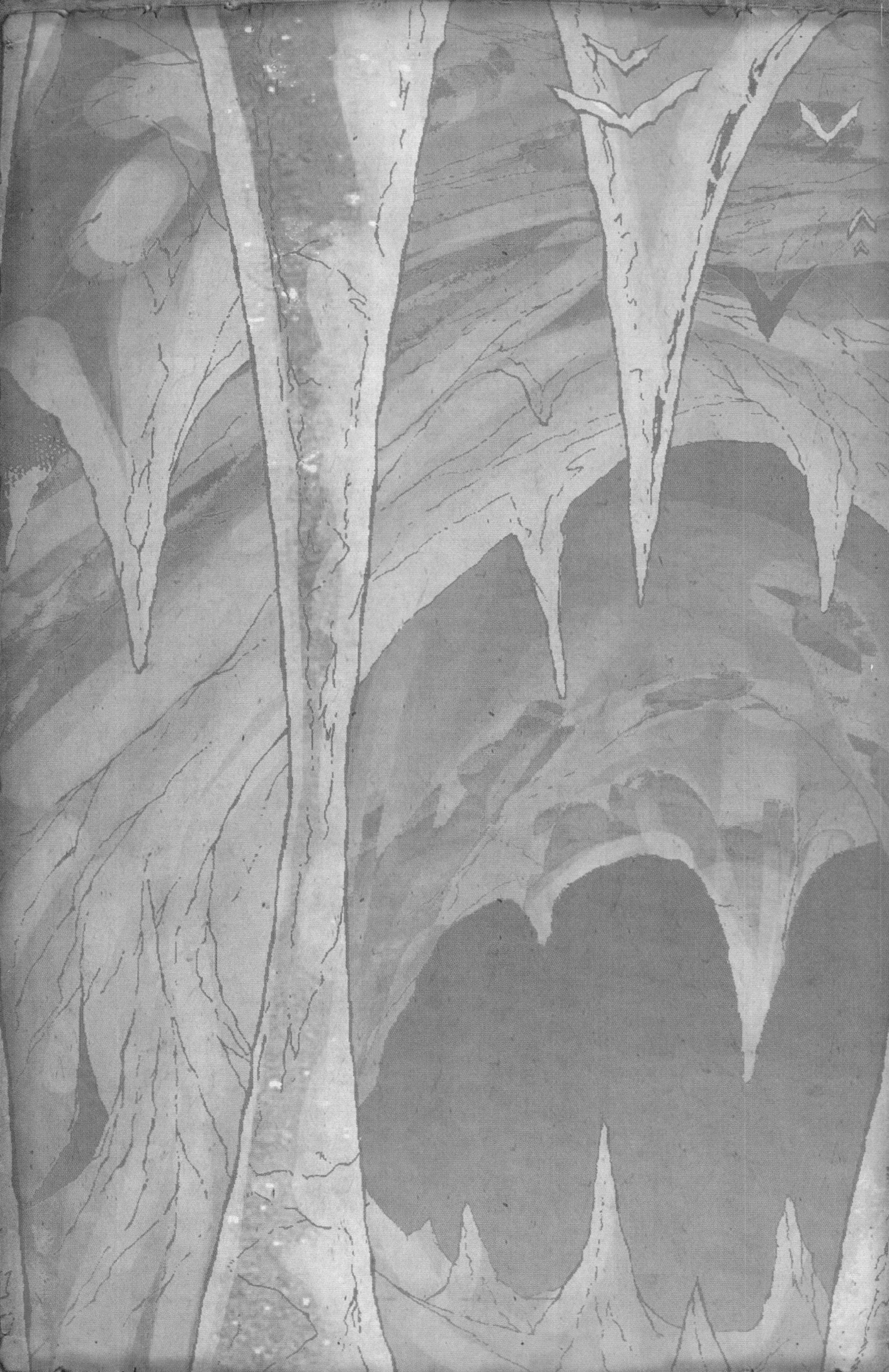

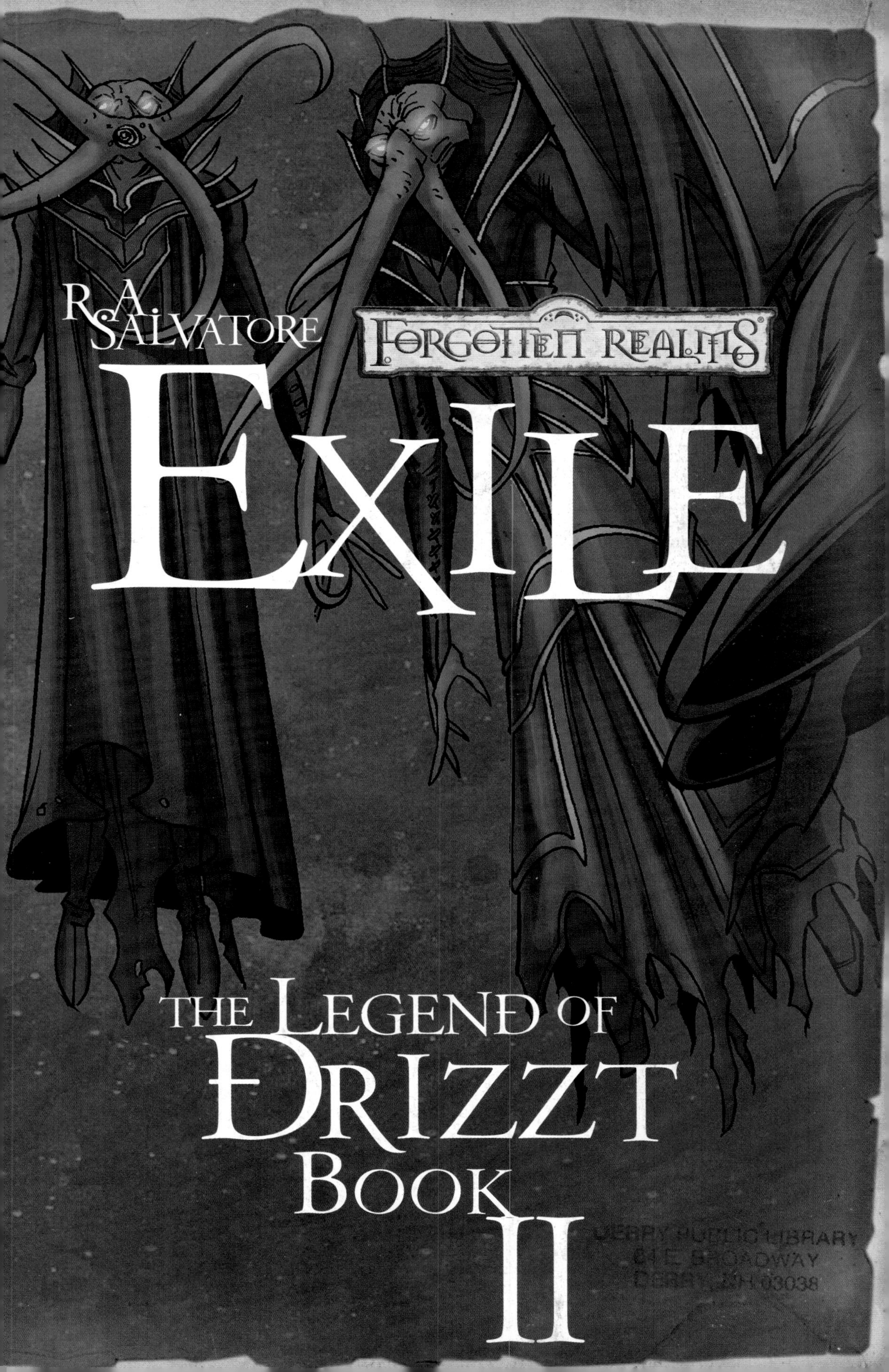
R.A. SALVATORE
FORGOTTEN REALMS®
EXILE
THE LEGEND OF DRIZZT
BOOK II

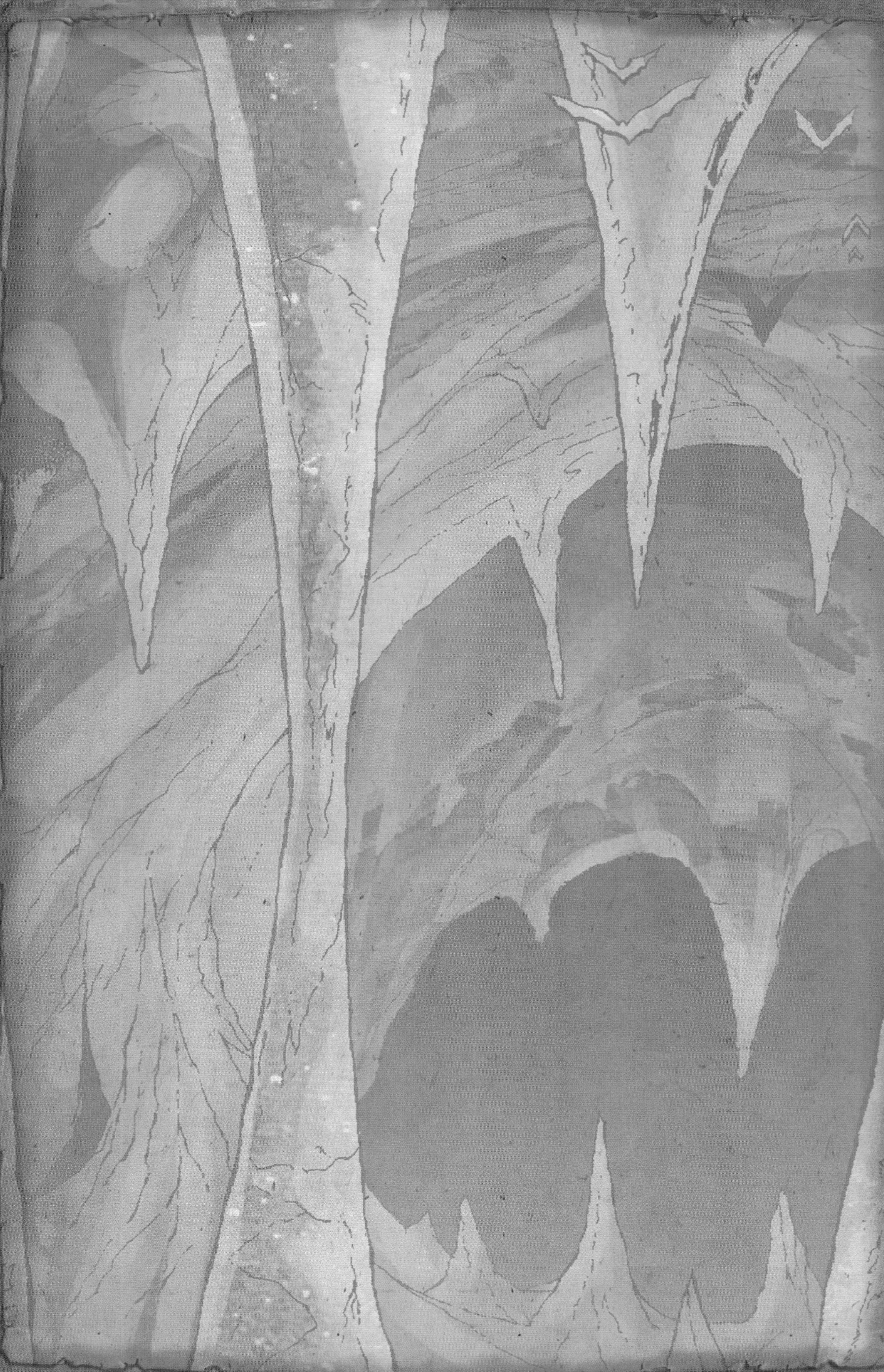

Foreword

ALMOST FORTY YEARS AGO NOW (yes, before there was a *Dungeons & Dragons® Game*), I started to create something called The Forgotten Realms. From the very first, it had an Underdark, though I called that vast and perilous subterranean world "the Realms Below" or (the dwarven term) "the Deep Realms." The Realms Below always had glows: magical radiations (that made mosses, lichens, and myconids grow with incredible speed) and fungi. And it had its lurking monsters. It even had (dead-pearly-white-skinned) evil elves, jaded and sophisticated—pointy-eared Borgias, if you will. Then came the *D&D®* game, and the classic series of adventures later collected and updated as *Queen of the Spiders,* that gave us obsidian-skinned, matriarchal, Lolth (or Lloth)-worshipping "Drow." And then came Drizzt Do'Urden, springing to vivid life from the pen of Bob Salvatore, and very soon the classic novel *Homeland,* that spread before us all the full dark glory of Menzoberranzan: Zaknafein, Matron Malice, House Baenrae, the entire fell city. It was alive. And as I've often said, the Forgotten Realms isn't places: it's people. People who live and breathe and come alive for the reader, even if they have scaly skins or pointed ears or revoltingly strange bodies and minds. Bob Salvatore has not only given fantasy a classic character in Drizzt, he's given us a line of great novels, some of them worthy of standing among the very best fantasy stories of all time, and every last one of them a gripping read. You hold in your hands a comic-book adaptation of one of Bob's most powerful tomes, *Exile,* the middle book of his classic Dark Elf trilogy, telling of Drizzt's youth and departure from Menzoberranzan. I had great fun crafting much of the *Menzoberranzan* boxed set for the *D&D®* game, and feel like I know its caverns and the Underdark around it. I'm also the guy who dreamed up the world above and around Lolth's dark city in the first place, so I'm a hard guy to please. Like Bob, I worry about someone tackling a great part of the Realms and "blowing it." I'm also a longtime comics fan. (How long? Well, monthly books had just gone up to 12 cents each when I started haunting the stands and shops. Yes, my beard is white.) I love comics.

Good comics, that is. Just as movies are a different medium than prose books (and so film adaptations of favorite books can be tricky; I'm sure we can all list pet horrors that "graced" the silver screen), comics are a different medium than prose books. It can be really hard to adapt a novel in a satisfying, successful way. And just as different actors doing the same Shakespeare play or different bands covering the same classic tune will take differing approaches that some folks will love and some folks will hate, not everyone will love every comics version of everything. (Boy, that's news, eh?) Myself, I was worried about bad art, about more than half the book hitting the cutting room floor to leave just frantic action scenes, and even that the Underdark and all that jet-black drow skin would collectively be too darned dark for my aging eyes to see what was going on.

I needn't have worried.

This is beautiful. Andrew Dabb, Tim Seeley, Mark Powers, everyone at Devil's Due: great job. Just like your take on *Homeland* (yes, I bought it, issue by issue: I'm not just the creator of the Realms, I'm its biggest fan!), the art is lovely, the storytelling moves and is elegantly spare, and the characters come alive. Er, until they die. The preceding joke is the only lame moment in this entire book you're holding. No, don't thank me. Really. I hope you'll join me in praising and thanking the Devil's Due team. I was wrong about everything I worried about (oh, except maybe the frantic action scenes: you did pack a lot of frantic action scenes into your adaptation), and I eagerly await *Sojourn.*

So to join the thumbs up I gave Bob a long time ago, here's another thumb. That's two thumbs, way, way—but no, I seem to have heard someone else saying that a time or ten, about movies. So I'll say it my way: Elminster approves, and Ed says thank you.

Can't wait for the next one.

—Ed Greenwood—

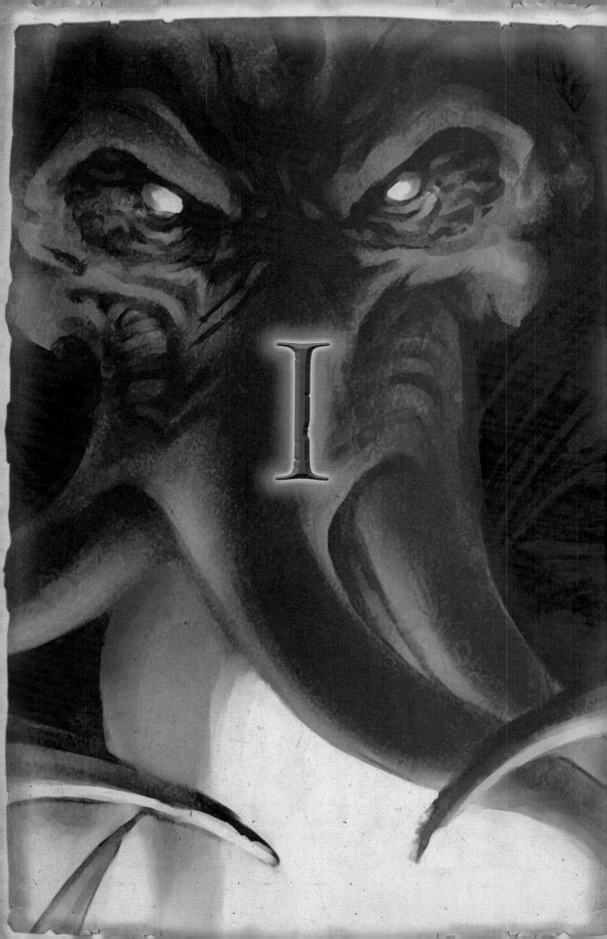

I

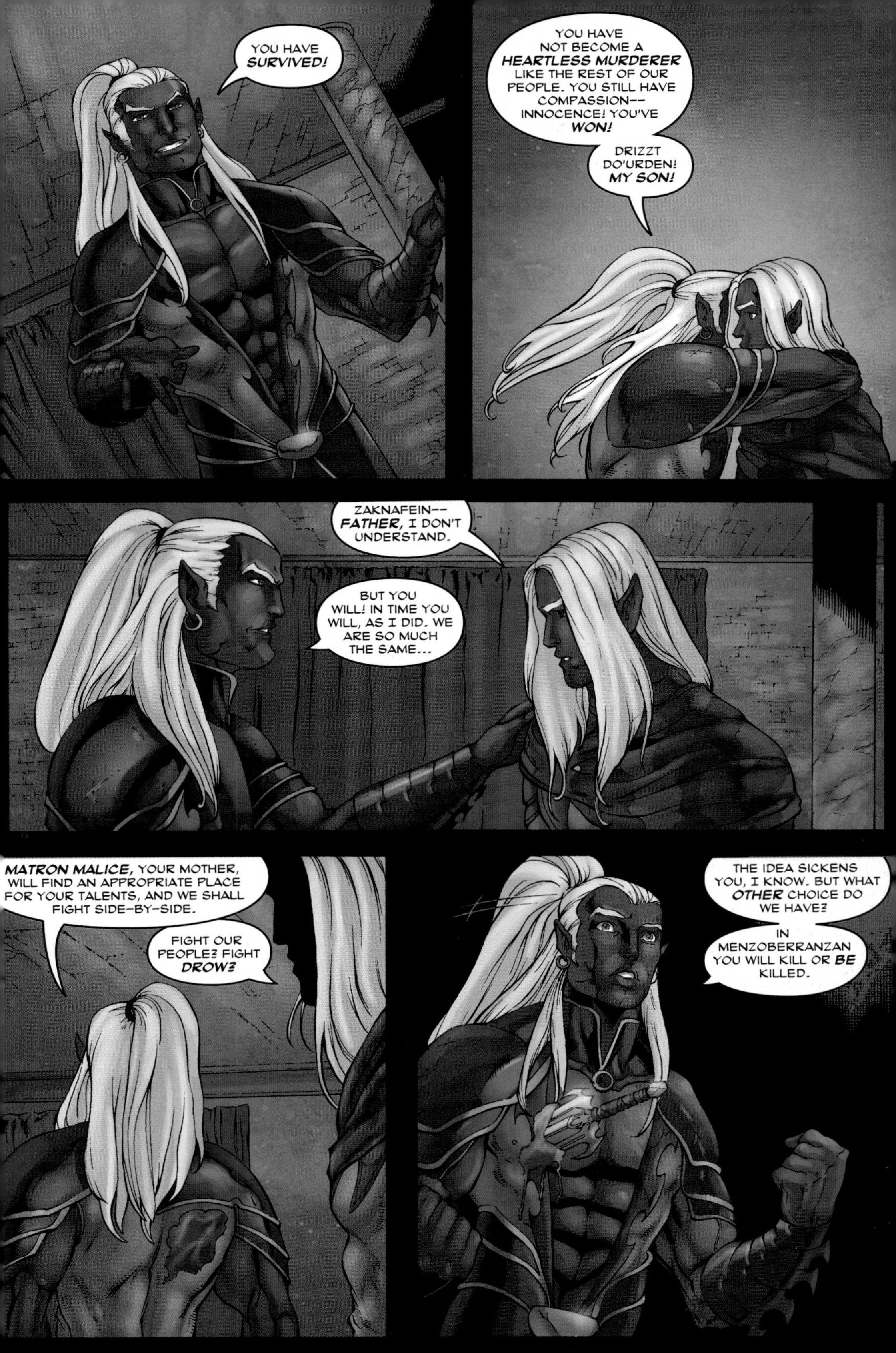
YOU HAVE SURVIVED!
YOU HAVE NOT BECOME A HEARTLESS MURDERER LIKE THE REST OF OUR PEOPLE. YOU STILL HAVE COMPASSION-- INNOCENCE! YOU'VE WON!
DRIZZT DO'URDEN! MY SON!
ZAKNAFEIN-- FATHER, I DON'T UNDERSTAND.
BUT YOU WILL! IN TIME YOU WILL, AS I DID. WE ARE SO MUCH THE SAME...
MATRON MALICE, YOUR MOTHER, WILL FIND AN APPROPRIATE PLACE FOR YOUR TALENTS, AND WE SHALL FIGHT SIDE-BY-SIDE.
FIGHT OUR PEOPLE? FIGHT DROW?
THE IDEA SICKENS YOU, I KNOW. BUT WHAT OTHER CHOICE DO WE HAVE?
IN MENZOBERRANZAN YOU WILL KILL OR BE KILLED.

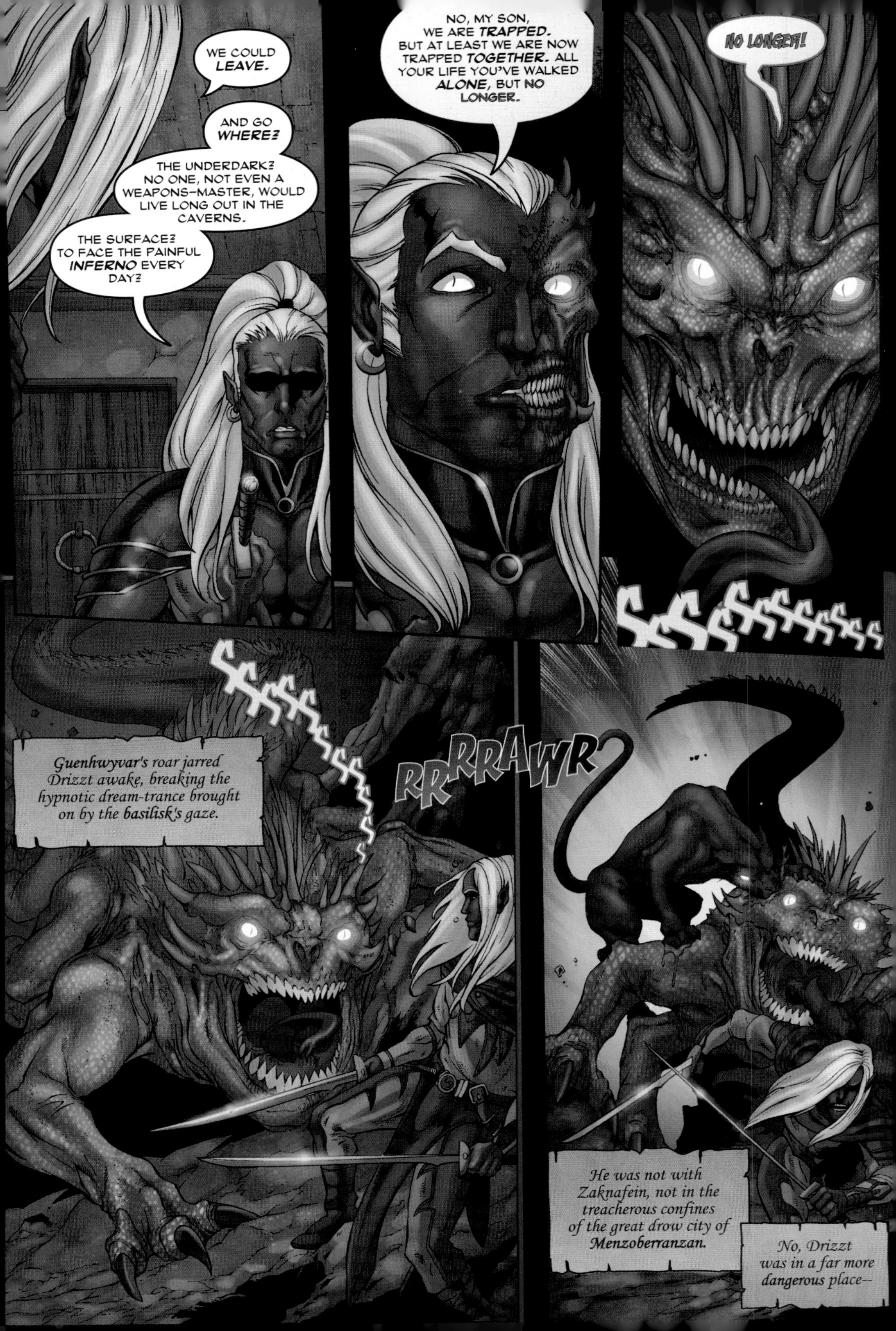
WE COULD LEAVE.
AND GO WHERE?
THE UNDERDARK? NO ONE, NOT EVEN A WEAPONS-MASTER, WOULD LIVE LONG OUT IN THE CAVERNS.
THE SURFACE? TO FACE THE PAINFUL INFERNO EVERY DAY?
NO, MY SON, WE ARE TRAPPED. BUT AT LEAST WE ARE NOW TRAPPED TOGETHER. ALL YOUR LIFE YOU'VE WALKED ALONE, BUT NO LONGER.
NO LONGER!
SSSSSSSSSSSS
Guenhwyvar's roar jarred Drizzt awake, breaking the hypnotic dream-trance brought on by the basilisk's gaze.
SSSSSSSSSSSSS
RRRRAWR
He was not with Zaknafein, not in the treacherous confines of the great drow city of Menzoberranzan.
No, Drizzt was in a far more dangerous place--

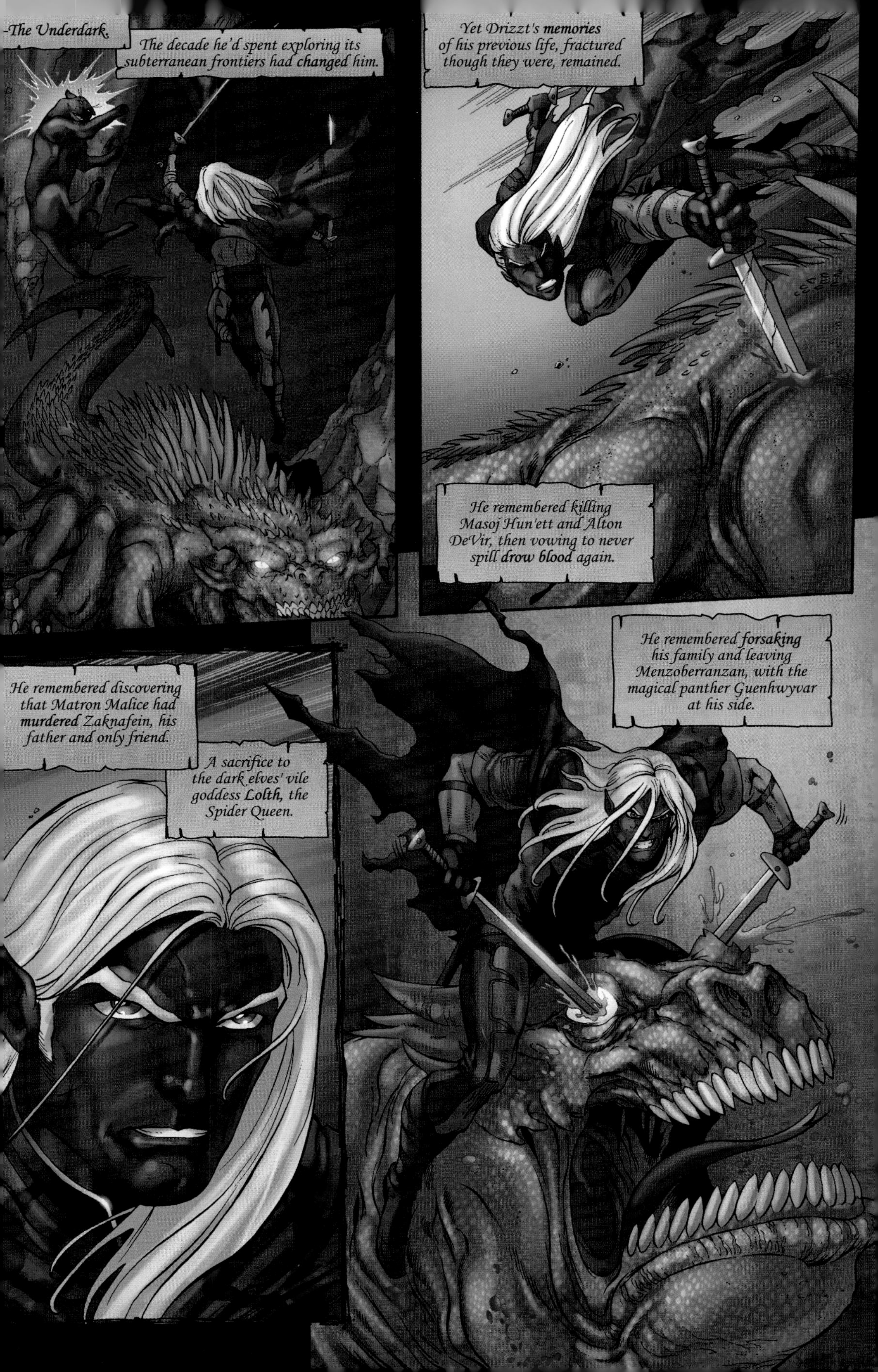

-The Underdark.
The decade he'd spent exploring its subterranean frontiers had changed him.
Yet Drizzt's memories of his previous life, fractured though they were, remained.
He remembered killing Masoj Hun'ett and Alton DeVir, then vowing to never spill drow blood again.
He remembered discovering that Matron Malice had murdered Zaknafein, his father and only friend.
A sacrifice to the dark elves' vile goddess Lolth, the Spider Queen.
He remembered forsaking his family and leaving Menzoberranzan, with the magical panther Guenhwyvar at his side.

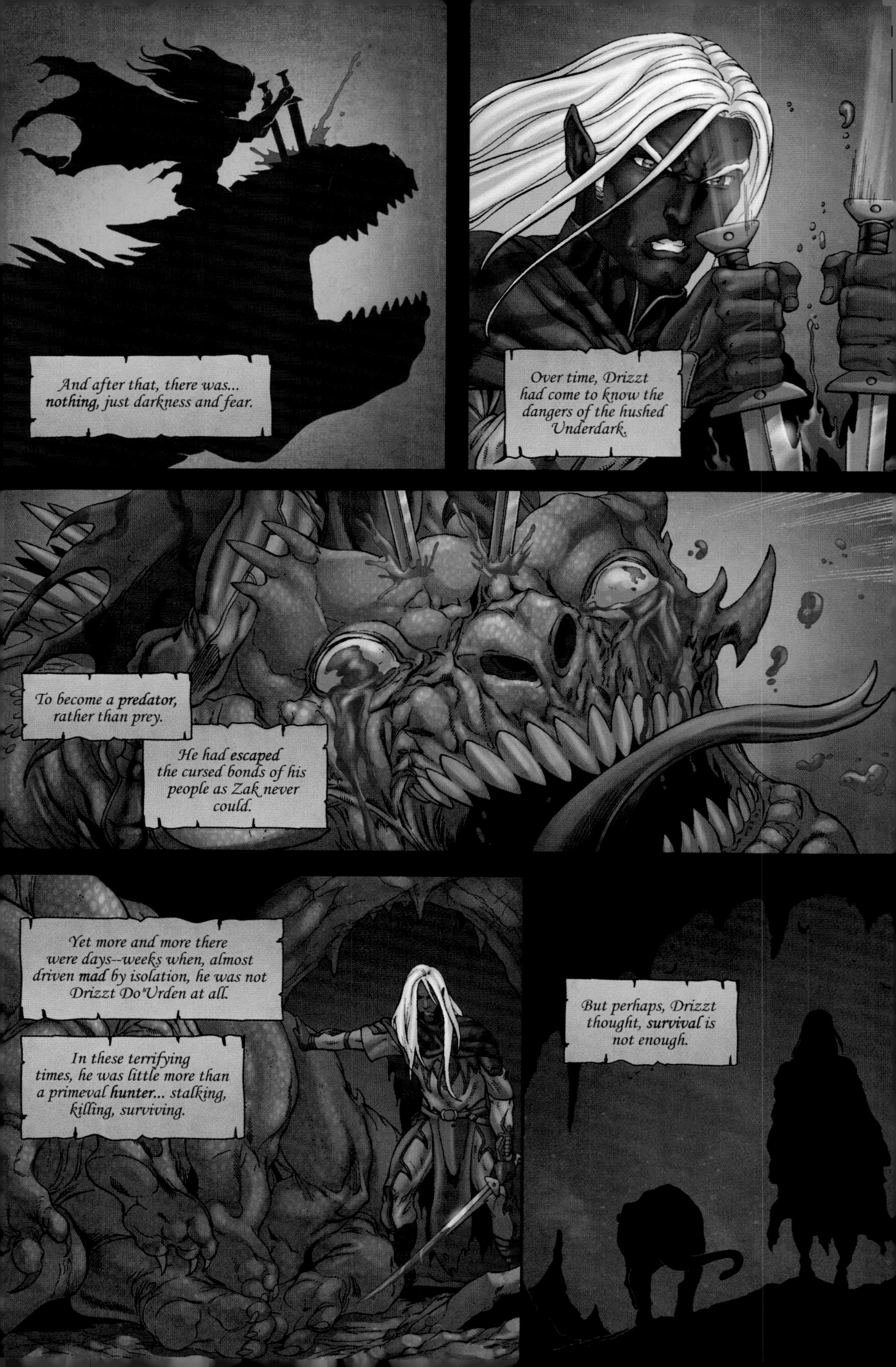
And after that, there was... nothing, just darkness and fear.
Over time, Drizzt had come to know the dangers of the hushed Underdark.
To become a predator, rather than prey.
He had escaped the cursed bonds of his people as Zak never could.
Yet more and more there were days--weeks when, almost driven mad by isolation, he was not Drizzt Do'Urden at all.
In these terrifying times, he was little more than a primeval hunter... stalking, killing, surviving.
But perhaps, Drizzt thought, survival is not enough.

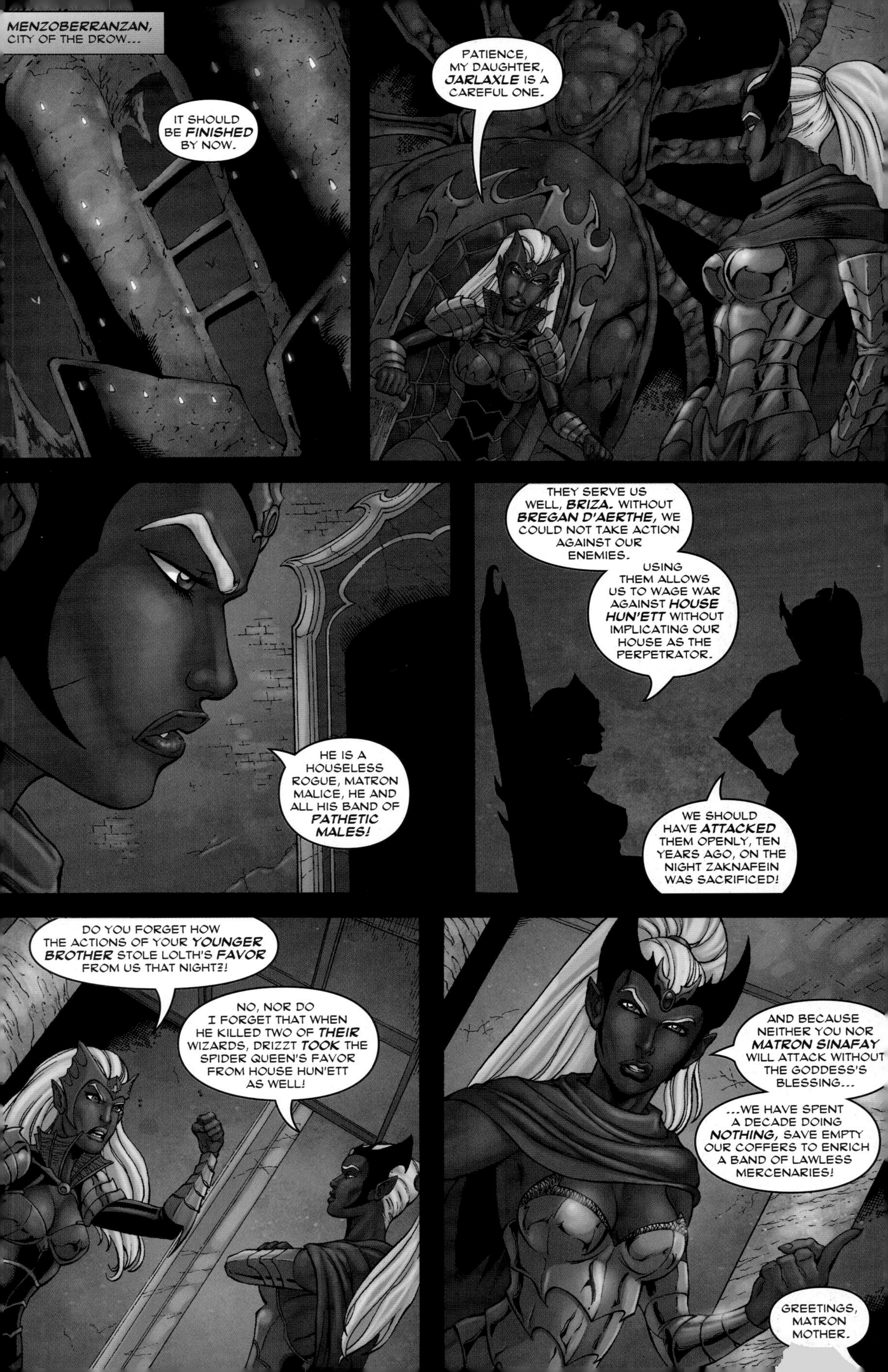
MENZOBERRANZAN, CITY OF THE DROW...
IT SHOULD BE FINISHED BY NOW.
PATIENCE, MY DAUGHTER, JARLAXLE IS A CAREFUL ONE.
HE IS A HOUSELESS ROGUE, MATRON MALICE, HE AND ALL HIS BAND OF PATHETIC MALES!
THEY SERVE US WELL, BRIZA. WITHOUT BREGAN D'AERTHE, WE COULD NOT TAKE ACTION AGAINST OUR ENEMIES.
USING THEM ALLOWS US TO WAGE WAR AGAINST HOUSE HUN'ETT WITHOUT IMPLICATING OUR HOUSE AS THE PERPETRATOR.
WE SHOULD HAVE ATTACKED THEM OPENLY, TEN YEARS AGO, ON THE NIGHT ZAKNAFEIN WAS SACRIFICED!
DO YOU FORGET HOW THE ACTIONS OF YOUR YOUNGER BROTHER STOLE LOLTH'S FAVOR FROM US THAT NIGHT?!
NO, NOR DO I FORGET THAT WHEN HE KILLED TWO OF THEIR WIZARDS, DRIZZT TOOK THE SPIDER QUEEN'S FAVOR FROM HOUSE HUN'ETT AS WELL!
AND BECAUSE NEITHER YOU NOR MATRON SINAFAY WILL ATTACK WITHOUT THE GODDESS'S BLESSING...
...WE HAVE SPENT A DECADE DOING NOTHING, SAVE EMPTY OUR COFFERS TO ENRICH A BAND OF LAWLESS MERCENARIES!
GREETINGS, MATRON MOTHER.

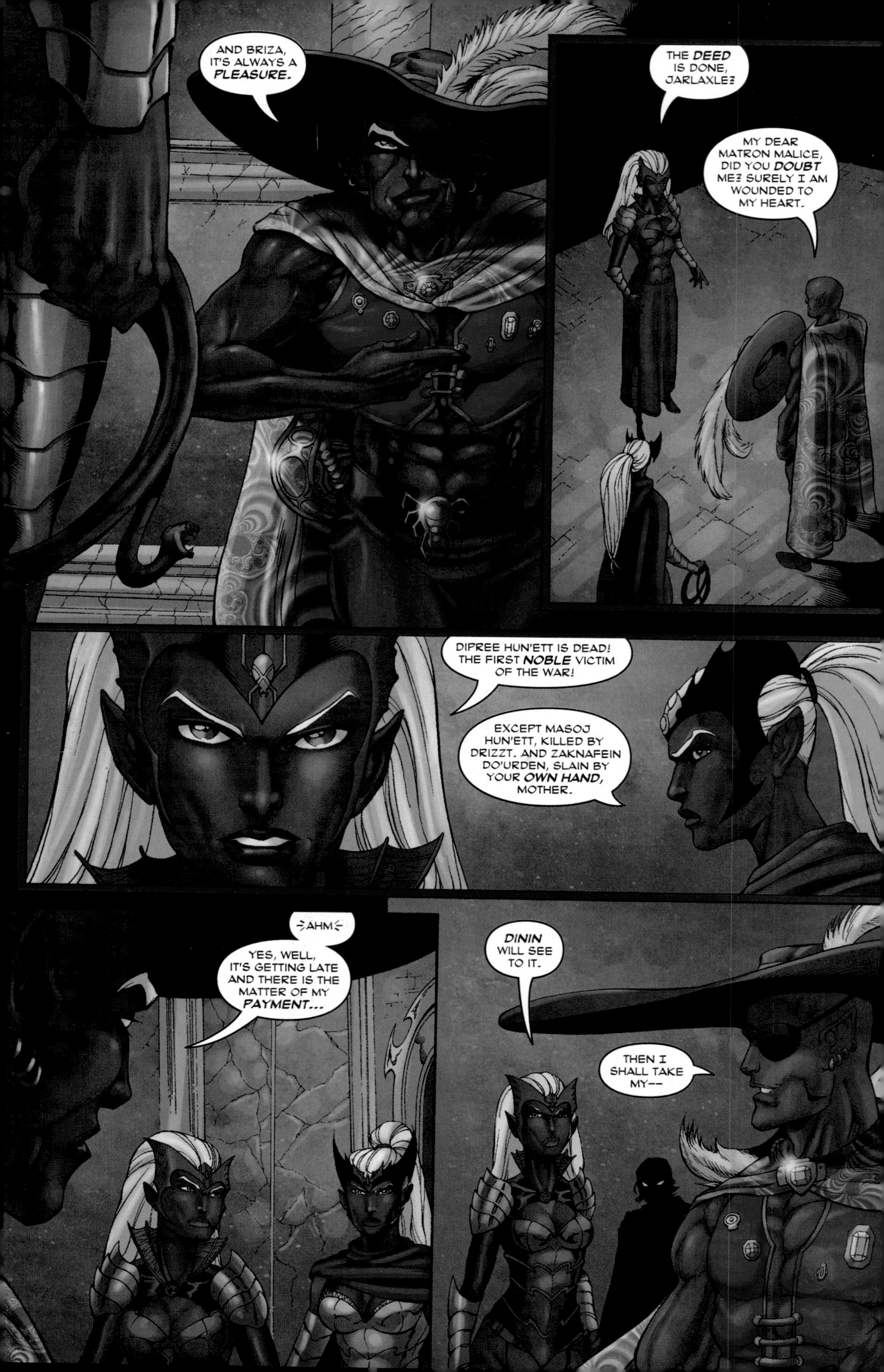
AND BRIZA, IT'S ALWAYS A PLEASURE.
THE DEED IS DONE, JARLAXLE?
MY DEAR MATRON MALICE, DID YOU DOUBT ME? SURELY I AM WOUNDED TO MY HEART.
DIPREE HUN'ETT IS DEAD! THE FIRST NOBLE VICTIM OF THE WAR!
EXCEPT MASOJ HUN'ETT, KILLED BY DRIZZT. AND ZAKNAFEIN DO'URDEN, SLAIN BY YOUR OWN HAND, MOTHER.
AHM
YES, WELL, IT'S GETTING LATE AND THERE IS THE MATTER OF MY PAYMENT...
DININ WILL SEE TO IT.
THEN I SHALL TAKE MY--

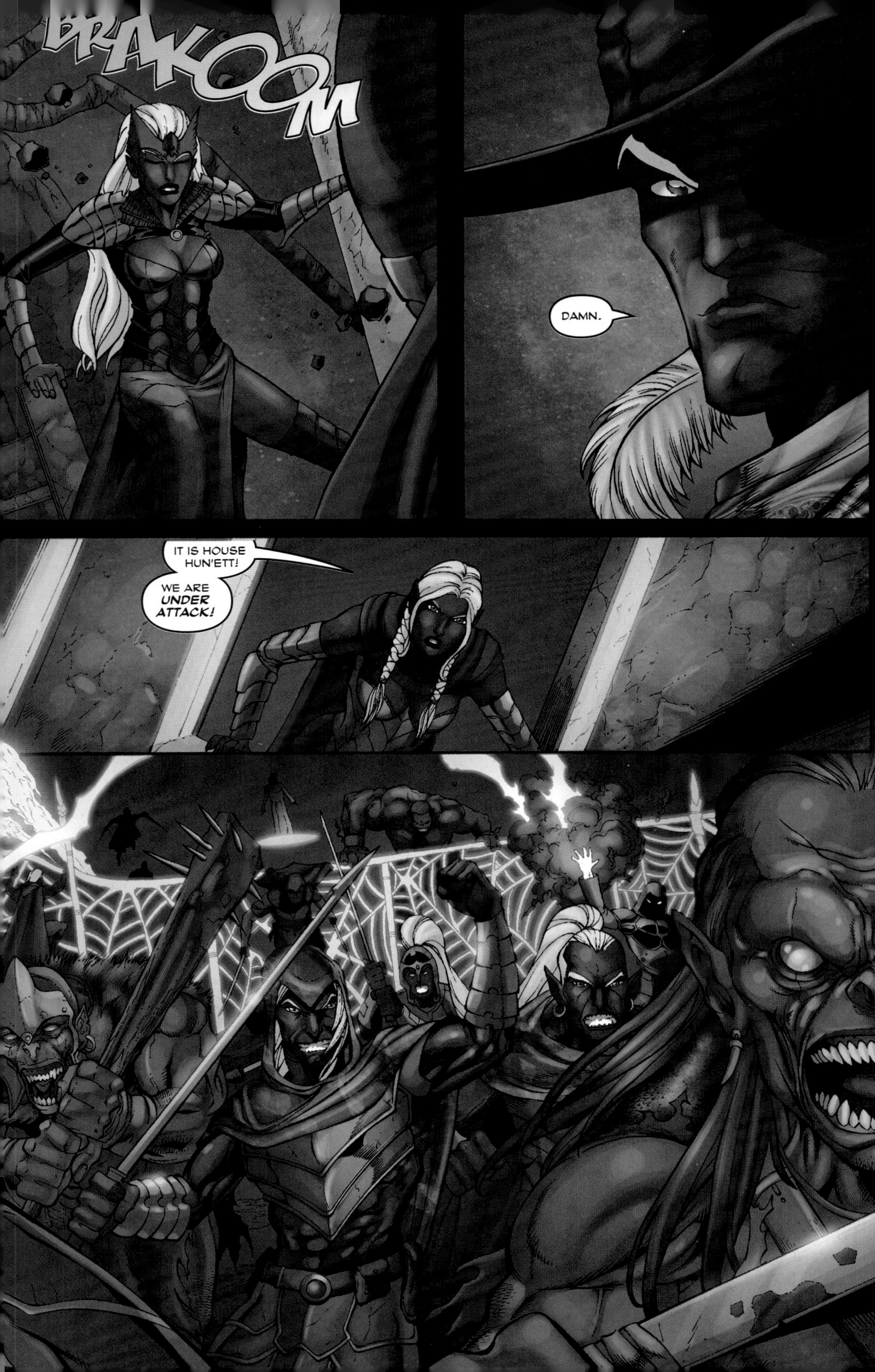
BRAKOOOM
DAMN.
IT IS HOUSE HUN'ETT!
WE ARE UNDER ATTACK!

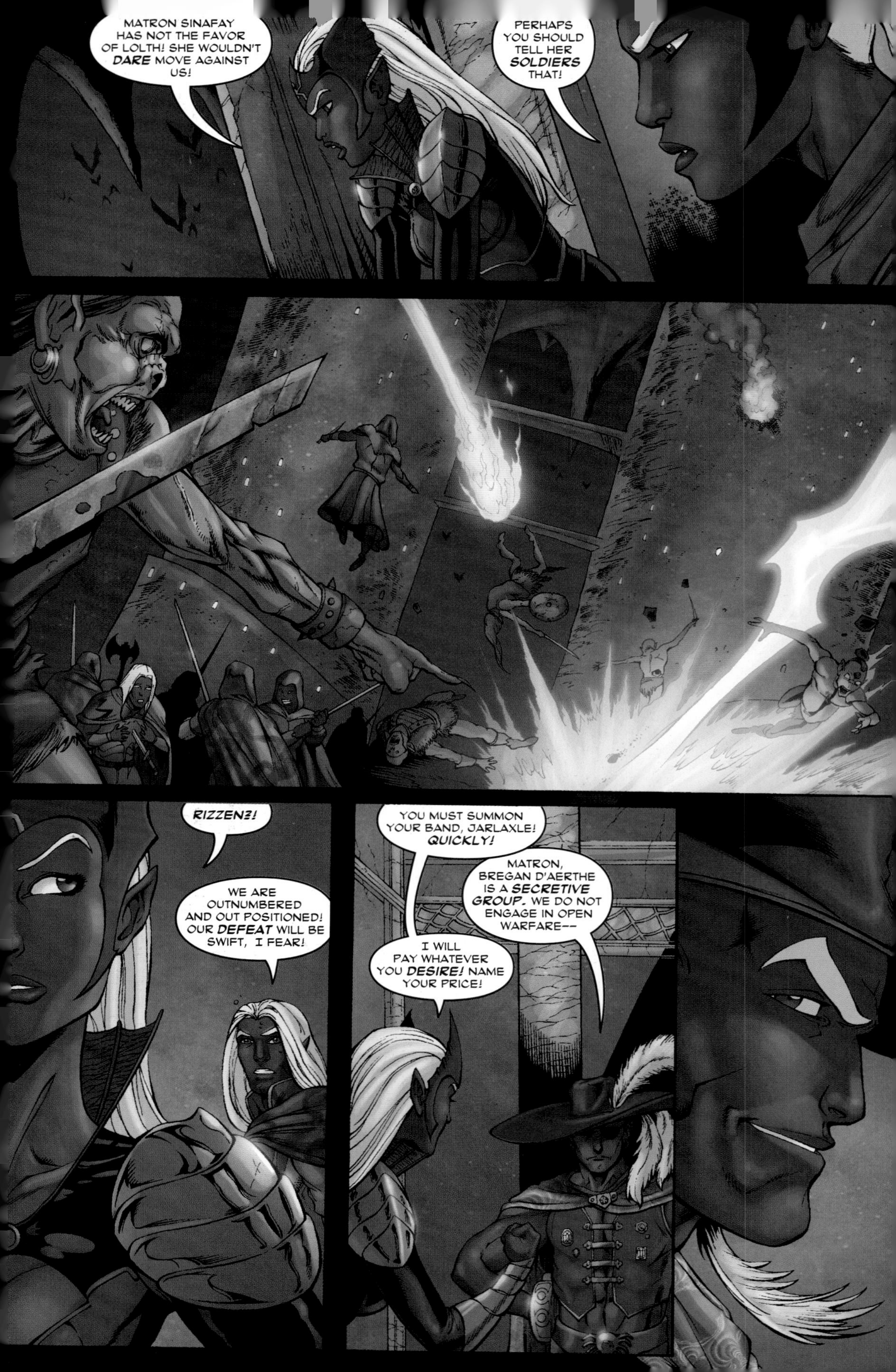
MATRON SINAFAY HAS NOT THE FAVOR OF LOLTH! SHE WOULDN'T DARE MOVE AGAINST US!
PERHAPS YOU SHOULD TELL HER SOLDIERS THAT!
RIZZEN?!
WE ARE OUTNUMBERED AND OUT POSITIONED! OUR DEFEAT WILL BE SWIFT, I FEAR!
YOU MUST SUMMON YOUR BAND, JARLAXLE! QUICKLY!
MATRON, BREGAN D'AERTHE IS A SECRETIVE GROUP. WE DO NOT ENGAGE IN OPEN WARFARE--
I WILL PAY WHATEVER YOU DESIRE! NAME YOUR PRICE!

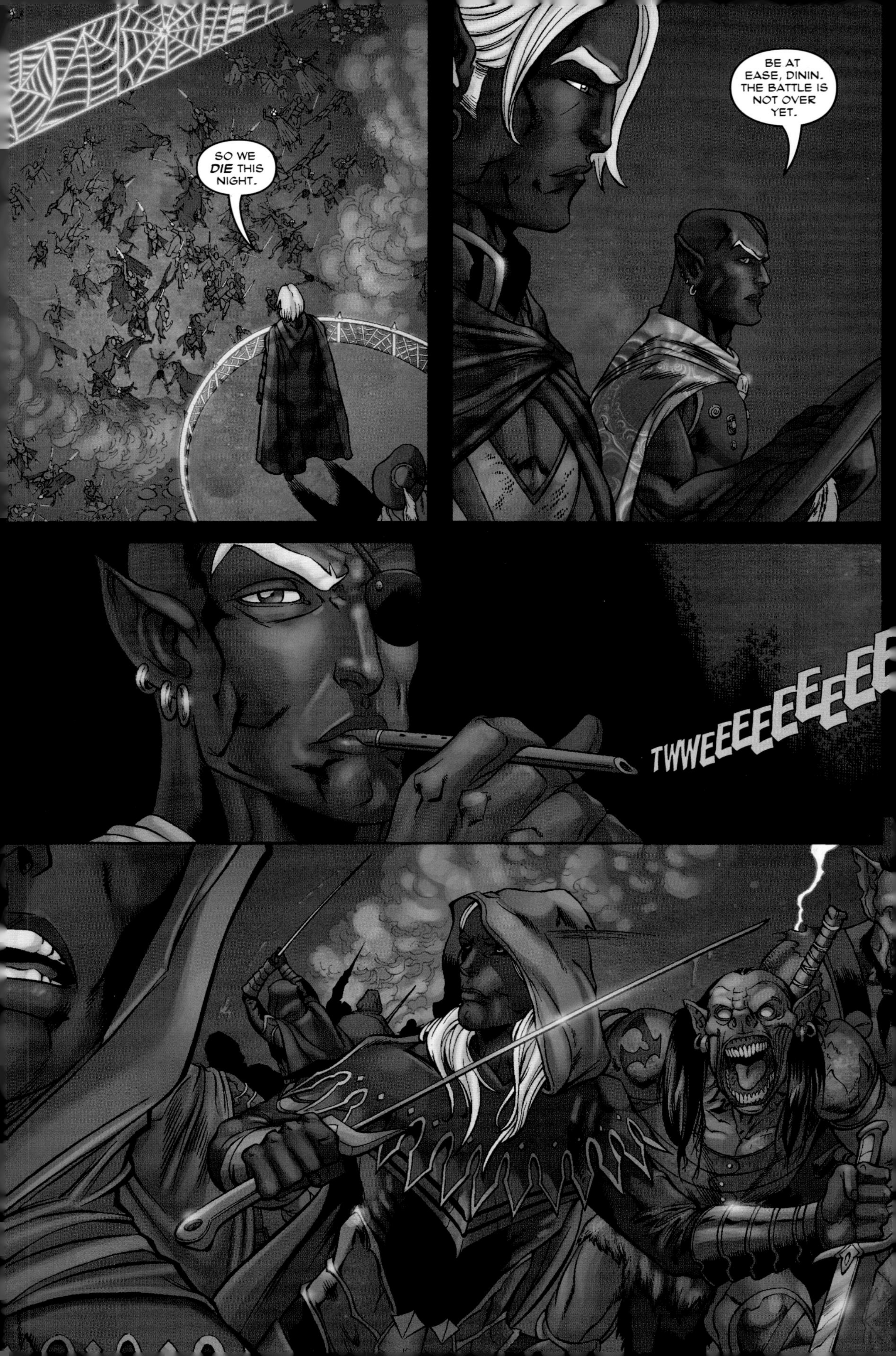
SO WE *DIE* THIS NIGHT.
BE AT EASE, DININ. THE BATTLE IS NOT OVER YET.
TWWEEEEEEEEEE

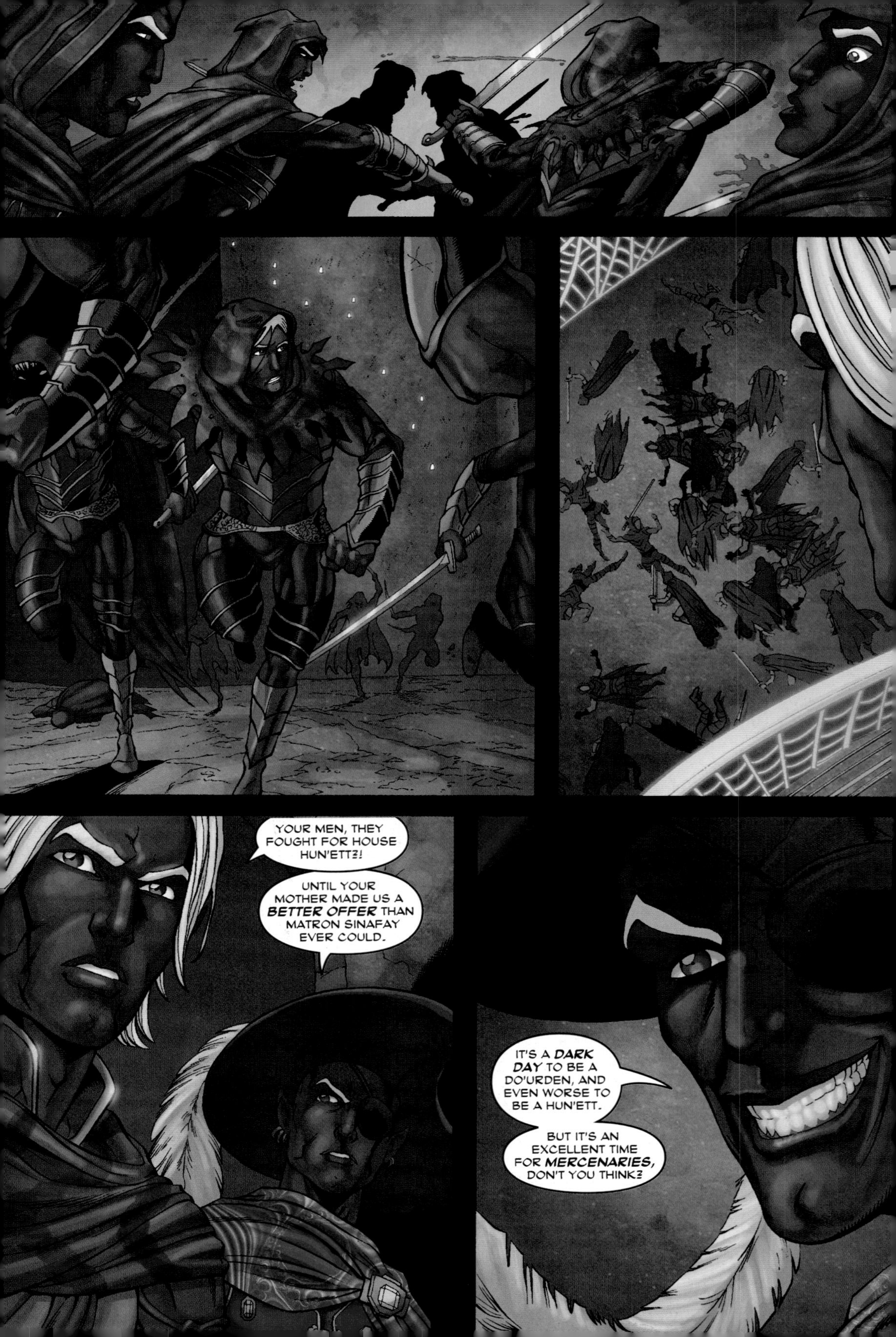
YOUR MEN, THEY FOUGHT FOR HOUSE HUN'ETT?!
UNTIL YOUR MOTHER MADE US A BETTER OFFER THAN MATRON SINAFAY EVER COULD.
IT'S A DARK DAY TO BE A DO'URDEN, AND EVEN WORSE TO BE A HUN'ETT.
BUT IT'S AN EXCELLENT TIME FOR MERCENARIES, DON'T YOU THINK?

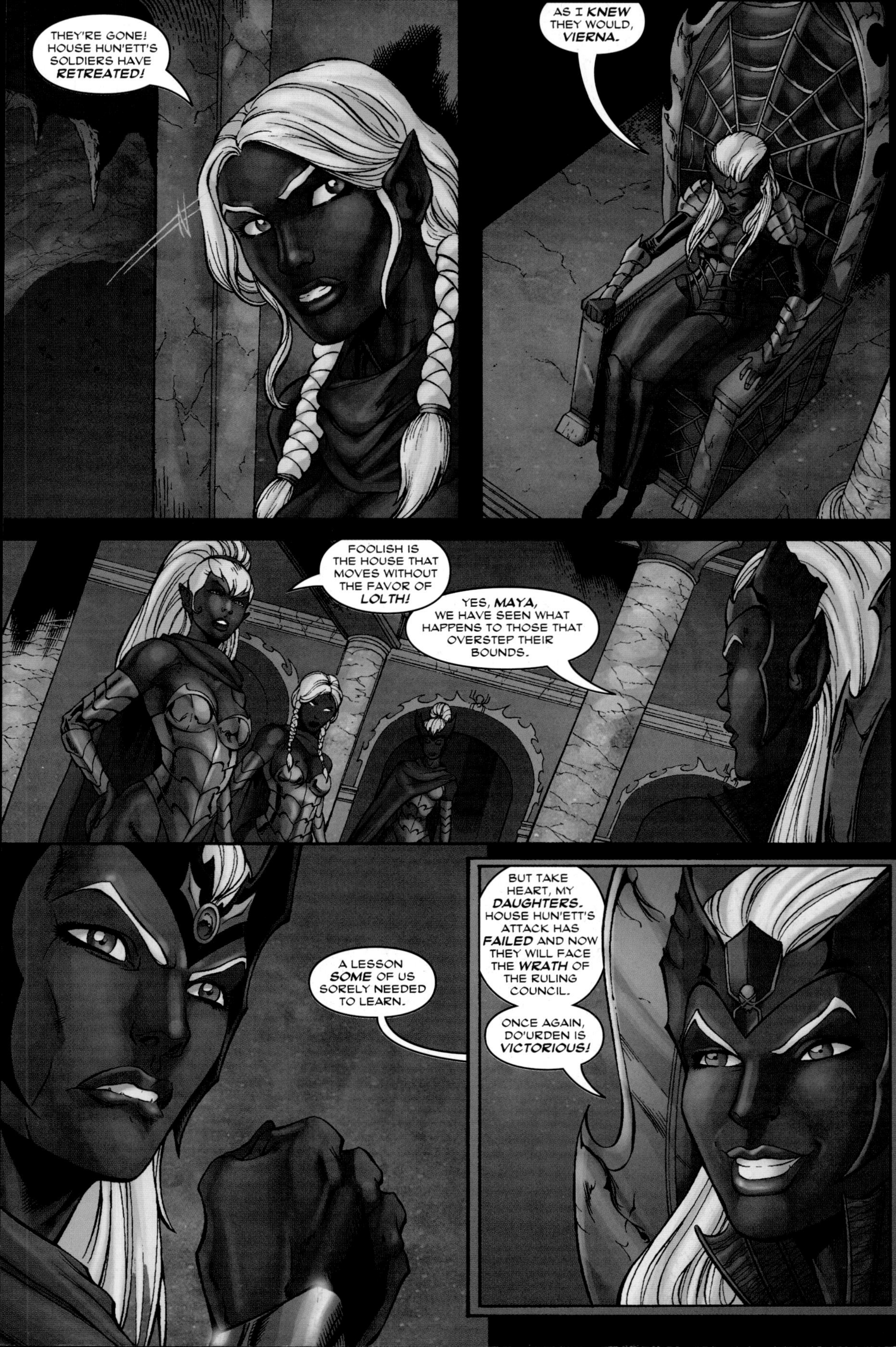
THEY'RE GONE! HOUSE HUN'ETT'S SOLDIERS HAVE RETREATED!
AS I KNEW THEY WOULD, VIERNA.
FOOLISH IS THE HOUSE THAT MOVES WITHOUT THE FAVOR OF LOLTH!
YES, MAYA, WE HAVE SEEN WHAT HAPPENS TO THOSE THAT OVERSTEP THEIR BOUNDS.
A LESSON SOME OF US SORELY NEEDED TO LEARN.
BUT TAKE HEART, MY DAUGHTERS. HOUSE HUN'ETT'S ATTACK HAS FAILED AND NOW THEY WILL FACE THE WRATH OF THE RULING COUNCIL.
ONCE AGAIN, DO'URDEN IS VICTORIOUS!

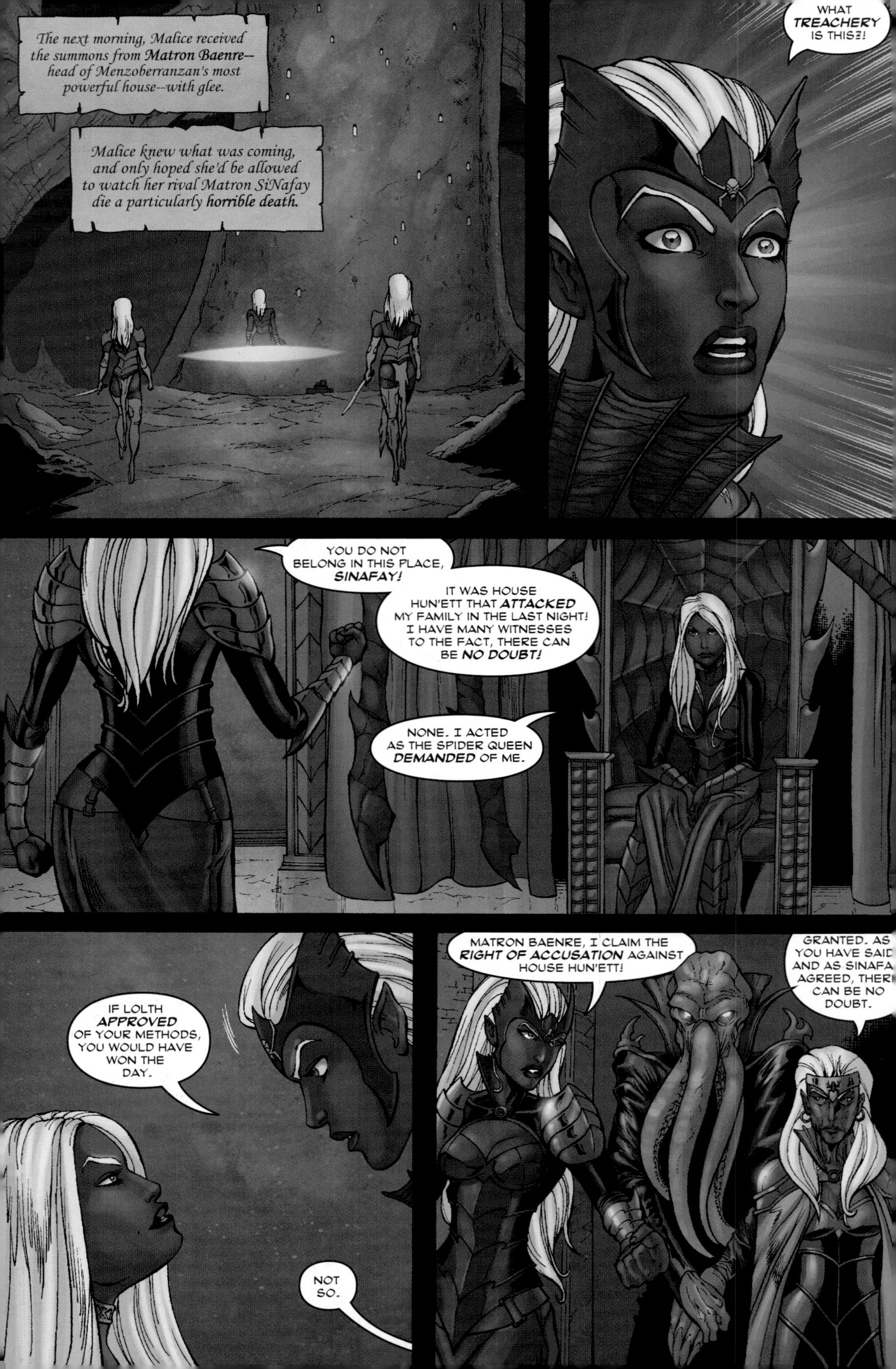

The next morning, Malice received the summons from Matron Baenre--head of Menzoberranzan's most powerful house--with glee.
Malice knew what was coming, and only hoped she'd be allowed to watch her rival Matron SiNafay die a particularly horrible death.
WHAT TREACHERY IS THIS?!
YOU DO NOT BELONG IN THIS PLACE, SINAFAY!
IT WAS HOUSE HUN'ETT THAT ATTACKED MY FAMILY IN THE LAST NIGHT! I HAVE MANY WITNESSES TO THE FACT, THERE CAN BE NO DOUBT!
NONE. I ACTED AS THE SPIDER QUEEN DEMANDED OF ME.
IF LOLTH APPROVED OF YOUR METHODS, YOU WOULD HAVE WON THE DAY.
NOT SO.
MATRON BAENRE, I CLAIM THE RIGHT OF ACCUSATION AGAINST HOUSE HUN'ETT!
GRANTED. AS YOU HAVE SAID AND AS SINAFA AGREED, THER CAN BE NO DOUBT.

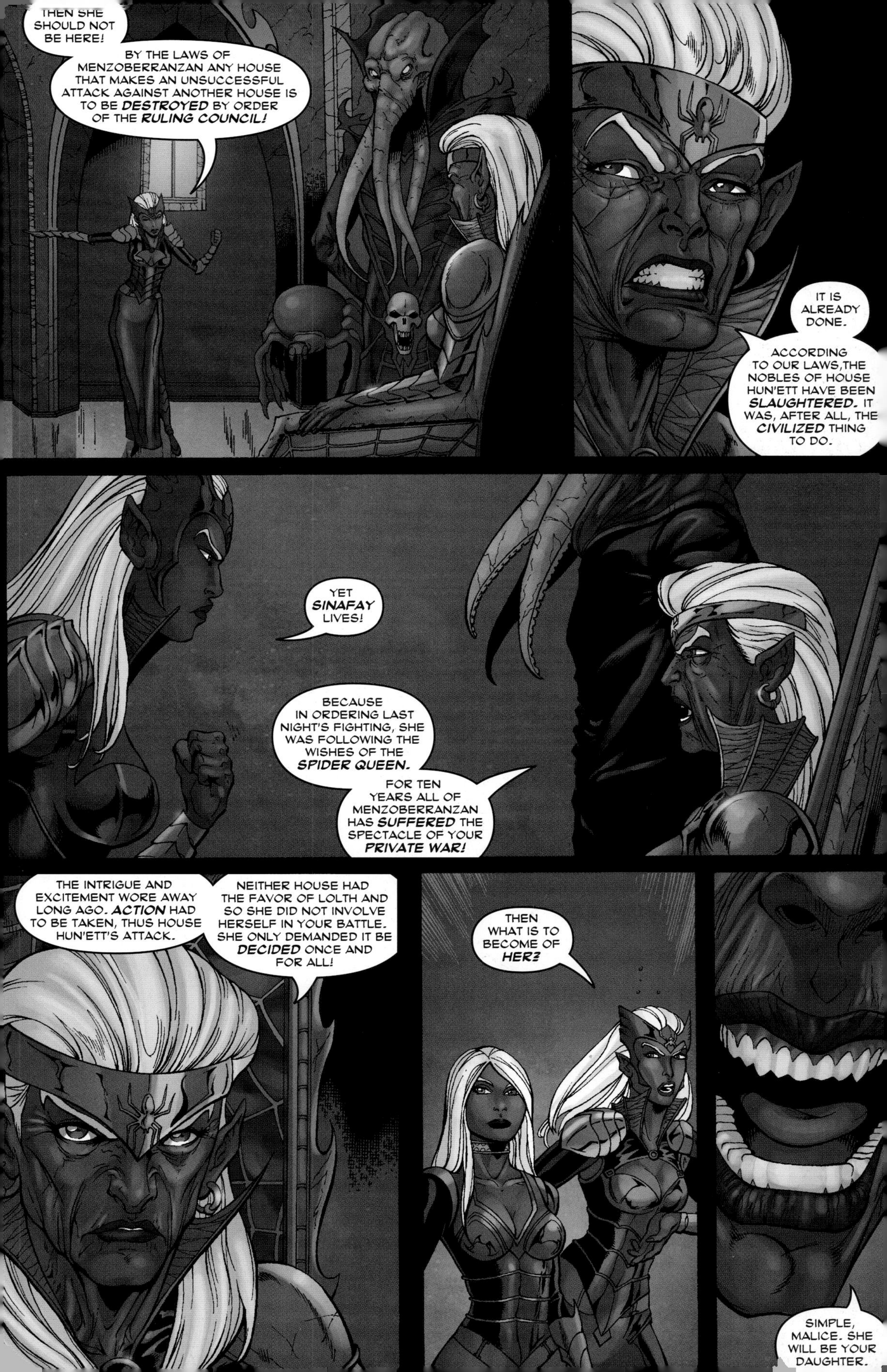
THEN SHE SHOULD NOT BE HERE!
BY THE LAWS OF MENZOBERRANZAN ANY HOUSE THAT MAKES AN UNSUCCESSFUL ATTACK AGAINST ANOTHER HOUSE IS TO BE DESTROYED BY ORDER OF THE RULING COUNCIL!
IT IS ALREADY DONE.
ACCORDING TO OUR LAWS, THE NOBLES OF HOUSE HUN'ETT HAVE BEEN SLAUGHTERED. IT WAS, AFTER ALL, THE CIVILIZED THING TO DO.
YET SINAFAY LIVES!
BECAUSE IN ORDERING LAST NIGHT'S FIGHTING, SHE WAS FOLLOWING THE WISHES OF THE SPIDER QUEEN.
FOR TEN YEARS ALL OF MENZOBERRANZAN HAS SUFFERED THE SPECTACLE OF YOUR PRIVATE WAR!
THE INTRIGUE AND EXCITEMENT WORE AWAY LONG AGO. ACTION HAD TO BE TAKEN, THUS HOUSE HUN'ETT'S ATTACK.
NEITHER HOUSE HAD THE FAVOR OF LOLTH AND SO SHE DID NOT INVOLVE HERSELF IN YOUR BATTLE. SHE ONLY DEMANDED IT BE DECIDED ONCE AND FOR ALL!
THEN WHAT IS TO BECOME OF HER?
SIMPLE, MALICE. SHE WILL BE YOUR DAUGHTER.

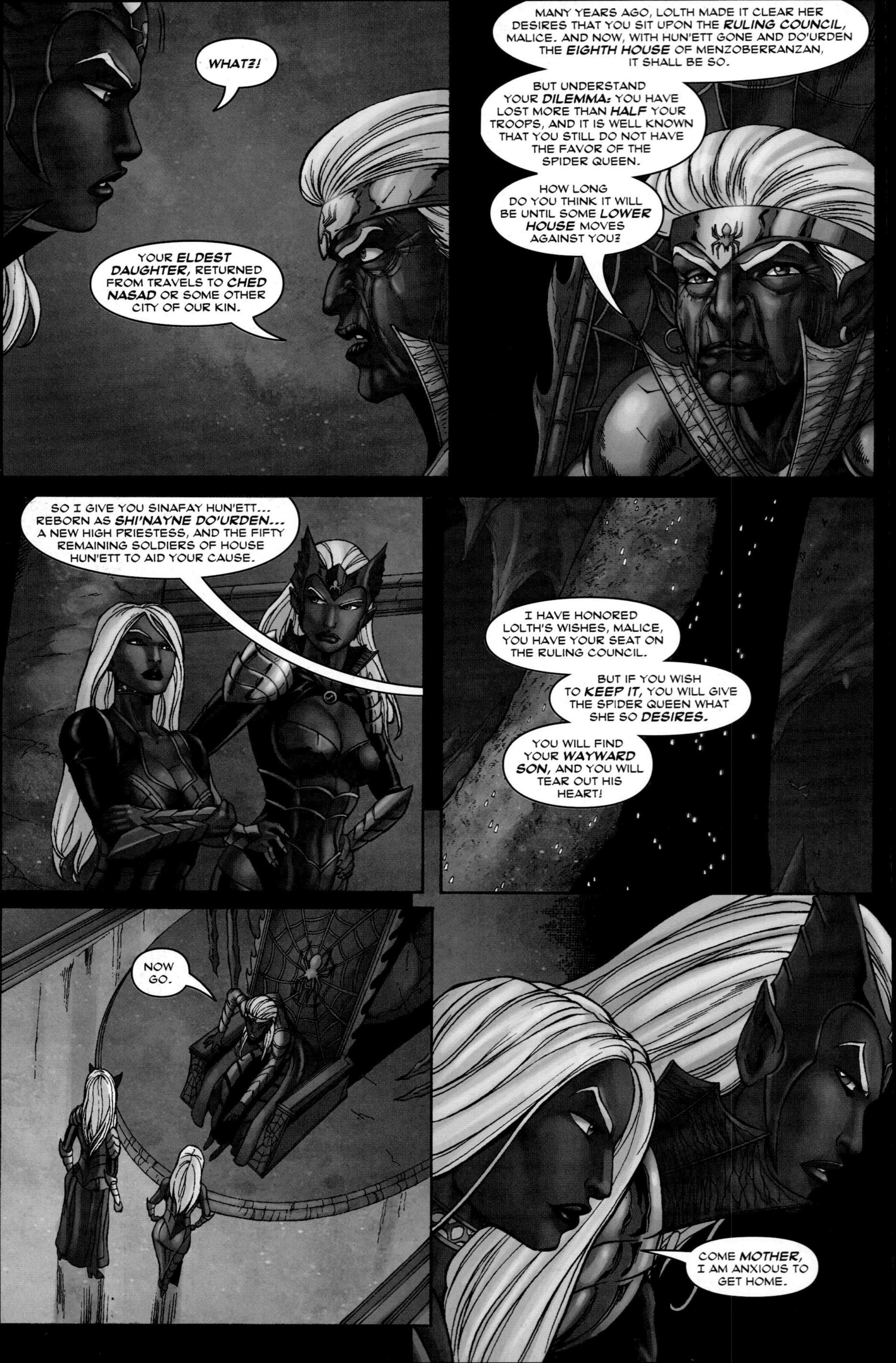
WHAT?!
YOUR ELDEST DAUGHTER, RETURNED FROM TRAVELS TO CHED NASAD OR SOME OTHER CITY OF OUR KIN.
MANY YEARS AGO, LOLTH MADE IT CLEAR HER DESIRES THAT YOU SIT UPON THE RULING COUNCIL, MALICE. AND NOW, WITH HUN'ETT GONE AND DO'URDEN THE EIGHTH HOUSE OF MENZOBERRANZAN, IT SHALL BE SO.
BUT UNDERSTAND YOUR DILEMMA: YOU HAVE LOST MORE THAN HALF YOUR TROOPS, AND IT IS WELL KNOWN THAT YOU STILL DO NOT HAVE THE FAVOR OF THE SPIDER QUEEN.
HOW LONG DO YOU THINK IT WILL BE UNTIL SOME LOWER HOUSE MOVES AGAINST YOU?
SO I GIVE YOU SINAFAY HUN'ETT... REBORN AS SHI'NAYNE DO'URDEN... A NEW HIGH PRIESTESS, AND THE FIFTY REMAINING SOLDIERS OF HOUSE HUN'ETT TO AID YOUR CAUSE.
I HAVE HONORED LOLTH'S WISHES, MALICE, YOU HAVE YOUR SEAT ON THE RULING COUNCIL.
BUT IF YOU WISH TO KEEP IT, YOU WILL GIVE THE SPIDER QUEEN WHAT SHE SO DESIRES.
YOU WILL FIND YOUR WAYWARD SON, AND YOU WILL TEAR OUT HIS HEART!
NOW GO.
COME MOTHER, I AM ANXIOUS TO GET HOME.

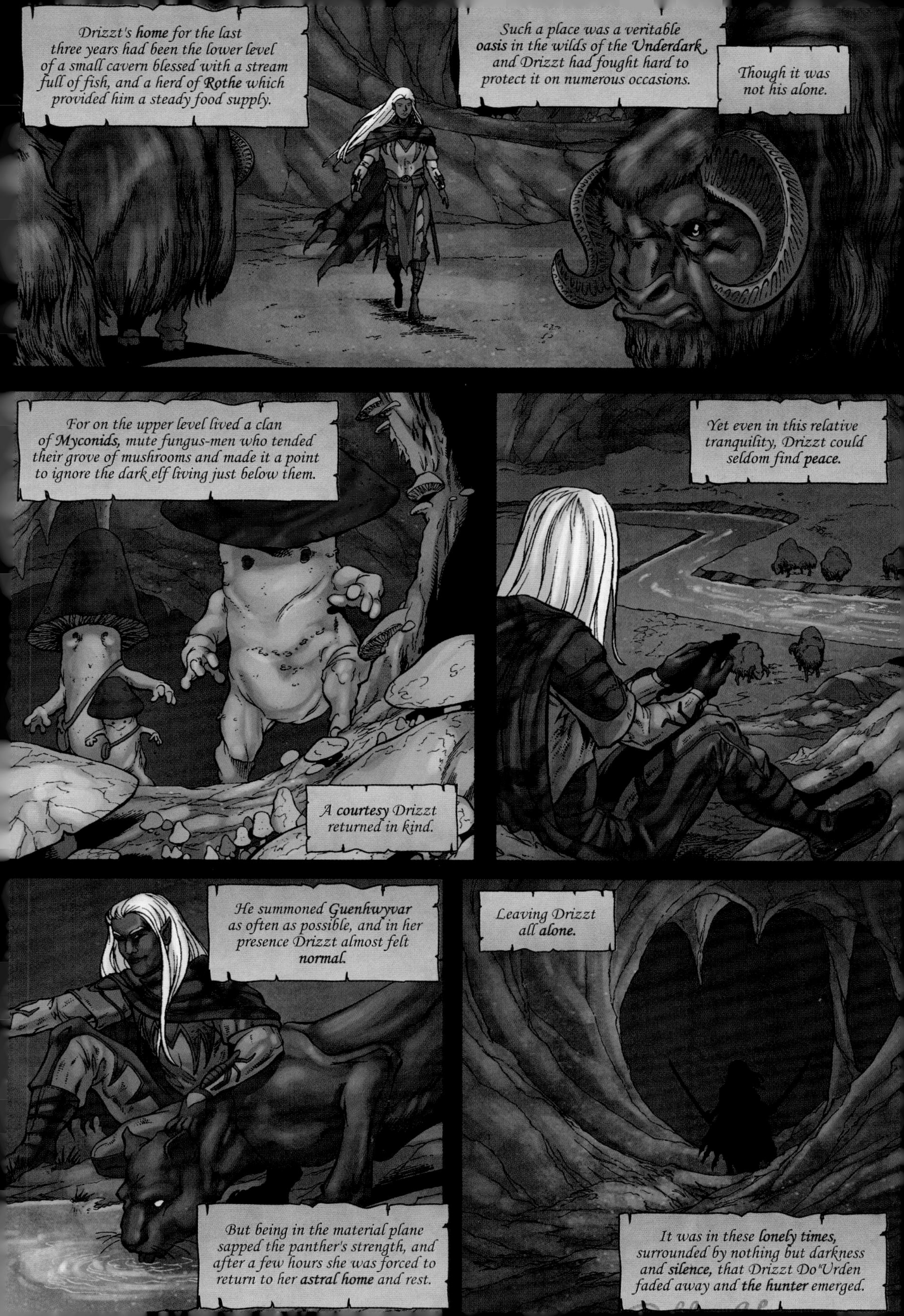
Drizzt's home for the last three years had been the lower level of a small cavern blessed with a stream full of fish, and a herd of Rothe which provided him a steady food supply.
Such a place was a veritable oasis in the wilds of the Underdark, and Drizzt had fought hard to protect it on numerous occasions.
Though it was not his alone.
For on the upper level lived a clan of Myconids, mute fungus-men who tended their grove of mushrooms and made it a point to ignore the dark elf living just below them.
A courtesy Drizzt returned in kind.
Yet even in this relative tranquility, Drizzt could seldom find peace.
He summoned Guenhwyvar as often as possible, and in her presence Drizzt almost felt normal.
But being in the material plane sapped the panther's strength, and after a few hours she was forced to return to her astral home and rest.
Leaving Drizzt all alone.
It was in these lonely times, surrounded by nothing but darkness and silence, that Drizzt Do'Urden faded away and the hunter emerged.

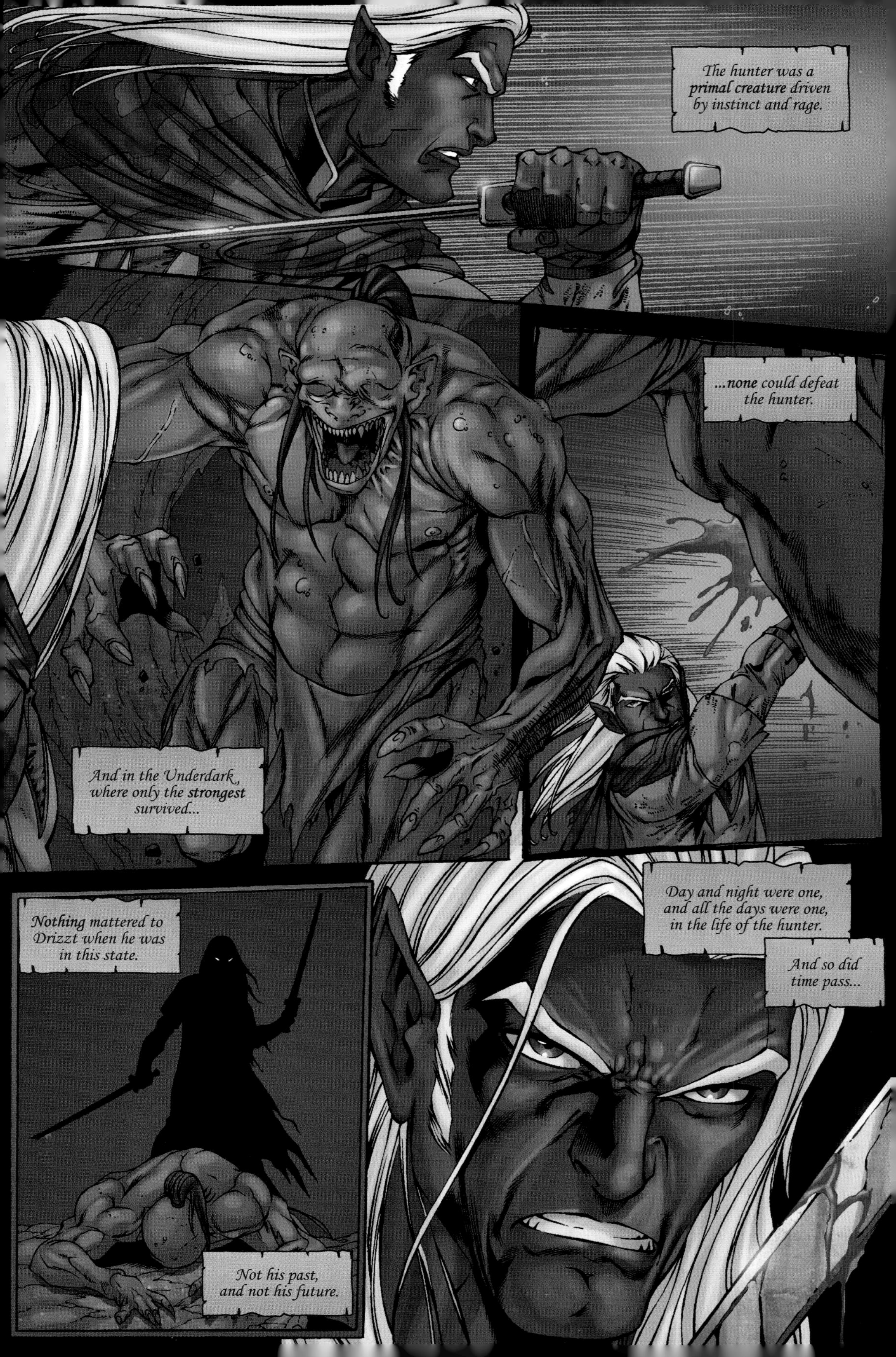
The hunter was a primal creature driven by instinct and rage.
And in the Underdark, where only the strongest survived...
...none could defeat the hunter.
Nothing mattered to Drizzt when he was in this state.
Not his past, and not his future.
Day and night were one, and all the days were one, in the life of the hunter.
And so did time pass...

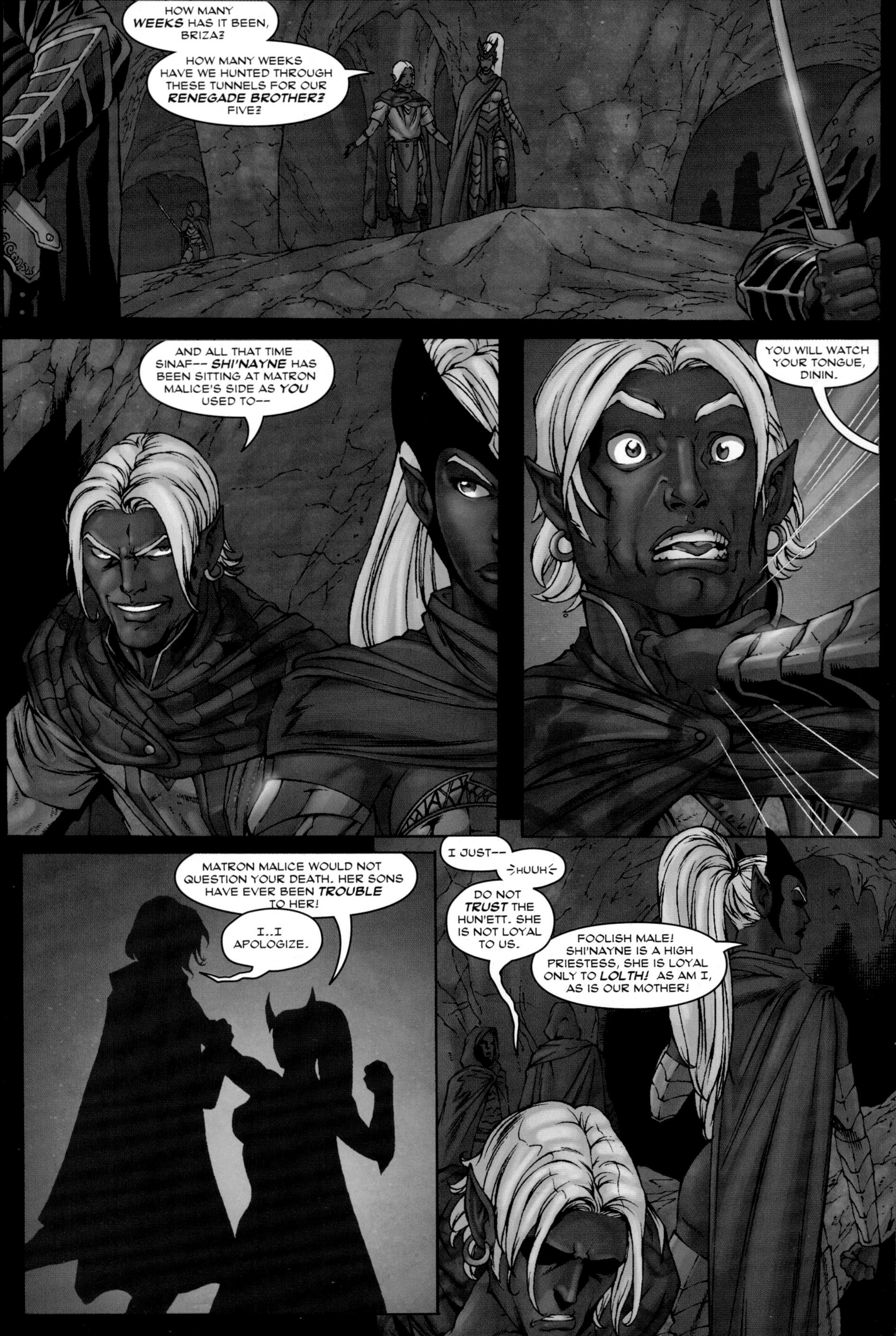
HOW MANY WEEKS HAS IT BEEN, BRIZA?
HOW MANY WEEKS HAVE WE HUNTED THROUGH THESE TUNNELS FOR OUR RENEGADE BROTHER? FIVE?
AND ALL THAT TIME SINAF-- SHI'NAYNE HAS BEEN SITTING AT MATRON MALICE'S SIDE AS YOU USED TO--
YOU WILL WATCH YOUR TONGUE, DININ.
MATRON MALICE WOULD NOT QUESTION YOUR DEATH. HER SONS HAVE EVER BEEN TROUBLE TO HER!
I..I APOLOGIZE.
I JUST--
HUUH
DO NOT TRUST THE HUN'ETT. SHE IS NOT LOYAL TO US.
FOOLISH MALE! SHI'NAYNE IS A HIGH PRIESTESS, SHE IS LOYAL ONLY TO LOLTH! AS AM I, AS IS OUR MOTHER!

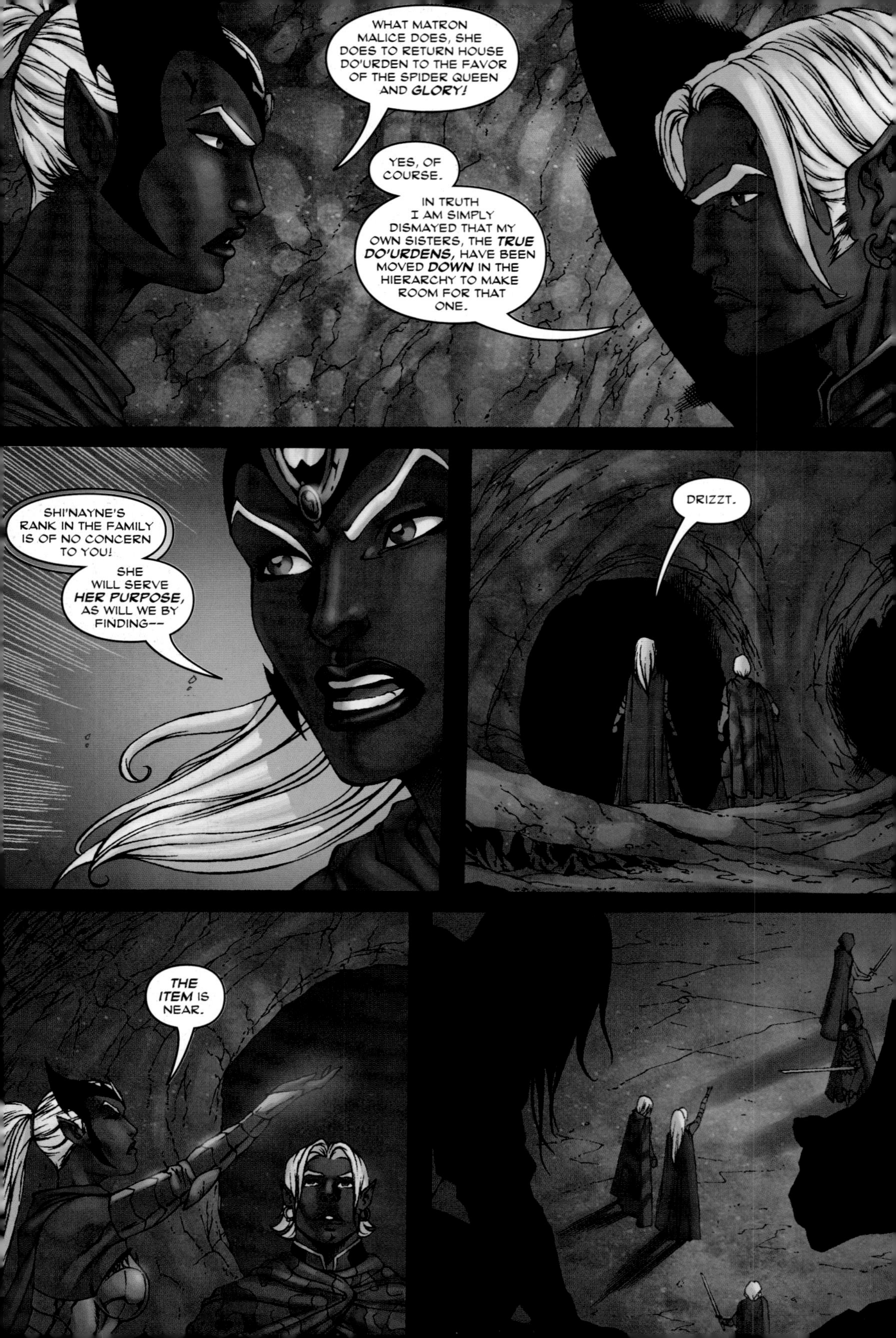
WHAT MATRON MALICE DOES, SHE DOES TO RETURN HOUSE DO'URDEN TO THE FAVOR OF THE SPIDER QUEEN AND *GLORY!*
YES, OF COURSE.
IN TRUTH I AM SIMPLY DISMAYED THAT MY OWN SISTERS, THE *TRUE DO'URDENS,* HAVE BEEN MOVED *DOWN* IN THE HIERARCHY TO MAKE ROOM FOR THAT ONE.
SHI'NAYNE'S RANK IN THE FAMILY IS OF NO CONCERN TO YOU!
SHE WILL SERVE *HER PURPOSE,* AS WILL WE BY FINDING--
DRIZZT.
THE ITEM IS NEAR.

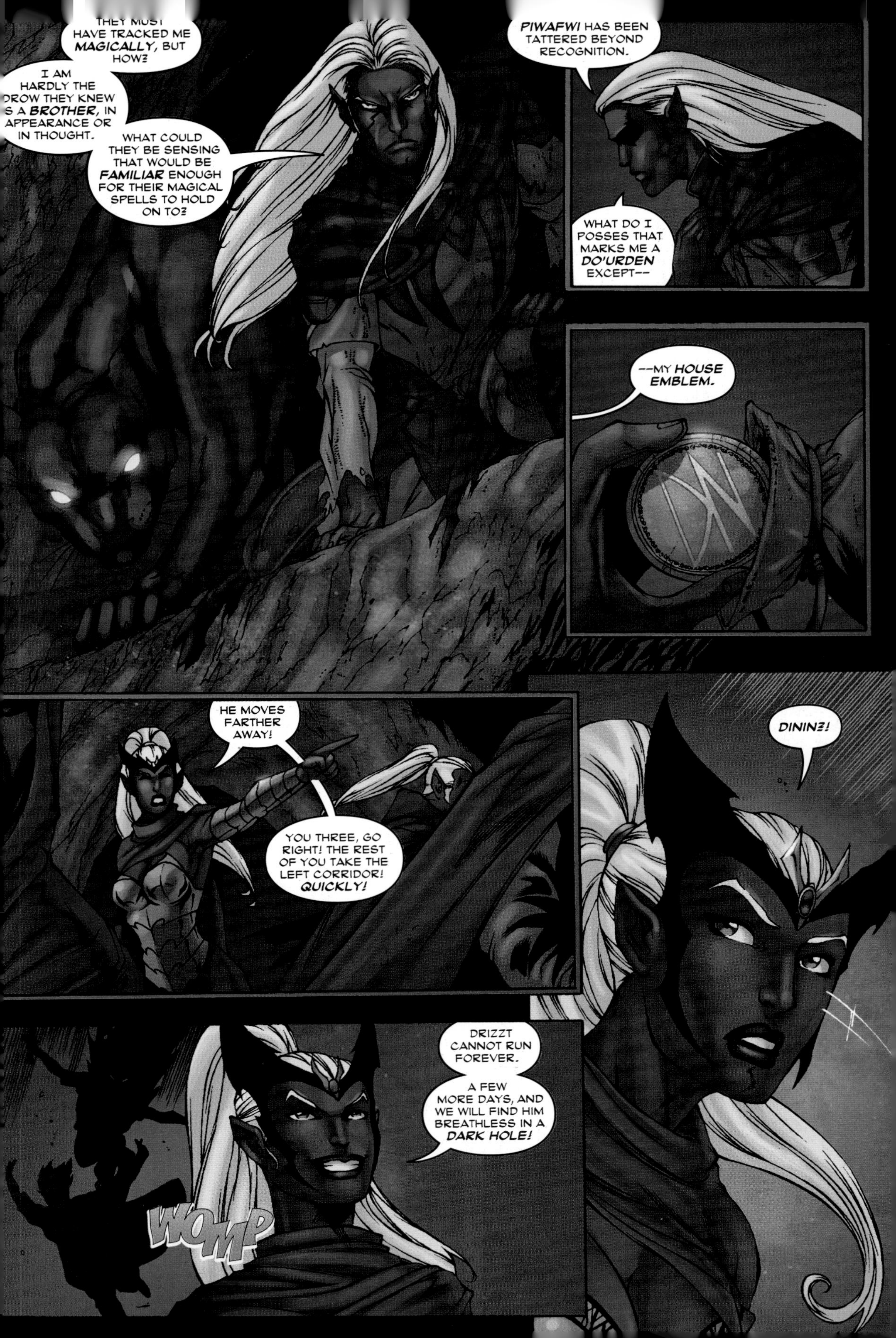
THEY MUST HAVE TRACKED ME MAGICALLY, BUT HOW?
I AM HARDLY THE DROW THEY KNEW AS A BROTHER, IN APPEARANCE OR IN THOUGHT.
WHAT COULD THEY BE SENSING THAT WOULD BE FAMILIAR ENOUGH FOR THEIR MAGICAL SPELLS TO HOLD ON TO?
PIWAFWI HAS BEEN TATTERED BEYOND RECOGNITION.
WHAT DO I POSSES THAT MARKS ME A DO'URDEN EXCEPT--
--MY HOUSE EMBLEM.
HE MOVES FARTHER AWAY!
YOU THREE, GO RIGHT! THE REST OF YOU TAKE THE LEFT CORRIDOR! QUICKLY!
DININ?!
DRIZZT CANNOT RUN FOREVER.
A FEW MORE DAYS, AND WE WILL FIND HIM BREATHLESS IN A DARK HOLE!
WOMP

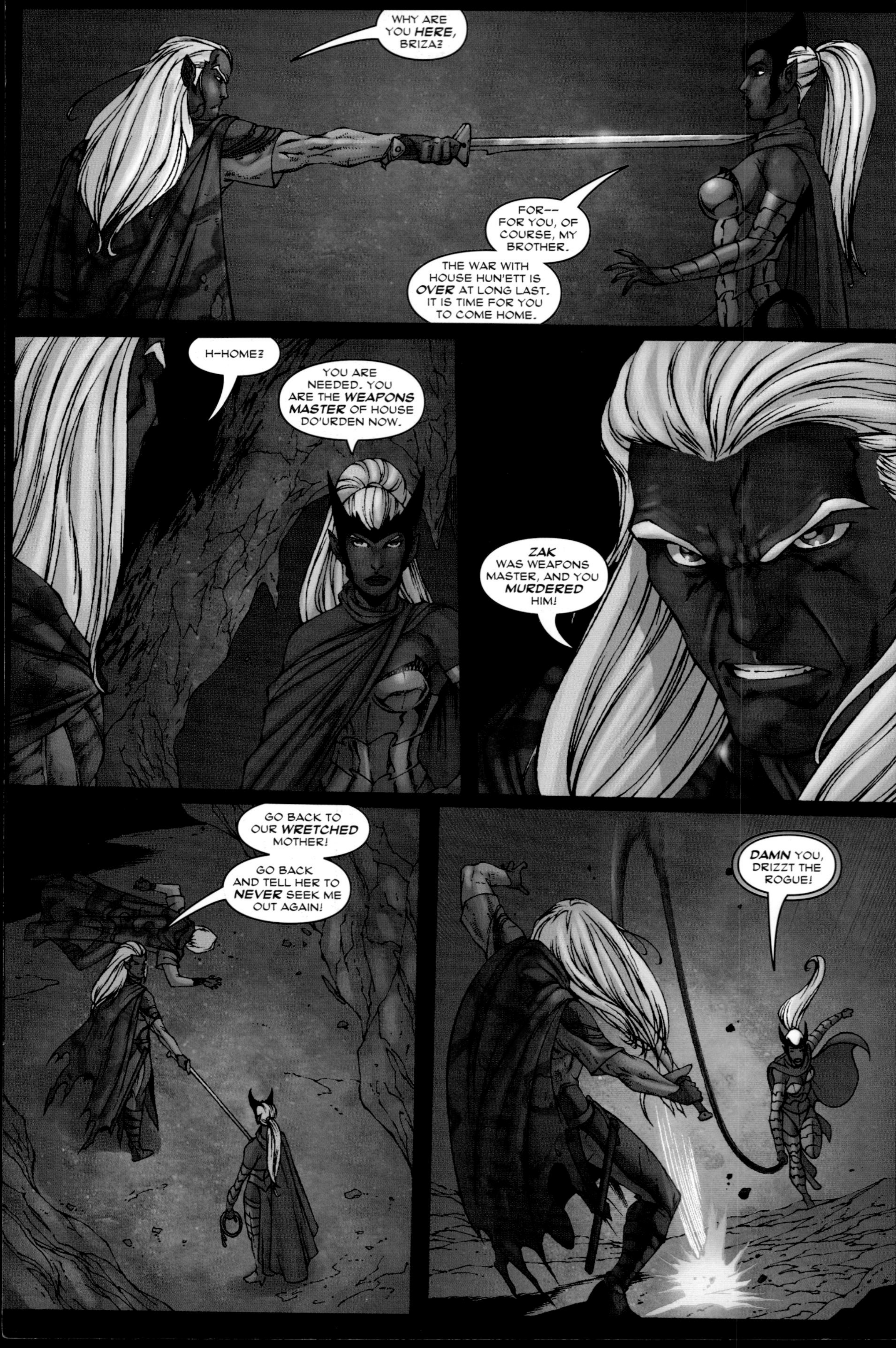
WHY ARE YOU HERE, BRIZA?
FOR-- FOR YOU, OF COURSE, MY BROTHER.
THE WAR WITH HOUSE HUN'ETT IS OVER AT LONG LAST. IT IS TIME FOR YOU TO COME HOME.
H-HOME?
YOU ARE NEEDED. YOU ARE THE WEAPONS MASTER OF HOUSE DO'URDEN NOW.
ZAK WAS WEAPONS MASTER, AND YOU MURDERED HIM!
GO BACK TO OUR WRETCHED MOTHER!
GO BACK AND TELL HER TO NEVER SEEK ME OUT AGAIN!
DAMN YOU, DRIZZT THE ROGUE!

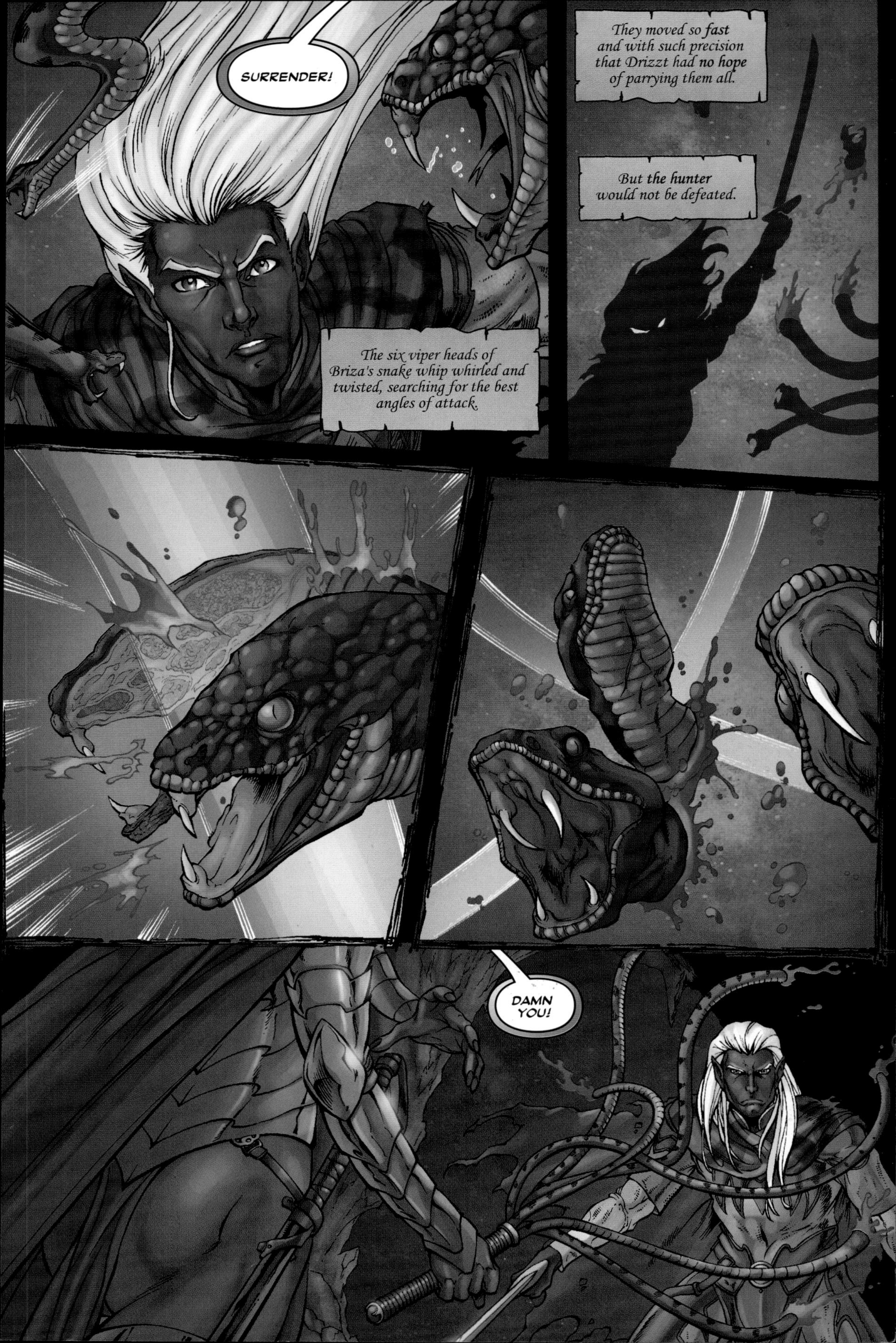
SURRENDER!
The six viper heads of Briza's snake whip whirled and twisted, searching for the best angles of attack.
They moved so fast and with such precision that Drizzt had no hope of parrying them all.
But the hunter would not be defeated.
DAMN YOU!

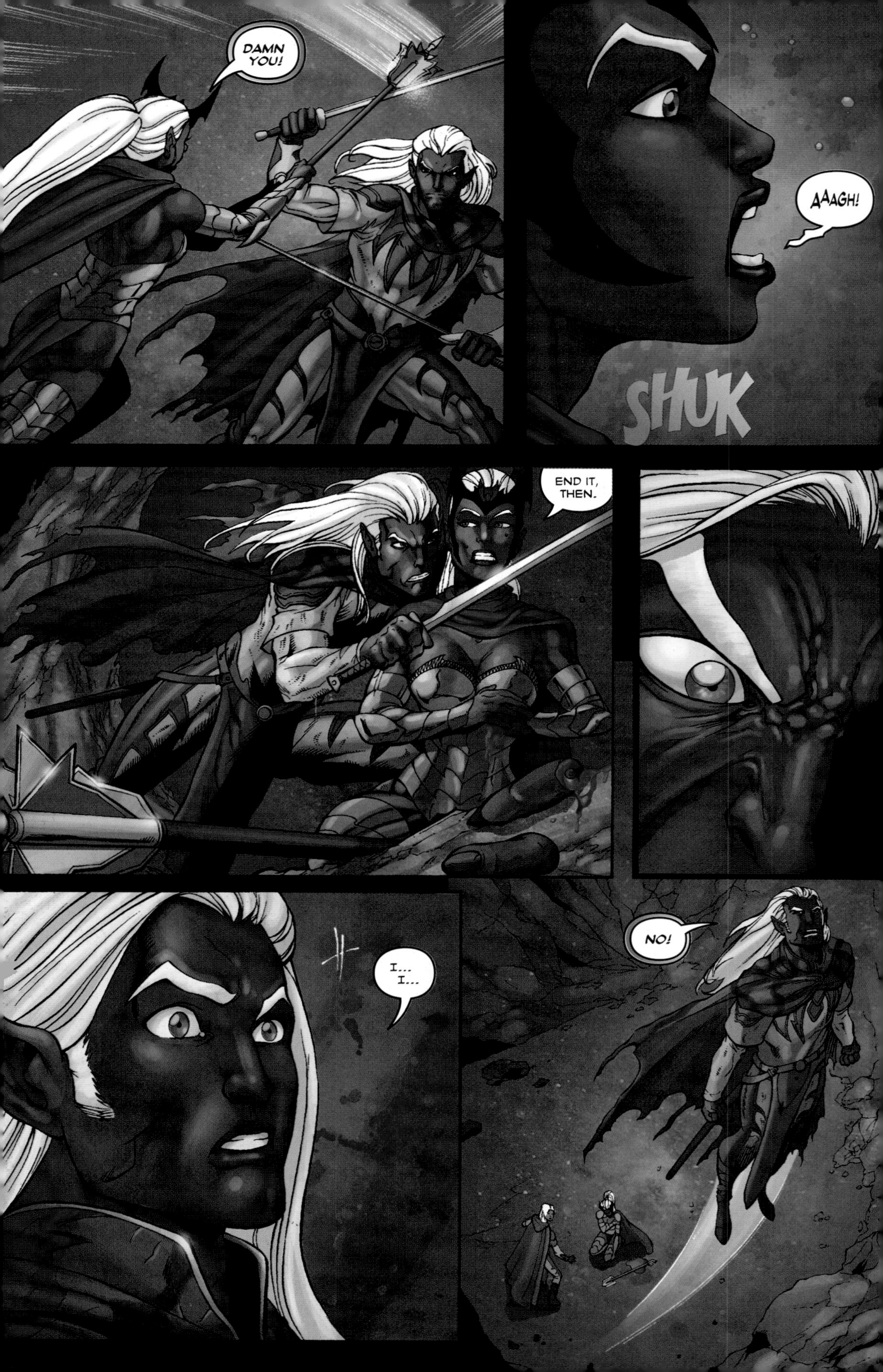
DAMN YOU!
AAAGH!
SHUK
END IT, THEN.
I... I...
NO!

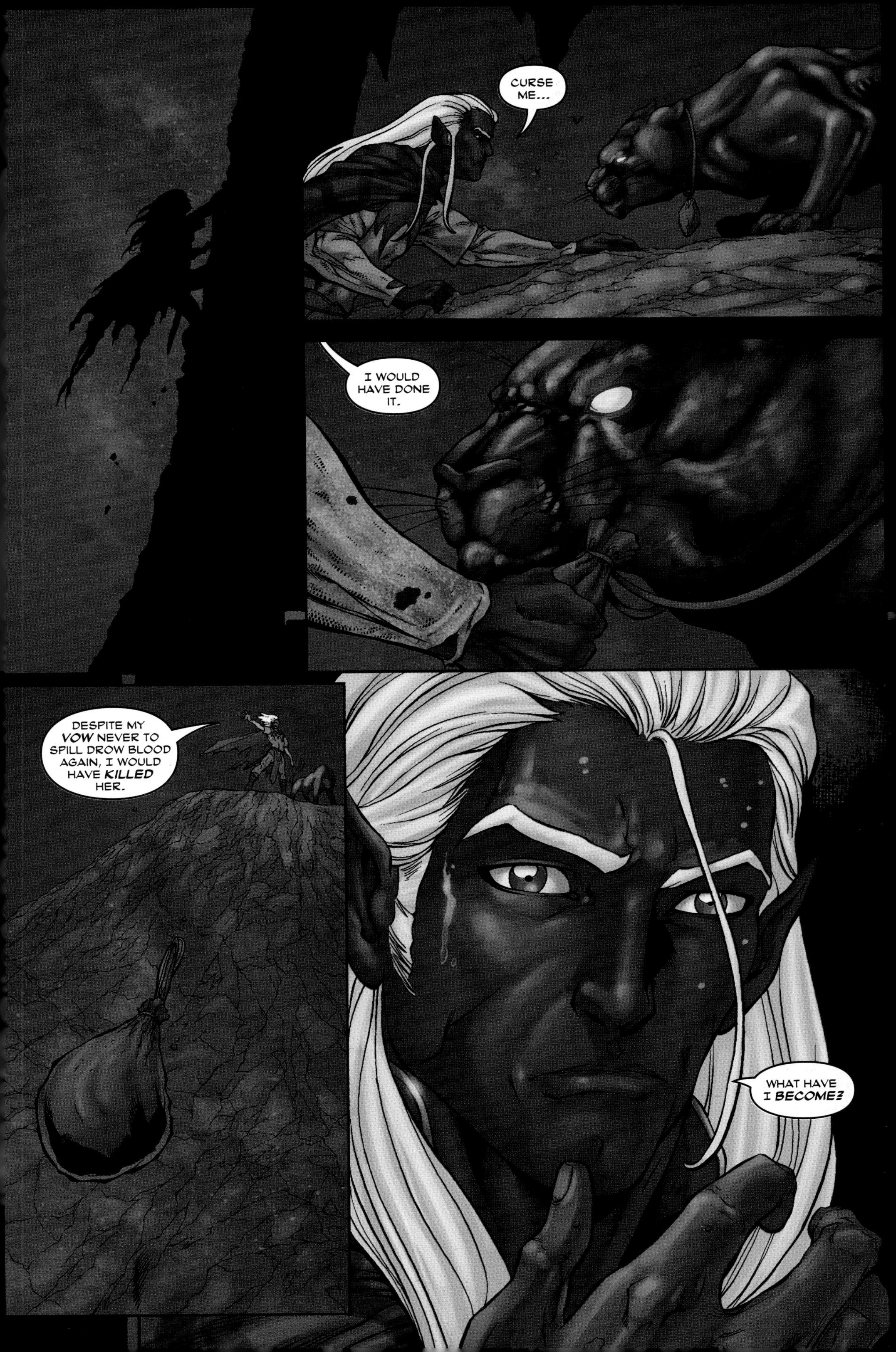
CURSE ME...
I WOULD HAVE DONE IT.
DESPITE MY VOW NEVER TO SPILL DROW BLOOD AGAIN, I WOULD HAVE KILLED HER.
WHAT HAVE I BECOME?

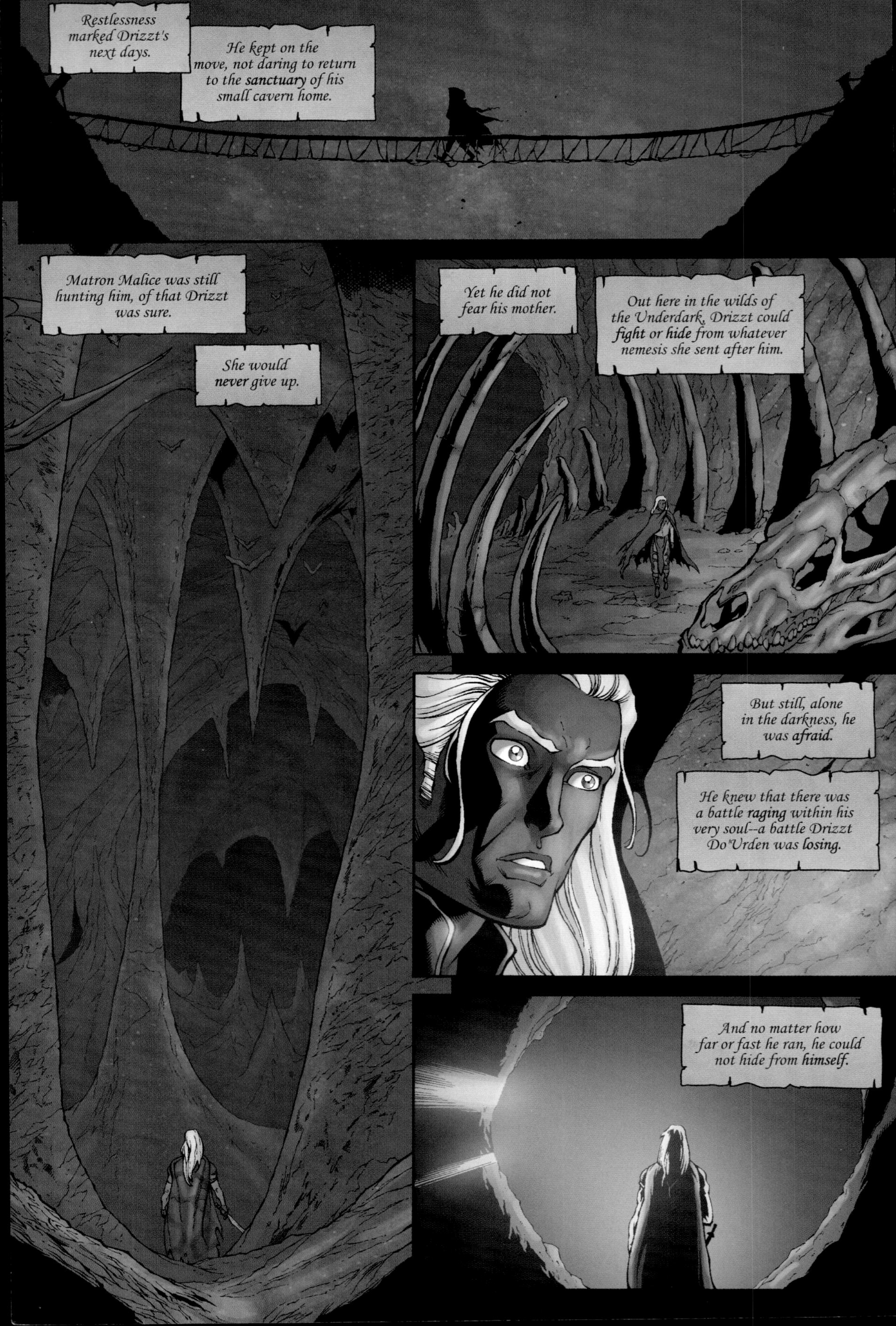
Restlessness marked Drizzt's next days.
He kept on the move, not daring to return to the sanctuary of his small cavern home.
Matron Malice was still hunting him, of that Drizzt was sure.
She would never give up.
Yet he did not fear his mother.
Out here in the wilds of the Underdark, Drizzt could fight or hide from whatever nemesis she sent after him.
But still, alone in the darkness, he was afraid.
He knew that there was a battle raging within his very soul--a battle Drizzt Do'Urden was losing.
And no matter how far or fast he ran, he could not hide from himself.

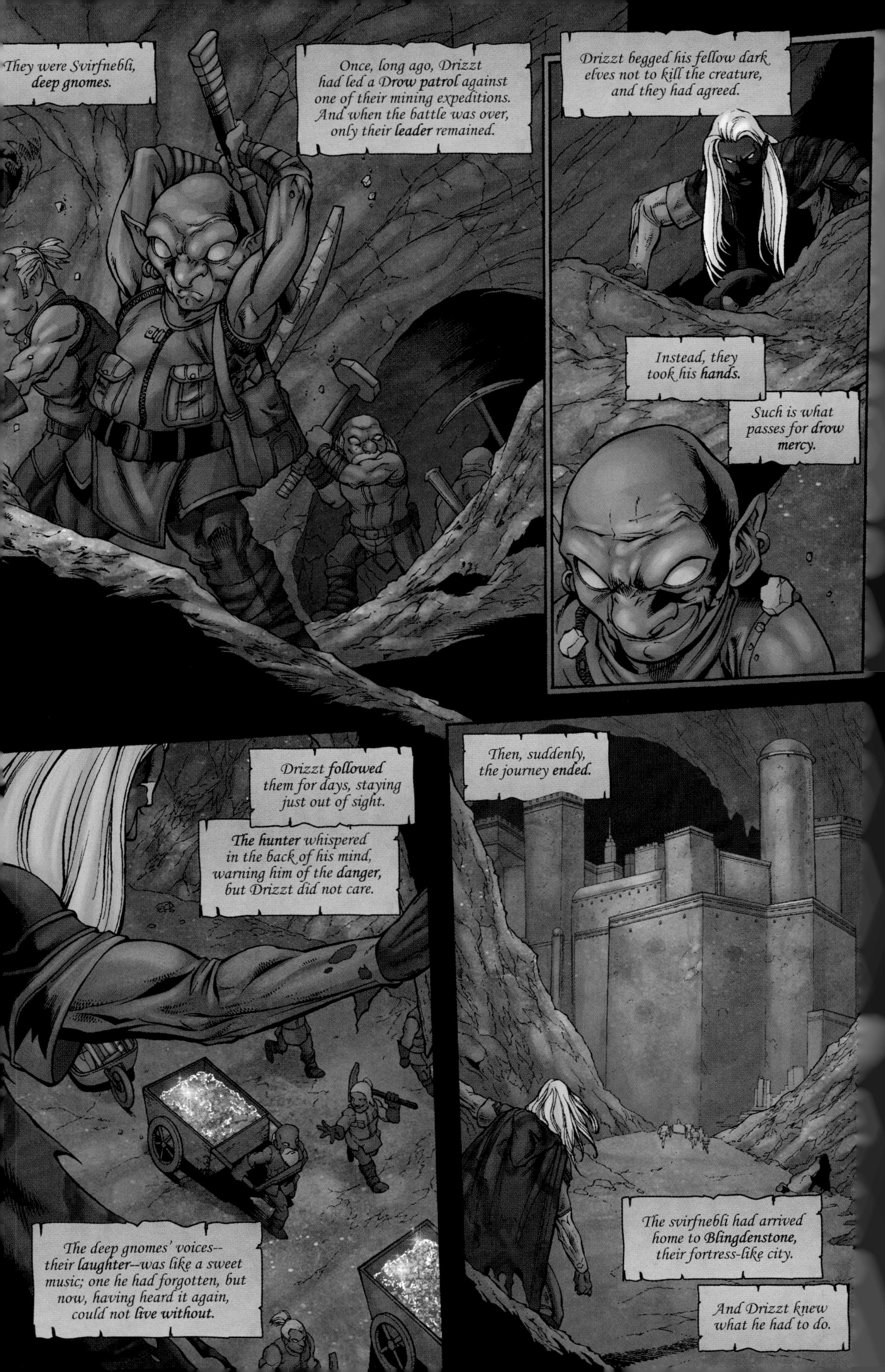
They were Svirfnebli, deep gnomes.
Once, long ago, Drizzt had led a Drow patrol against one of their mining expeditions. And when the battle was over, only their leader remained.
Drizzt begged his fellow dark elves not to kill the creature, and they had agreed.
Instead, they took his hands.
Such is what passes for drow mercy.
Drizzt followed them for days, staying just out of sight.
The hunter whispered in the back of his mind, warning him of the danger, but Drizzt did not care.
The deep gnomes' voices--their laughter--was like a sweet music; one he had forgotten, but now, having heard it again, could not live without.
Then, suddenly, the journey ended.
The svirfnebli had arrived home to Blingdenstone, their fortress-like city.
And Drizzt knew what he had to do.

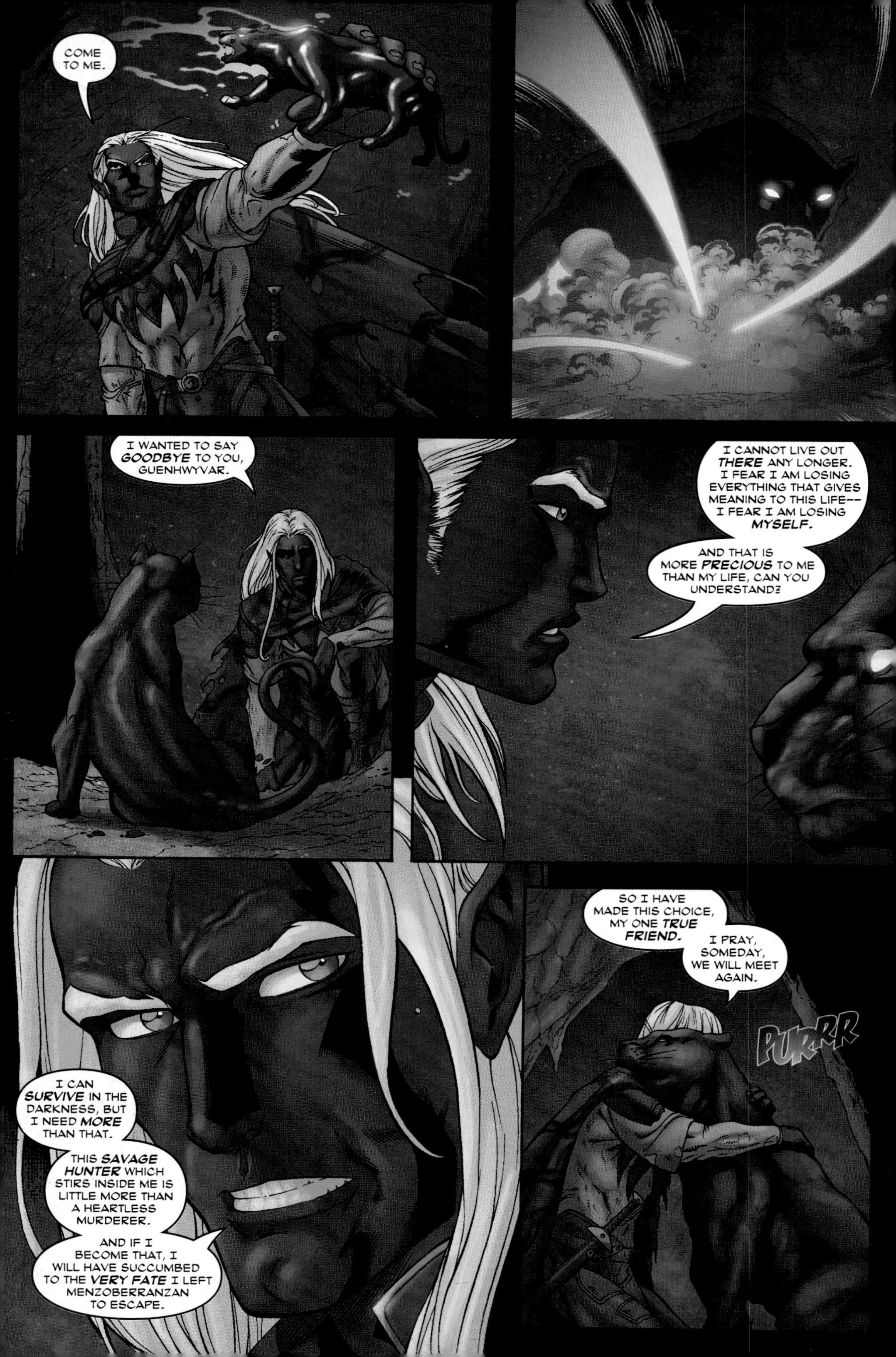

COME TO ME.
I WANTED TO SAY GOODBYE TO YOU, GUENHWYVAR.
I CANNOT LIVE OUT THERE ANY LONGER. I FEAR I AM LOSING EVERYTHING THAT GIVES MEANING TO THIS LIFE-- I FEAR I AM LOSING MYSELF.
AND THAT IS MORE PRECIOUS TO ME THAN MY LIFE, CAN YOU UNDERSTAND?
I CAN SURVIVE IN THE DARKNESS, BUT I NEED MORE THAN THAT.
THIS SAVAGE HUNTER WHICH STIRS INSIDE ME IS LITTLE MORE THAN A HEARTLESS MURDERER.
AND IF I BECOME THAT, I WILL HAVE SUCCUMBED TO THE VERY FATE I LEFT MENZOBERRANZAN TO ESCAPE.
SO I HAVE MADE THIS CHOICE, MY ONE TRUE FRIEND.
I PRAY, SOMEDAY, WE WILL MEET AGAIN.
PURRR

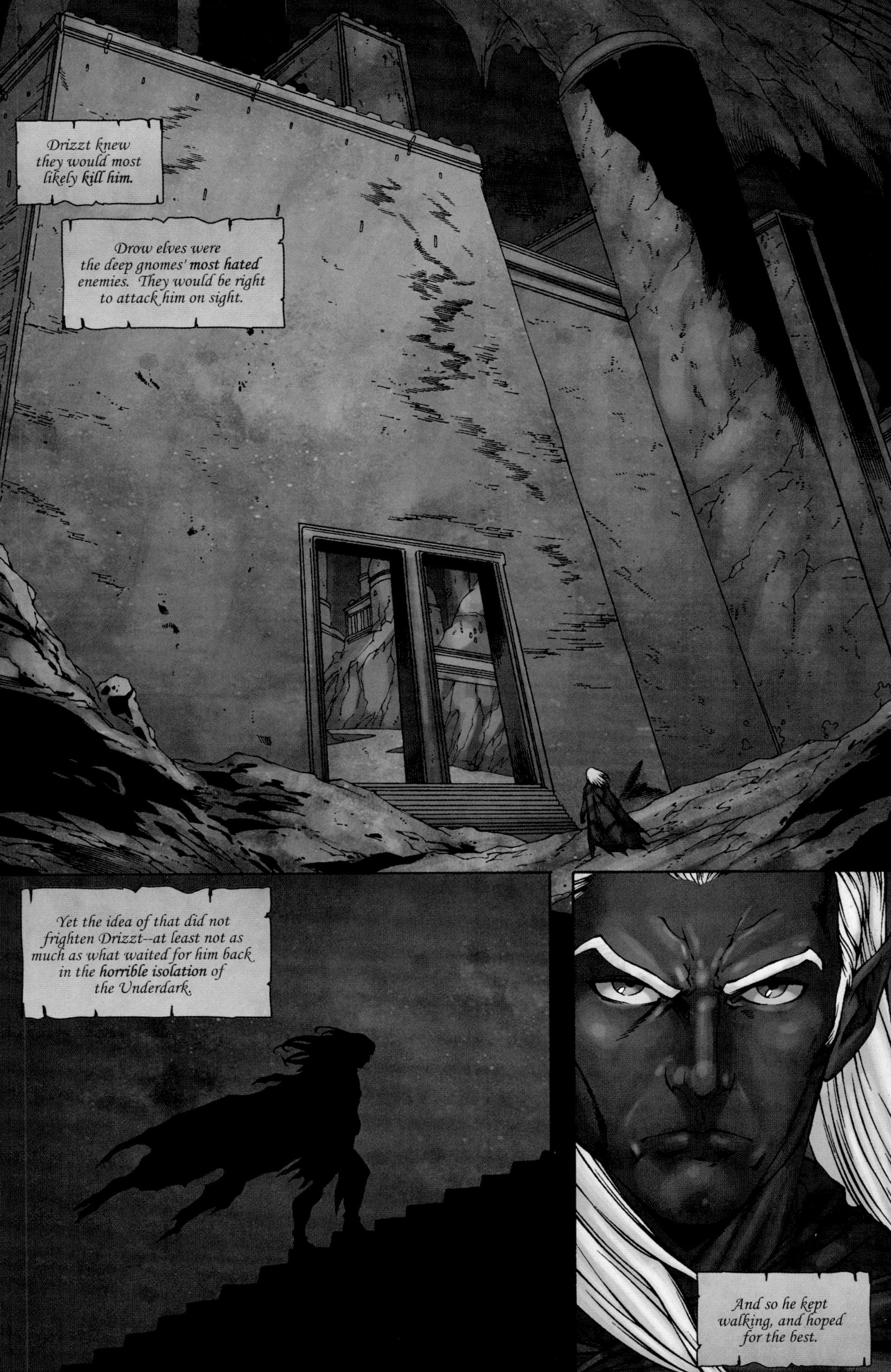
Drizzt knew they would most likely kill him.
Drow elves were the deep gnomes' most hated enemies. They would be right to attack him on sight.
Yet the idea of that did not frighten Drizzt--at least not as much as what waited for him back in the horrible isolation of the Underdark.
And so he kept walking, and hoped for the best.

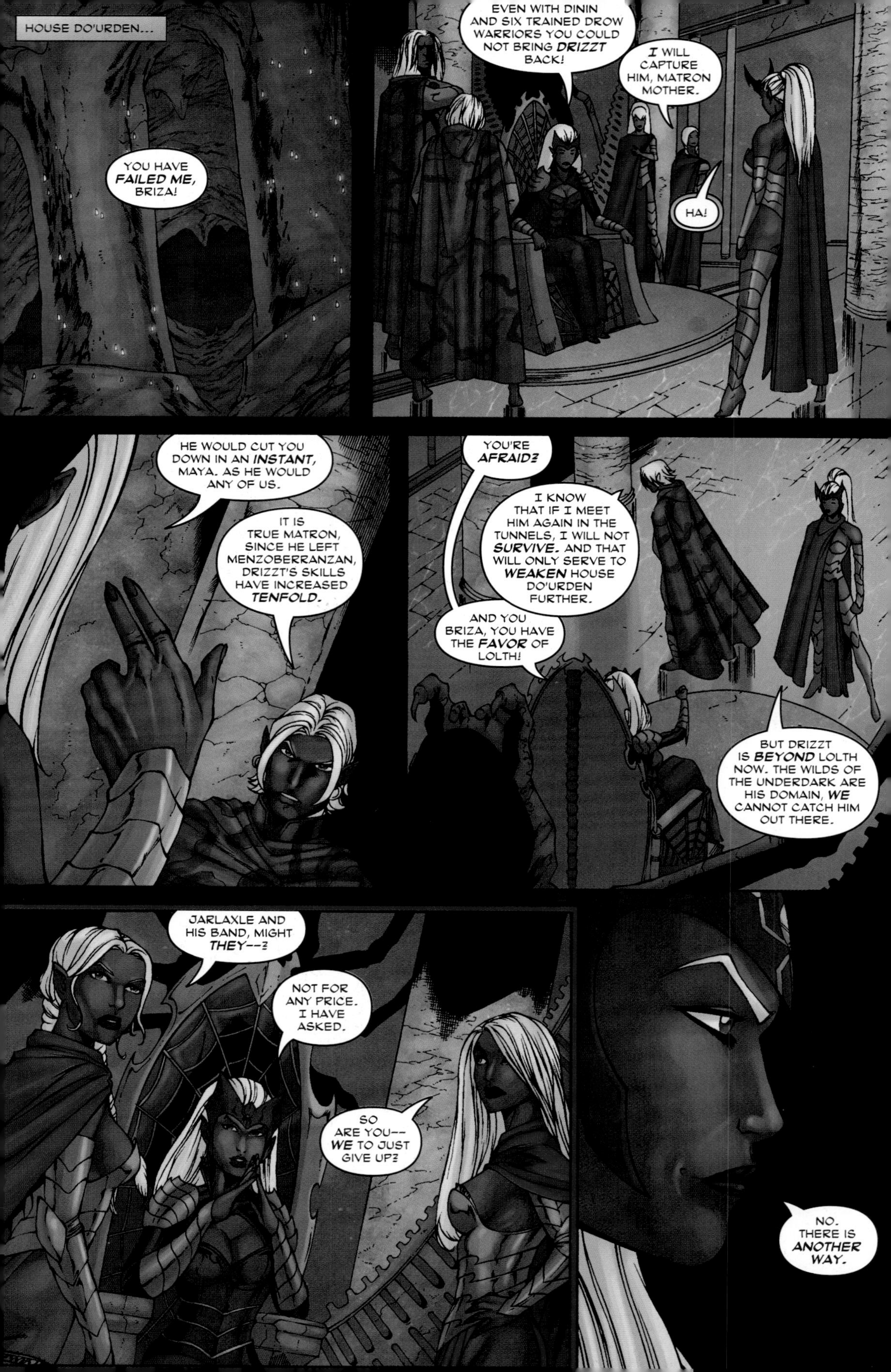
HOUSE DO'URDEN...
YOU HAVE FAILED ME, BRIZA!
EVEN WITH DININ AND SIX TRAINED DROW WARRIORS YOU COULD NOT BRING DRIZZT BACK!
I WILL CAPTURE HIM, MATRON MOTHER.
HA!
HE WOULD CUT YOU DOWN IN AN INSTANT, MAYA. AS HE WOULD ANY OF US.
IT IS TRUE MATRON, SINCE HE LEFT MENZOBERRANZAN, DRIZZT'S SKILLS HAVE INCREASED TENFOLD.
YOU'RE AFRAID?
I KNOW THAT IF I MEET HIM AGAIN IN THE TUNNELS, I WILL NOT SURVIVE. AND THAT WILL ONLY SERVE TO WEAKEN HOUSE DO'URDEN FURTHER.
AND YOU BRIZA, YOU HAVE THE FAVOR OF LOLTH!
BUT DRIZZT IS BEYOND LOLTH NOW. THE WILDS OF THE UNDERDARK ARE HIS DOMAIN, WE CANNOT CATCH HIM OUT THERE.
JARLAXLE AND HIS BAND, MIGHT THEY--?
NOT FOR ANY PRICE. I HAVE ASKED.
SO ARE YOU-- WE TO JUST GIVE UP?
NO. THERE IS ANOTHER WAY.

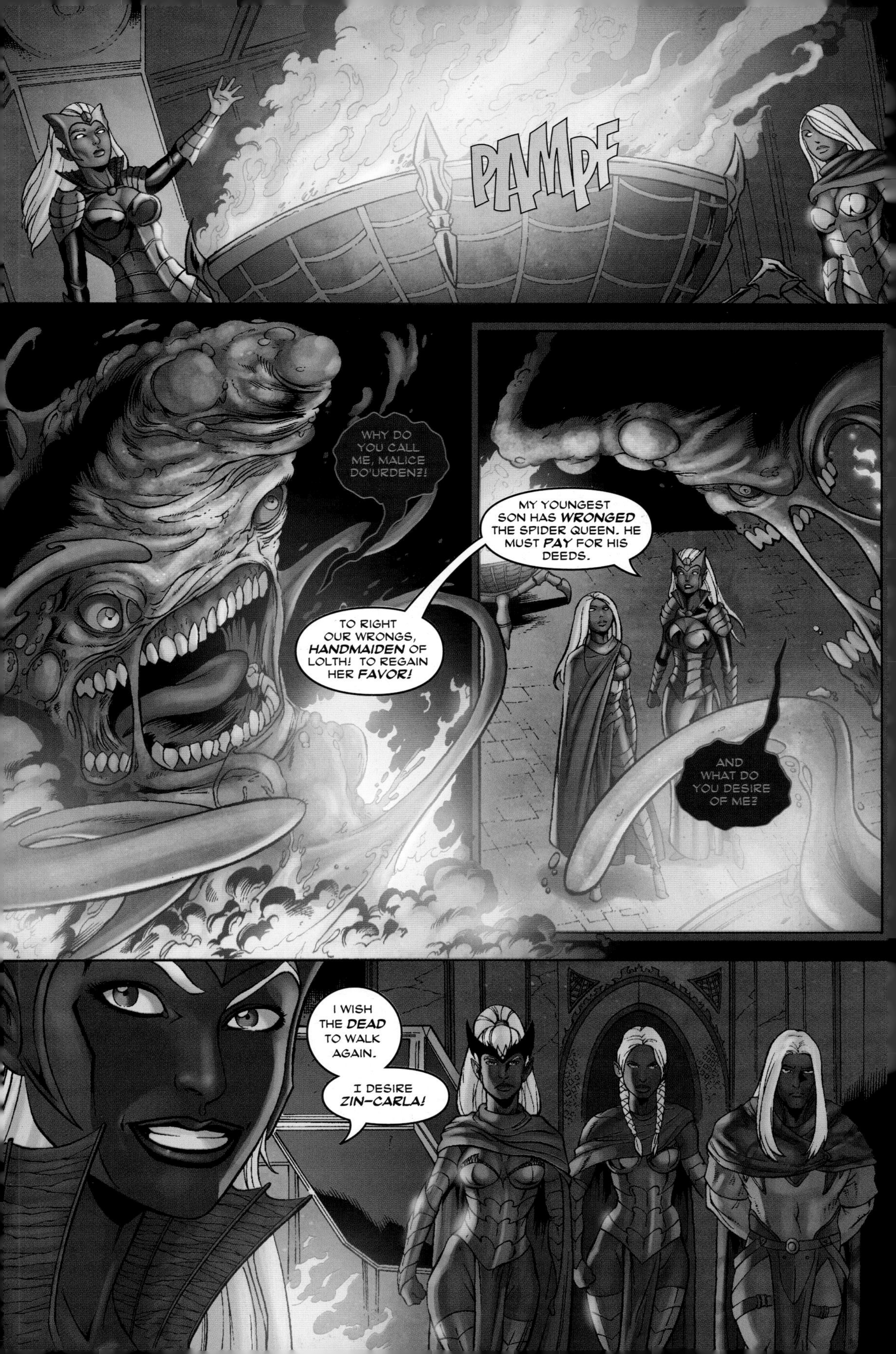
PAMPF
WHY DO YOU CALL ME, MALICE DO'URDEN?!
MY YOUNGEST SON HAS WRONGED THE SPIDER QUEEN. HE MUST PAY FOR HIS DEEDS.
TO RIGHT OUR WRONGS, HANDMAIDEN OF LOLTH! TO REGAIN HER FAVOR!
AND WHAT DO YOU DESIRE OF ME?
I WISH THE DEAD TO WALK AGAIN.
I DESIRE ZIN-CARLA!

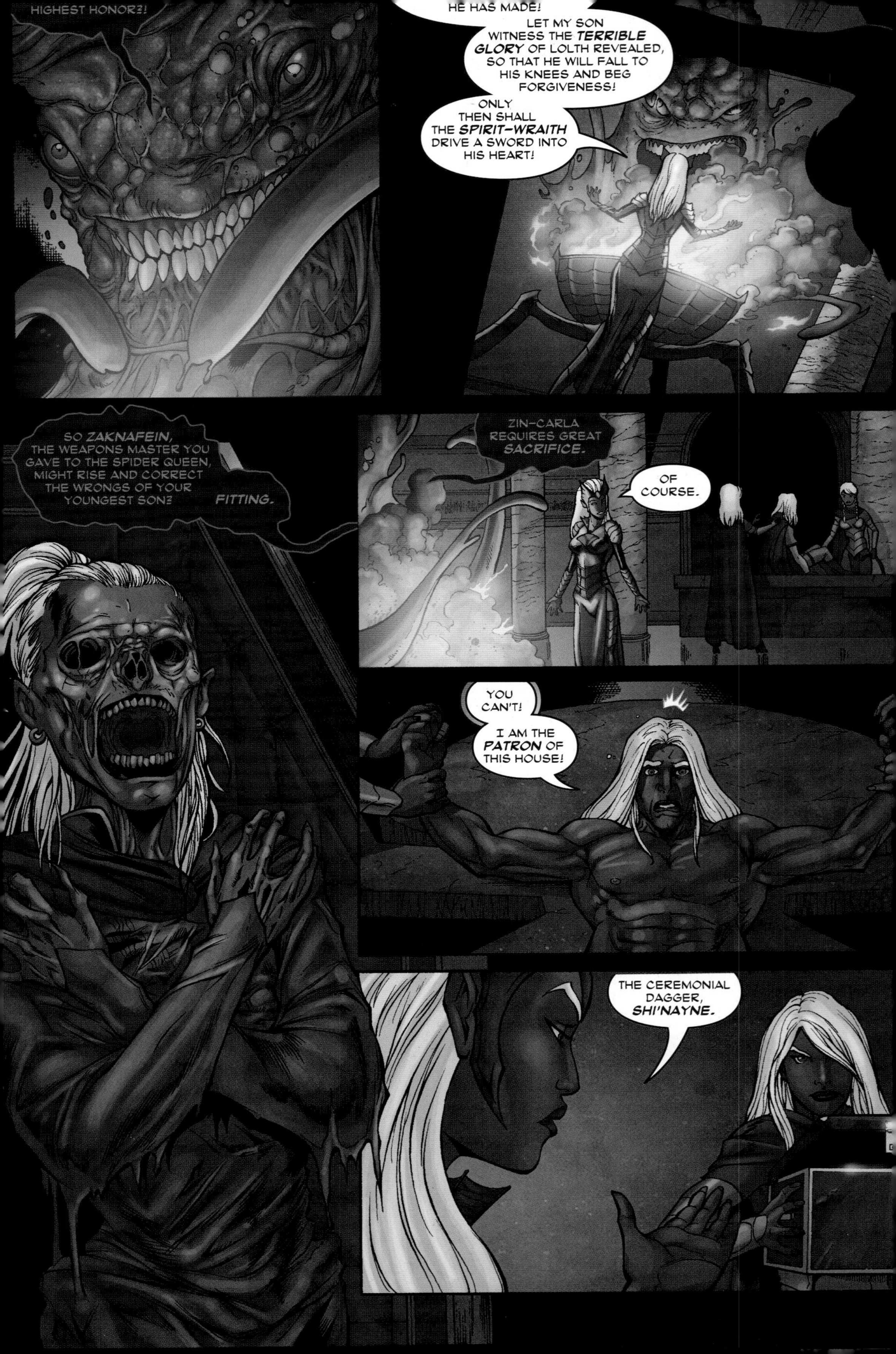
HIGHEST HONOR?!
HE HAS MADE!
LET MY SON WITNESS THE TERRIBLE GLORY OF LOLTH REVEALED, SO THAT HE WILL FALL TO HIS KNEES AND BEG FORGIVENESS!
ONLY THEN SHALL THE SPIRIT-WRAITH DRIVE A SWORD INTO HIS HEART!
SO ZAKNAFEIN, THE WEAPONS MASTER YOU GAVE TO THE SPIDER QUEEN, MIGHT RISE AND CORRECT THE WRONGS OF YOUR YOUNGEST SON? FITTING.
ZIN-CARLA REQUIRES GREAT SACRIFICE.
OF COURSE.
YOU CAN'T!
I AM THE PATRON OF THIS HOUSE!
THE CEREMONIAL DAGGER, SHI'NAYNE.

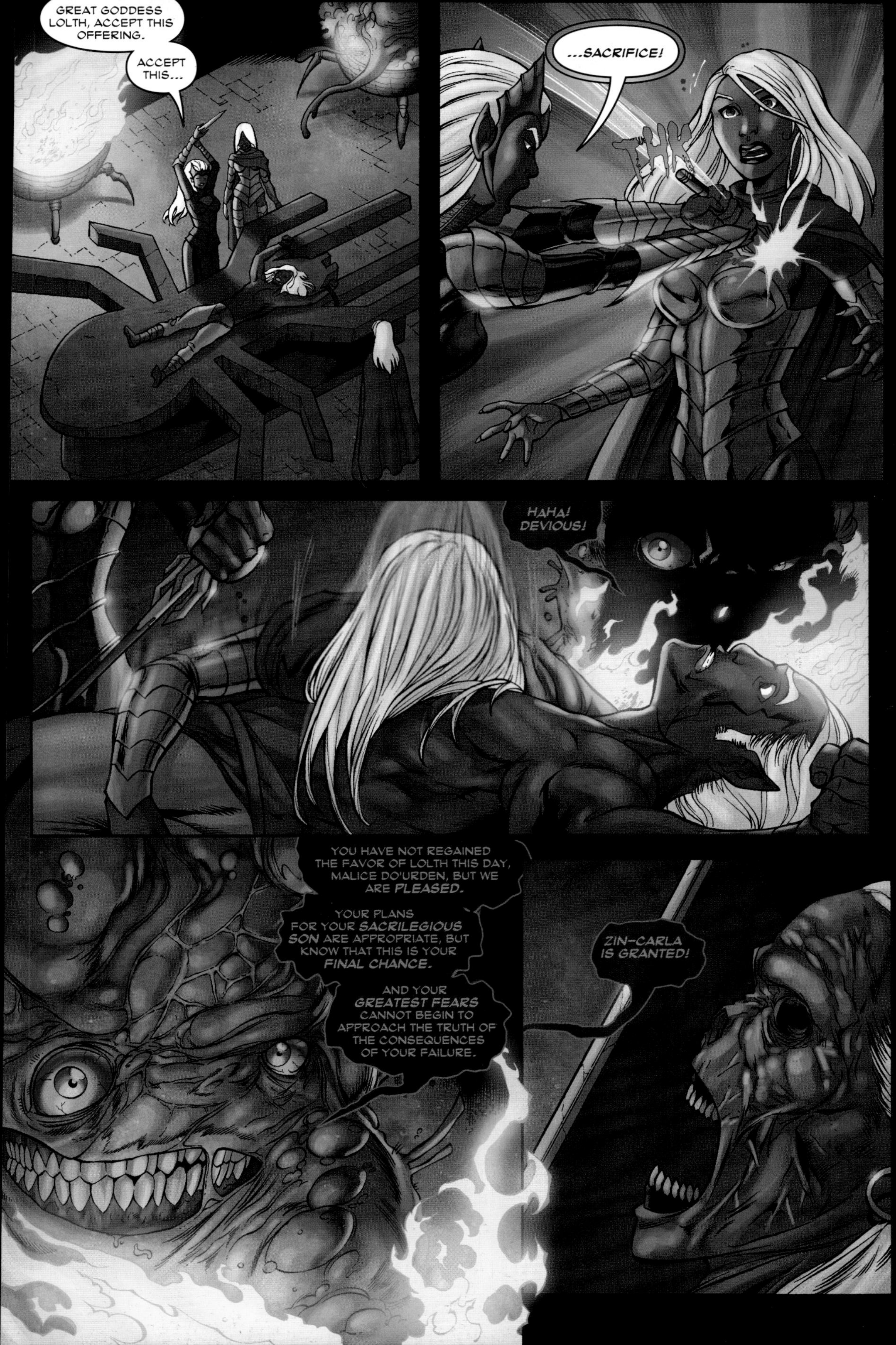
GREAT GODDESS LOLTH, ACCEPT THIS OFFERING.
ACCEPT THIS...
...SACRIFICE!
THK
HAHA! DEVIOUS!
YOU HAVE NOT REGAINED THE FAVOR OF LOLTH THIS DAY, MALICE DO'URDEN, BUT WE ARE PLEASED.
YOUR PLANS FOR YOUR SACRILEGIOUS SON ARE APPROPRIATE, BUT KNOW THAT THIS IS YOUR FINAL CHANCE.
AND YOUR GREATEST FEARS CANNOT BEGIN TO APPROACH THE TRUTH OF THE CONSEQUENCES OF YOUR FAILURE.
ZIN-CARLA IS GRANTED!

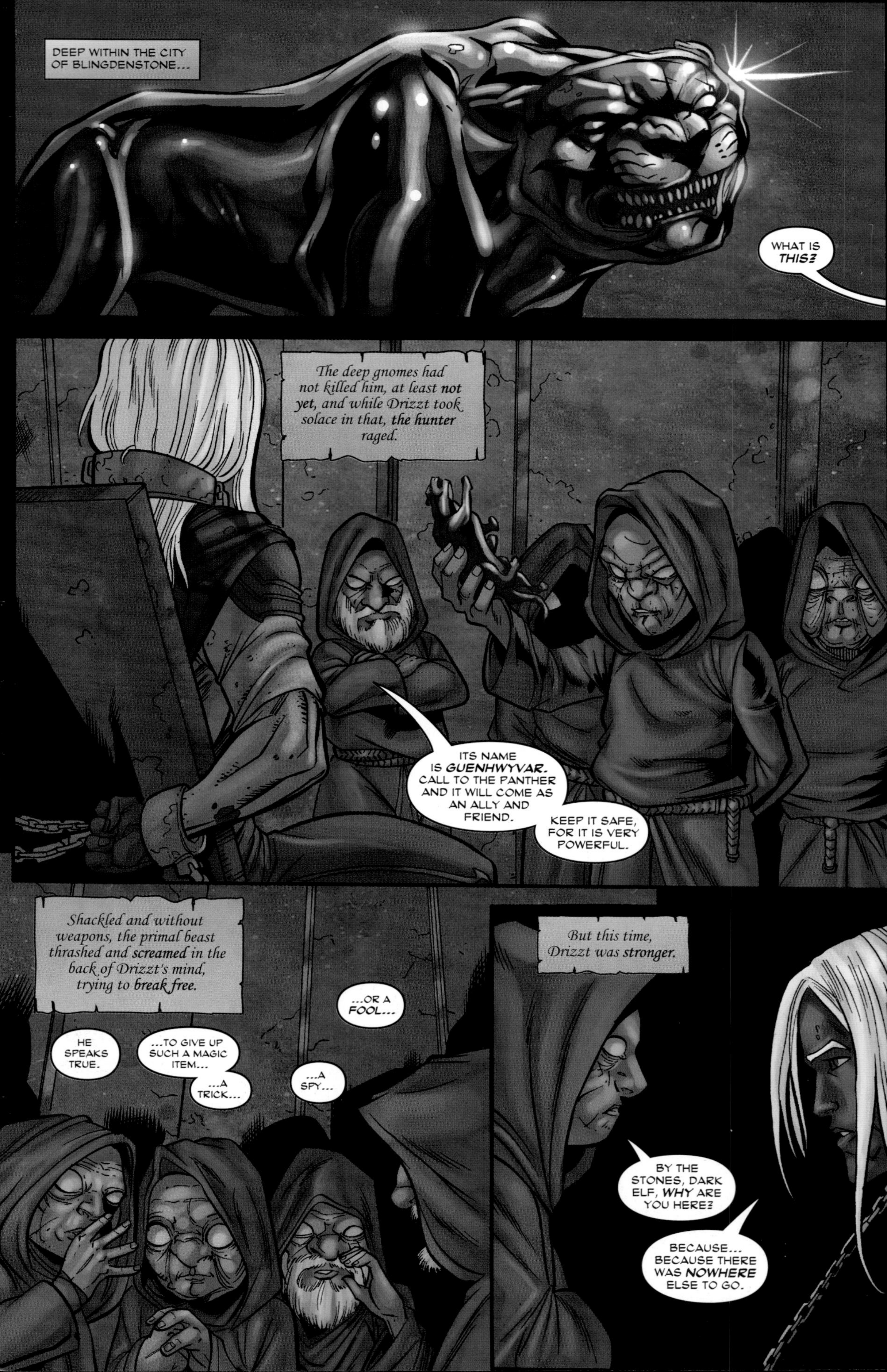

DEEP WITHIN THE CITY OF BLINGDENSTONE...
WHAT IS *THIS?*
The deep gnomes had not killed him, at least **not yet**, and while Drizzt took solace in that, **the hunter** raged.
ITS NAME IS ***GUENHWYVAR.*** CALL TO THE PANTHER AND IT WILL COME AS AN ALLY AND FRIEND.
KEEP IT SAFE, FOR IT IS VERY POWERFUL.
Shackled and without weapons, the primal beast thrashed and **screamed** in the back of Drizzt's mind, trying to **break free.**
HE SPEAKS TRUE.
...TO GIVE UP SUCH A MAGIC ITEM...
...A TRICK...
...A SPY...
...OR A **FOOL...**
But this time, Drizzt was **stronger.**
BY THE STONES, DARK ELF, ***WHY*** ARE YOU HERE?
BECAUSE... BECAUSE THERE WAS ***NOWHERE*** ELSE TO GO.

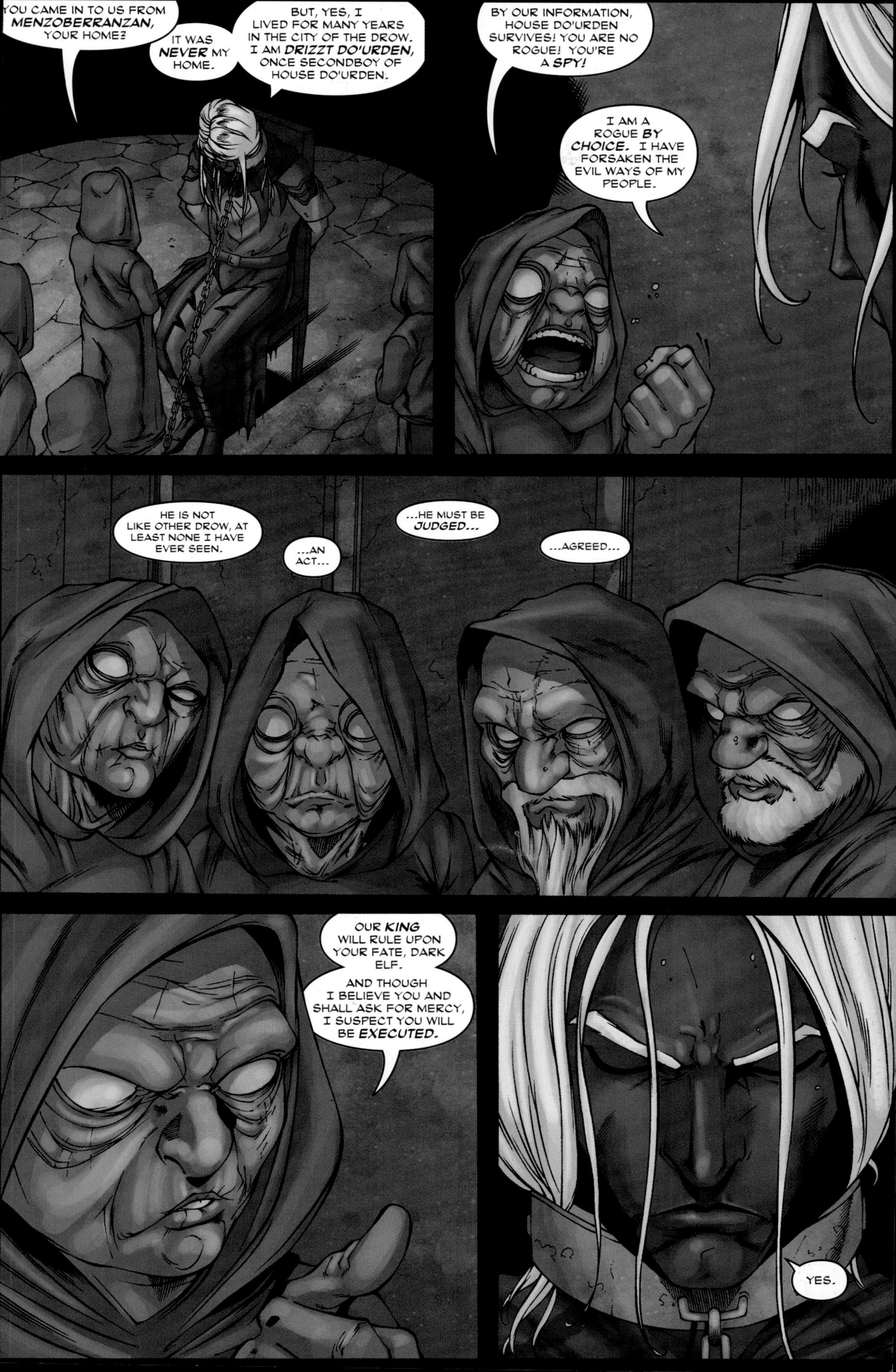
YOU CAME IN TO US FROM MENZOBERRANZAN, YOUR HOME?
IT WAS NEVER MY HOME.
BUT, YES, I LIVED FOR MANY YEARS IN THE CITY OF THE DROW. I AM DRIZZT DO'URDEN, ONCE SECONDBOY OF HOUSE DO'URDEN.
BY OUR INFORMATION, HOUSE DO'URDEN SURVIVES! YOU ARE NO ROGUE! YOU'RE A SPY!
I AM A ROGUE BY CHOICE. I HAVE FORSAKEN THE EVIL WAYS OF MY PEOPLE.
HE IS NOT LIKE OTHER DROW, AT LEAST NONE I HAVE EVER SEEN.
...AN ACT...
...HE MUST BE JUDGED...
...AGREED...
OUR KING WILL RULE UPON YOUR FATE, DARK ELF.
AND THOUGH I BELIEVE YOU AND SHALL ASK FOR MERCY, I SUSPECT YOU WILL BE EXECUTED.
YES.

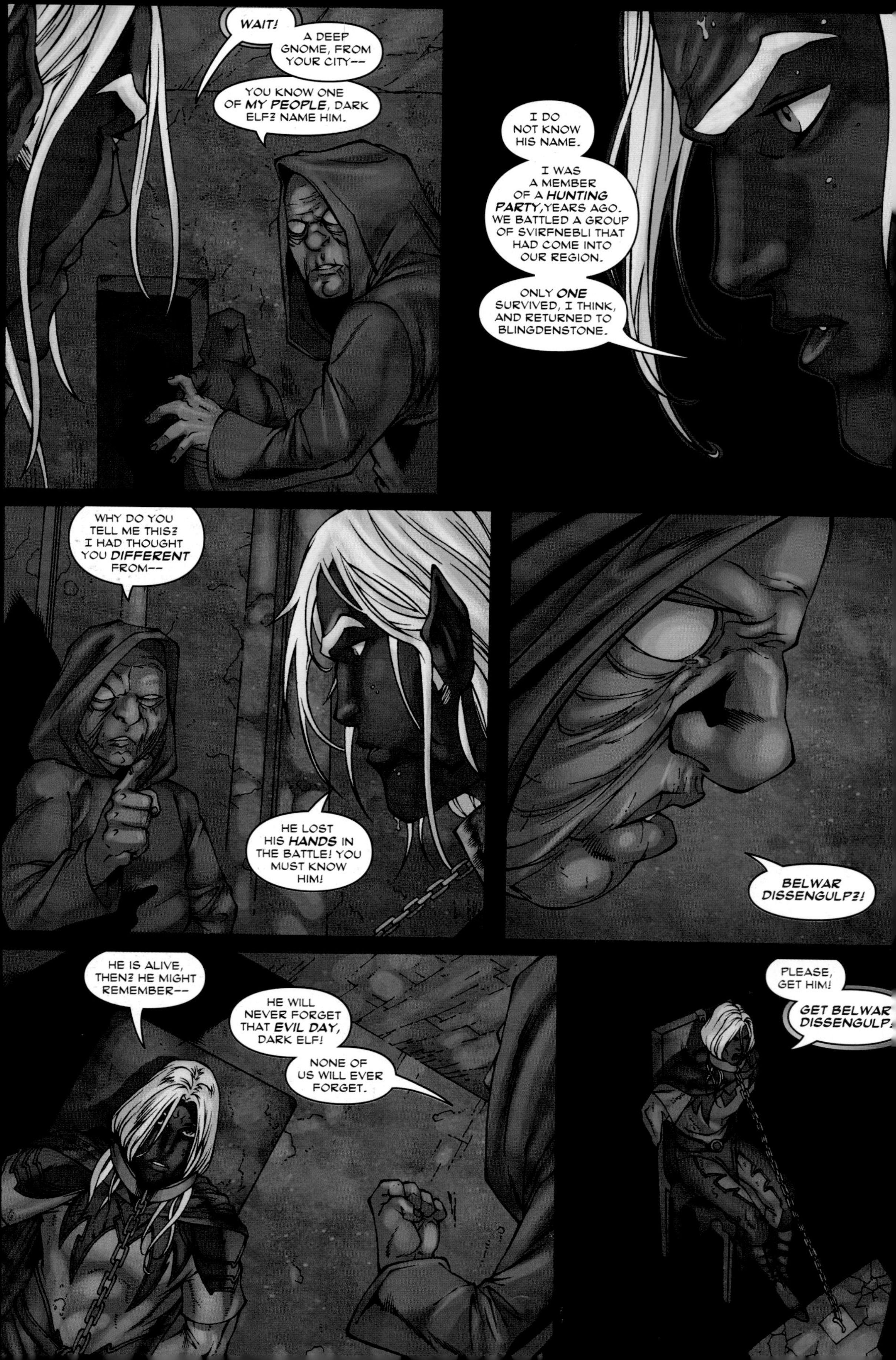
WAIT!
A DEEP GNOME, FROM YOUR CITY--
YOU KNOW ONE OF MY PEOPLE, DARK ELF? NAME HIM.
I DO NOT KNOW HIS NAME.
I WAS A MEMBER OF A HUNTING PARTY, YEARS AGO. WE BATTLED A GROUP OF SVIRFNEBLI THAT HAD COME INTO OUR REGION.
ONLY ONE SURVIVED, I THINK, AND RETURNED TO BLINGDENSTONE.
WHY DO YOU TELL ME THIS? I HAD THOUGHT YOU DIFFERENT FROM--
HE LOST HIS HANDS IN THE BATTLE! YOU MUST KNOW HIM!
BELWAR DISSENGULP?!
HE IS ALIVE, THEN? HE MIGHT REMEMBER--
HE WILL NEVER FORGET THAT EVIL DAY, DARK ELF!
NONE OF US WILL EVER FORGET.
PLEASE, GET HIM!
GET BELWAR DISSENGULP!

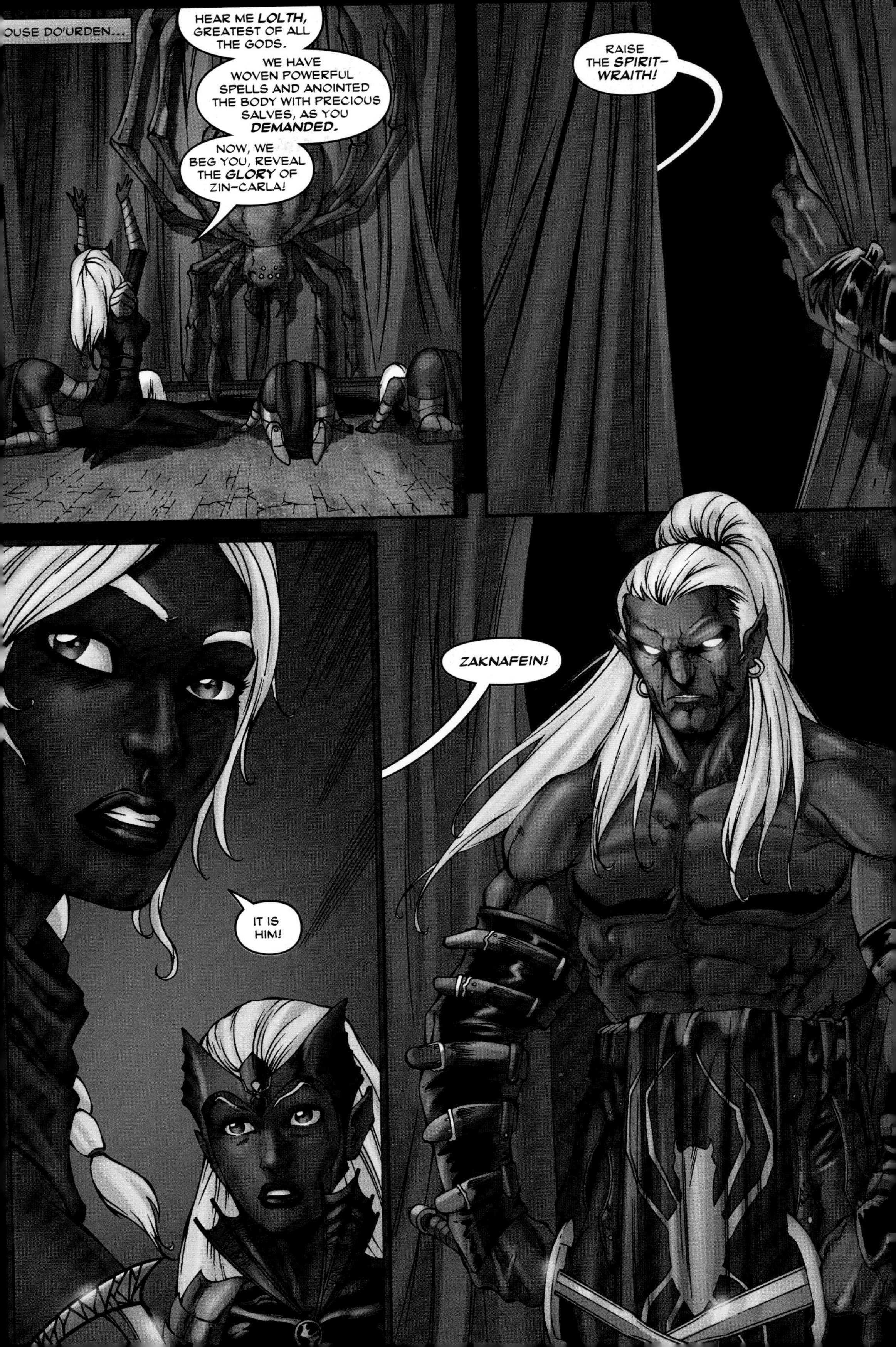
OUSE DO'URDEN...
HEAR ME LOLTH, GREATEST OF ALL THE GODS.
WE HAVE WOVEN POWERFUL SPELLS AND ANOINTED THE BODY WITH PRECIOUS SALVES, AS YOU DEMANDED.
NOW, WE BEG YOU, REVEAL THE GLORY OF ZIN-CARLA!
RAISE THE SPIRIT-WRAITH!
ZAKNAFEIN!
IT IS HIM!

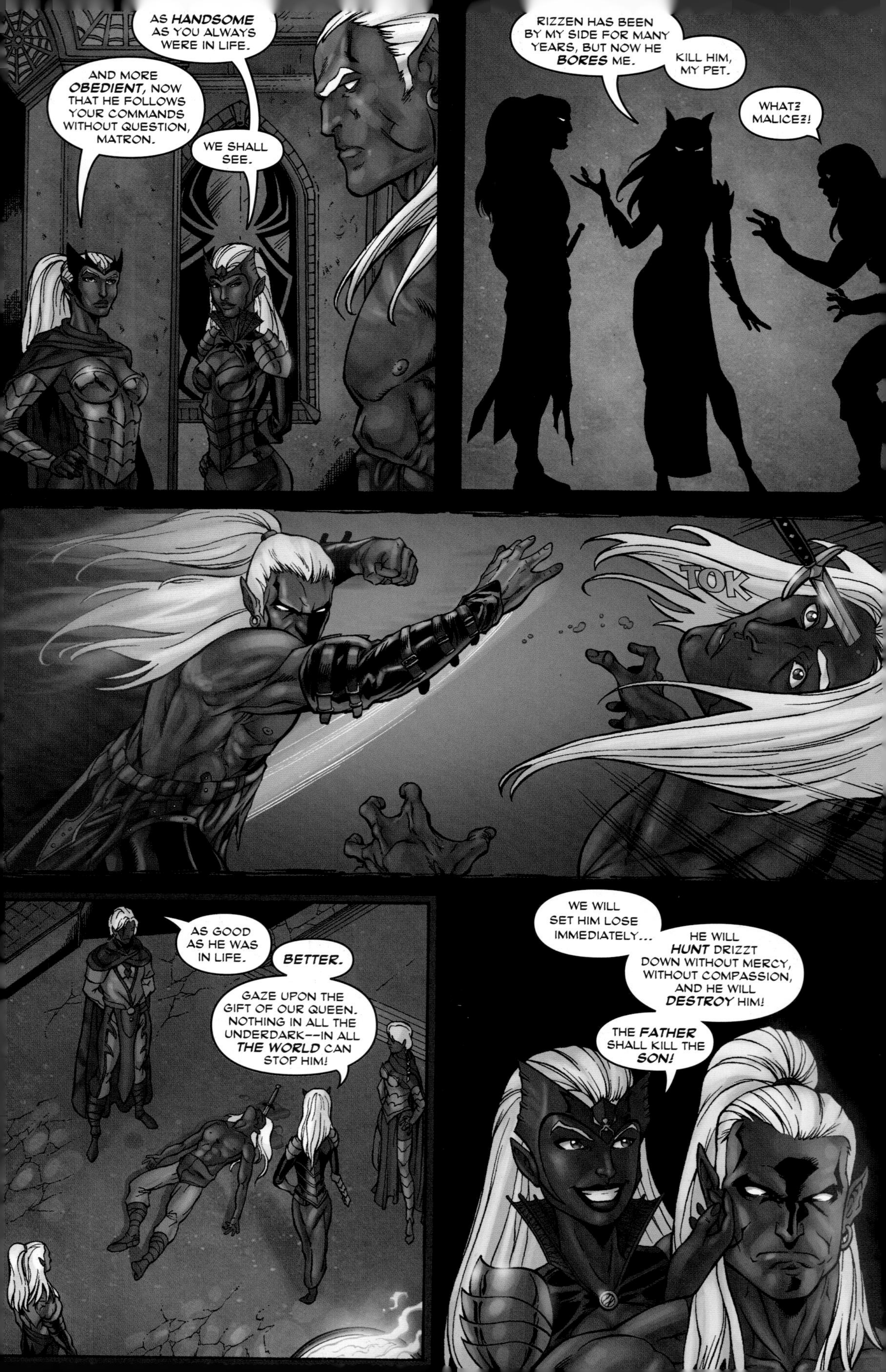
AS HANDSOME AS YOU ALWAYS WERE IN LIFE.
AND MORE OBEDIENT, NOW THAT HE FOLLOWS YOUR COMMANDS WITHOUT QUESTION, MATRON.
WE SHALL SEE.
RIZZEN HAS BEEN BY MY SIDE FOR MANY YEARS, BUT NOW HE BORES ME.
KILL HIM, MY PET.
WHAT? MALICE?!
TOK
AS GOOD AS HE WAS IN LIFE.
BETTER.
GAZE UPON THE GIFT OF OUR QUEEN. NOTHING IN ALL THE UNDERDARK--IN ALL THE WORLD CAN STOP HIM!
WE WILL SET HIM LOSE IMMEDIATELY...
HE WILL HUNT DRIZZT DOWN WITHOUT MERCY, WITHOUT COMPASSION, AND HE WILL DESTROY HIM!
THE FATHER SHALL KILL THE SON!

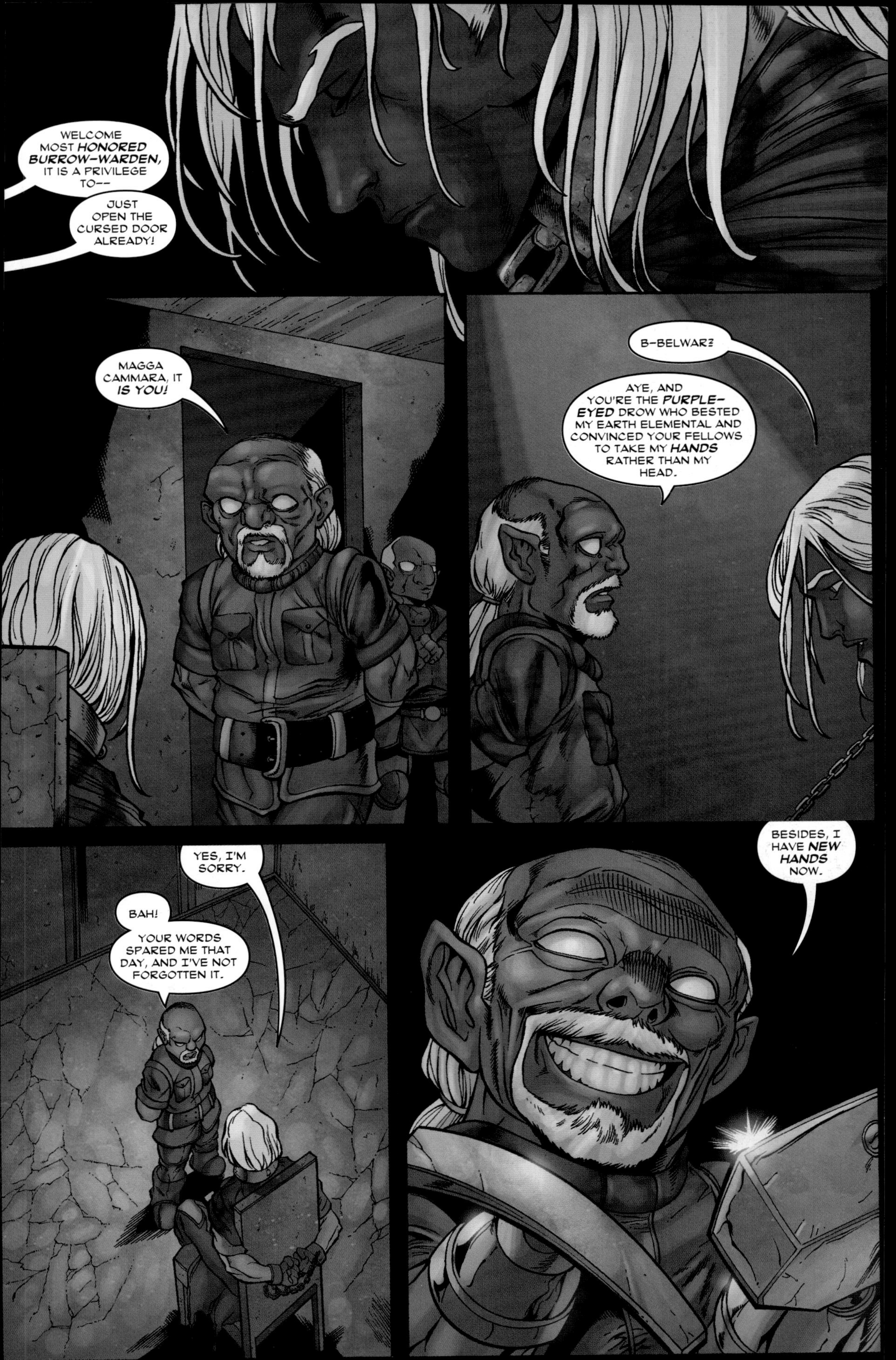
WELCOME MOST HONORED BURROW-WARDEN, IT IS A PRIVILEGE TO--
JUST OPEN THE CURSED DOOR ALREADY!
MAGGA CAMMARA, IT IS YOU!
B-BELWAR?
AYE, AND YOU'RE THE PURPLE-EYED DROW WHO BESTED MY EARTH ELEMENTAL AND CONVINCED YOUR FELLOWS TO TAKE MY HANDS RATHER THAN MY HEAD.
YES, I'M SORRY.
BAH!
YOUR WORDS SPARED ME THAT DAY, AND I'VE NOT FORGOTTEN IT.
BESIDES, I HAVE NEW HANDS NOW.

IT WAS THE DECISION OF *KING SCHNICKTICK* THAT YOU BE *EXECUTED*. HE BELIEVED YOU MEANT US NO HARM, BUT THE DANGER OF HAVING A DARK ELF IN BLINGDENSTONE WAS TOO GREAT.

I GUESSED AS MUCH. I WILL OFFER NO RESISTANCE.

NO, *YOU WON'T*, FOR YOU'LL NOT DIE THIS DAY.

WHAT?

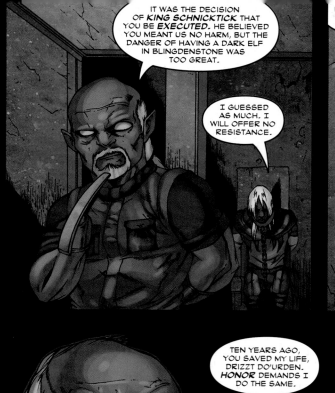

TEN YEARS AGO, YOU SAVED MY LIFE, DRIZZT DO'URDEN. *HONOR* DEMANDS I DO THE SAME.

I'VE ACCEPTED THE *RESPONSIBILITY* OF KEEPING YOU.

YOU'LL BE A GUEST IN MY HOME AT FIRST, THEN WHO KNOWS?

SO... SO I'M *NOT* TO DIE?

NOT UNLESS YOU BRING DEATH UPON YOURSELF.

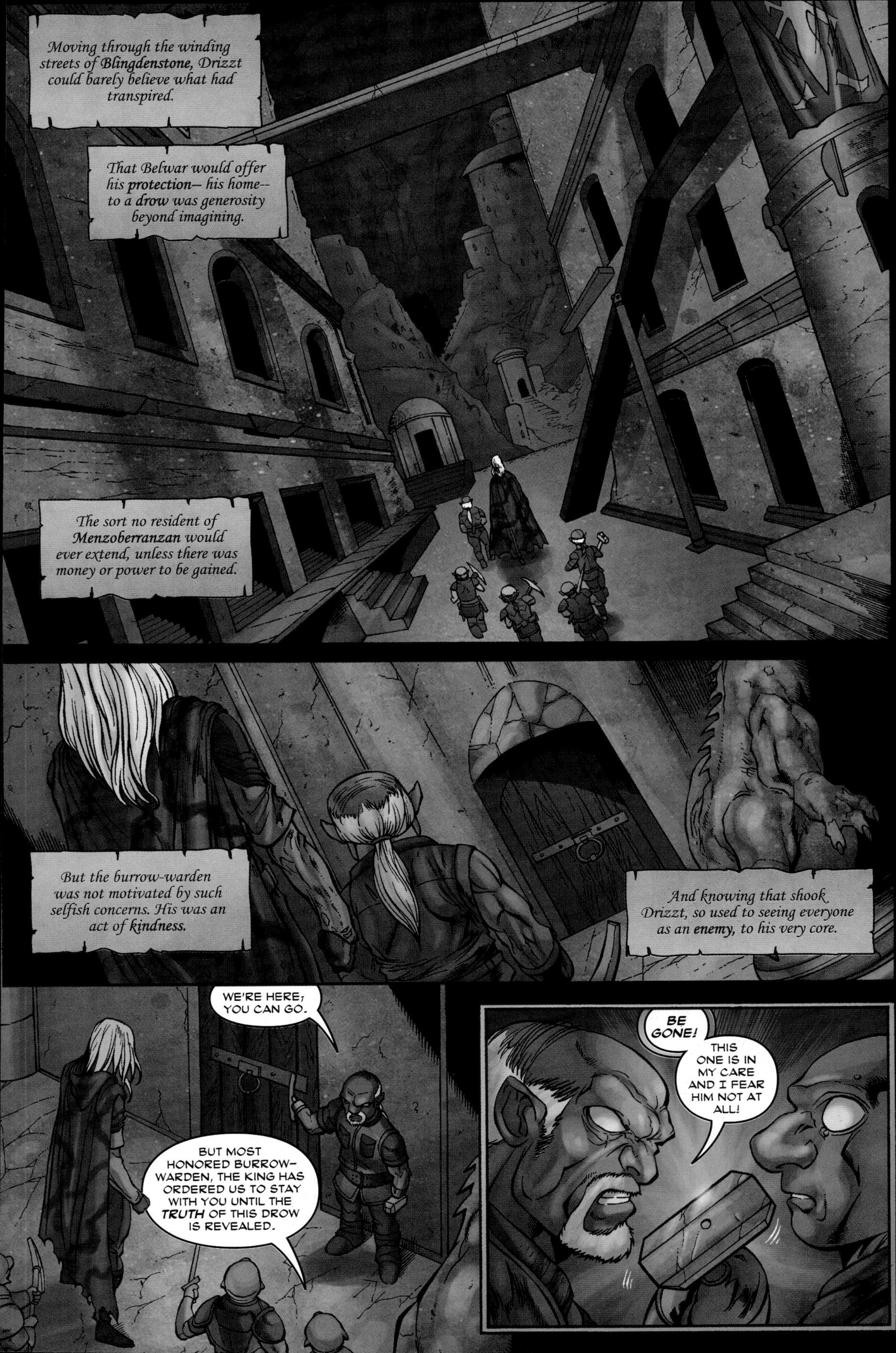
Moving through the winding streets of Blingdenstone, Drizzt could barely believe what had transpired.
That Belwar would offer his protection-- his home-- to a drow was generosity beyond imagining.
The sort no resident of Menzoberranzan would ever extend, unless there was money or power to be gained.
But the burrow-warden was not motivated by such selfish concerns. His was an act of kindness.
And knowing that shook Drizzt, so used to seeing everyone as an enemy, to his very core.
WE'RE HERE; YOU CAN GO.
BUT MOST HONORED BURROW-WARDEN, THE KING HAS ORDERED US TO STAY WITH YOU UNTIL THE TRUTH OF THIS DROW IS REVEALED.
BE GONE!
THIS ONE IS IN MY CARE AND I FEAR HIM NOT AT ALL!

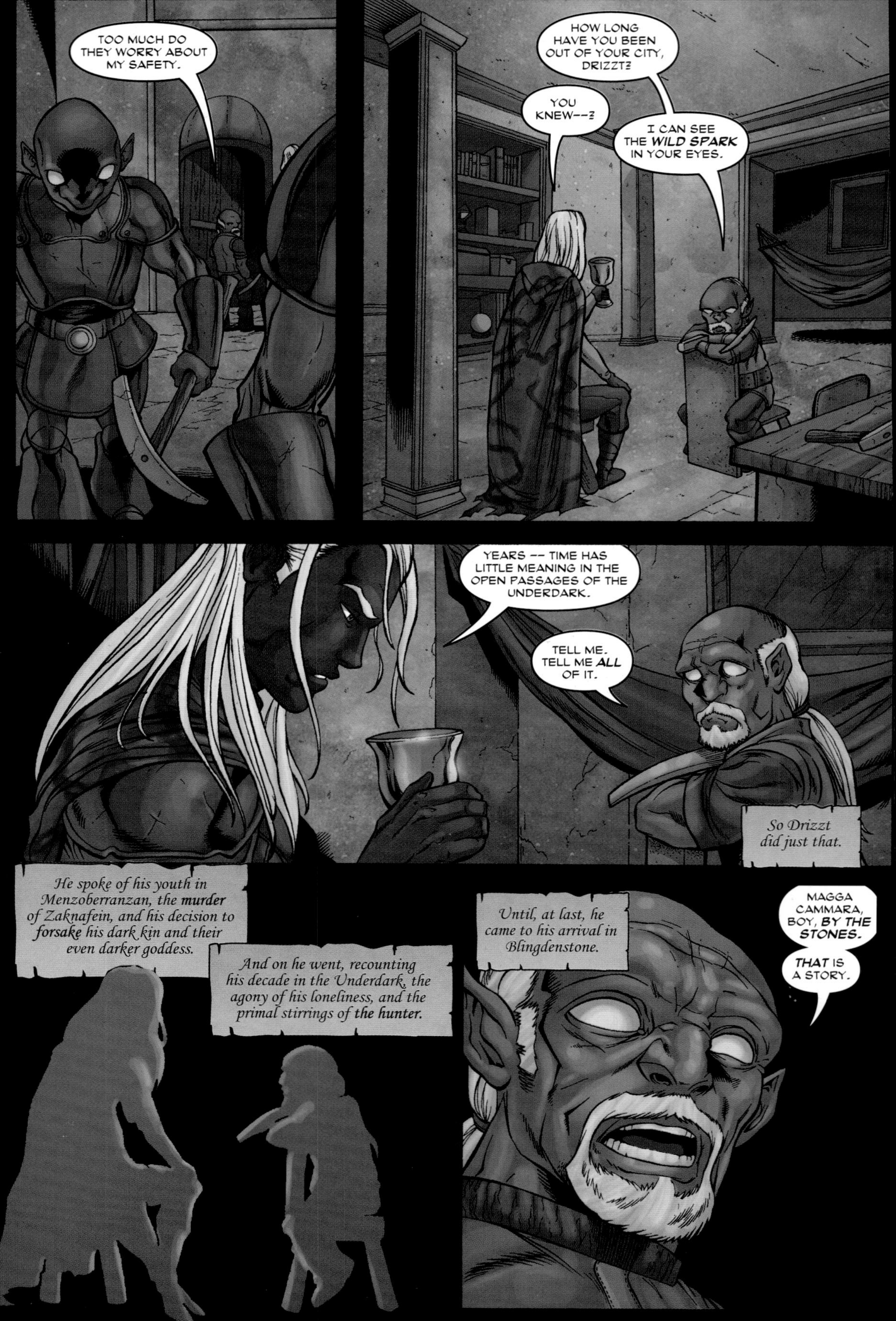
TOO MUCH DO THEY WORRY ABOUT MY SAFETY.
HOW LONG HAVE YOU BEEN OUT OF YOUR CITY, DRIZZT?
YOU KNEW--?
I CAN SEE THE WILD SPARK IN YOUR EYES.
YEARS -- TIME HAS LITTLE MEANING IN THE OPEN PASSAGES OF THE UNDERDARK.
TELL ME. TELL ME ALL OF IT.
So Drizzt did just that.
He spoke of his youth in Menzoberranzan, the murder of Zaknafein, and his decision to forsake his dark kin and their even darker goddess.
And on he went, recounting his decade in the Underdark, the agony of his loneliness, and the primal stirrings of the hunter.
Until, at last, he came to his arrival in Blingdenstone.
MAGGA CAMMARA, BOY, BY THE STONES.
THAT IS A STORY.

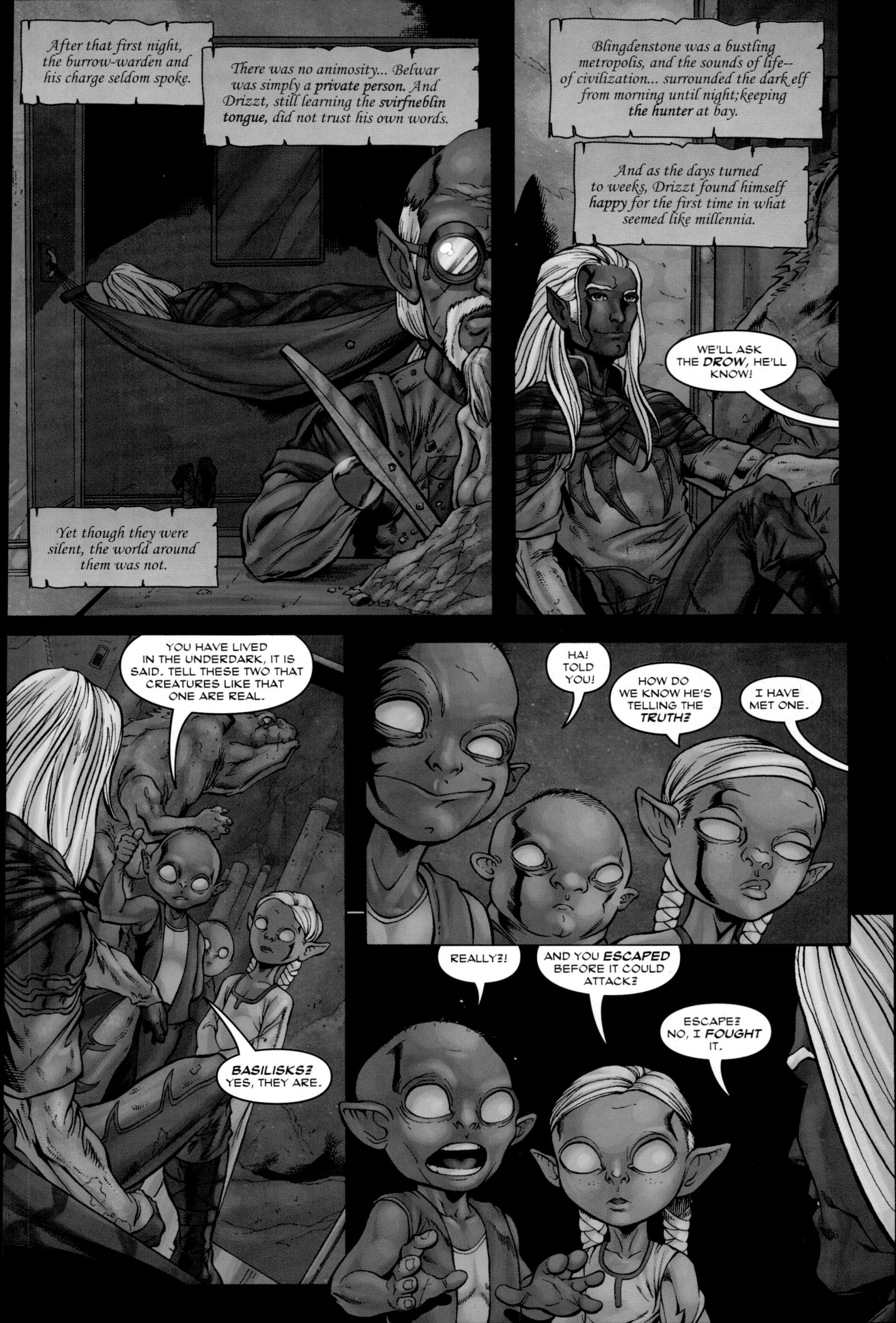

After that first night, the burrow-warden and his charge seldom spoke.
There was no animosity... Belwar was simply a private person. And Drizzt, still learning the svirfneblin tongue, did not trust his own words.
Yet though they were silent, the world around them was not.
Blingdenstone was a bustling metropolis, and the sounds of life-- of civilization... surrounded the dark elf from morning until night; keeping the hunter at bay.
And as the days turned to weeks, Drizzt found himself happy for the first time in what seemed like millennia.
WE'LL ASK THE DROW, HE'LL KNOW!
YOU HAVE LIVED IN THE UNDERDARK, IT IS SAID. TELL THESE TWO THAT CREATURES LIKE THAT ONE ARE REAL.
BASILISKS? YES, THEY ARE.
HA! TOLD YOU!
HOW DO WE KNOW HE'S TELLING THE TRUTH?
I HAVE MET ONE.
REALLY?!
AND YOU ESCAPED BEFORE IT COULD ATTACK?
ESCAPE? NO, I FOUGHT IT.

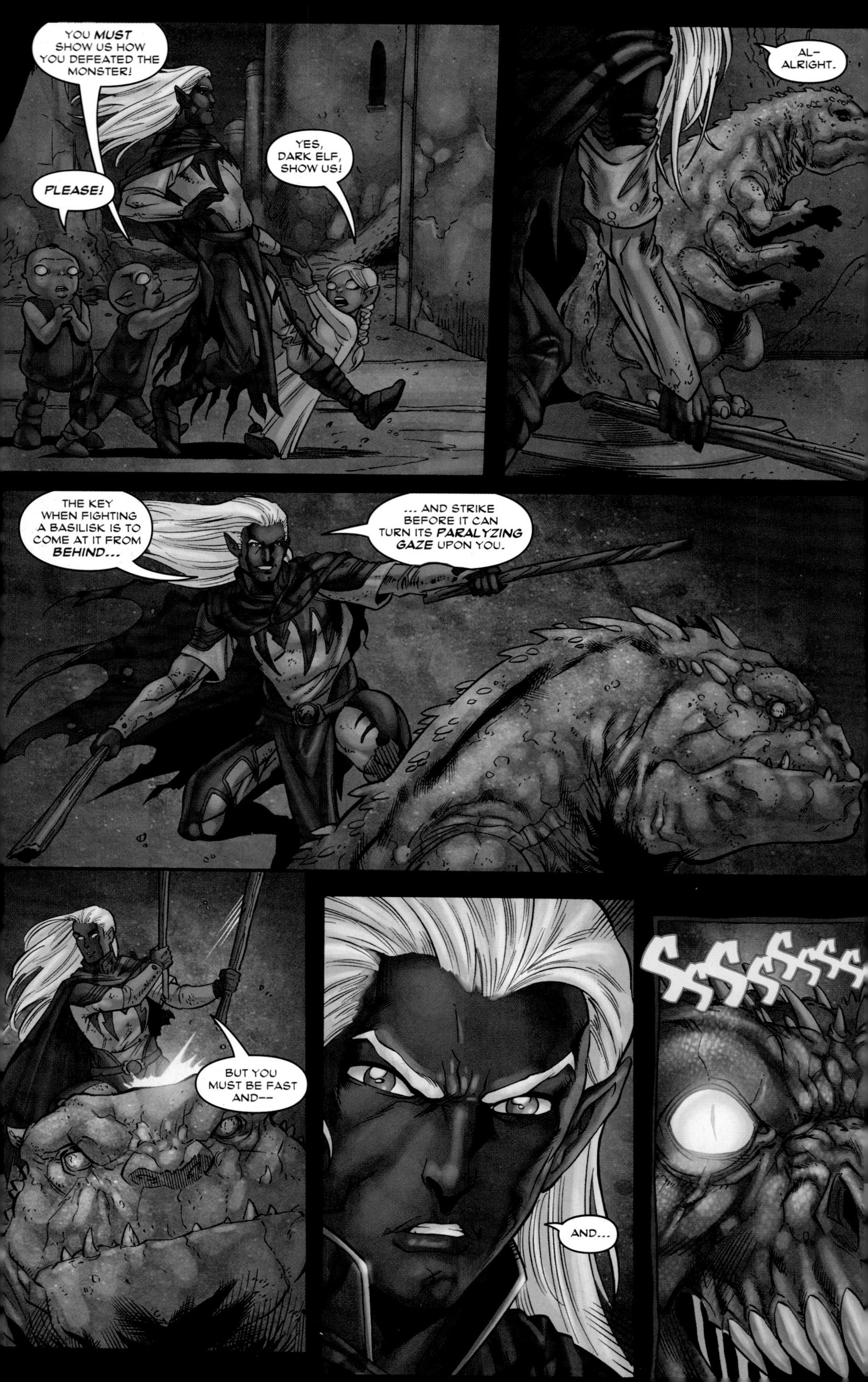
YOU MUST SHOW US HOW YOU DEFEATED THE MONSTER!
PLEASE!
YES, DARK ELF, SHOW US!
AL-ALRIGHT.
THE KEY WHEN FIGHTING A BASILISK IS TO COME AT IT FROM BEHIND...
... AND STRIKE BEFORE IT CAN TURN ITS PARALYZING GAZE UPON YOU.
BUT YOU MUST BE FAST AND--
AND...
SSSSSSS

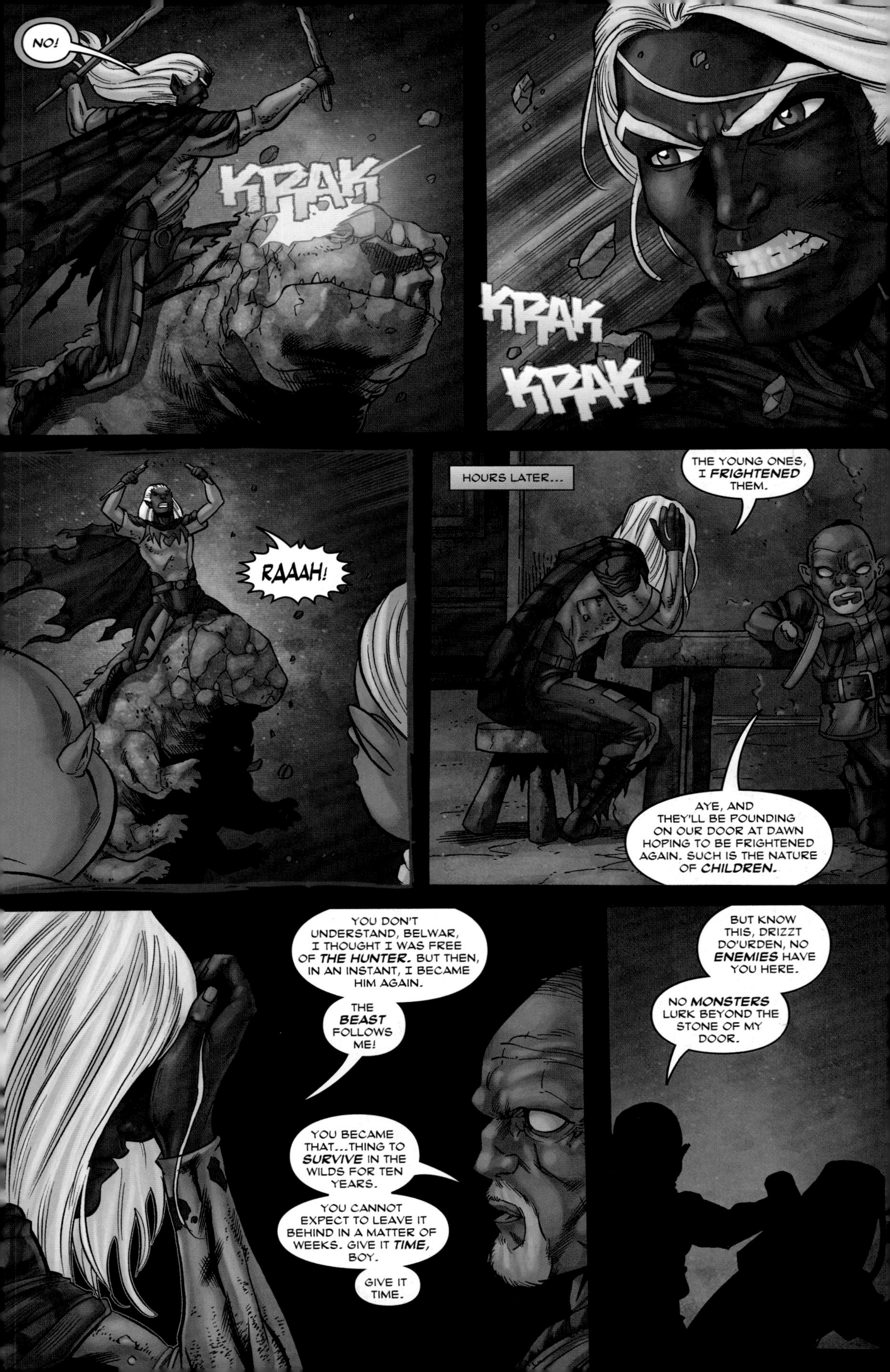
NO!
KRAK
KRAK
KRAK
RAAAH!
HOURS LATER...
THE YOUNG ONES, I FRIGHTENED THEM.
AYE, AND THEY'LL BE POUNDING ON OUR DOOR AT DAWN HOPING TO BE FRIGHTENED AGAIN. SUCH IS THE NATURE OF CHILDREN.
YOU DON'T UNDERSTAND, BELWAR, I THOUGHT I WAS FREE OF THE HUNTER. BUT THEN, IN AN INSTANT, I BECAME HIM AGAIN.
THE BEAST FOLLOWS ME!
YOU BECAME THAT...THING TO SURVIVE IN THE WILDS FOR TEN YEARS.
YOU CANNOT EXPECT TO LEAVE IT BEHIND IN A MATTER OF WEEKS. GIVE IT TIME, BOY.
GIVE IT TIME.
BUT KNOW THIS, DRIZZT DO'URDEN, NO ENEMIES HAVE YOU HERE.
NO MONSTERS LURK BEYOND THE STONE OF MY DOOR.

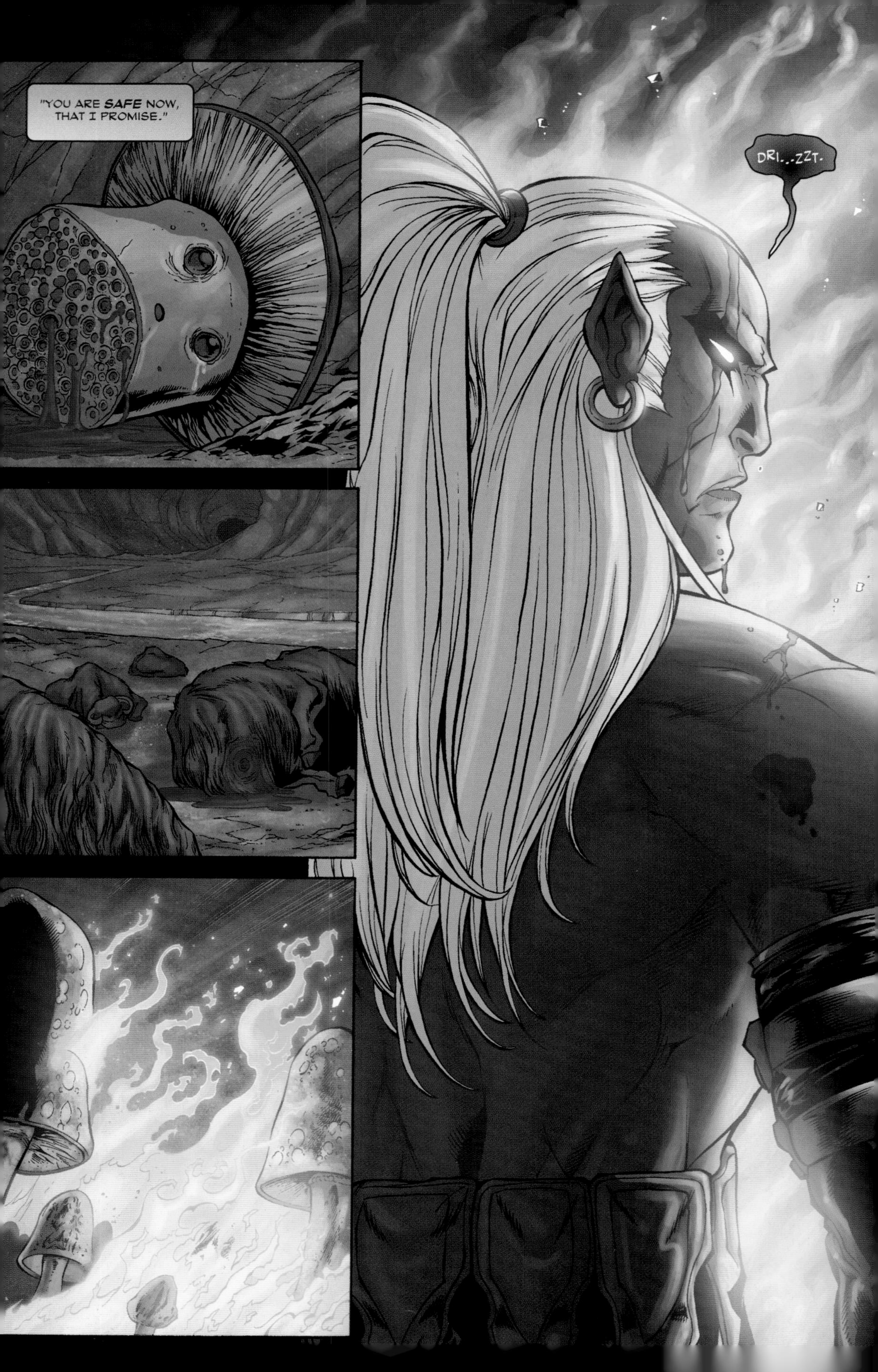
"YOU ARE SAFE NOW, THAT I PROMISE."
DRI...ZZT.

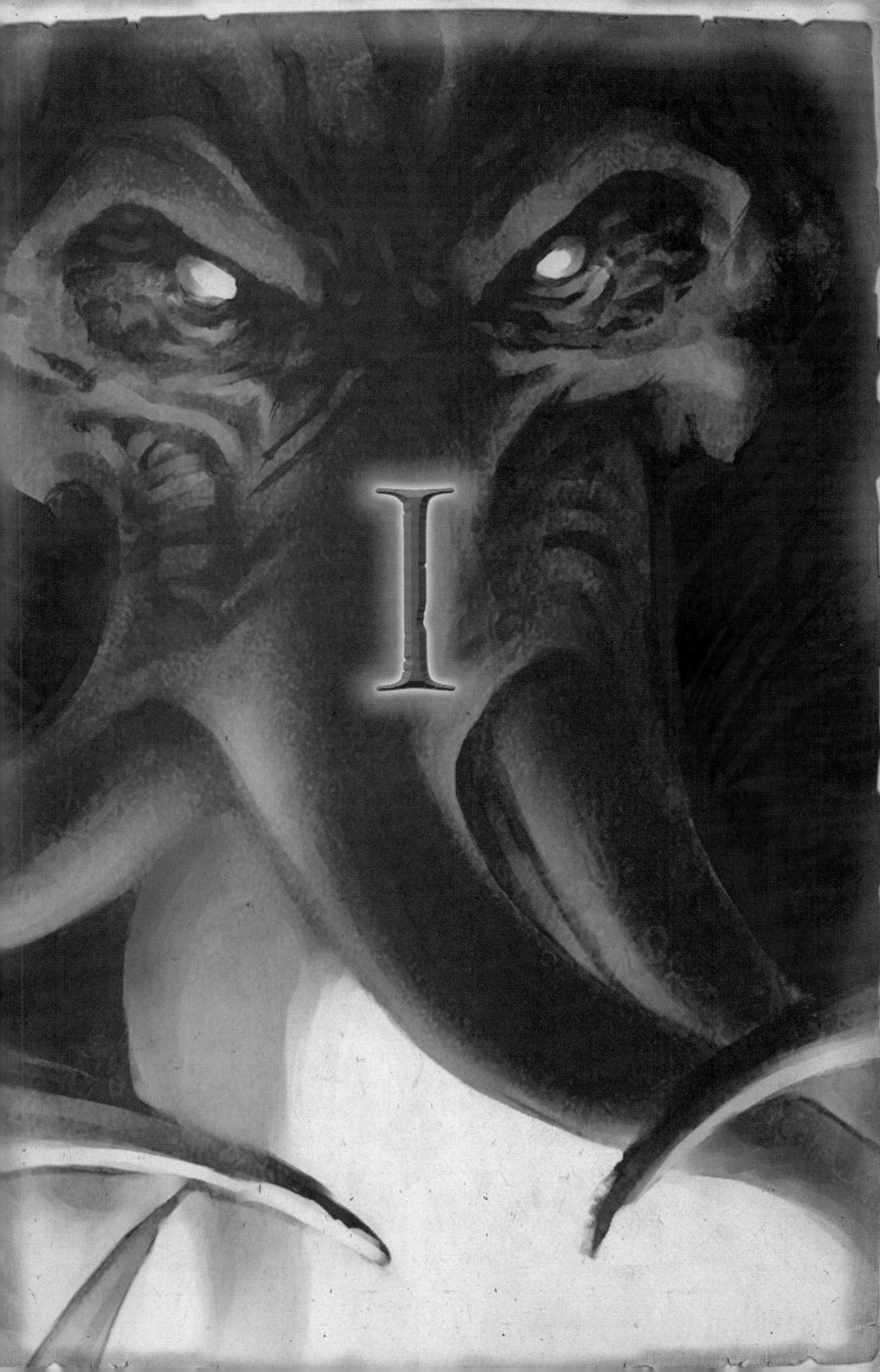
I

II

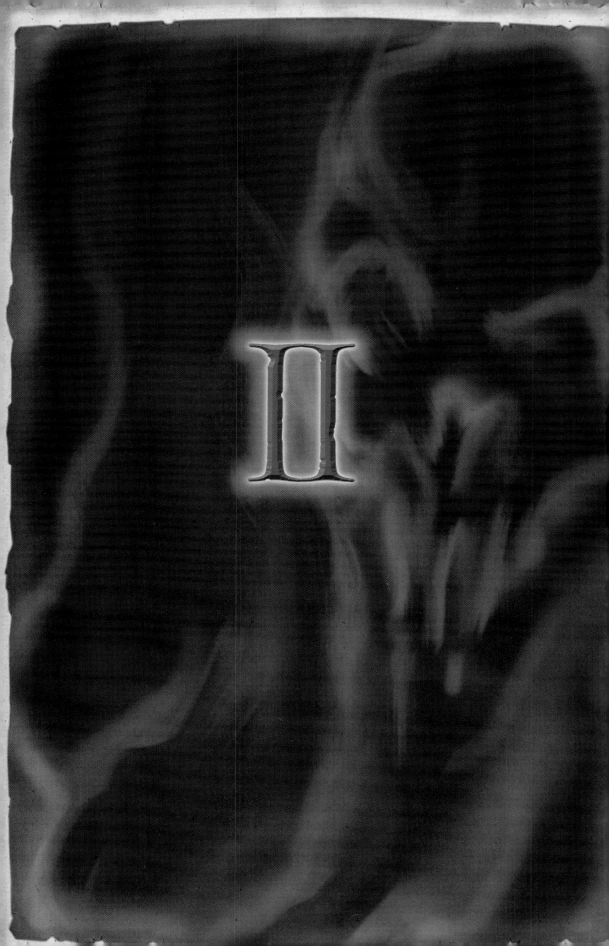

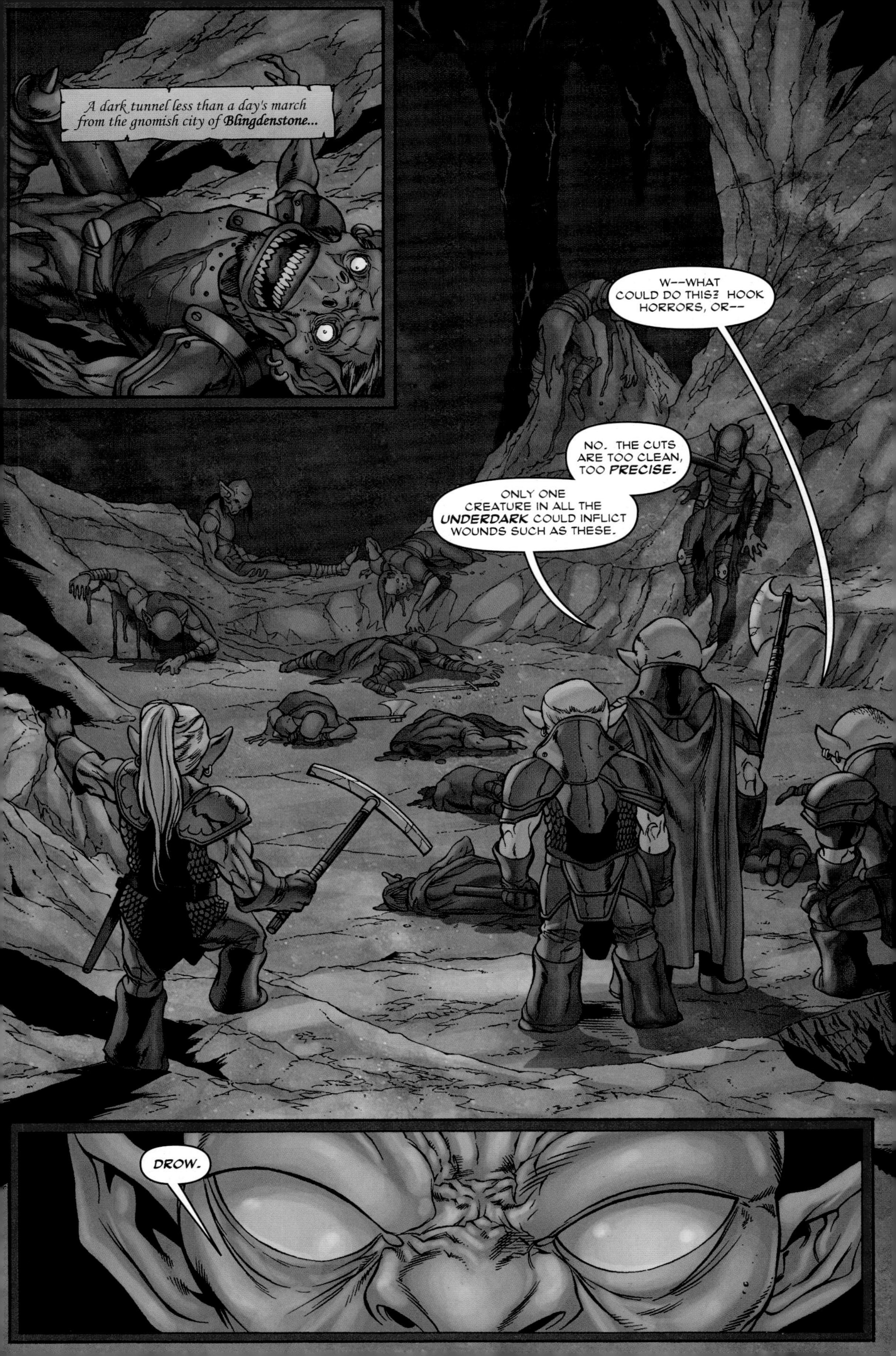
A dark tunnel less than a day's march from the gnomish city of **Blingdenstone...**
W--WHAT COULD DO THIS? HOOK HORRORS, OR--
NO. THE CUTS ARE TOO CLEAN, TOO ***PRECISE.***
ONLY ONE CREATURE IN ALL THE ***UNDERDARK*** COULD INFLICT WOUNDS SUCH AS THESE.
DROW.

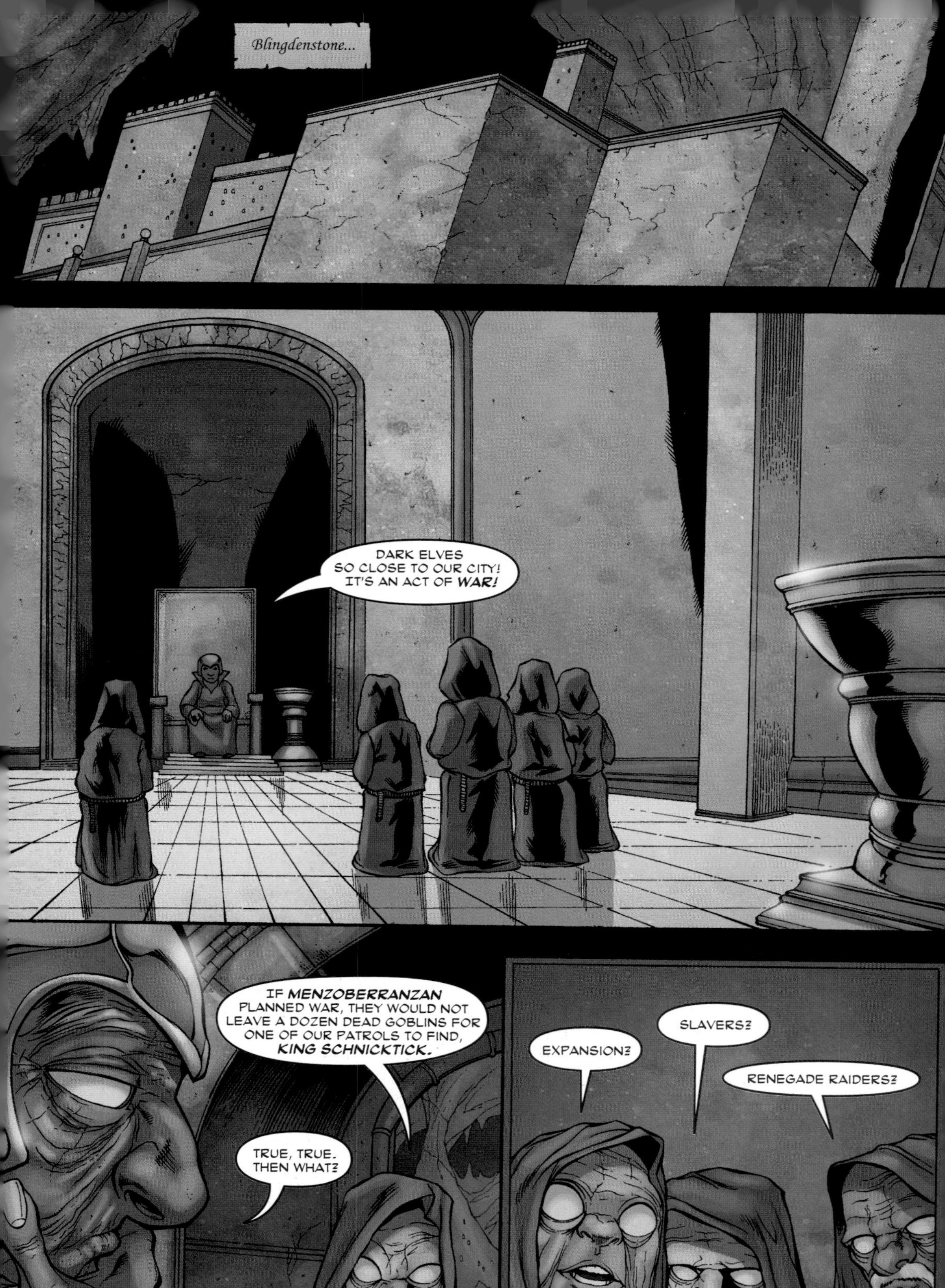

Blingdenstone...
DARK ELVES SO CLOSE TO OUR CITY! IT'S AN ACT OF WAR!
IF MENZOBERRANZAN PLANNED WAR, THEY WOULD NOT LEAVE A DOZEN DEAD GOBLINS FOR ONE OF OUR PATROLS TO FIND, KING SCHNICKTICK.
TRUE, TRUE. THEN WHAT?
EXPANSION?
SLAVERS?
RENEGADE RAIDERS?

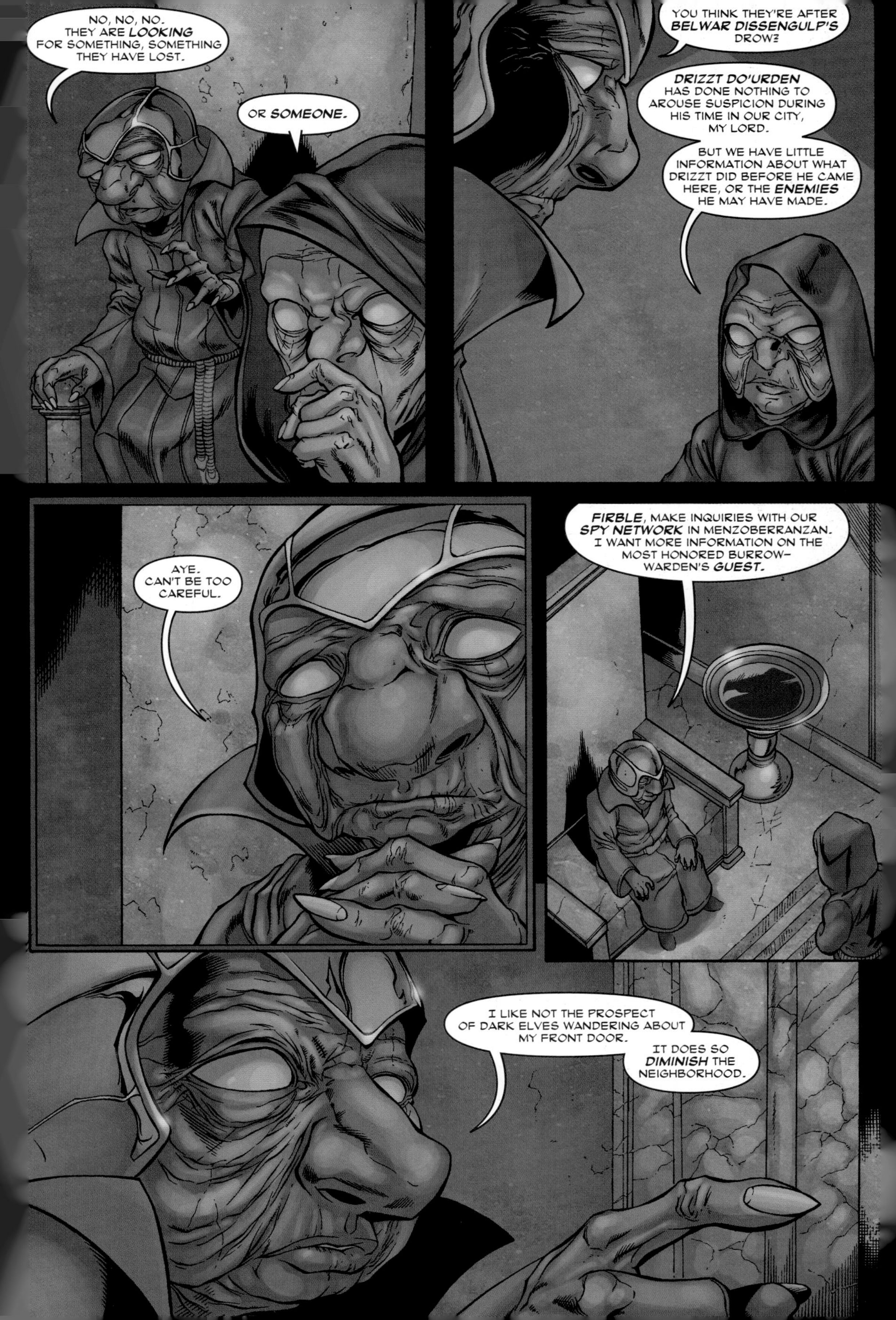
NO, NO, NO. THEY ARE LOOKING FOR SOMETHING, SOMETHING THEY HAVE LOST.
OR SOMEONE.
YOU THINK THEY'RE AFTER BELWAR DISSENGULP'S DROW?
DRIZZT DO'URDEN HAS DONE NOTHING TO AROUSE SUSPICION DURING HIS TIME IN OUR CITY, MY LORD.
BUT WE HAVE LITTLE INFORMATION ABOUT WHAT DRIZZT DID BEFORE HE CAME HERE, OR THE ENEMIES HE MAY HAVE MADE.
AYE. CAN'T BE TOO CAREFUL.
FIRBLE, MAKE INQUIRIES WITH OUR SPY NETWORK IN MENZOBERRANZAN. I WANT MORE INFORMATION ON THE MOST HONORED BURROW-WARDEN'S GUEST.
I LIKE NOT THE PROSPECT OF DARK ELVES WANDERING ABOUT MY FRONT DOOR.
IT DOES SO DIMINISH THE NEIGHBORHOOD.

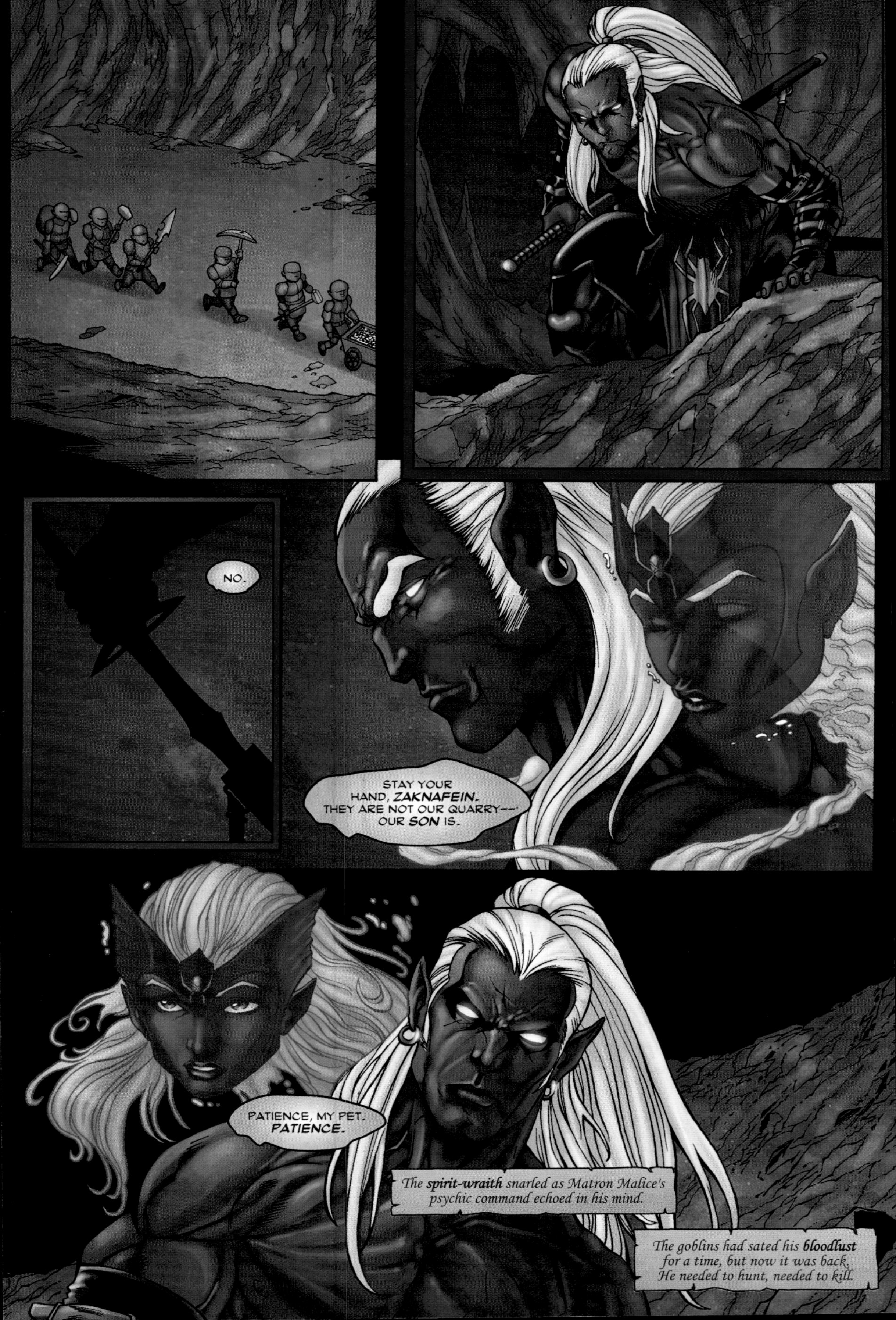
NO.
STAY YOUR HAND, ZAKNAFEIN. THEY ARE NOT OUR QUARRY--- OUR SON IS.
PATIENCE, MY PET. PATIENCE.
The spirit-wraith snarled as Matron Malice's psychic command echoed in his mind.
The goblins had sated his bloodlust for a time, but now it was back. He needed to hunt, needed to kill.

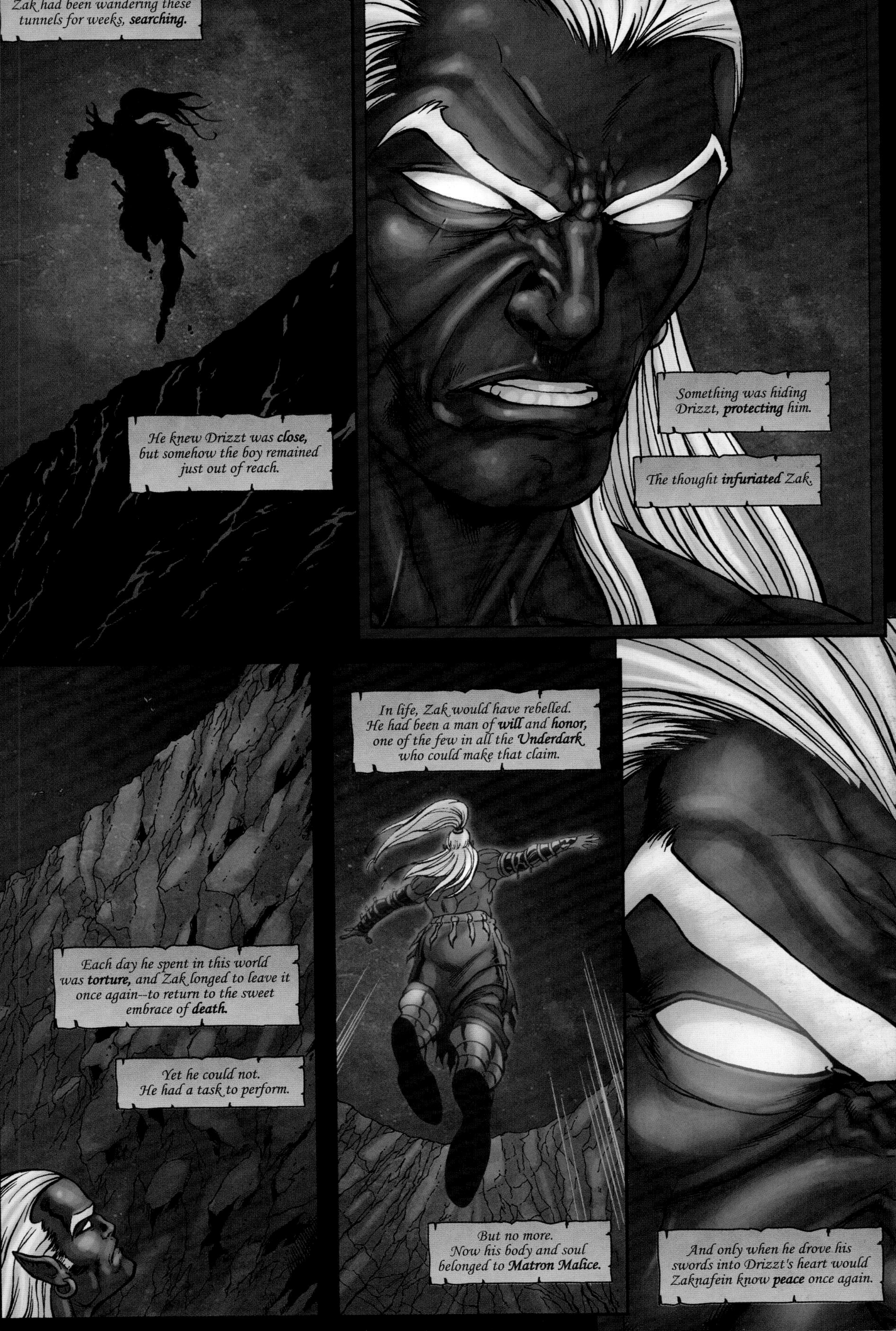

Zak had been wandering these tunnels for weeks, searching.
He knew Drizzt was close, but somehow the boy remained just out of reach.
Something was hiding Drizzt, protecting him.
The thought infuriated Zak.
Each day he spent in this world was torture, and Zak longed to leave it once again--to return to the sweet embrace of death.
Yet he could not. He had a task to perform.
In life, Zak would have rebelled. He had been a man of will and honor, one of the few in all the Underdark who could make that claim.
But no more. Now his body and soul belonged to Matron Malice.
And only when he drove his swords into Drizzt's heart would Zaknafein know peace once again.

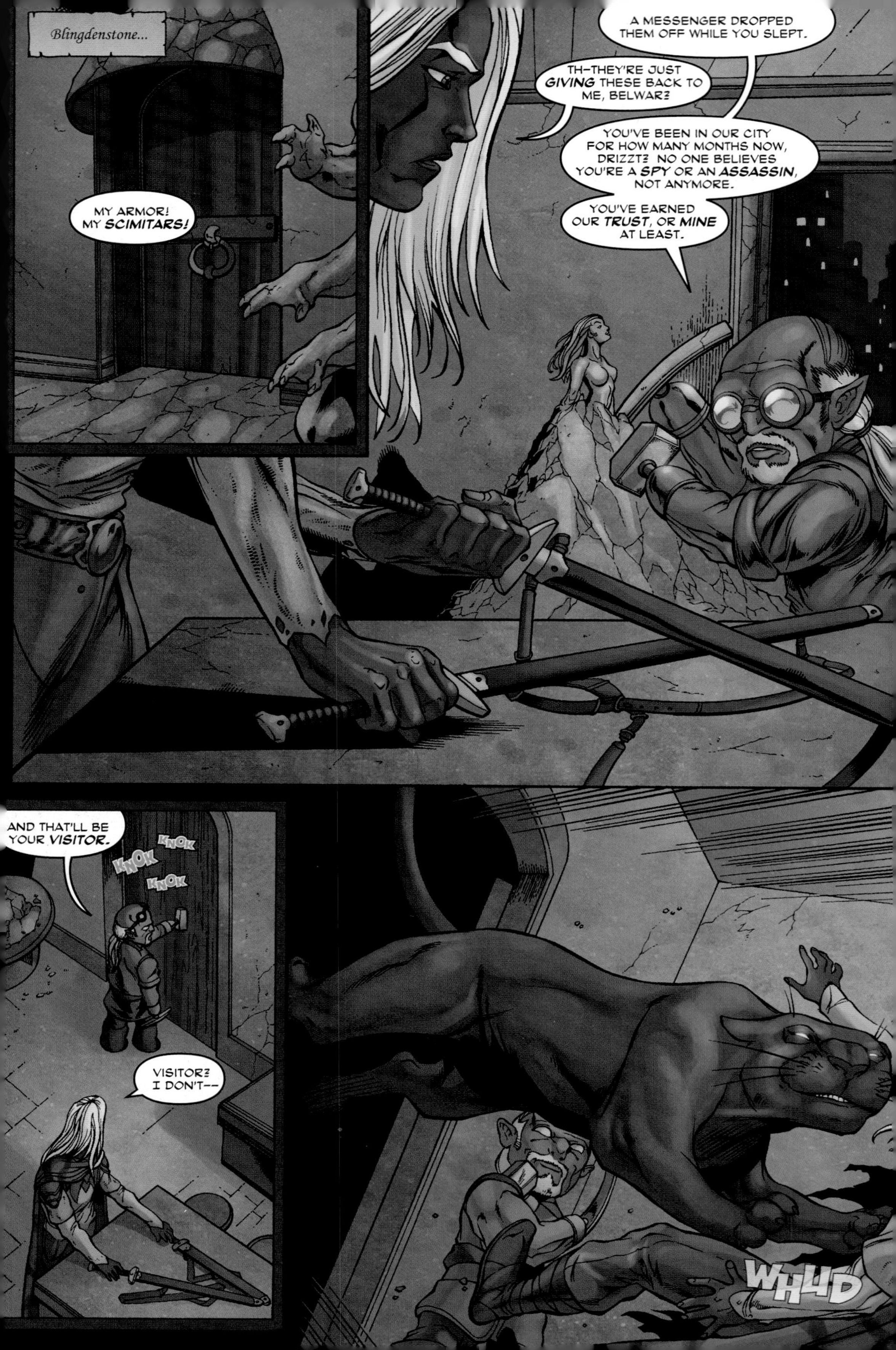
Blingdenstone...
MY ARMOR! MY SCIMITARS!
TH--THEY'RE JUST GIVING THESE BACK TO ME, BELWAR?
A MESSENGER DROPPED THEM OFF WHILE YOU SLEPT.
YOU'VE BEEN IN OUR CITY FOR HOW MANY MONTHS NOW, DRIZZT? NO ONE BELIEVES YOU'RE A SPY OR AN ASSASSIN, NOT ANYMORE.
YOU'VE EARNED OUR TRUST, OR MINE AT LEAST.
AND THAT'LL BE YOUR VISITOR.
KNOK
KNOK
KNOK
VISITOR? I DON'T--
WHUD

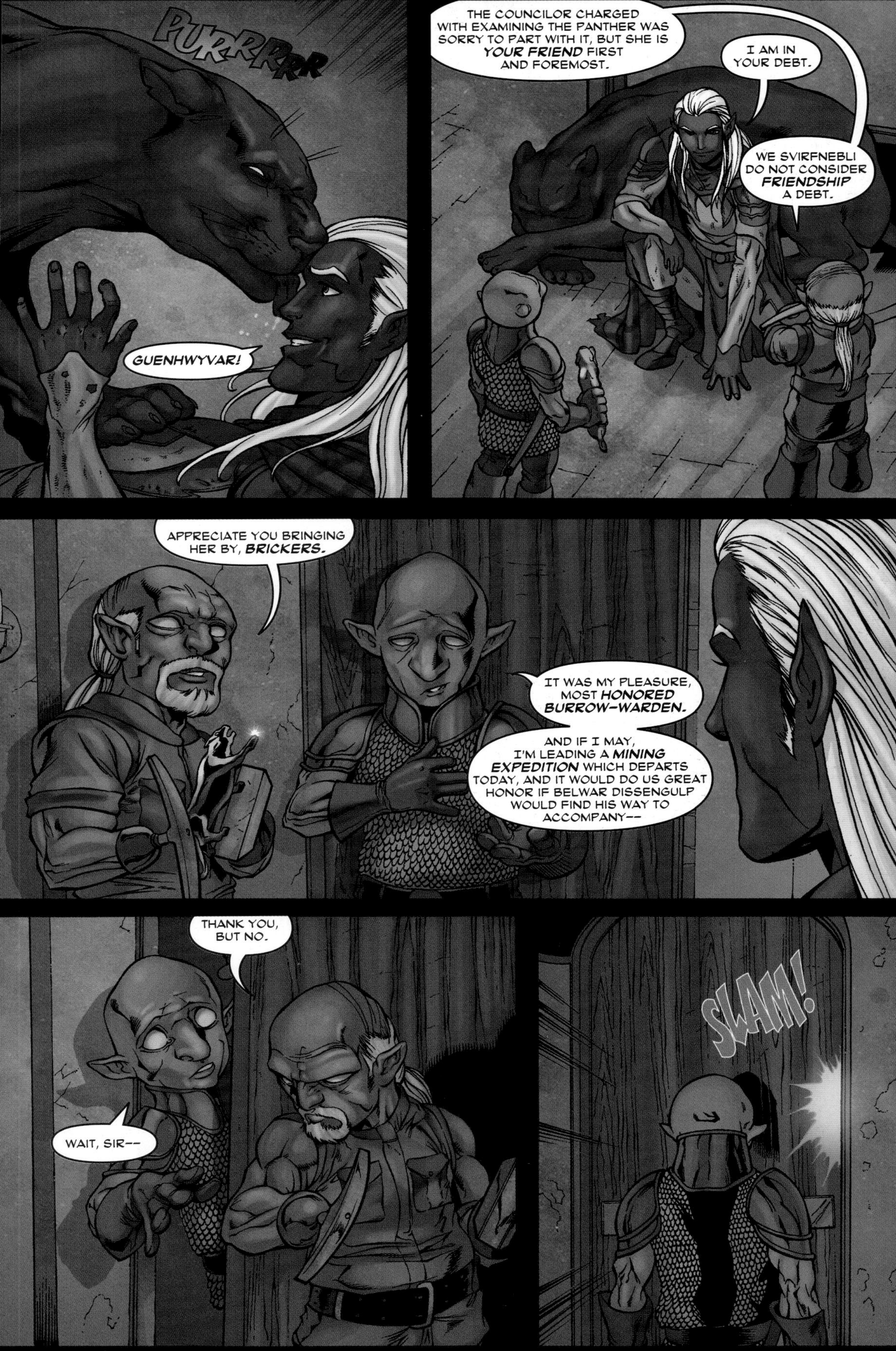
PURRRRRR
GUENHWYVAR!
THE COUNCILOR CHARGED WITH EXAMINING THE PANTHER WAS SORRY TO PART WITH IT, BUT SHE IS YOUR FRIEND FIRST AND FOREMOST.
I AM IN YOUR DEBT.
WE SVIRFNEBLI DO NOT CONSIDER FRIENDSHIP A DEBT.
APPRECIATE YOU BRINGING HER BY, BRICKERS.
IT WAS MY PLEASURE, MOST HONORED BURROW-WARDEN.
AND IF I MAY, I'M LEADING A MINING EXPEDITION WHICH DEPARTS TODAY, AND IT WOULD DO US GREAT HONOR IF BELWAR DISSENGULP WOULD FIND HIS WAY TO ACCOMPANY--
THANK YOU, BUT NO.
WAIT, SIR--
SLAM!

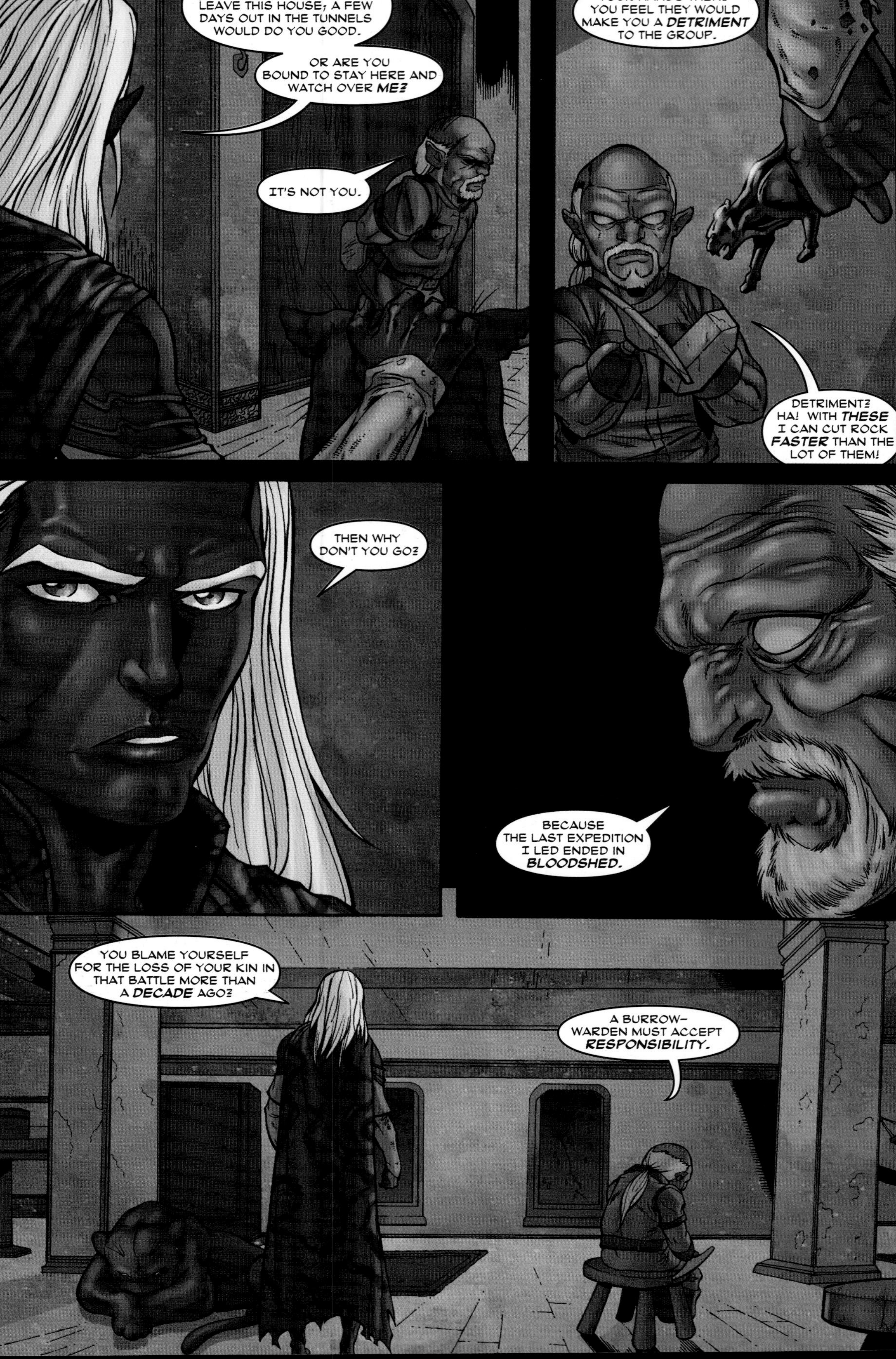
LEAVE THIS HOUSE; A FEW DAYS OUT IN THE TUNNELS WOULD DO YOU GOOD.
OR ARE YOU BOUND TO STAY HERE AND WATCH OVER ME?
IT'S NOT YOU.
YOU FEEL THEY WOULD MAKE YOU A DETRIMENT TO THE GROUP.
DETRIMENT? HA! WITH THESE I CAN CUT ROCK FASTER THAN THE LOT OF THEM!
THEN WHY DON'T YOU GO?
BECAUSE THE LAST EXPEDITION I LED ENDED IN BLOODSHED.
YOU BLAME YOURSELF FOR THE LOSS OF YOUR KIN IN THAT BATTLE MORE THAN A DECADE AGO?
A BURROW-WARDEN MUST ACCEPT RESPONSIBILITY.

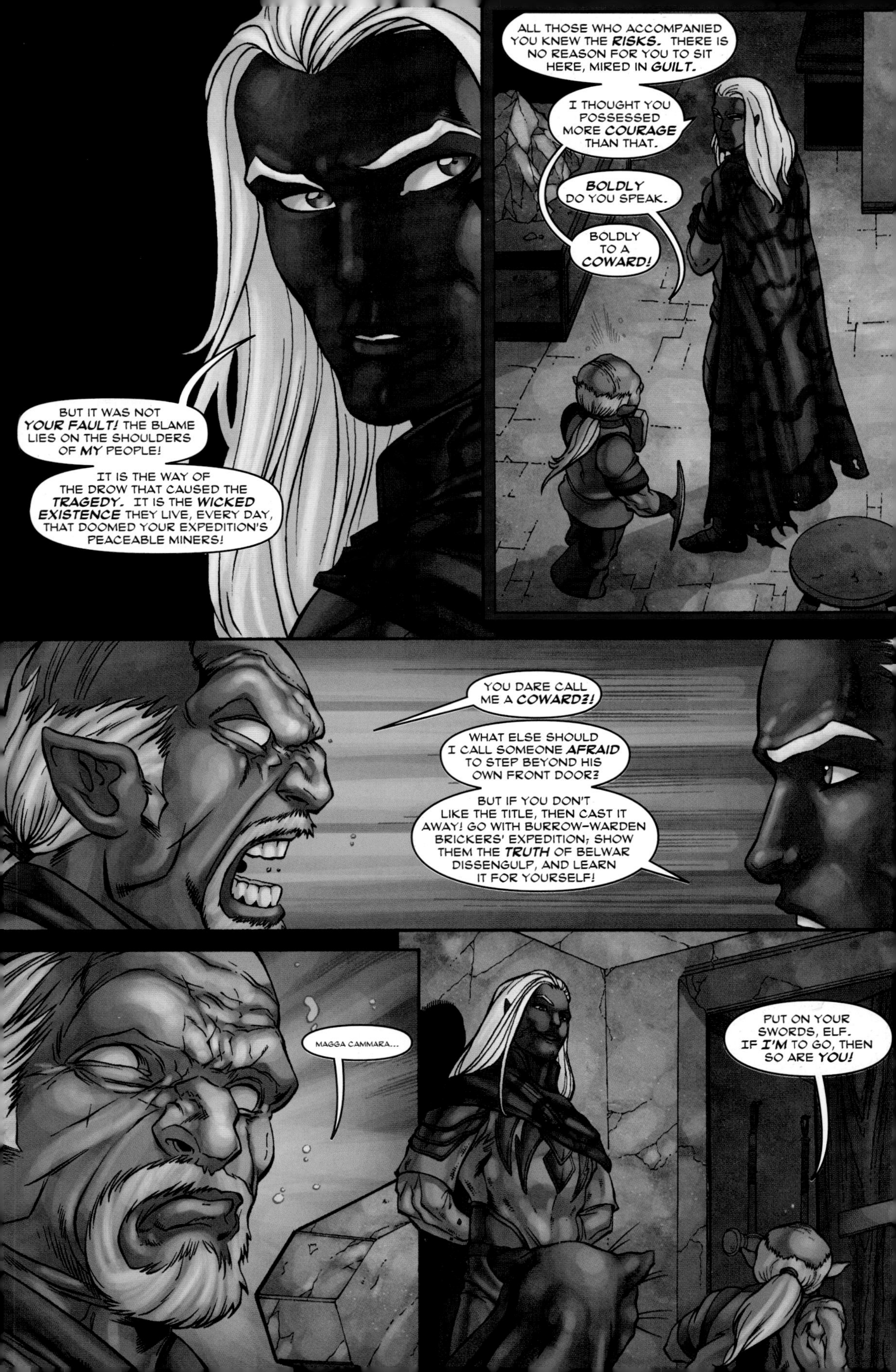
BUT IT WAS NOT YOUR FAULT! THE BLAME LIES ON THE SHOULDERS OF MY PEOPLE!
IT IS THE WAY OF THE DROW THAT CAUSED THE TRAGEDY. IT IS THE WICKED EXISTENCE THEY LIVE, EVERY DAY, THAT DOOMED YOUR EXPEDITION'S PEACEABLE MINERS!
ALL THOSE WHO ACCOMPANIED YOU KNEW THE RISKS. THERE IS NO REASON FOR YOU TO SIT HERE, MIRED IN GUILT.
I THOUGHT YOU POSSESSED MORE COURAGE THAN THAT.
BOLDLY DO YOU SPEAK.
BOLDLY TO A COWARD!
YOU DARE CALL ME A COWARD?!
WHAT ELSE SHOULD I CALL SOMEONE AFRAID TO STEP BEYOND HIS OWN FRONT DOOR?
BUT IF YOU DON'T LIKE THE TITLE, THEN CAST IT AWAY! GO WITH BURROW-WARDEN BRICKERS' EXPEDITION; SHOW THEM THE TRUTH OF BELWAR DISSENGULP, AND LEARN IT FOR YOURSELF!
MAGGA CAMMARA...
PUT ON YOUR SWORDS, ELF. IF I'M TO GO, THEN SO ARE YOU!

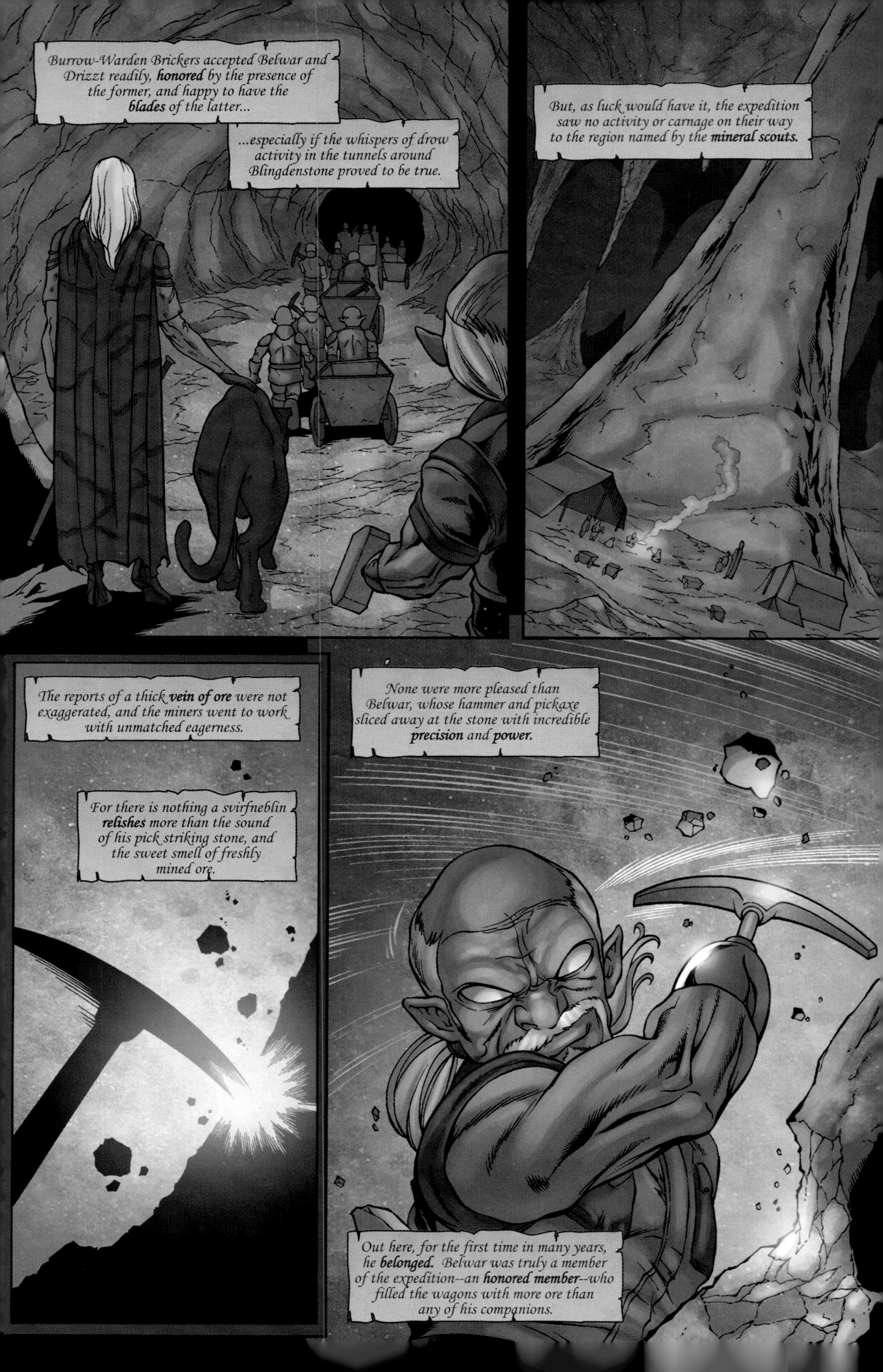
Burrow-Warden Brickers accepted Belwar and Drizzt readily, **honored** by the presence of the former, and happy to have the **blades** of the latter...
...especially if the whispers of drow activity in the tunnels around Blingdenstone proved to be true.
But, as luck would have it, the expedition saw no activity or carnage on their way to the region named by the **mineral scouts.**
The reports of a thick **vein of ore** were not exaggerated, and the miners went to work with unmatched eagerness.
For there is nothing a svirfneblin **relishes** more than the sound of his pick striking stone, and the sweet smell of freshly mined ore.
None were more pleased than Belwar, whose hammer and pickaxe sliced away at the stone with incredible **precision** and **power.**
Out here, for the first time in many years, he **belonged.** Belwar was truly a member of the expedition--an **honored member**--who filled the wagons with more ore than any of his companions.

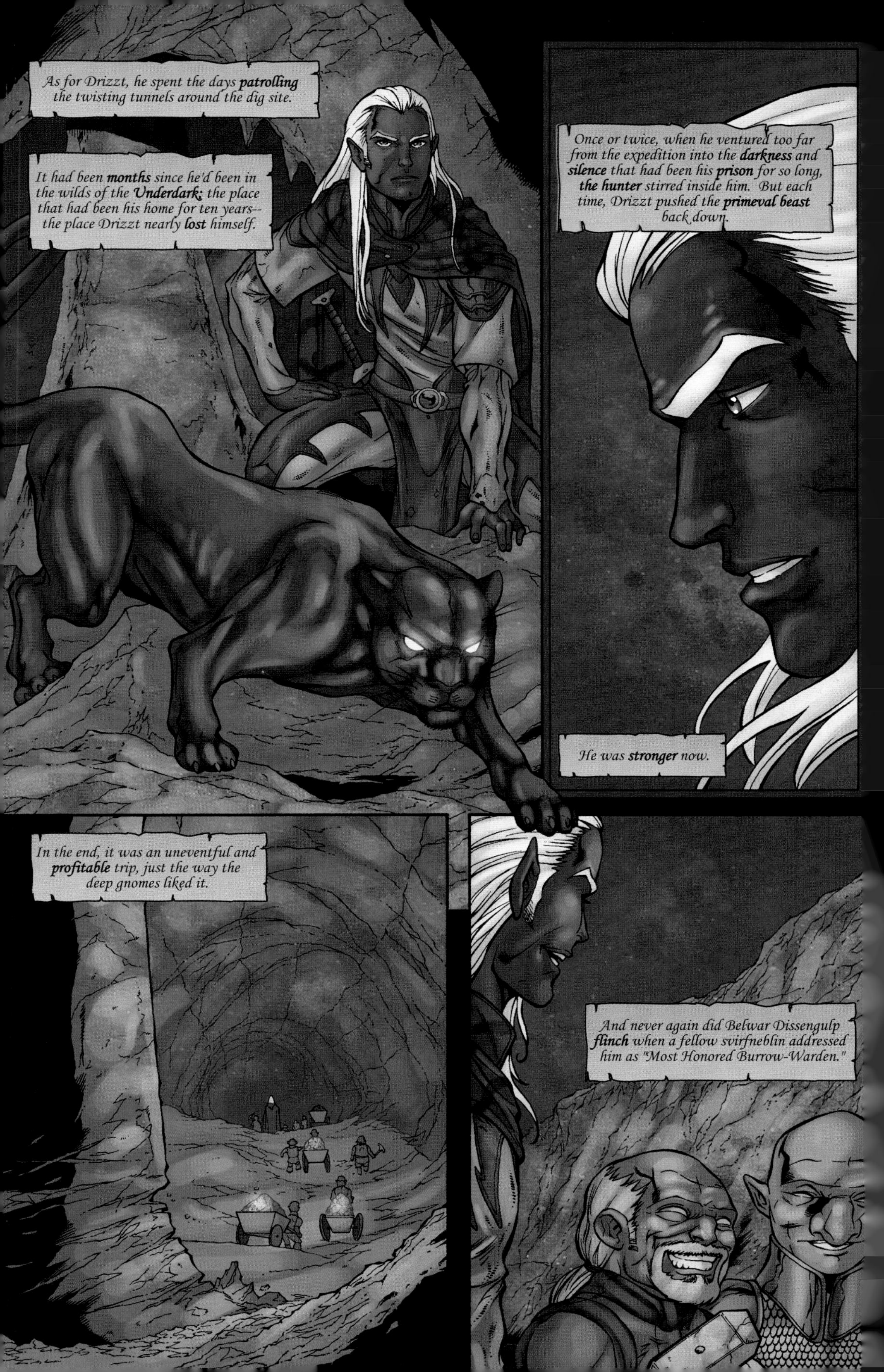

As for Drizzt, he spent the days patrolling the twisting tunnels around the dig site.
It had been months since he'd been in the wilds of the Underdark; the place that had been his home for ten years--the place Drizzt nearly lost himself.
Once or twice, when he ventured too far from the expedition into the darkness and silence that had been his prison for so long, the hunter stirred inside him. But each time, Drizzt pushed the primeval beast back down.
He was stronger now.
In the end, it was an uneventful and profitable trip, just the way the deep gnomes liked it.
And never again did Belwar Dissengulp flinch when a fellow svirfneblin addressed him as "Most Honored Burrow-Warden."

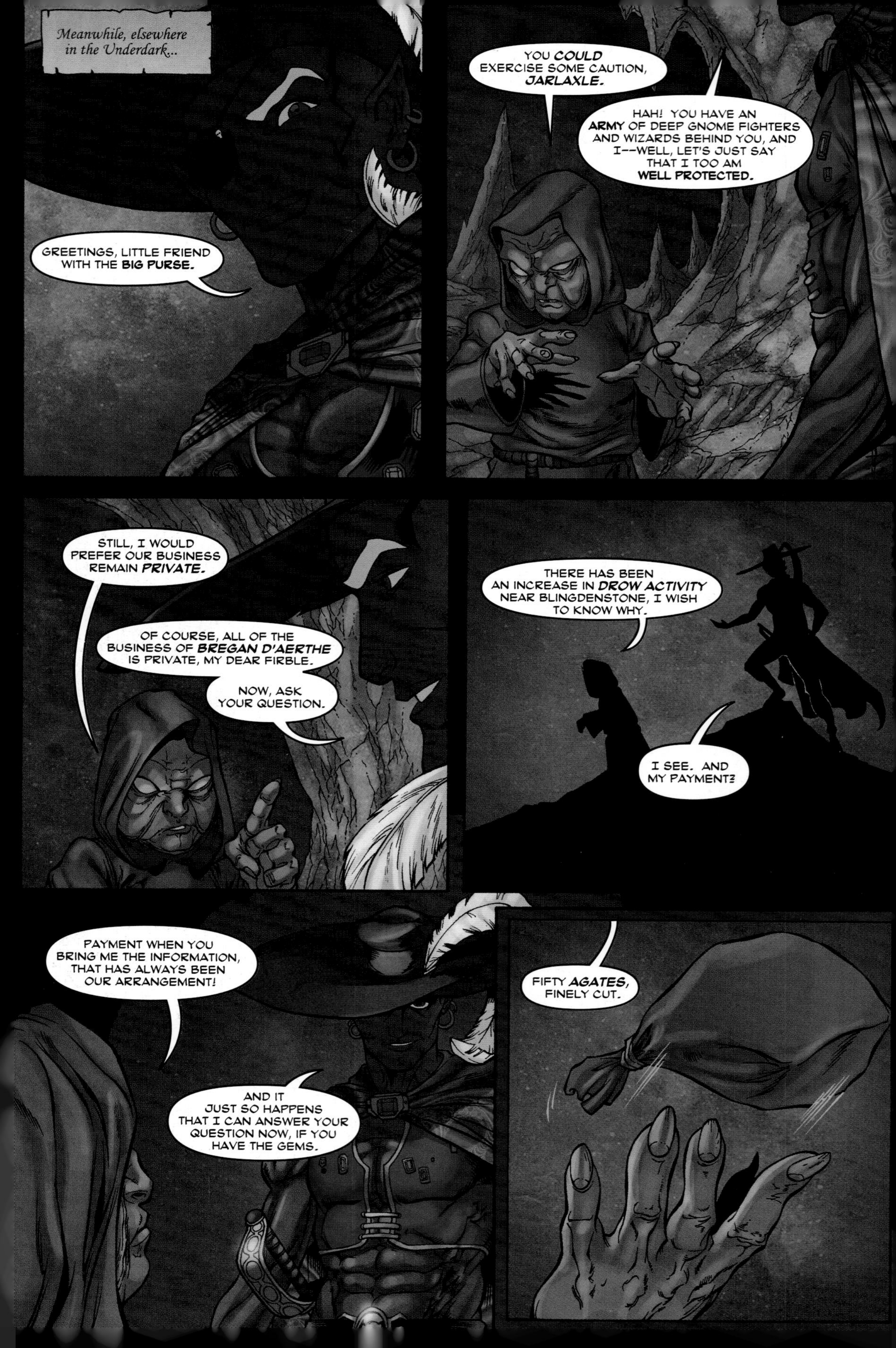
Meanwhile, elsewhere in the Underdark...
GREETINGS, LITTLE FRIEND WITH THE BIG PURSE.
YOU COULD EXERCISE SOME CAUTION, JARLAXLE.
HAH! YOU HAVE AN ARMY OF DEEP GNOME FIGHTERS AND WIZARDS BEHIND YOU, AND I--WELL, LET'S JUST SAY THAT I TOO AM WELL PROTECTED.
STILL, I WOULD PREFER OUR BUSINESS REMAIN PRIVATE.
OF COURSE, ALL OF THE BUSINESS OF BREGAN D'AERTHE IS PRIVATE, MY DEAR FIRBLE.
NOW, ASK YOUR QUESTION.
THERE HAS BEEN AN INCREASE IN DROW ACTIVITY NEAR BLINGDENSTONE, I WISH TO KNOW WHY.
I SEE. AND MY PAYMENT?
PAYMENT WHEN YOU BRING ME THE INFORMATION, THAT HAS ALWAYS BEEN OUR ARRANGEMENT!
AND IT JUST SO HAPPENS THAT I CAN ANSWER YOUR QUESTION NOW, IF YOU HAVE THE GEMS.
FIFTY AGATES, FINELY CUT.

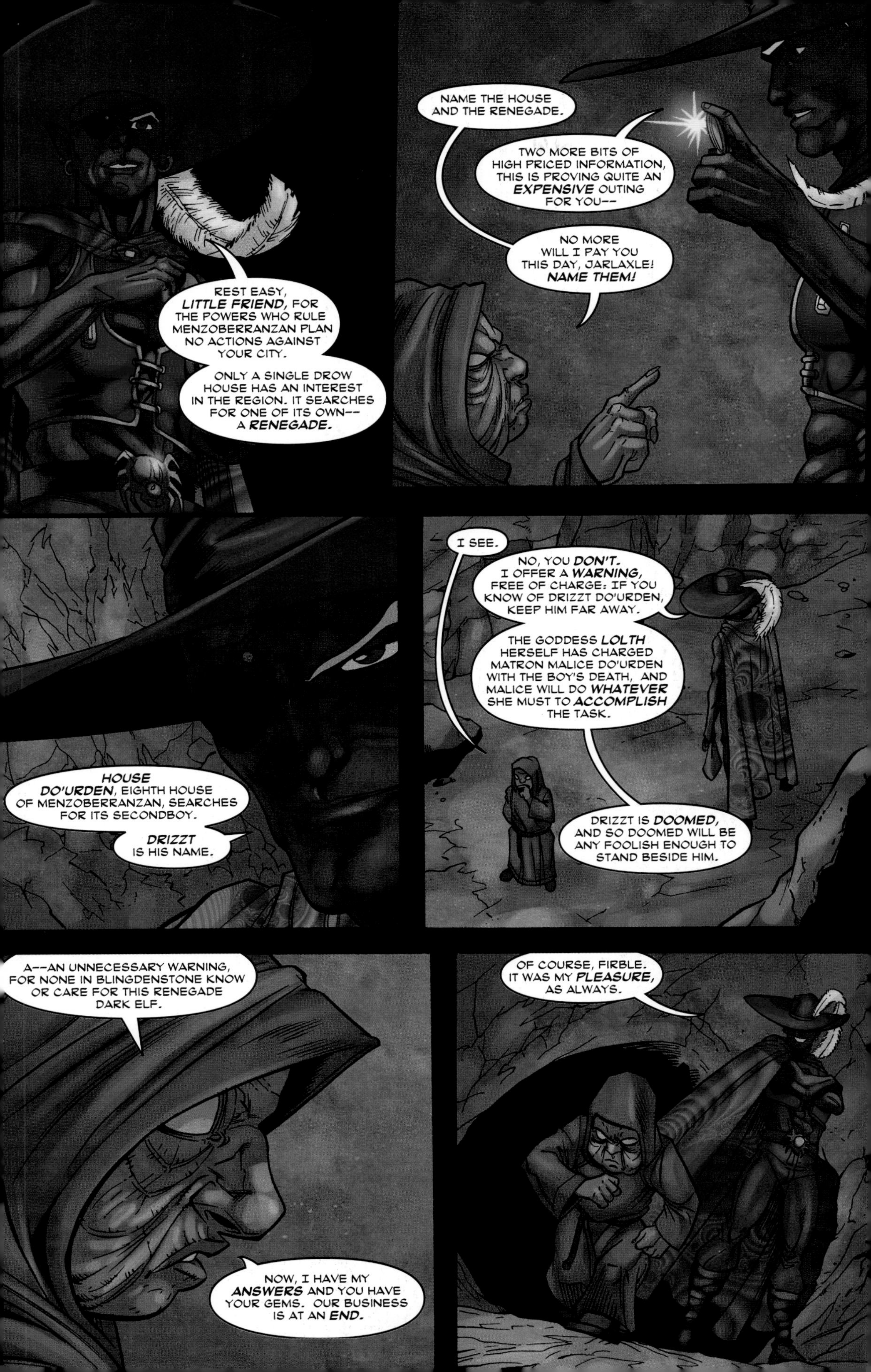
REST EASY, LITTLE FRIEND, FOR THE POWERS WHO RULE MENZOBERRANZAN PLAN NO ACTIONS AGAINST YOUR CITY.
ONLY A SINGLE DROW HOUSE HAS AN INTEREST IN THE REGION. IT SEARCHES FOR ONE OF ITS OWN-- A RENEGADE.
NAME THE HOUSE AND THE RENEGADE.
TWO MORE BITS OF HIGH PRICED INFORMATION, THIS IS PROVING QUITE AN EXPENSIVE OUTING FOR YOU--
NO MORE WILL I PAY YOU THIS DAY, JARLAXLE! NAME THEM!
HOUSE DO'URDEN, EIGHTH HOUSE OF MENZOBERRANZAN, SEARCHES FOR ITS SECONDBOY.
DRIZZT IS HIS NAME.
I SEE.
NO, YOU DON'T. I OFFER A WARNING, FREE OF CHARGE: IF YOU KNOW OF DRIZZT DO'URDEN, KEEP HIM FAR AWAY.
THE GODDESS LOLTH HERSELF HAS CHARGED MATRON MALICE DO'URDEN WITH THE BOY'S DEATH, AND MALICE WILL DO WHATEVER SHE MUST TO ACCOMPLISH THE TASK.
DRIZZT IS DOOMED, AND SO DOOMED WILL BE ANY FOOLISH ENOUGH TO STAND BESIDE HIM.
A--AN UNNECESSARY WARNING, FOR NONE IN BLINGDENSTONE KNOW OR CARE FOR THIS RENEGADE DARK ELF.
NOW, I HAVE MY ANSWERS AND YOU HAVE YOUR GEMS. OUR BUSINESS IS AT AN END.
OF COURSE, FIRBLE. IT WAS MY PLEASURE, AS ALWAYS.

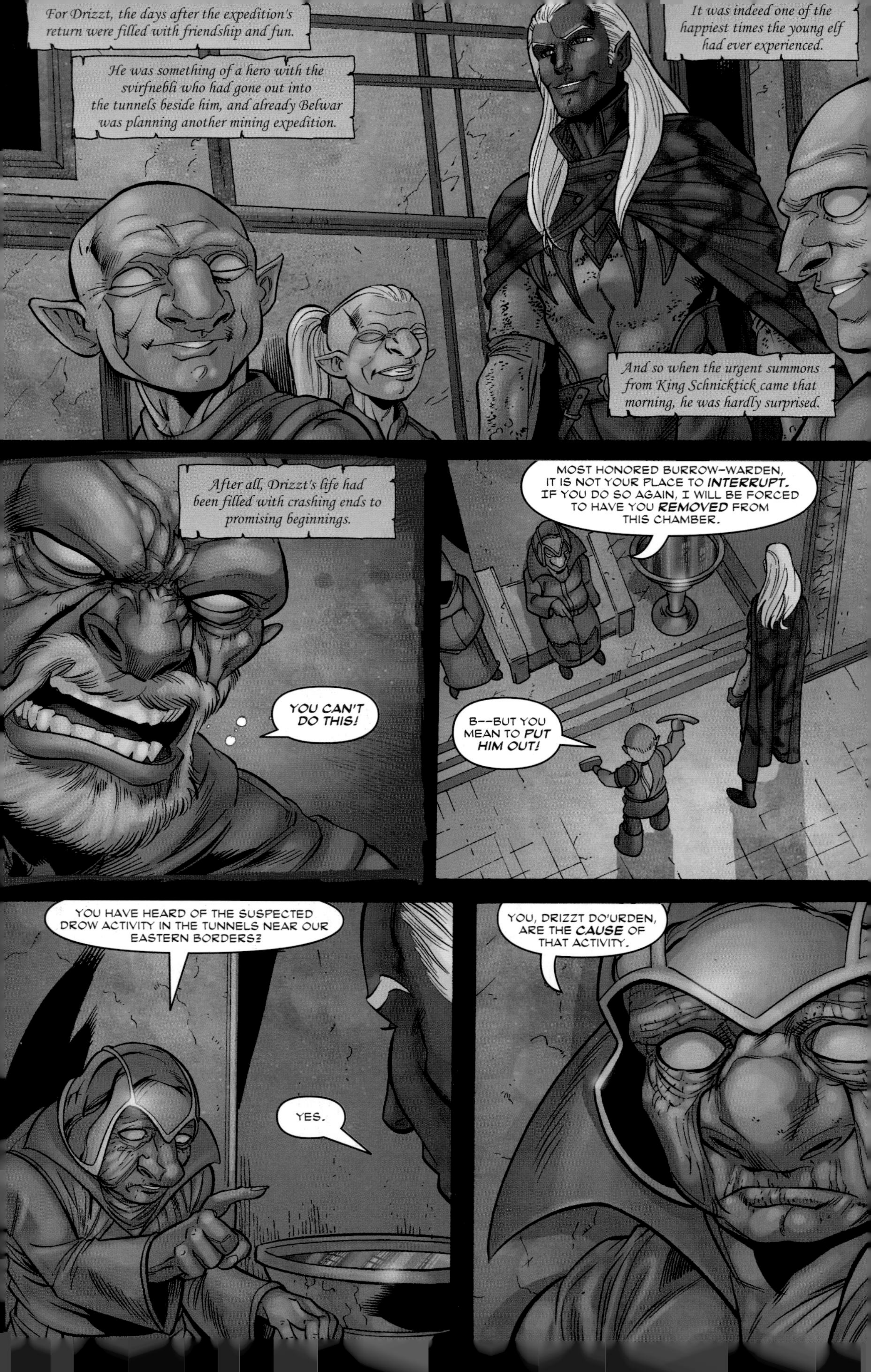
For Drizzt, the days after the expedition's return were filled with friendship and fun.
He was something of a hero with the svirfnebli who had gone out into the tunnels beside him, and already Belwar was planning another mining expedition.
It was indeed one of the happiest times the young elf had ever experienced.
And so when the urgent summons from King Schnicktick came that morning, he was hardly surprised.
After all, Drizzt's life had been filled with crashing ends to promising beginnings.
YOU CAN'T DO THIS!
MOST HONORED BURROW-WARDEN, IT IS NOT YOUR PLACE TO INTERRUPT. IF YOU DO SO AGAIN, I WILL BE FORCED TO HAVE YOU REMOVED FROM THIS CHAMBER.
B--BUT YOU MEAN TO PUT HIM OUT!
YOU HAVE HEARD OF THE SUSPECTED DROW ACTIVITY IN THE TUNNELS NEAR OUR EASTERN BORDERS?
YES.
YOU, DRIZZT DO'URDEN, ARE THE CAUSE OF THAT ACTIVITY.

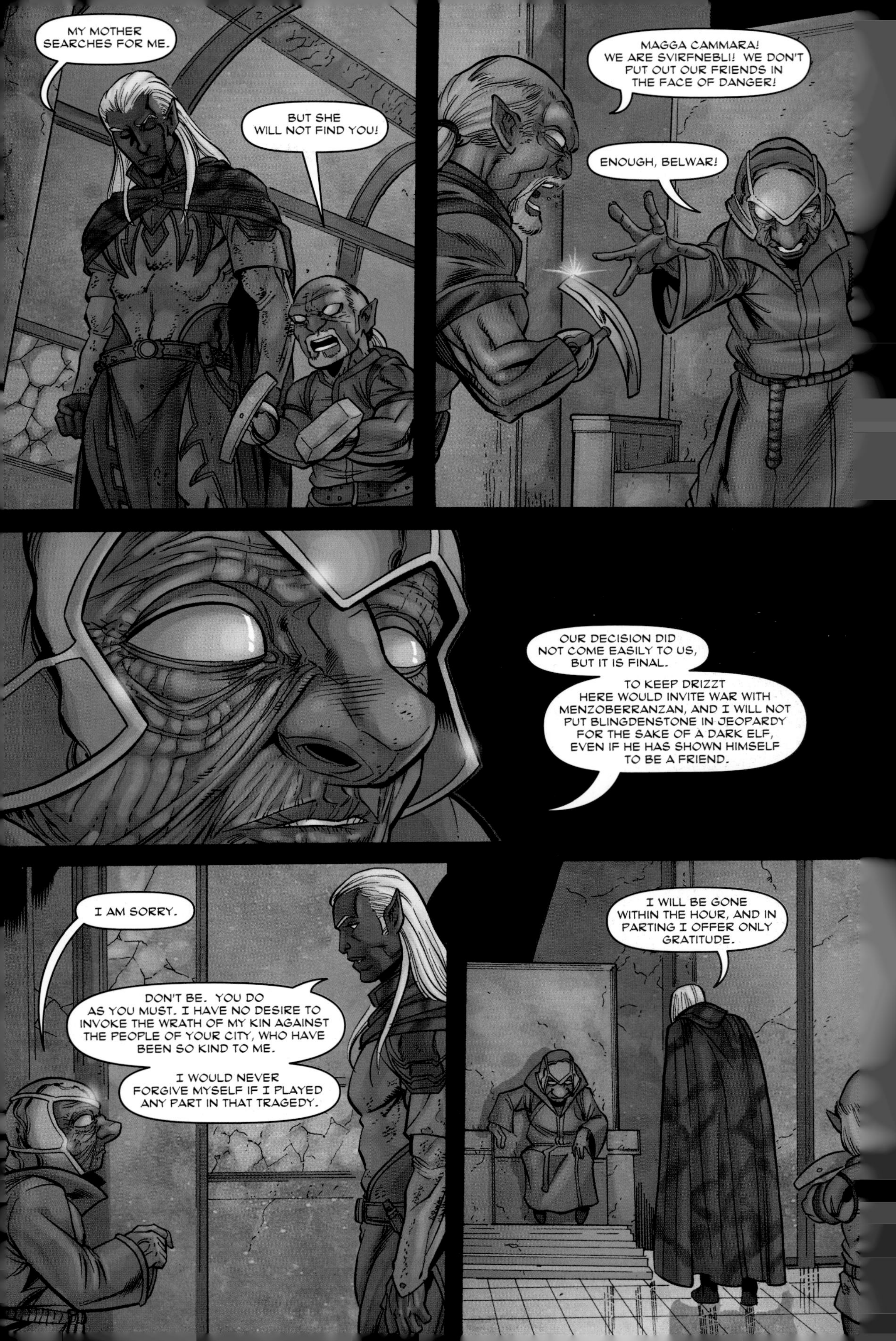
MY MOTHER SEARCHES FOR ME.
BUT SHE WILL NOT FIND YOU!
MAGGA CAMMARA! WE ARE SVIRFNEBLI! WE DON'T PUT OUT OUR FRIENDS IN THE FACE OF DANGER!
ENOUGH, BELWAR!
OUR DECISION DID NOT COME EASILY TO US, BUT IT IS FINAL.
TO KEEP DRIZZT HERE WOULD INVITE WAR WITH MENZOBERRANZAN, AND I WILL NOT PUT BLINGDENSTONE IN JEOPARDY FOR THE SAKE OF A DARK ELF, EVEN IF HE HAS SHOWN HIMSELF TO BE A FRIEND.
I AM SORRY.
DON'T BE. YOU DO AS YOU MUST. I HAVE NO DESIRE TO INVOKE THE WRATH OF MY KIN AGAINST THE PEOPLE OF YOUR CITY, WHO HAVE BEEN SO KIND TO ME.
I WOULD NEVER FORGIVE MYSELF IF I PLAYED ANY PART IN THAT TRAGEDY.
I WILL BE GONE WITHIN THE HOUR, AND IN PARTING I OFFER ONLY GRATITUDE.

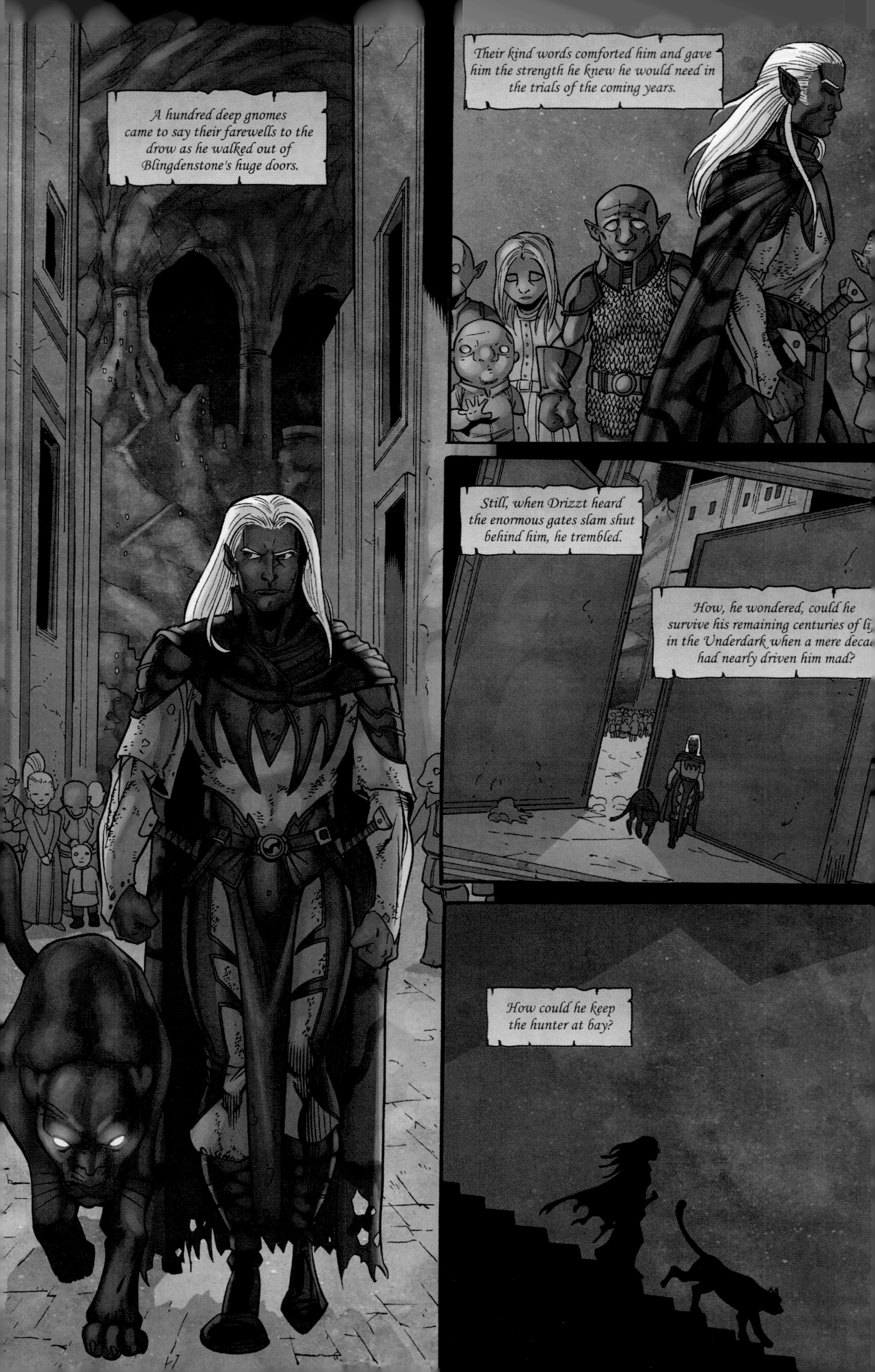
A hundred deep gnomes came to say their farewells to the drow as he walked out of Blingdenstone's huge doors.
Their kind words comforted him and gave him the strength he knew he would need in the trials of the coming years.
Still, when Drizzt heard the enormous gates slam shut behind him, he trembled.
How, he wondered, could he survive his remaining centuries of li in the Underdark when a mere deca had nearly driven him mad?
How could he keep the hunter at bay?

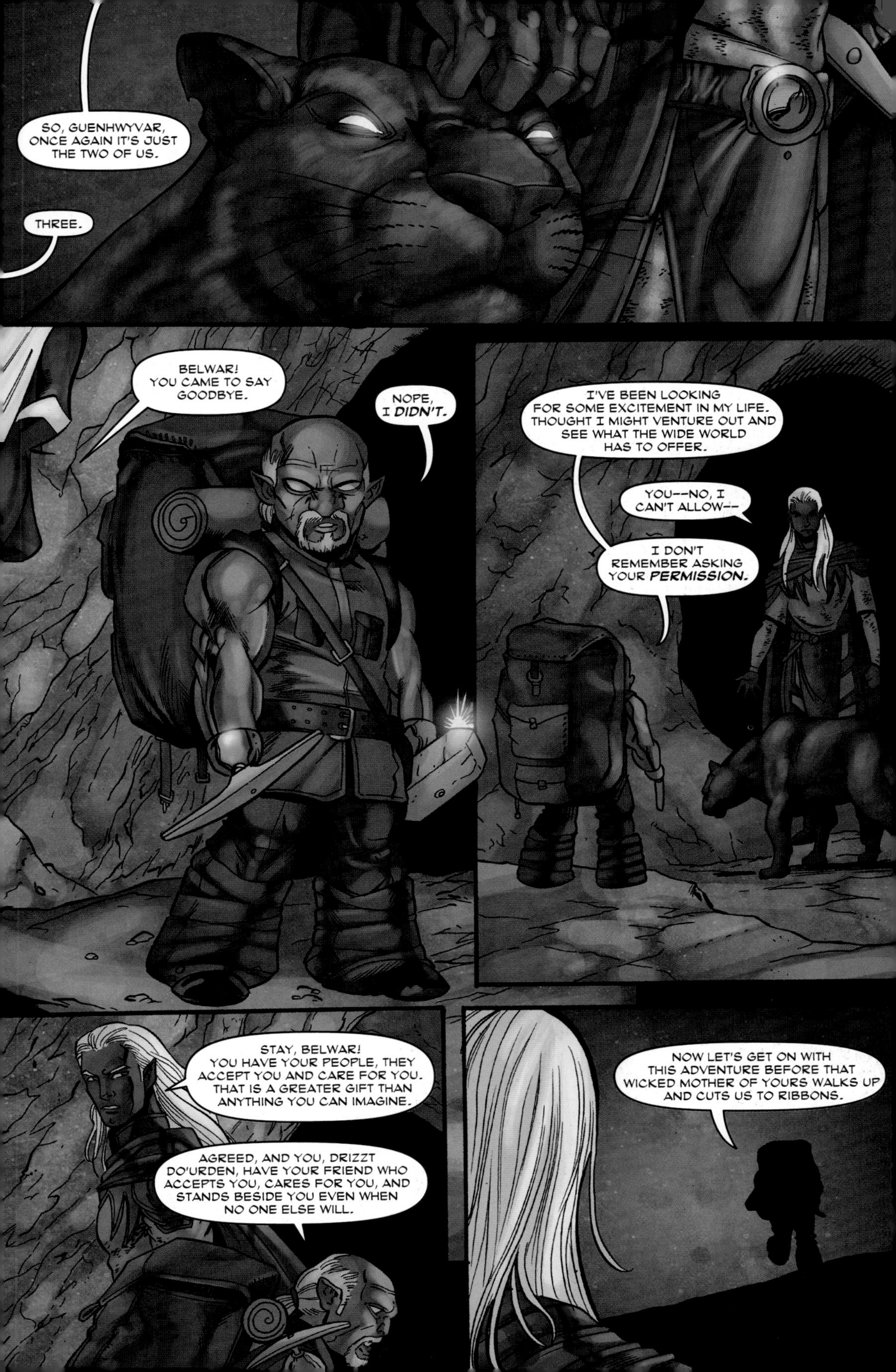
SO, GUENHWYVAR, ONCE AGAIN IT'S JUST THE TWO OF US.
THREE.
BELWAR! YOU CAME TO SAY GOODBYE.
NOPE, I **DIDN'T.**
I'VE BEEN LOOKING FOR SOME EXCITEMENT IN MY LIFE. THOUGHT I MIGHT VENTURE OUT AND SEE WHAT THE WIDE WORLD HAS TO OFFER.
YOU--NO, I CAN'T ALLOW--
I DON'T REMEMBER ASKING YOUR **PERMISSION.**
STAY, BELWAR! YOU HAVE YOUR PEOPLE, THEY ACCEPT YOU AND CARE FOR YOU. THAT IS A GREATER GIFT THAN ANYTHING YOU CAN IMAGINE.
AGREED, AND YOU, DRIZZT DO'URDEN, HAVE YOUR FRIEND WHO ACCEPTS YOU, CARES FOR YOU, AND STANDS BESIDE YOU EVEN WHEN NO ONE ELSE WILL.
NOW LET'S GET ON WITH THIS ADVENTURE BEFORE THAT WICKED MOTHER OF YOURS WALKS UP AND CUTS US TO RIBBONS.

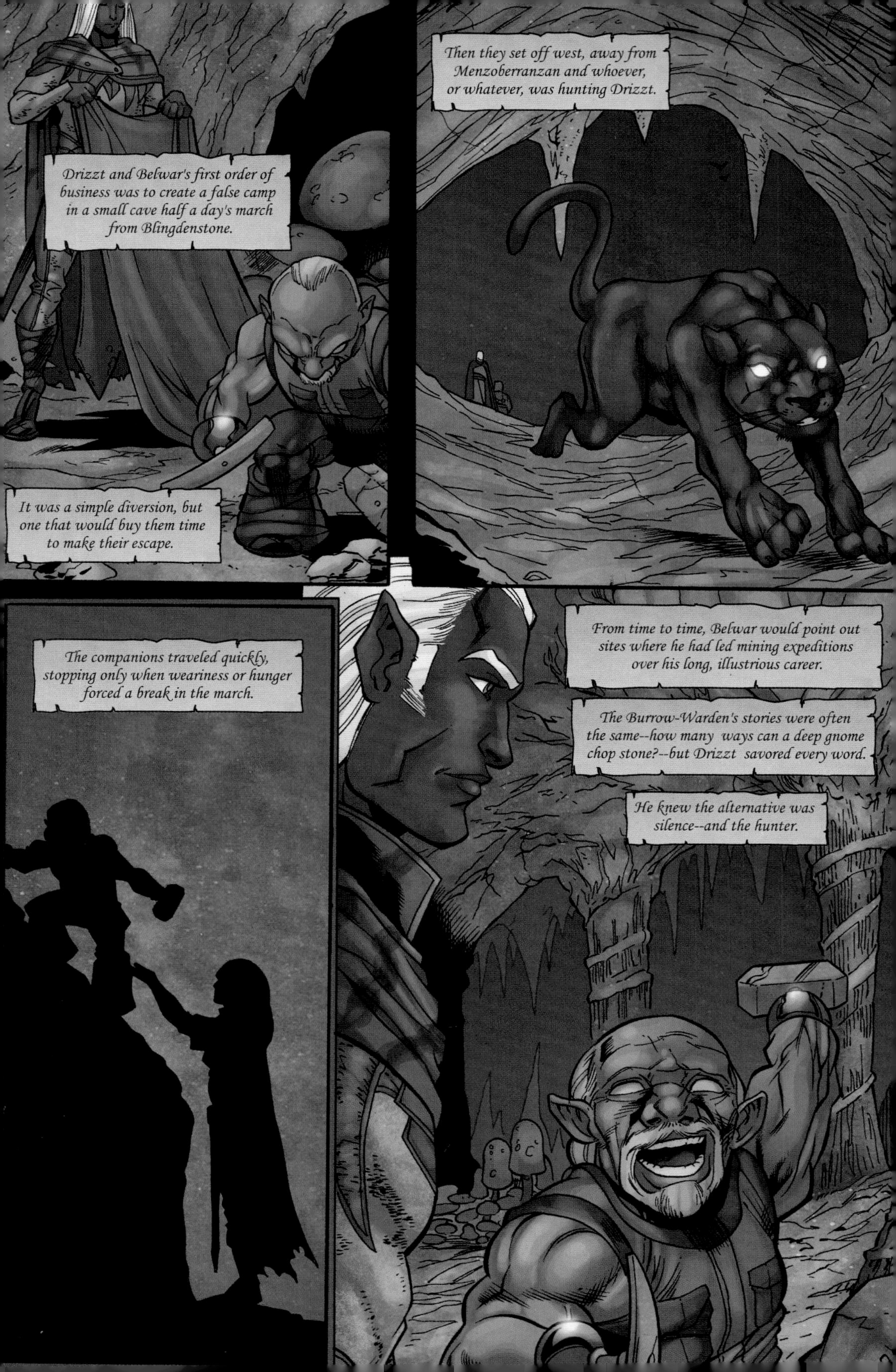
Drizzt and Belwar's first order of business was to create a false camp in a small cave half a day's march from Blingdenstone.
It was a simple diversion, but one that would buy them time to make their escape.
Then they set off west, away from Menzoberranzan and whoever, or whatever, was hunting Drizzt.
The companions traveled quickly, stopping only when weariness or hunger forced a break in the march.
From time to time, Belwar would point out sites where he had led mining expeditions over his long, illustrious career.
The Burrow-Warden's stories were often the same--how many ways can a deep gnome chop stone?--but Drizzt savored every word.
He knew the alternative was silence--and the hunter.

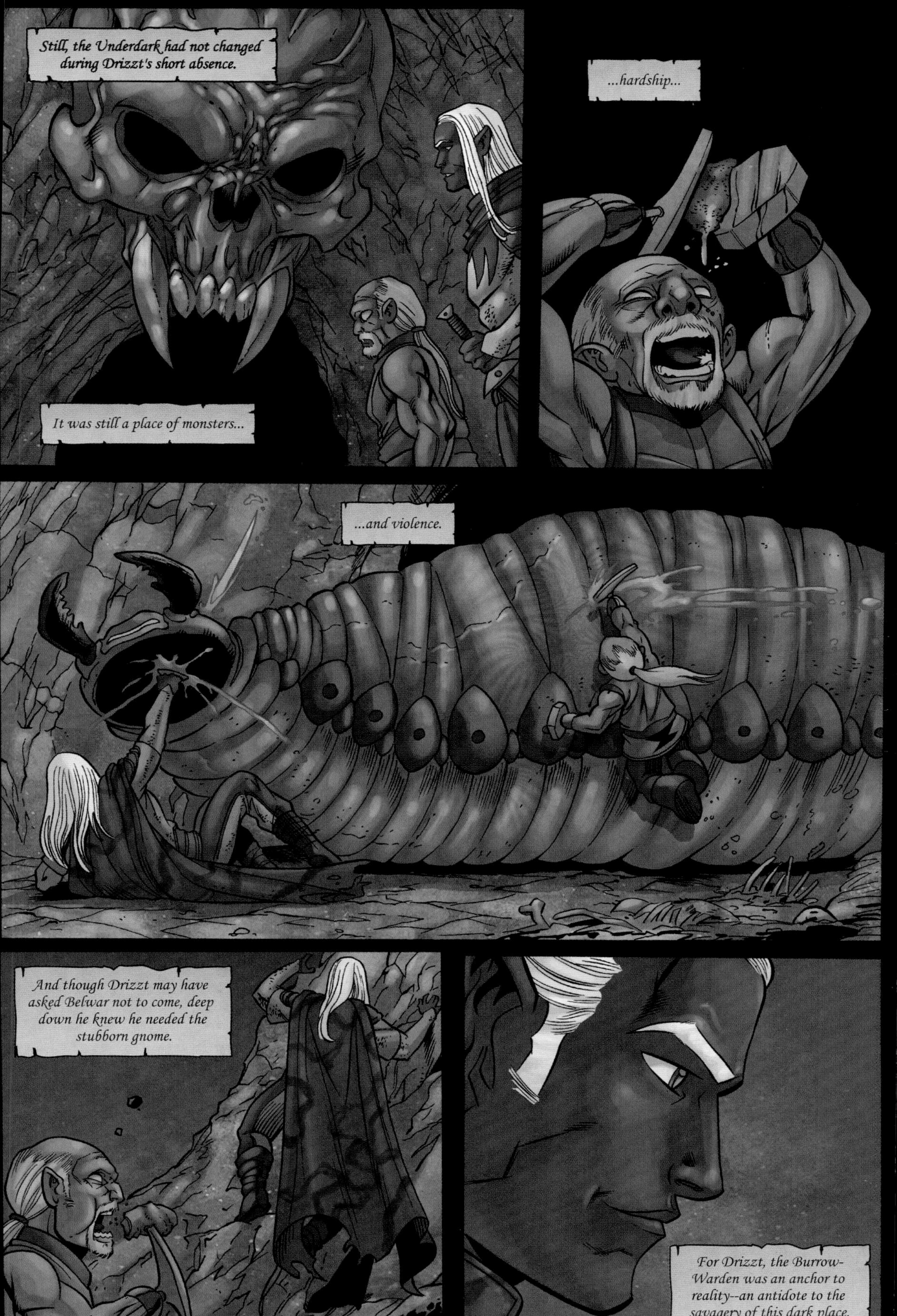

Still, the Underdark had not changed during Drizzt's short absence.
It was still a place of monsters...
...hardship...
...and violence.
And though Drizzt may have asked Belwar not to come, deep down he knew he needed the stubborn gnome.
For Drizzt, the Burrow-Warden was an anchor to reality--an antidote to the savagery of this dark place.

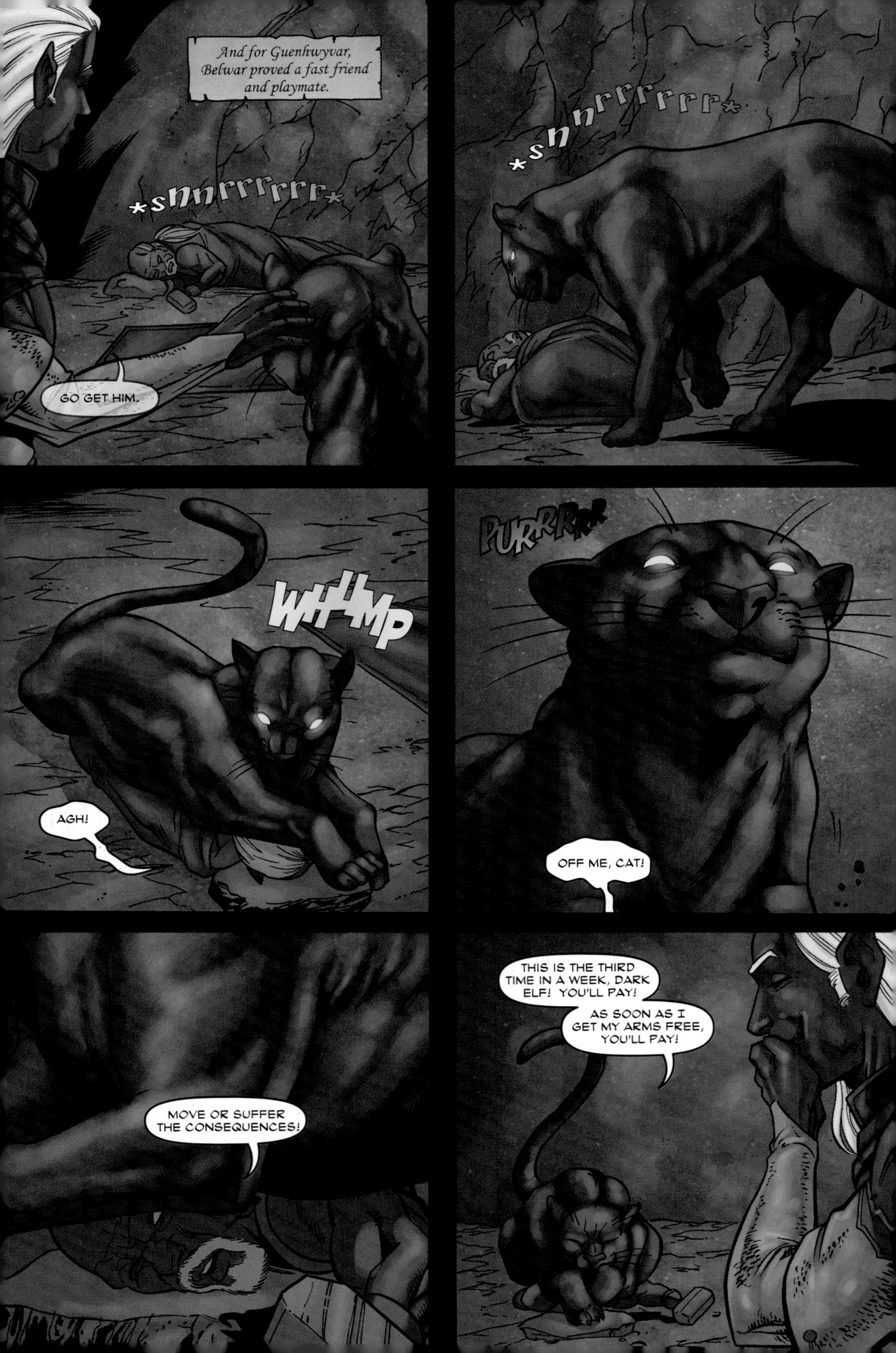
And for Guenhwyvar, Belwar proved a fast friend and playmate.
snnrrrrrrr
GO GET HIM.
snnrrrrrrr
WHUMP
AGH!
PURRRRR
OFF ME, CAT!
MOVE OR SUFFER THE CONSEQUENCES!
THIS IS THE THIRD TIME IN A WEEK, DARK ELF! YOU'LL PAY!
AS SOON AS I GET MY ARMS FREE, YOU'LL PAY!

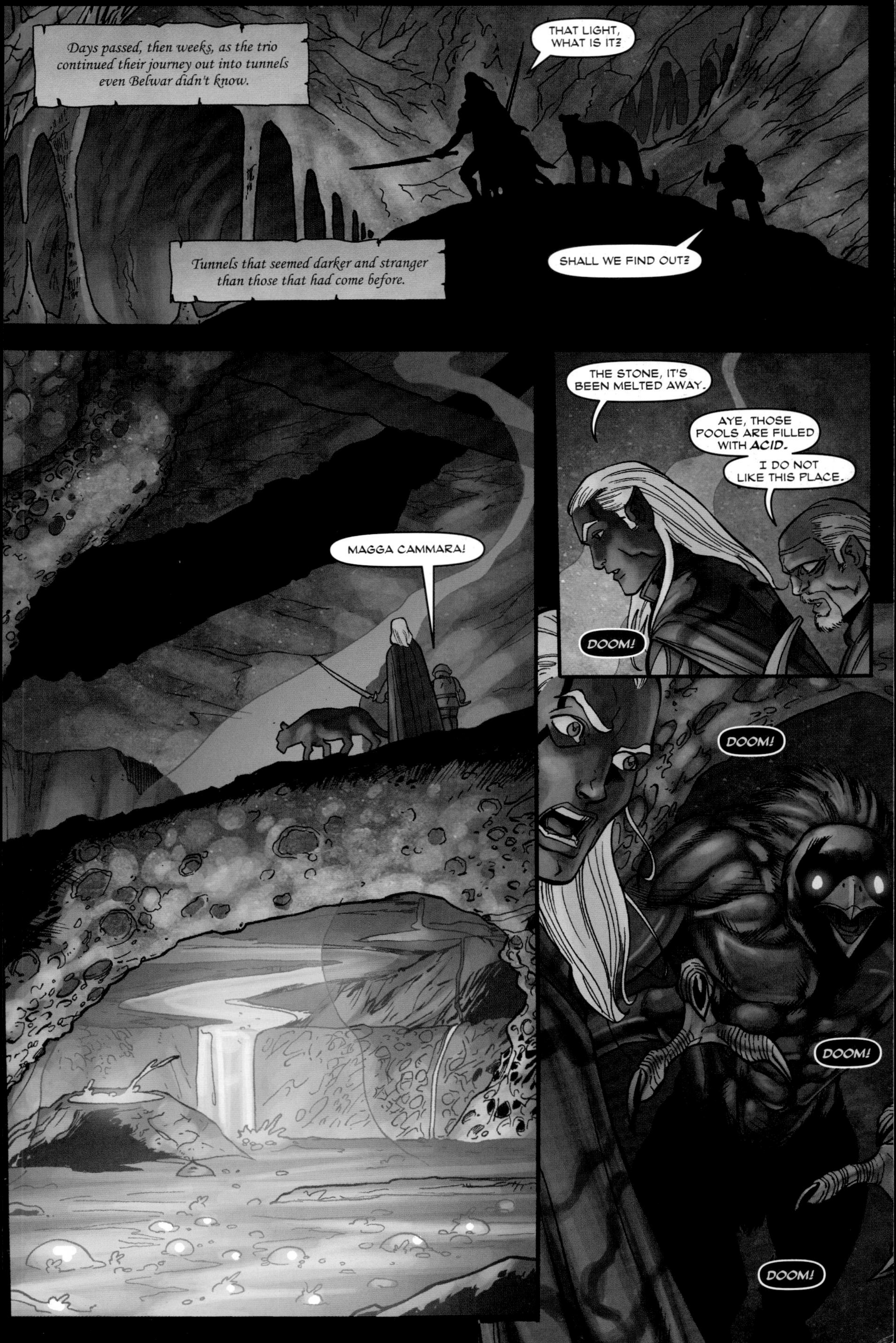

Days passed, then weeks, as the trio continued their journey out into tunnels even Belwar didn't know.
THAT LIGHT, WHAT IS IT?
Tunnels that seemed darker and stranger than those that had come before.
SHALL WE FIND OUT?
MAGGA CAMMARA!
THE STONE, IT'S BEEN MELTED AWAY.
AYE, THOSE POOLS ARE FILLED WITH ACID.
I DO NOT LIKE THIS PLACE.
DOOM!
DOOM!
DOOM!
DOOM!

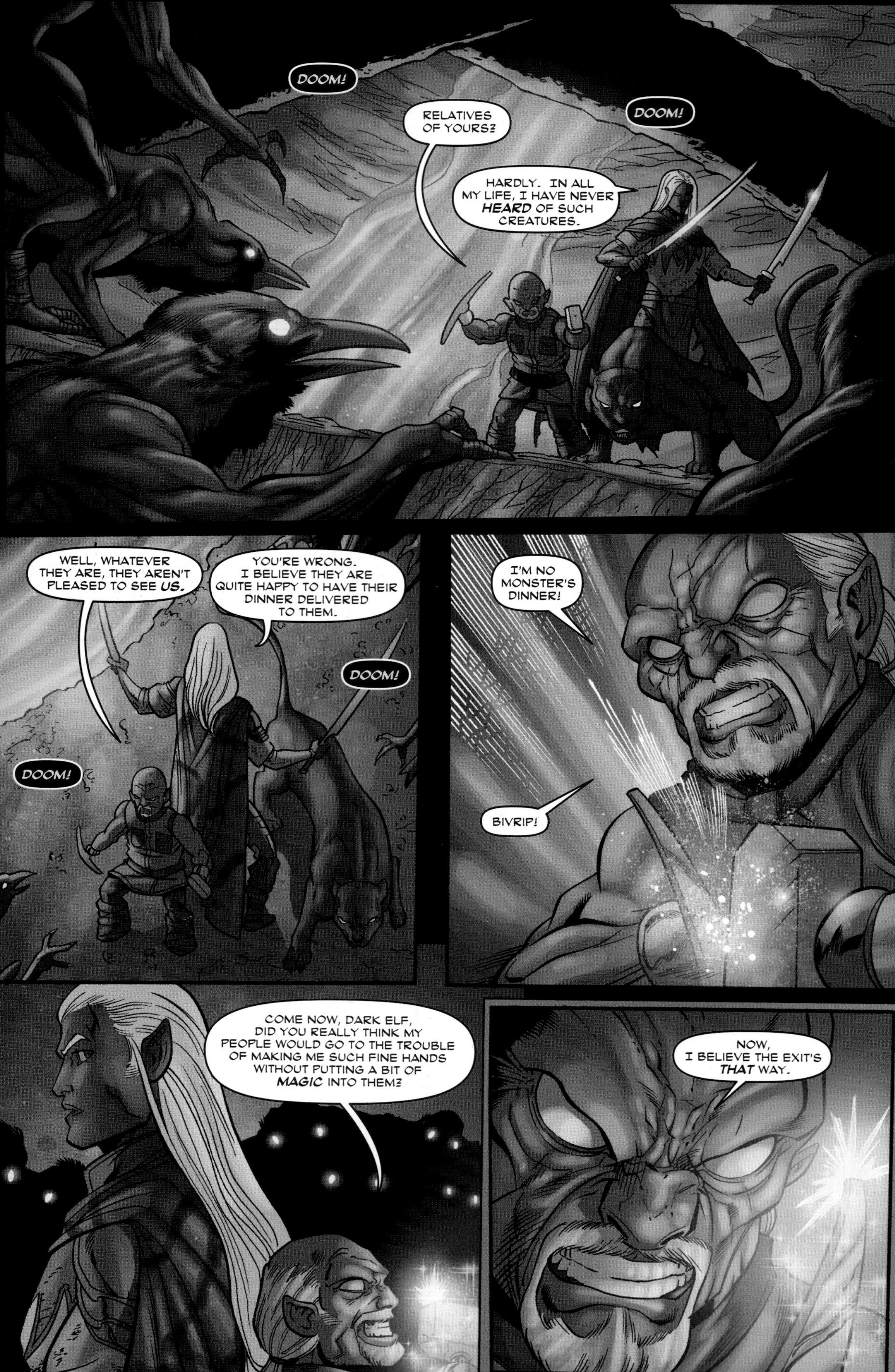
DOOM!
RELATIVES OF YOURS?
DOOM!
HARDLY. IN ALL MY LIFE, I HAVE NEVER HEARD OF SUCH CREATURES.
WELL, WHATEVER THEY ARE, THEY AREN'T PLEASED TO SEE US.
YOU'RE WRONG. I BELIEVE THEY ARE QUITE HAPPY TO HAVE THEIR DINNER DELIVERED TO THEM.
DOOM!
DOOM!
I'M NO MONSTER'S DINNER!
BIVRIP!
COME NOW, DARK ELF, DID YOU REALLY THINK MY PEOPLE WOULD GO TO THE TROUBLE OF MAKING ME SUCH FINE HANDS WITHOUT PUTTING A BIT OF MAGIC INTO THEM?
NOW, I BELIEVE THE EXIT'S THAT WAY.

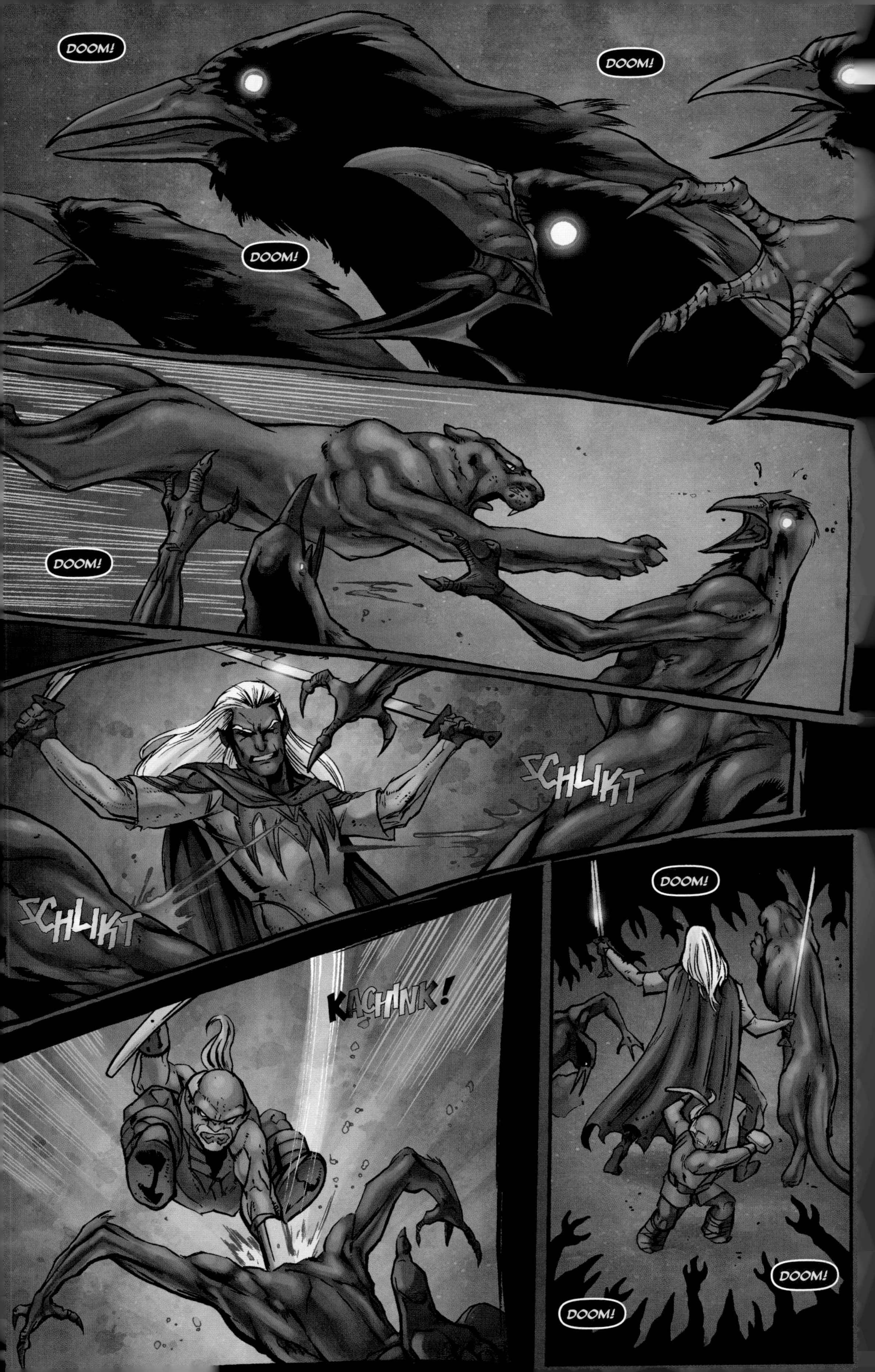
DOOM!
DOOM!
DOOM!
DOOM!
SCHLIKT
SCHLIKT
KACHINK!
DOOM!
DOOM!
DOOM!

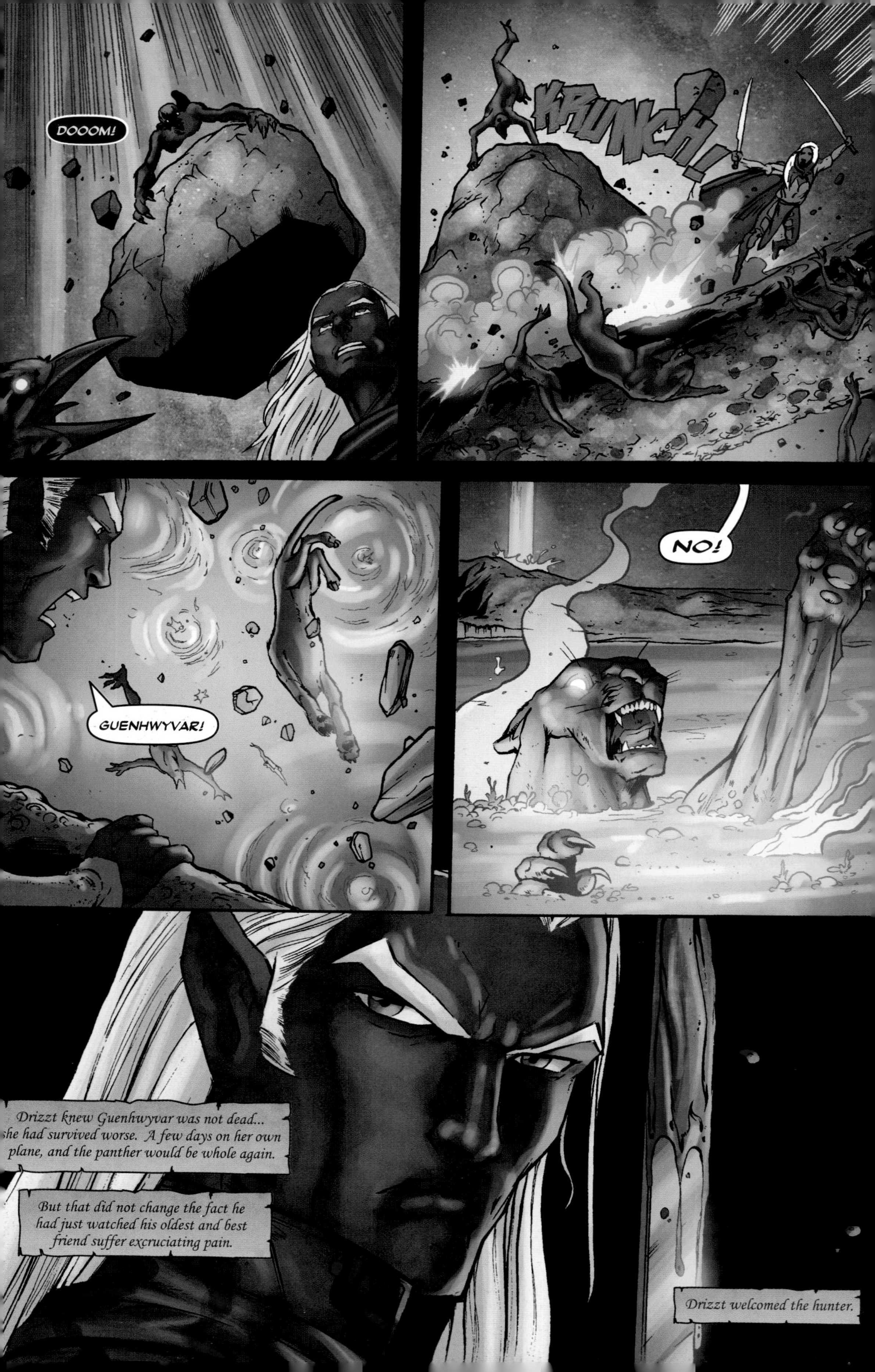
DOOOM!
KRUNCH!
GUENHWYVAR!
NO!
Drizzt knew Guenhwyvar was not dead... she had survived worse. A few days on her own plane, and the panther would be whole again.
But that did not change the fact he had just watched his oldest and best friend suffer excruciating pain.
Drizzt welcomed the hunter.

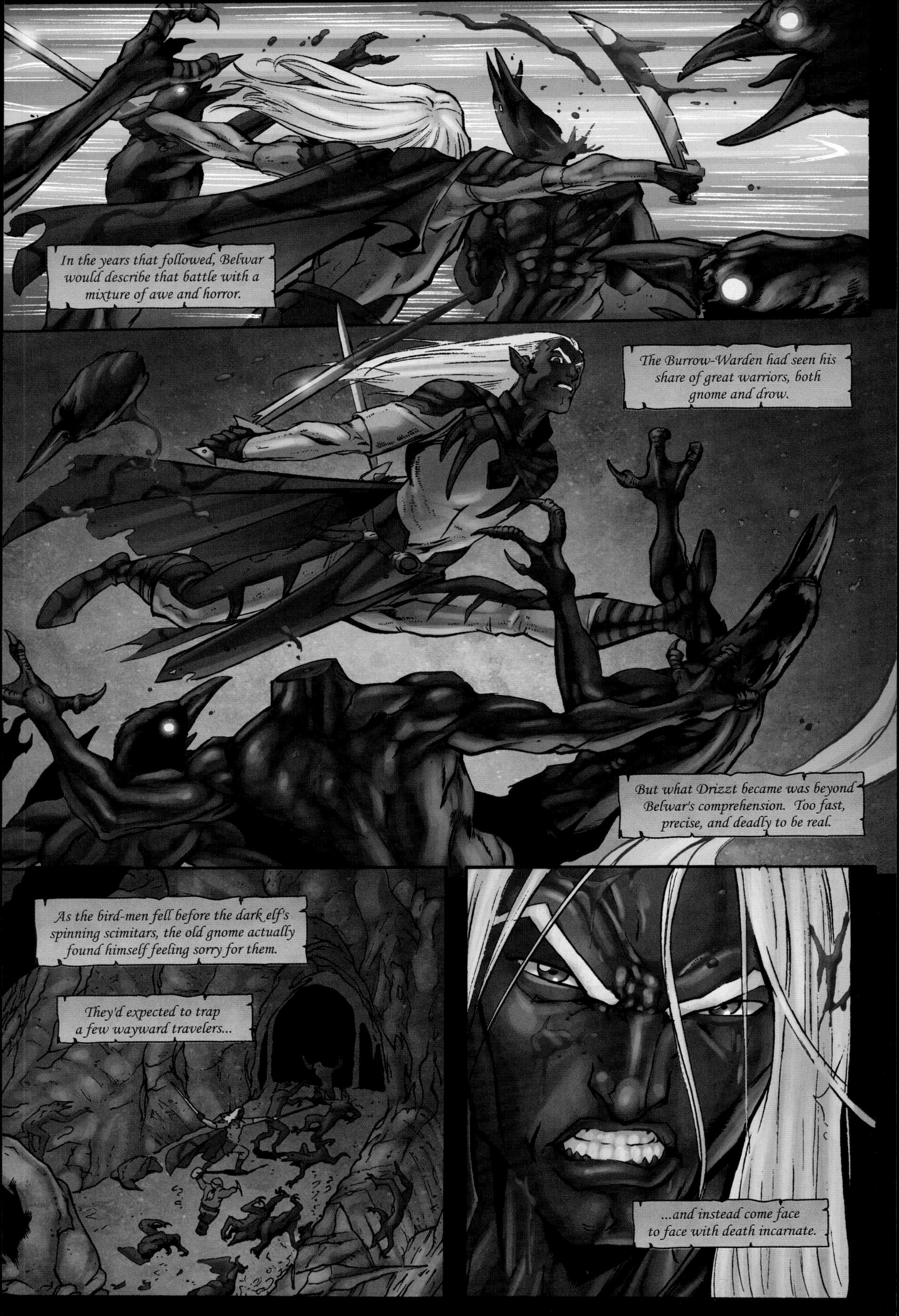

In the years that followed, Belwar would describe that battle with a mixture of awe and horror.
The Burrow-Warden had seen his share of great warriors, both gnome and drow.
But what Drizzt became was beyond Belwar's comprehension. Too fast, precise, and deadly to be real.
As the bird-men fell before the dark elf's spinning scimitars, the old gnome actually found himself feeling sorry for them.
They'd expected to trap a few wayward travelers...
...and instead come face to face with death incarnate.

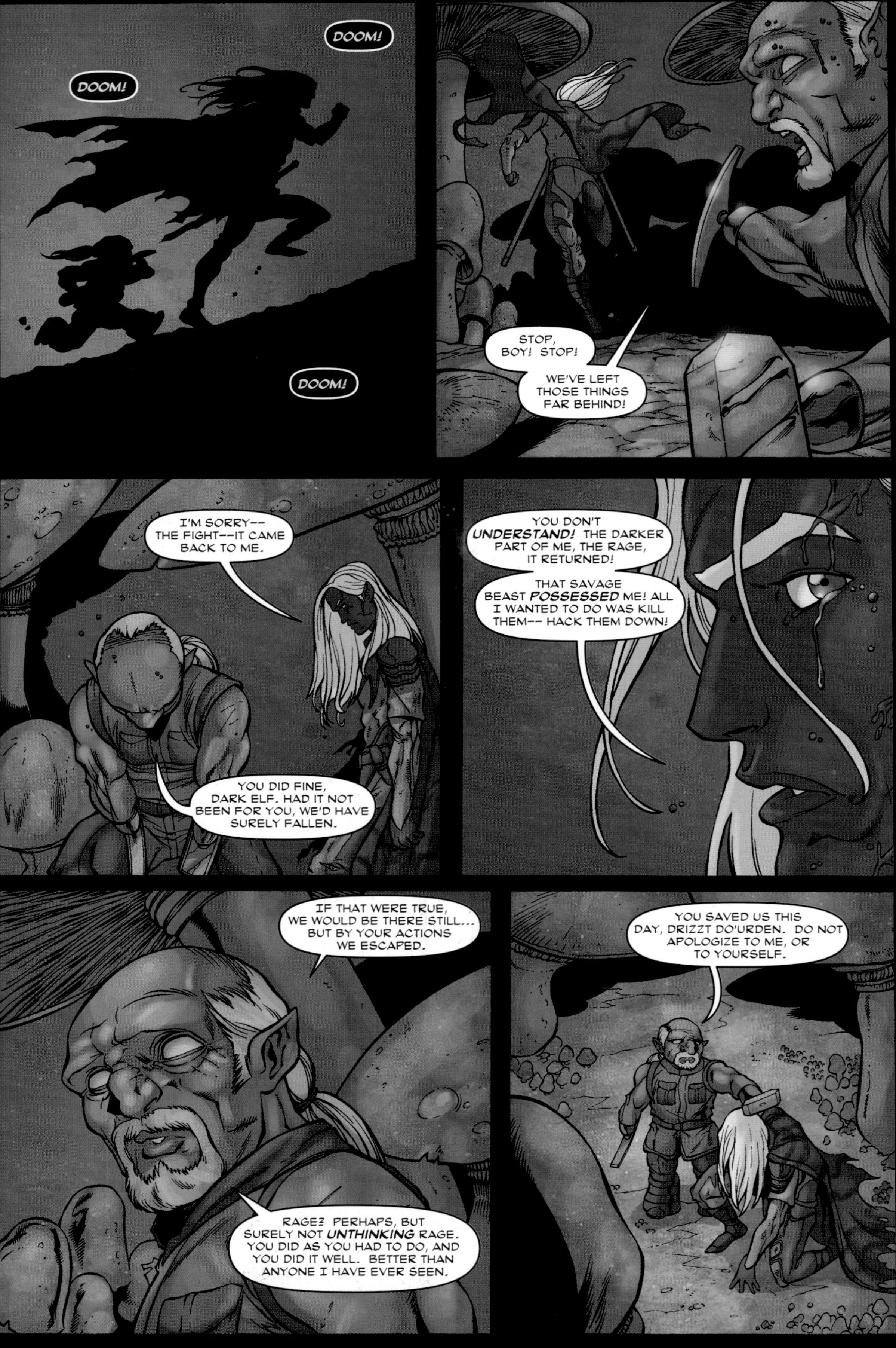
DOOM!
DOOM!
DOOM!
STOP, BOY! STOP!
WE'VE LEFT THOSE THINGS FAR BEHIND!
I'M SORRY-- THE FIGHT--IT CAME BACK TO ME.
YOU DID FINE, DARK ELF. HAD IT NOT BEEN FOR YOU, WE'D HAVE SURELY FALLEN.
YOU DON'T UNDERSTAND! THE DARKER PART OF ME, THE RAGE, IT RETURNED!
THAT SAVAGE BEAST POSSESSED ME! ALL I WANTED TO DO WAS KILL THEM-- HACK THEM DOWN!
IF THAT WERE TRUE, WE WOULD BE THERE STILL... BUT BY YOUR ACTIONS WE ESCAPED.
RAGE? PERHAPS, BUT SURELY NOT UNTHINKING RAGE. YOU DID AS YOU HAD TO DO, AND YOU DID IT WELL. BETTER THAN ANYONE I HAVE EVER SEEN.
YOU SAVED US THIS DAY, DRIZZT DO'URDEN. DO NOT APOLOGIZE TO ME, OR TO YOURSELF.

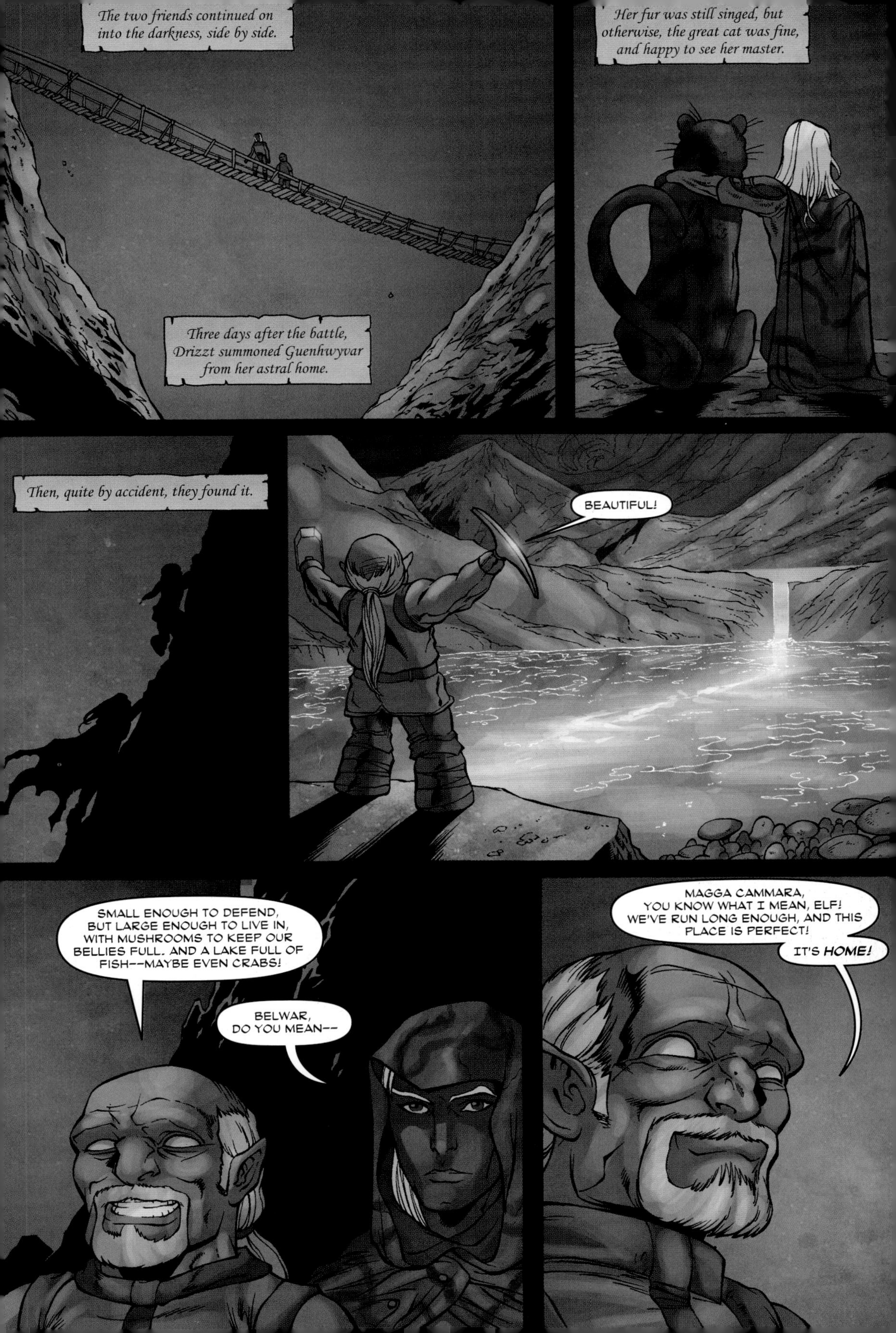
The two friends continued on into the darkness, side by side.
Three days after the battle, Drizzt summoned Guenhwyvar from her astral home.
Her fur was still singed, but otherwise, the great cat was fine, and happy to see her master.
Then, quite by accident, they found it.
BEAUTIFUL!
SMALL ENOUGH TO DEFEND, BUT LARGE ENOUGH TO LIVE IN, WITH MUSHROOMS TO KEEP OUR BELLIES FULL. AND A LAKE FULL OF FISH--MAYBE EVEN CRABS!
BELWAR, DO YOU MEAN--
MAGGA CAMMARA, YOU KNOW WHAT I MEAN, ELF! WE'VE RUN LONG ENOUGH, AND THIS PLACE IS PERFECT!
IT'S *HOME!*

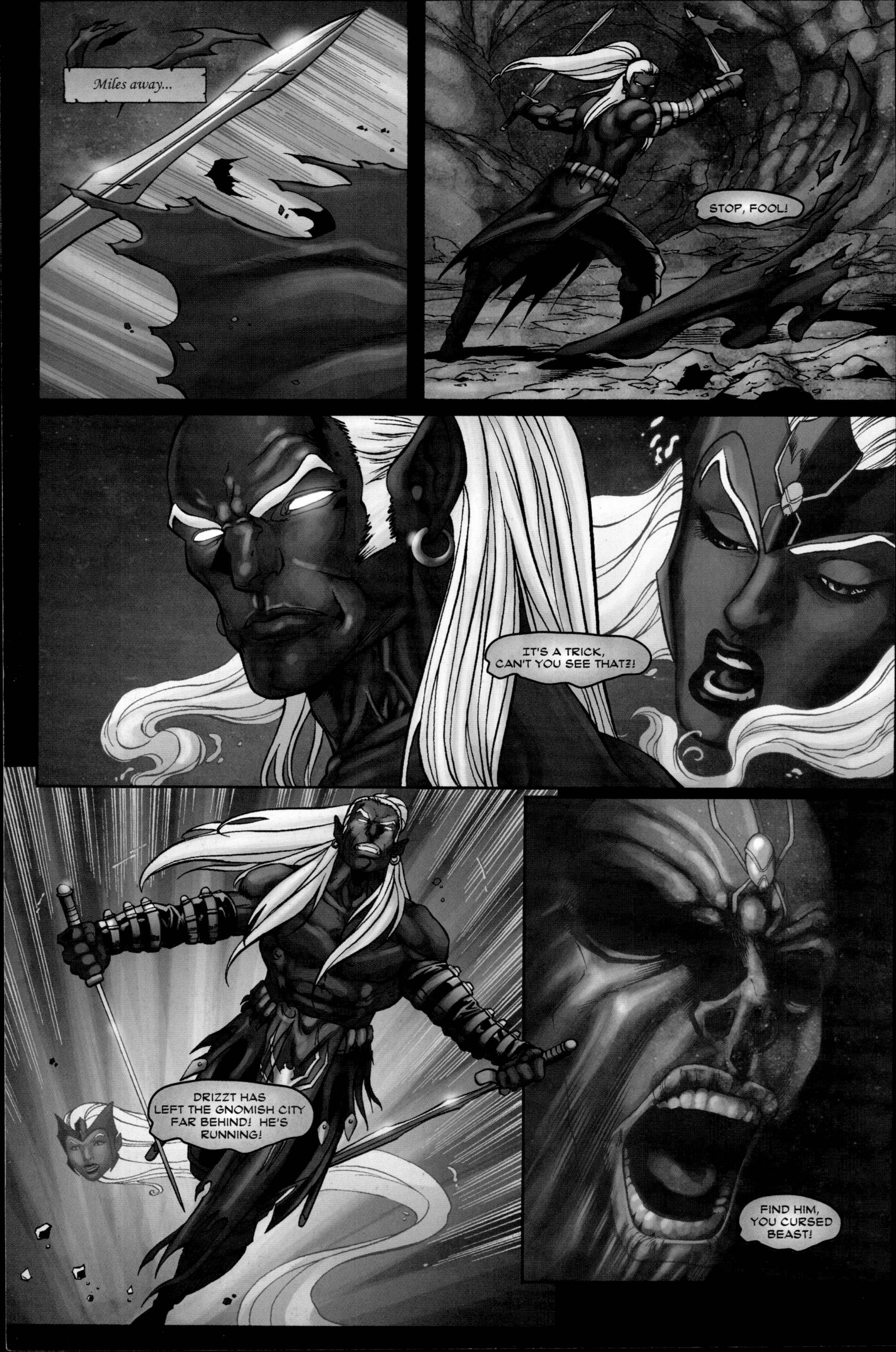
Miles away...
STOP, FOOL!
IT'S A TRICK, CAN'T YOU SEE THAT?!
DRIZZT HAS LEFT THE GNOMISH CITY FAR BEHIND! HE'S RUNNING!
FIND HIM, YOU CURSED BEAST!

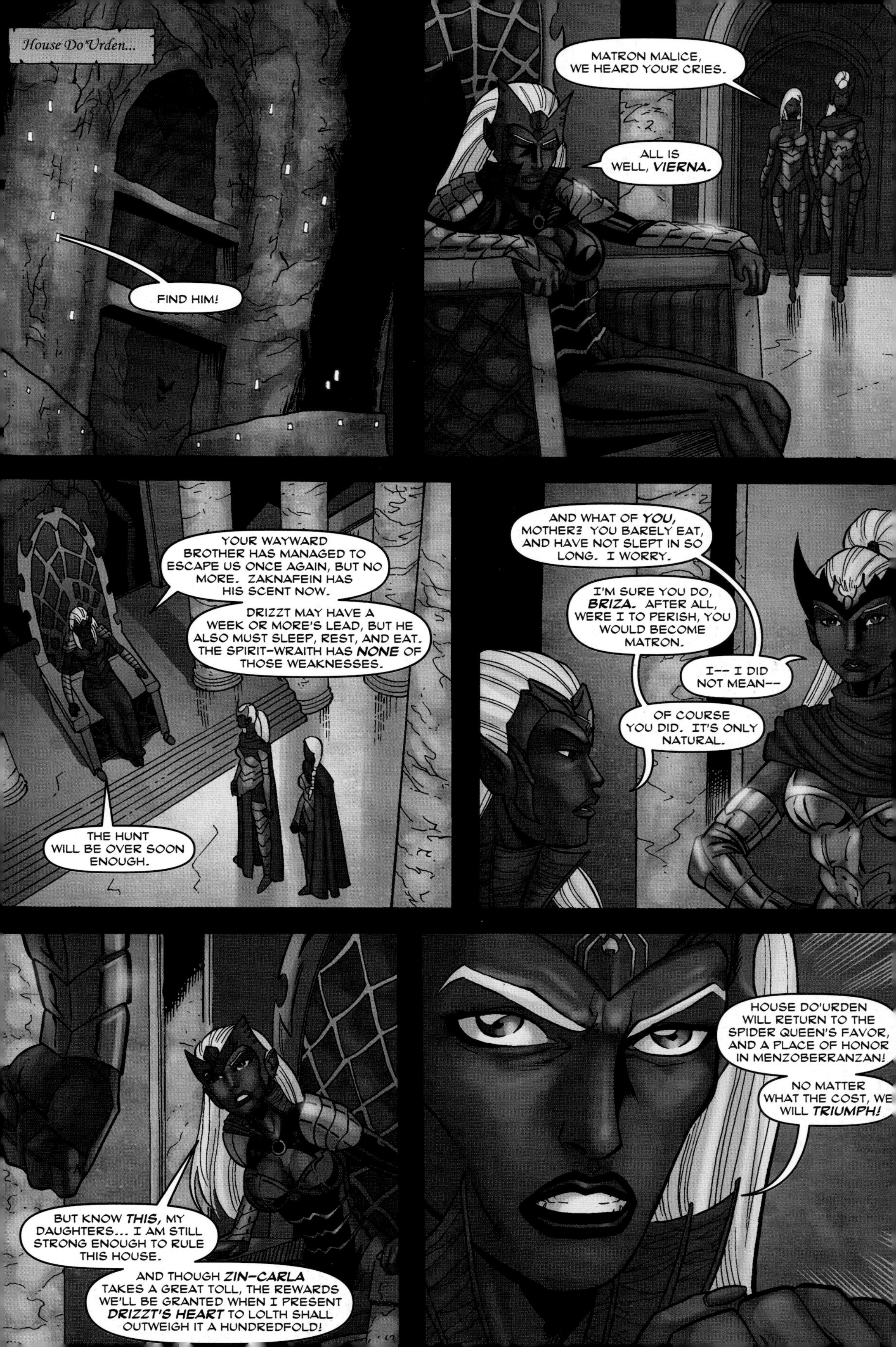
House Do'Urden...
FIND HIM!
MATRON MALICE, WE HEARD YOUR CRIES.
ALL IS WELL, VIERNA.
YOUR WAYWARD BROTHER HAS MANAGED TO ESCAPE US ONCE AGAIN, BUT NO MORE. ZAKNAFEIN HAS HIS SCENT NOW.
DRIZZT MAY HAVE A WEEK OR MORE'S LEAD, BUT HE ALSO MUST SLEEP, REST, AND EAT. THE SPIRIT-WRAITH HAS NONE OF THOSE WEAKNESSES.
THE HUNT WILL BE OVER SOON ENOUGH.
AND WHAT OF YOU, MOTHER? YOU BARELY EAT, AND HAVE NOT SLEPT IN SO LONG. I WORRY.
I'M SURE YOU DO, BRIZA. AFTER ALL, WERE I TO PERISH, YOU WOULD BECOME MATRON.
I-- I DID NOT MEAN--
OF COURSE YOU DID. IT'S ONLY NATURAL.
BUT KNOW THIS, MY DAUGHTERS... I AM STILL STRONG ENOUGH TO RULE THIS HOUSE.
AND THOUGH ZIN-CARLA TAKES A GREAT TOLL, THE REWARDS WE'LL BE GRANTED WHEN I PRESENT DRIZZT'S HEART TO LOLTH SHALL OUTWEIGH IT A HUNDREDFOLD!
HOUSE DO'URDEN WILL RETURN TO THE SPIDER QUEEN'S FAVOR, AND A PLACE OF HONOR IN MENZOBERRANZAN!
NO MATTER WHAT THE COST, WE WILL TRIUMPH!

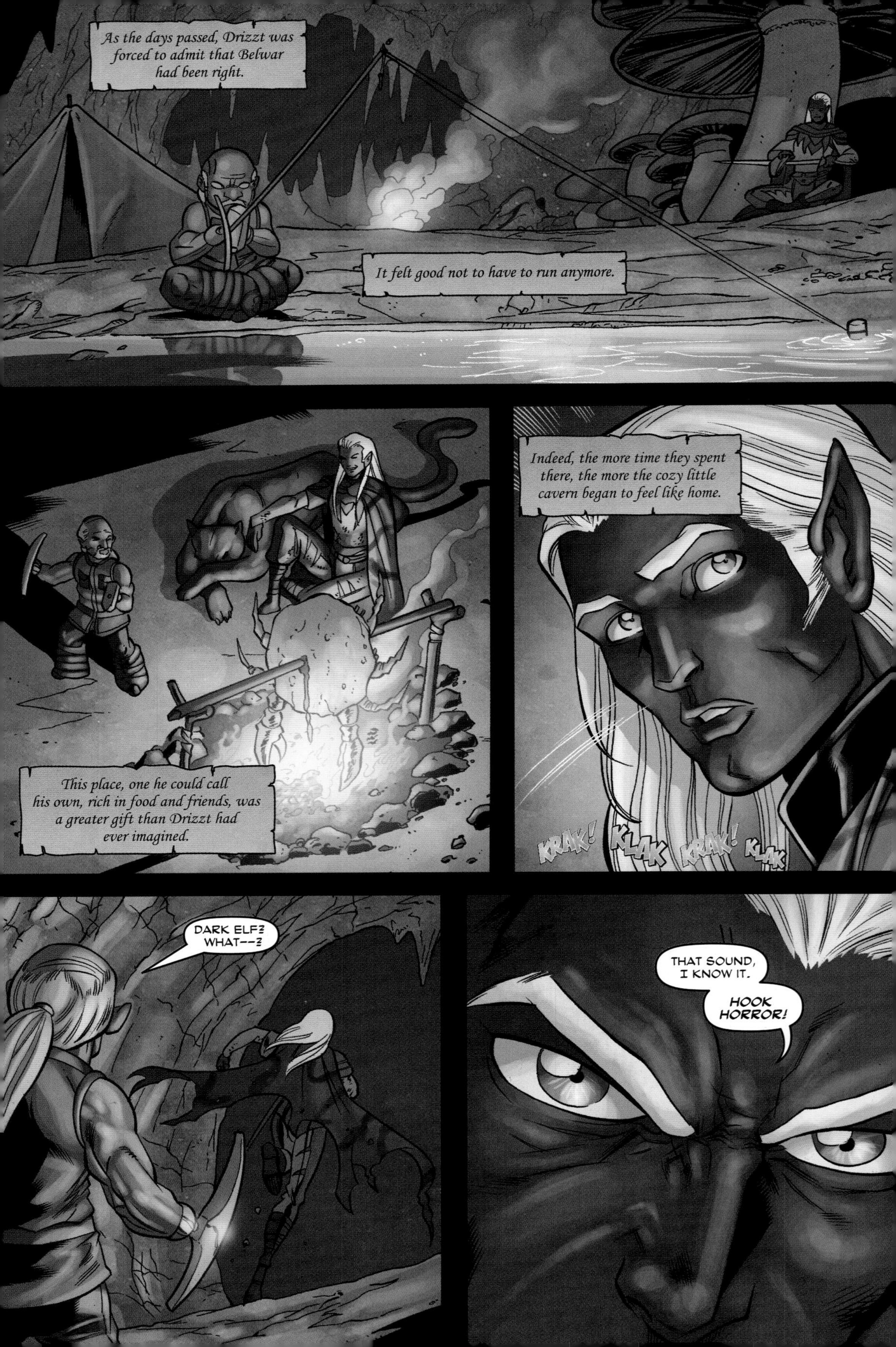
As the days passed, Drizzt was forced to admit that Belwar had been right.
It felt good not to have to run anymore.
This place, one he could call his own, rich in food and friends, was a greater gift than Drizzt had ever imagined.
Indeed, the more time they spent there, the more the cozy little cavern began to feel like home.
KRAK! KLAK KRAK! KLAK
DARK ELF? WHAT--?
THAT SOUND, I KNOW IT.
HOOK HORROR!

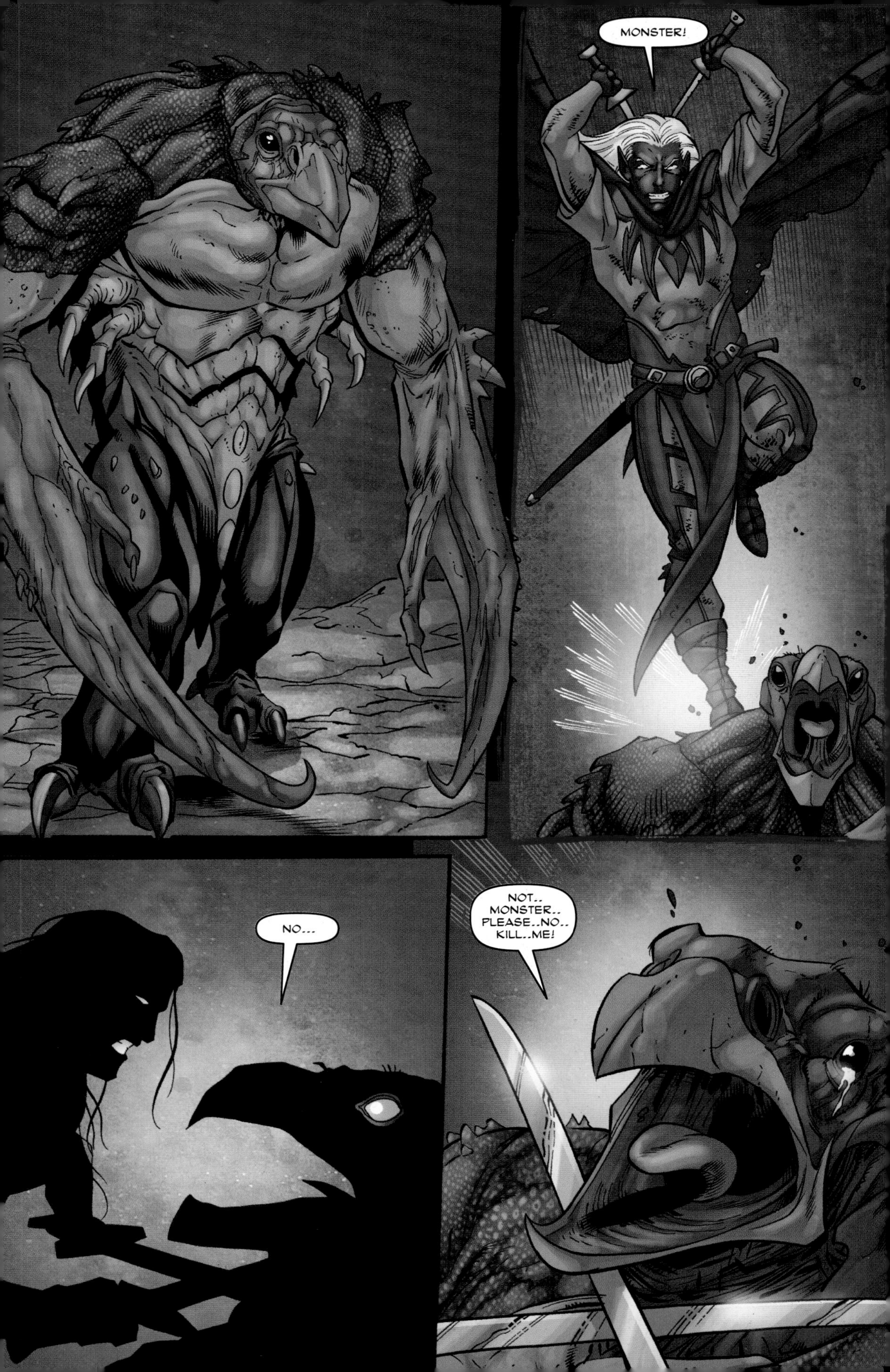
MONSTER!
NO...
NOT.. MONSTER.. PLEASE..NO.. KILL..ME!

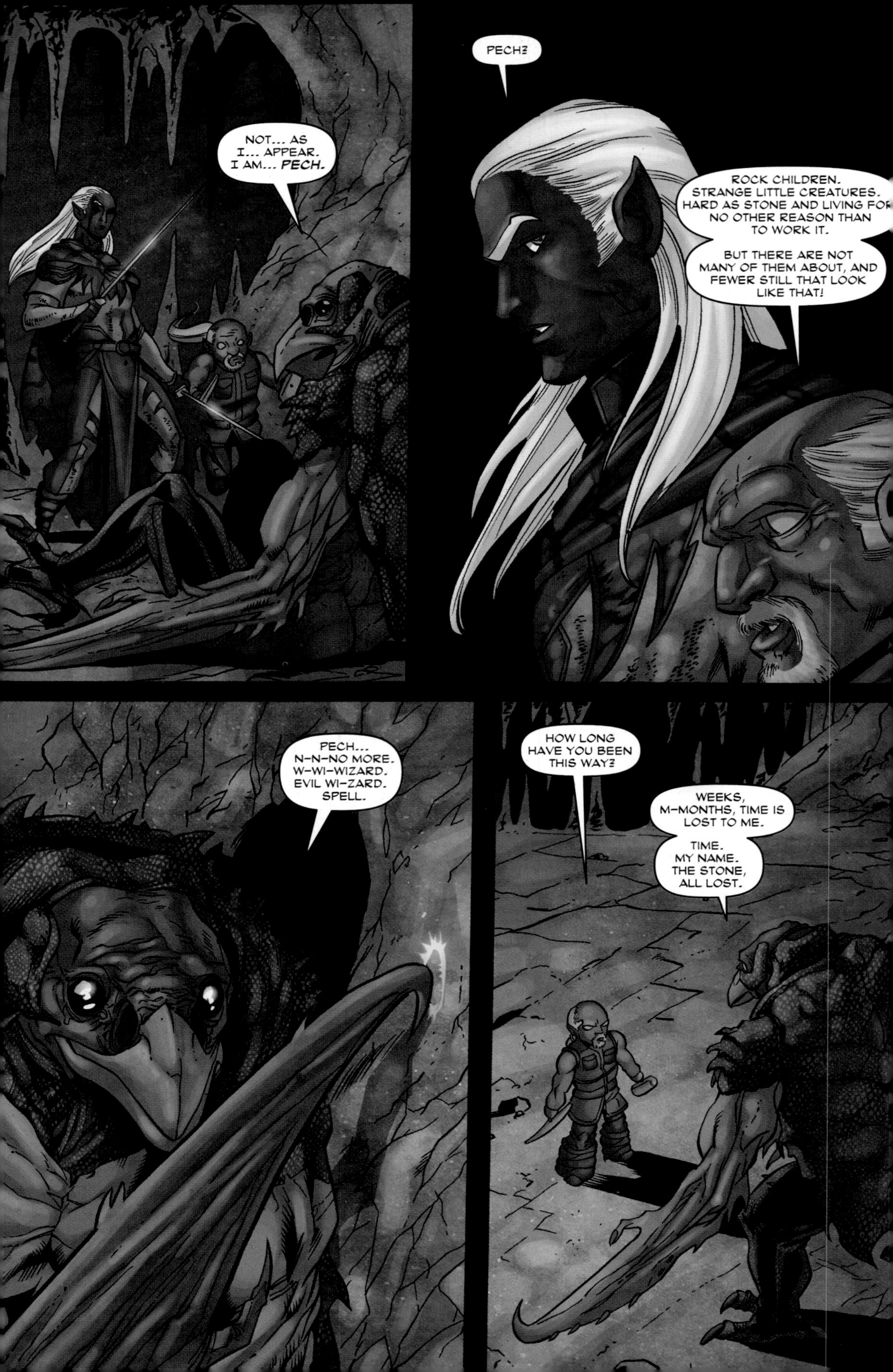
NOT... AS I... APPEAR. I AM... PECH.
PECH?
ROCK CHILDREN. STRANGE LITTLE CREATURES. HARD AS STONE AND LIVING FOR NO OTHER REASON THAN TO WORK IT.
BUT THERE ARE NOT MANY OF THEM ABOUT, AND FEWER STILL THAT LOOK LIKE THAT!
PECH... N-N-NO MORE. W-WI-WIZARD. EVIL WI-ZARD. SPELL.
HOW LONG HAVE YOU BEEN THIS WAY?
WEEKS, M-MONTHS, TIME IS LOST TO ME.
TIME. MY NAME. THE STONE, ALL LOST.

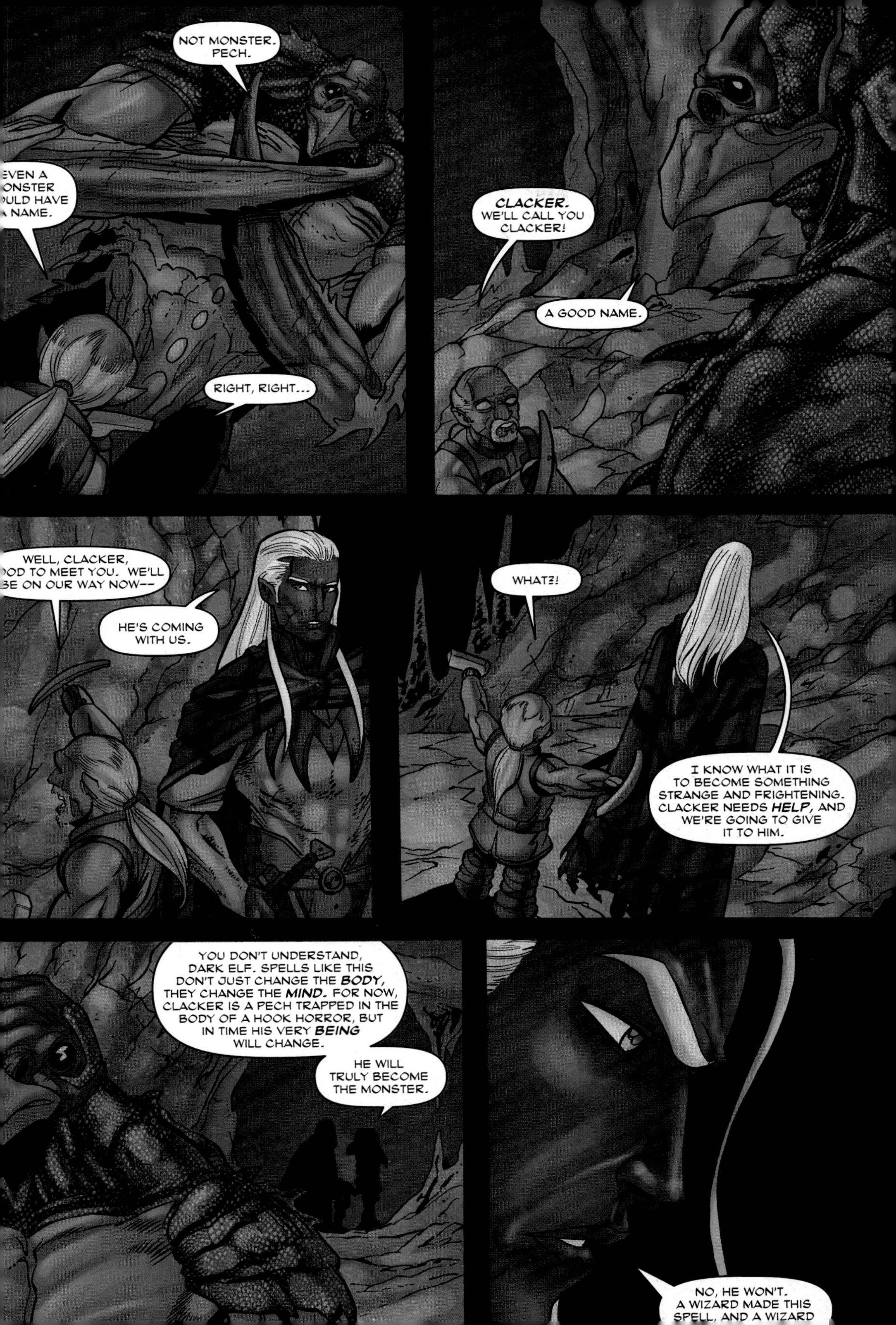
NOT MONSTER. PECH.
EVEN A MONSTER OULD HAVE A NAME.
RIGHT, RIGHT...
CLACKER. WE'LL CALL YOU CLACKER!
A GOOD NAME.
WELL, CLACKER, OOD TO MEET YOU. WE'LL BE ON OUR WAY NOW--
HE'S COMING WITH US.
WHAT?!
I KNOW WHAT IT IS TO BECOME SOMETHING STRANGE AND FRIGHTENING. CLACKER NEEDS HELP, AND WE'RE GOING TO GIVE IT TO HIM.
YOU DON'T UNDERSTAND, DARK ELF. SPELLS LIKE THIS DON'T JUST CHANGE THE BODY, THEY CHANGE THE MIND. FOR NOW, CLACKER IS A PECH TRAPPED IN THE BODY OF A HOOK HORROR, BUT IN TIME HIS VERY BEING WILL CHANGE.
HE WILL TRULY BECOME THE MONSTER.
NO, HE WON'T. A WIZARD MADE THIS SPELL, AND A WIZARD

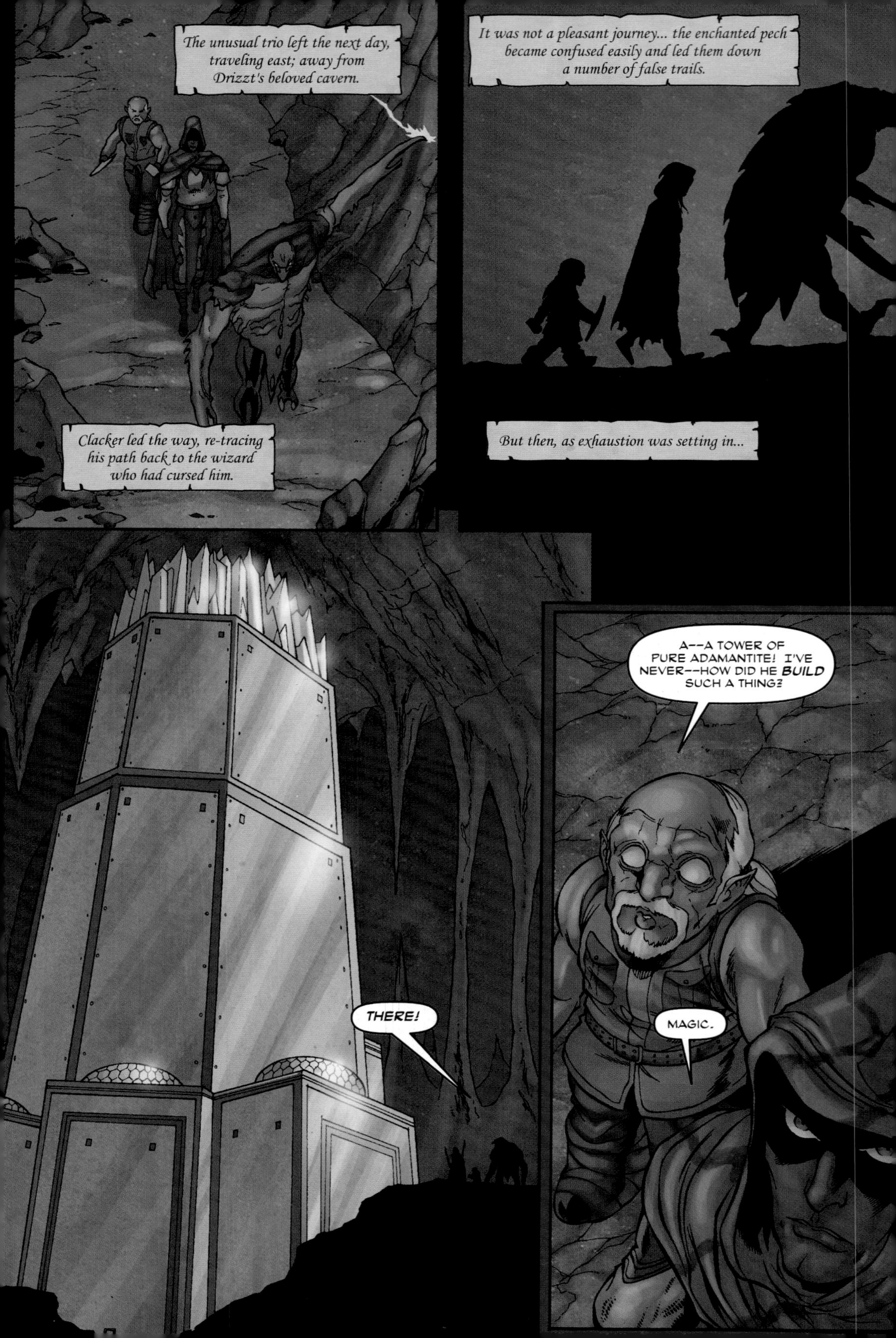
The unusual trio left the next day, traveling east; away from Drizzt's beloved cavern.
Clacker led the way, re-tracing his path back to the wizard who had cursed him.
It was not a pleasant journey... the enchanted pech became confused easily and led them down a number of false trails.
But then, as exhaustion was setting in...
THERE!
A--A TOWER OF PURE ADAMANTITE! I'VE NEVER--HOW DID HE BUILD SUCH A THING?
MAGIC.

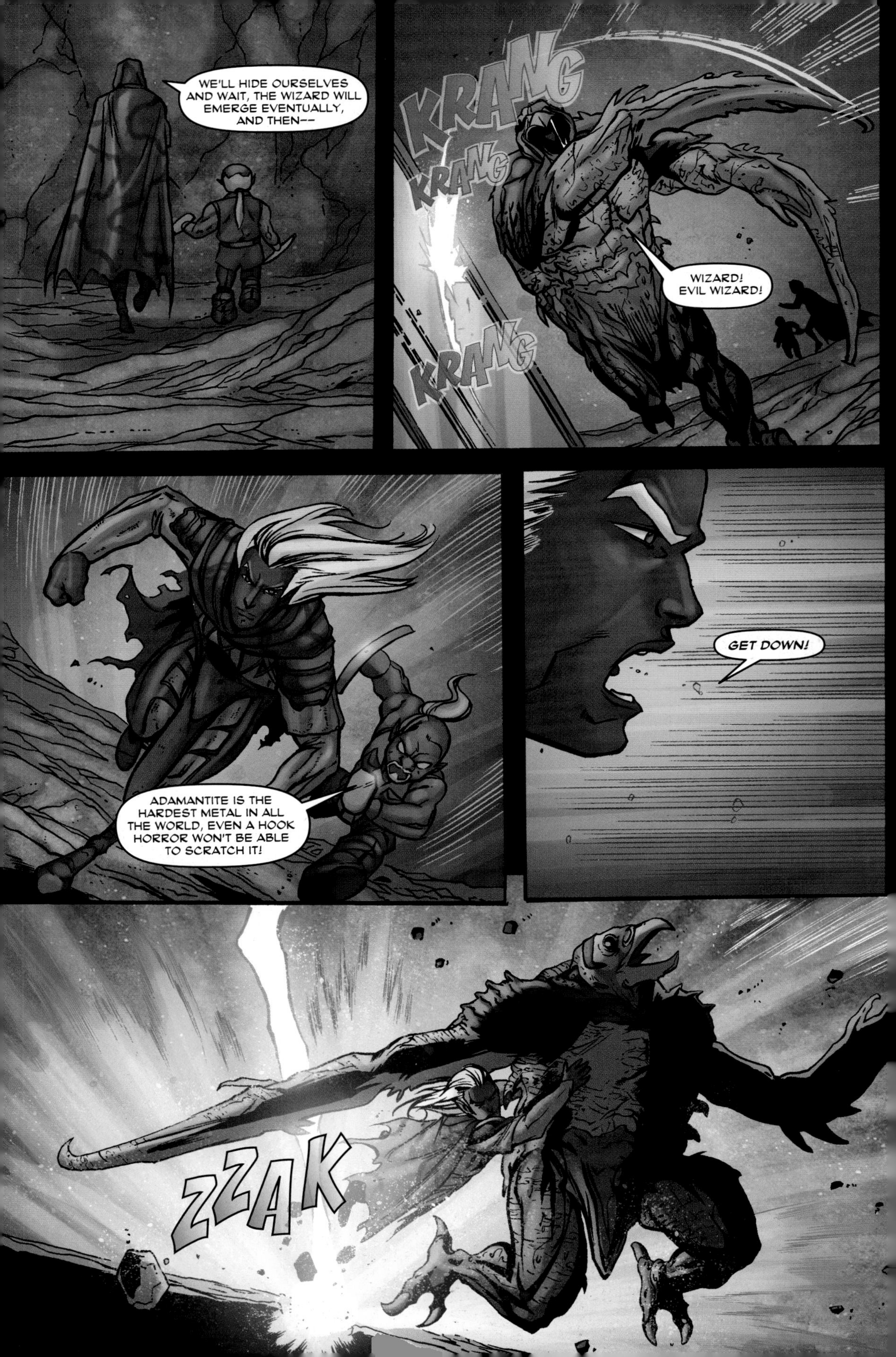
WE'LL HIDE OURSELVES AND WAIT, THE WIZARD WILL EMERGE EVENTUALLY, AND THEN--
KRANG
KRANG
KRANG
WIZARD! EVIL WIZARD!
ADAMANTITE IS THE HARDEST METAL IN ALL THE WORLD, EVEN A HOOK HORROR WON'T BE ABLE TO SCRATCH IT!
GET DOWN!
ZZAK

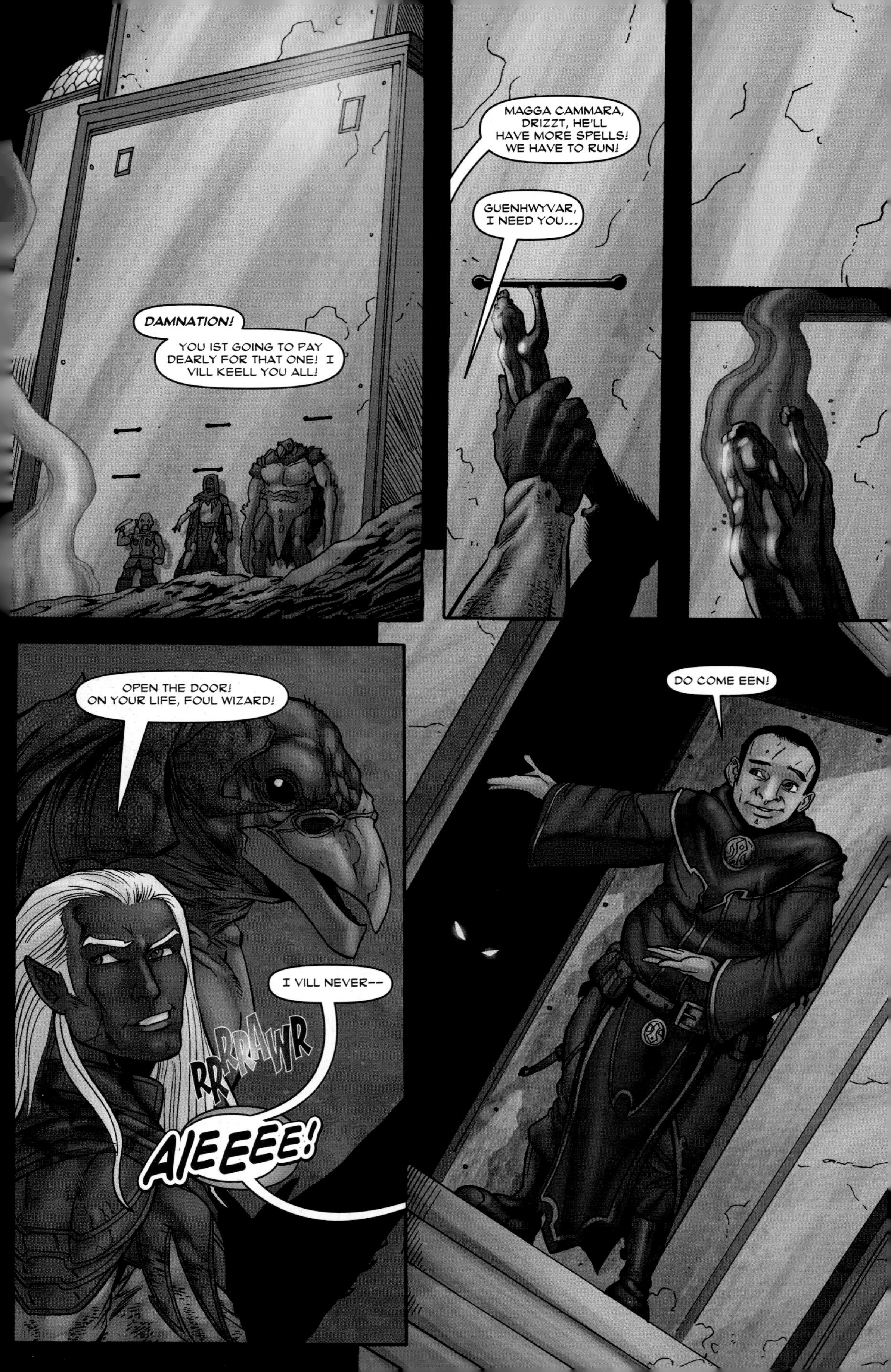
DAMNATION!
YOU IST GOING TO PAY DEARLY FOR THAT ONE! I VILL KEELL YOU ALL!
MAGGA CAMMARA, DRIZZT, HE'LL HAVE MORE SPELLS! WE HAVE TO RUN!
GUENHWYVAR, I NEED YOU...
OPEN THE DOOR! ON YOUR LIFE, FOUL WIZARD!
I VILL NEVER--
RRRRAWR
AIEEEE!
DO COME EEN!

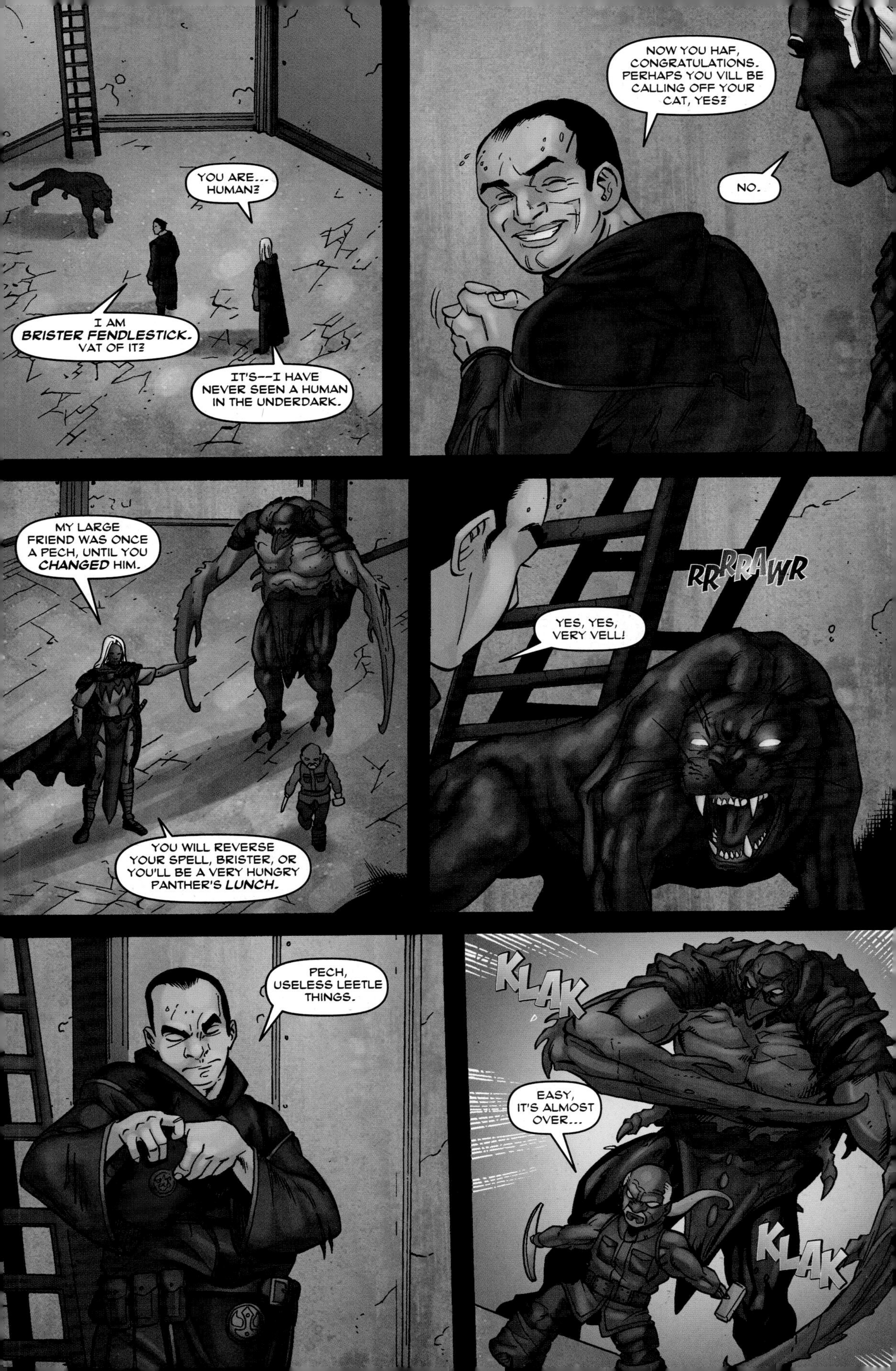
YOU ARE... HUMAN?
I AM BRISTER FENDLESTICK. VAT OF IT?
IT'S--I HAVE NEVER SEEN A HUMAN IN THE UNDERDARK.
NOW YOU HAF, CONGRATULATIONS. PERHAPS YOU VILL BE CALLING OFF YOUR CAT, YES?
NO.
MY LARGE FRIEND WAS ONCE A PECH, UNTIL YOU CHANGED HIM.
YOU WILL REVERSE YOUR SPELL, BRISTER, OR YOU'LL BE A VERY HUNGRY PANTHER'S LUNCH.
RRRRAWR
YES, YES, VERY VELL!
PECH, USELESS LEETLE THINGS.
KLAK
EASY, IT'S ALMOST OVER...
KLAK

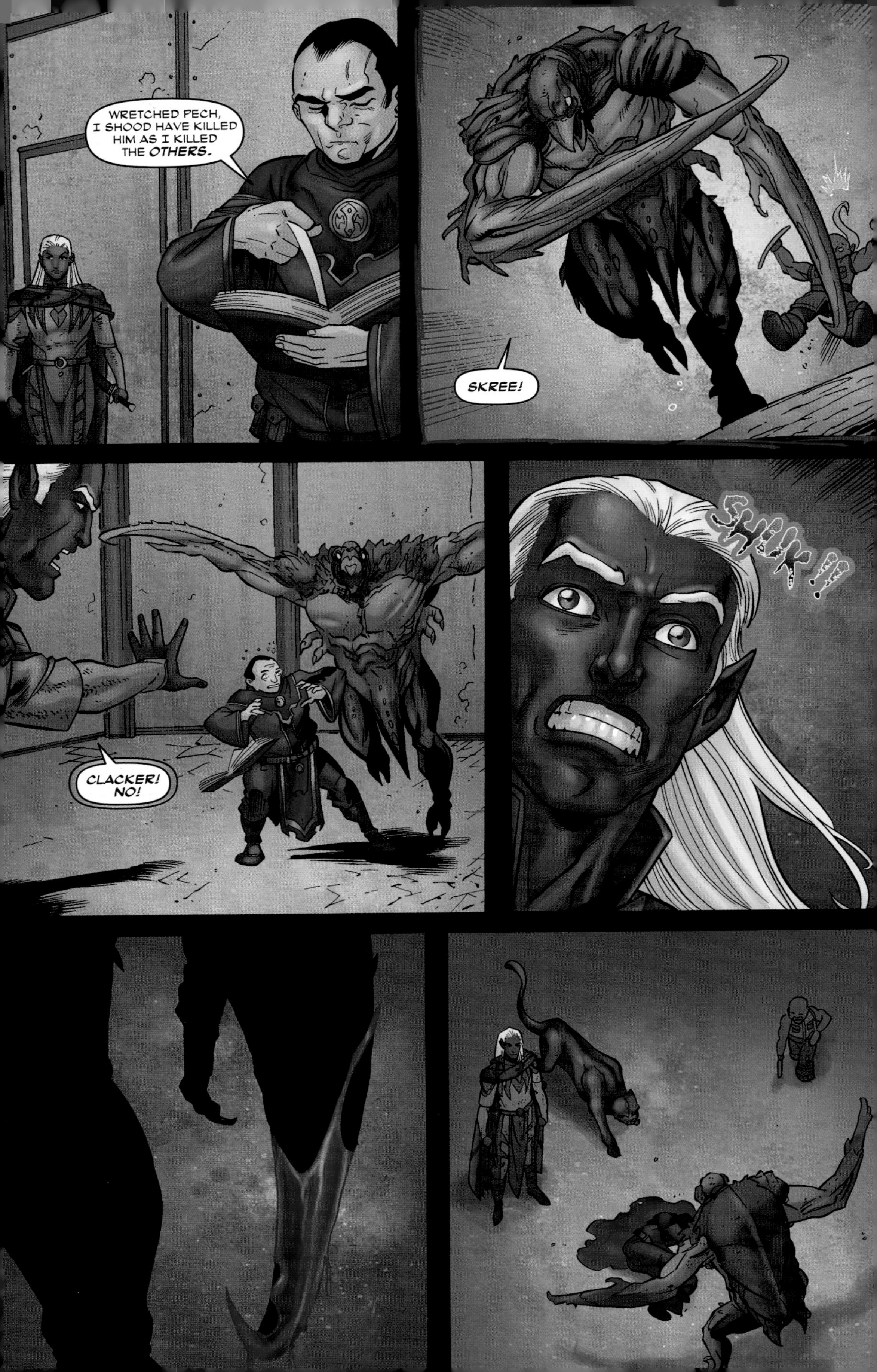
WRETCHED PECH, I SHOOD HAVE KILLED HIM AS I KILLED THE OTHERS.
SKREE!
CLACKER! NO!
SHHK!!

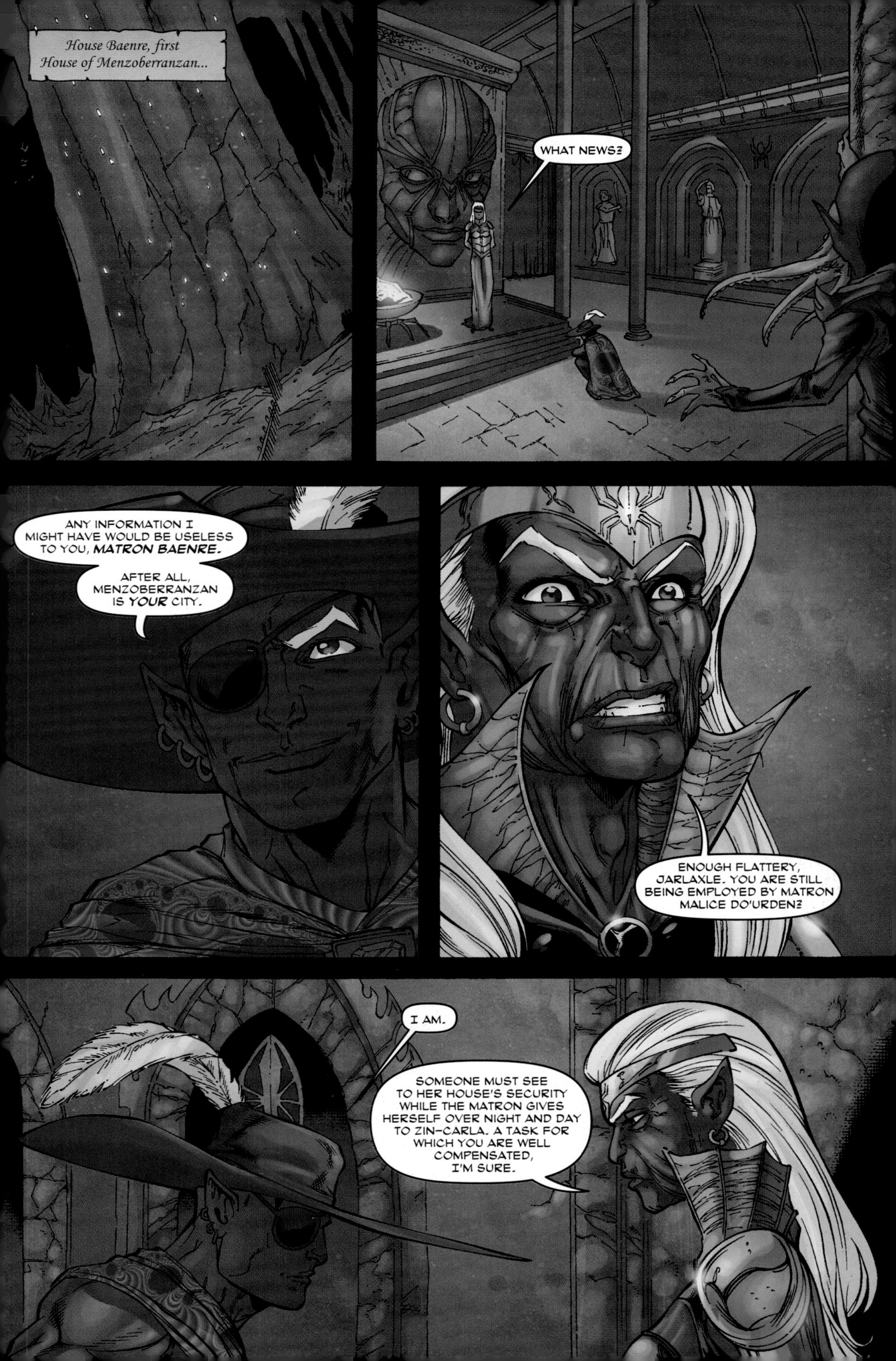
House Baenre, first House of Menzoberranzan...
WHAT NEWS?
ANY INFORMATION I MIGHT HAVE WOULD BE USELESS TO YOU, MATRON BAENRE.
AFTER ALL, MENZOBERRANZAN IS YOUR CITY.
ENOUGH FLATTERY, JARLAXLE. YOU ARE STILL BEING EMPLOYED BY MATRON MALICE DO'URDEN?
I AM.
SOMEONE MUST SEE TO HER HOUSE'S SECURITY WHILE THE MATRON GIVES HERSELF OVER NIGHT AND DAY TO ZIN-CARLA. A TASK FOR WHICH YOU ARE WELL COMPENSATED, I'M SURE.

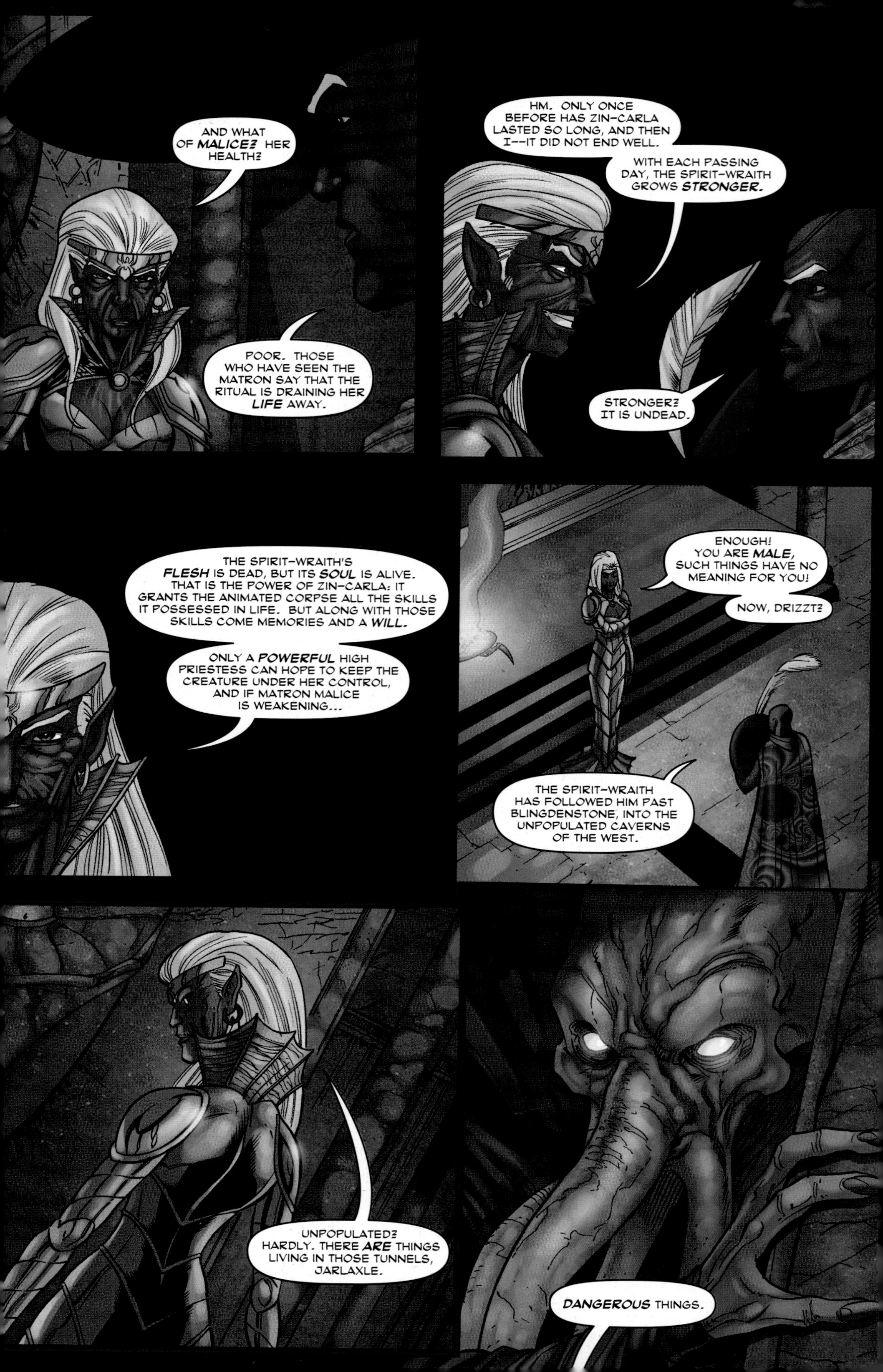
AND WHAT OF MALICE? HER HEALTH?
POOR. THOSE WHO HAVE SEEN THE MATRON SAY THAT THE RITUAL IS DRAINING HER LIFE AWAY.
HM. ONLY ONCE BEFORE HAS ZIN-CARLA LASTED SO LONG, AND THEN I--IT DID NOT END WELL.
WITH EACH PASSING DAY, THE SPIRIT-WRAITH GROWS STRONGER.
STRONGER? IT IS UNDEAD.
THE SPIRIT-WRAITH'S FLESH IS DEAD, BUT ITS SOUL IS ALIVE. THAT IS THE POWER OF ZIN-CARLA: IT GRANTS THE ANIMATED CORPSE ALL THE SKILLS IT POSSESSED IN LIFE. BUT ALONG WITH THOSE SKILLS COME MEMORIES AND A WILL.
ONLY A POWERFUL HIGH PRIESTESS CAN HOPE TO KEEP THE CREATURE UNDER HER CONTROL, AND IF MATRON MALICE IS WEAKENING...
ENOUGH! YOU ARE MALE, SUCH THINGS HAVE NO MEANING FOR YOU!
NOW, DRIZZT?
THE SPIRIT-WRAITH HAS FOLLOWED HIM PAST BLINGDENSTONE, INTO THE UNPOPULATED CAVERNS OF THE WEST.
UNPOPULATED? HARDLY. THERE ARE THINGS LIVING IN THOSE TUNNELS, JARLAXLE.
DANGEROUS THINGS.

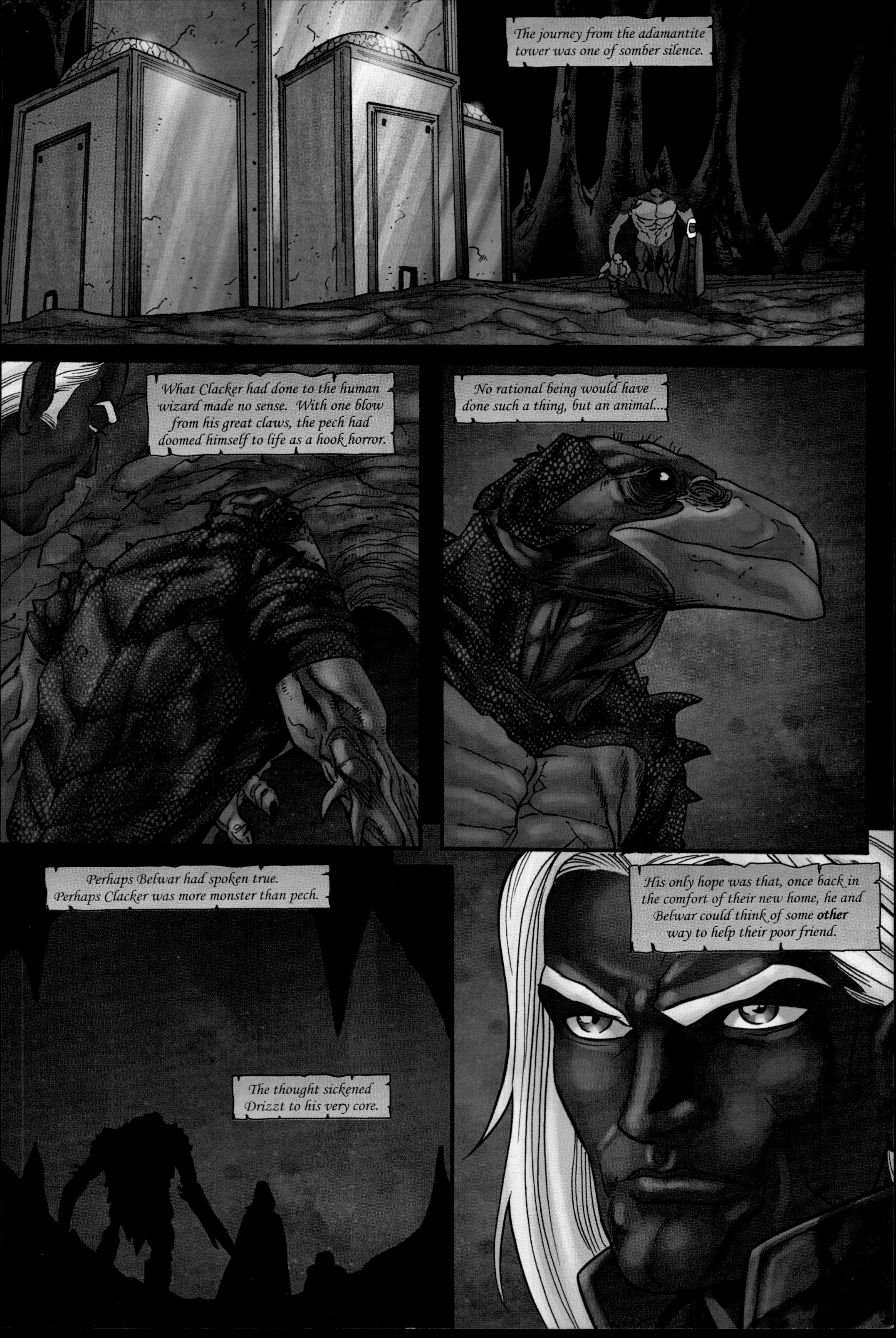
The journey from the adamantite tower was one of somber silence.
What Clacker had done to the human wizard made no sense. With one blow from his great claws, the pech had doomed himself to life as a hook horror.
No rational being would have done such a thing, but an animal...
Perhaps Belwar had spoken true. Perhaps Clacker was more monster than pech.
The thought sickened Drizzt to his very core.
His only hope was that, once back in the comfort of their new home, he and Belwar could think of some **other** way to help their poor friend.

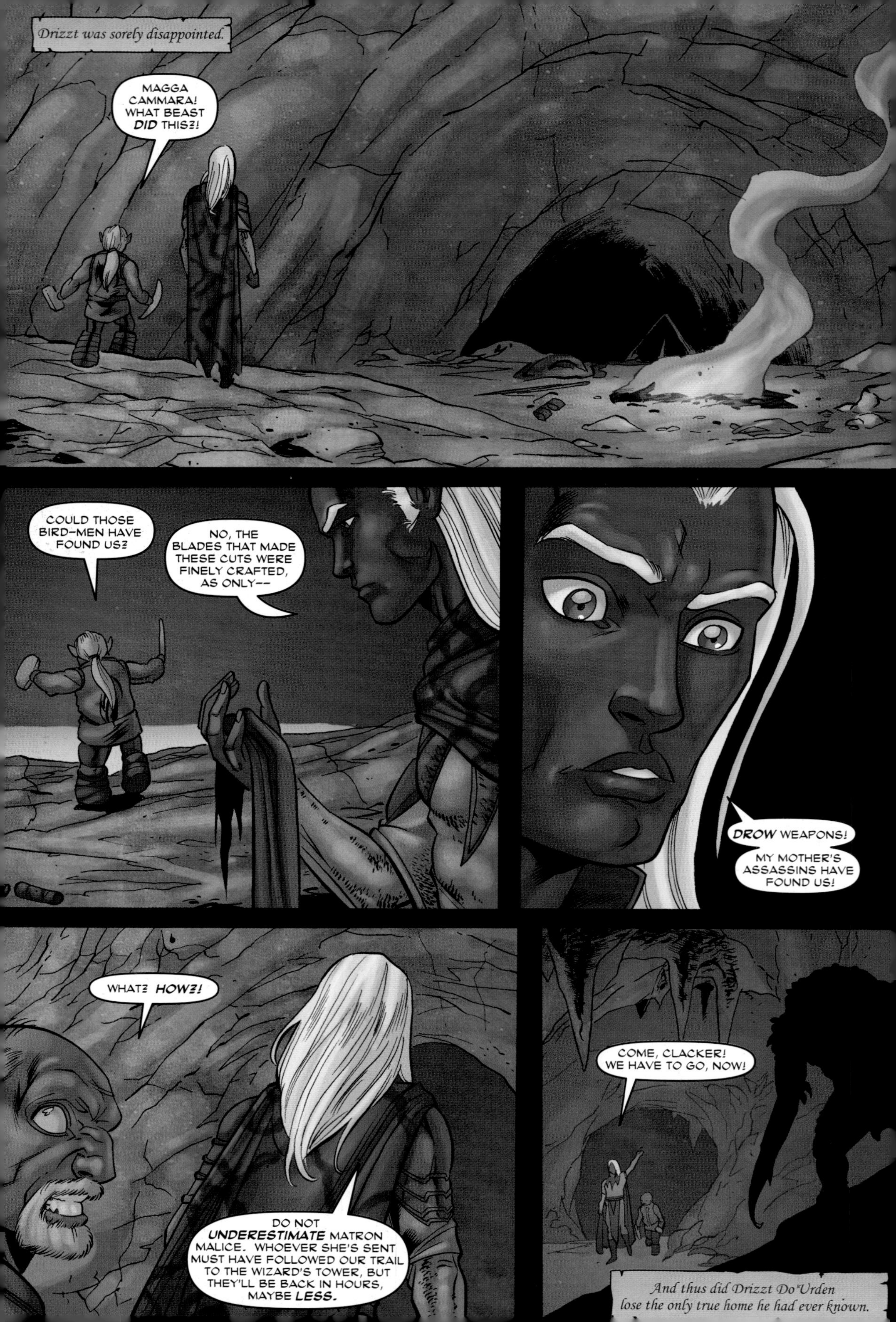
Drizzt was sorely disappointed.
MAGGA CAMMARA! WHAT BEAST DID THIS?!
COULD THOSE BIRD-MEN HAVE FOUND US?
NO, THE BLADES THAT MADE THESE CUTS WERE FINELY CRAFTED, AS ONLY--
DROW WEAPONS!
MY MOTHER'S ASSASSINS HAVE FOUND US!
WHAT? HOW?!
DO NOT UNDERESTIMATE MATRON MALICE. WHOEVER SHE'S SENT MUST HAVE FOLLOWED OUR TRAIL TO THE WIZARD'S TOWER, BUT THEY'LL BE BACK IN HOURS, MAYBE LESS.
COME, CLACKER! WE HAVE TO GO, NOW!
And thus did Drizzt Do'Urden lose the only true home he had ever known.

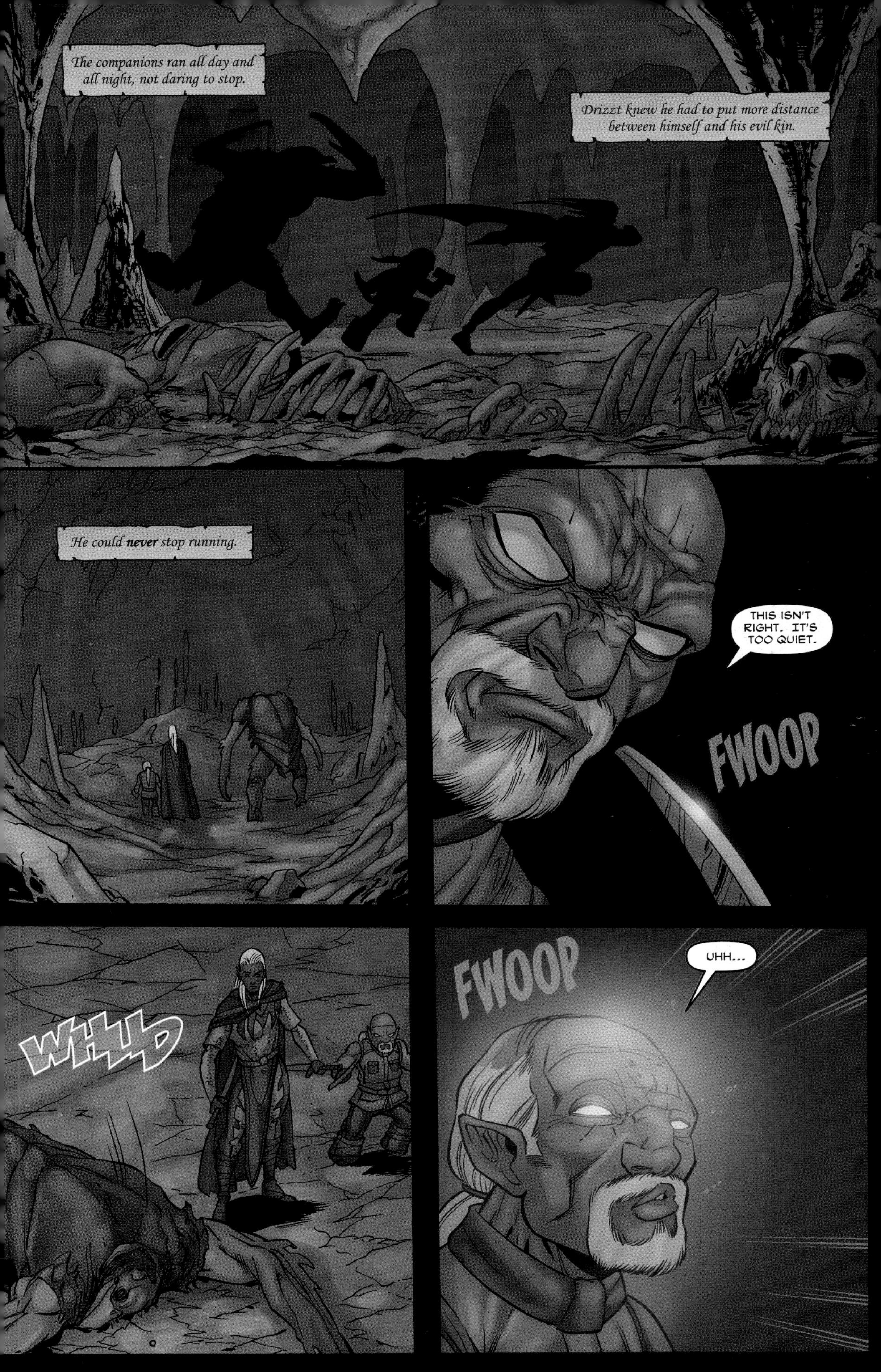
The companions ran all day and all night, not daring to stop.
Drizzt knew he had to put more distance between himself and his evil kin.
He could **never** stop running.
THIS ISN'T RIGHT. IT'S TOO QUIET.
FWOOP
WHUD
FWOOP
UHH...

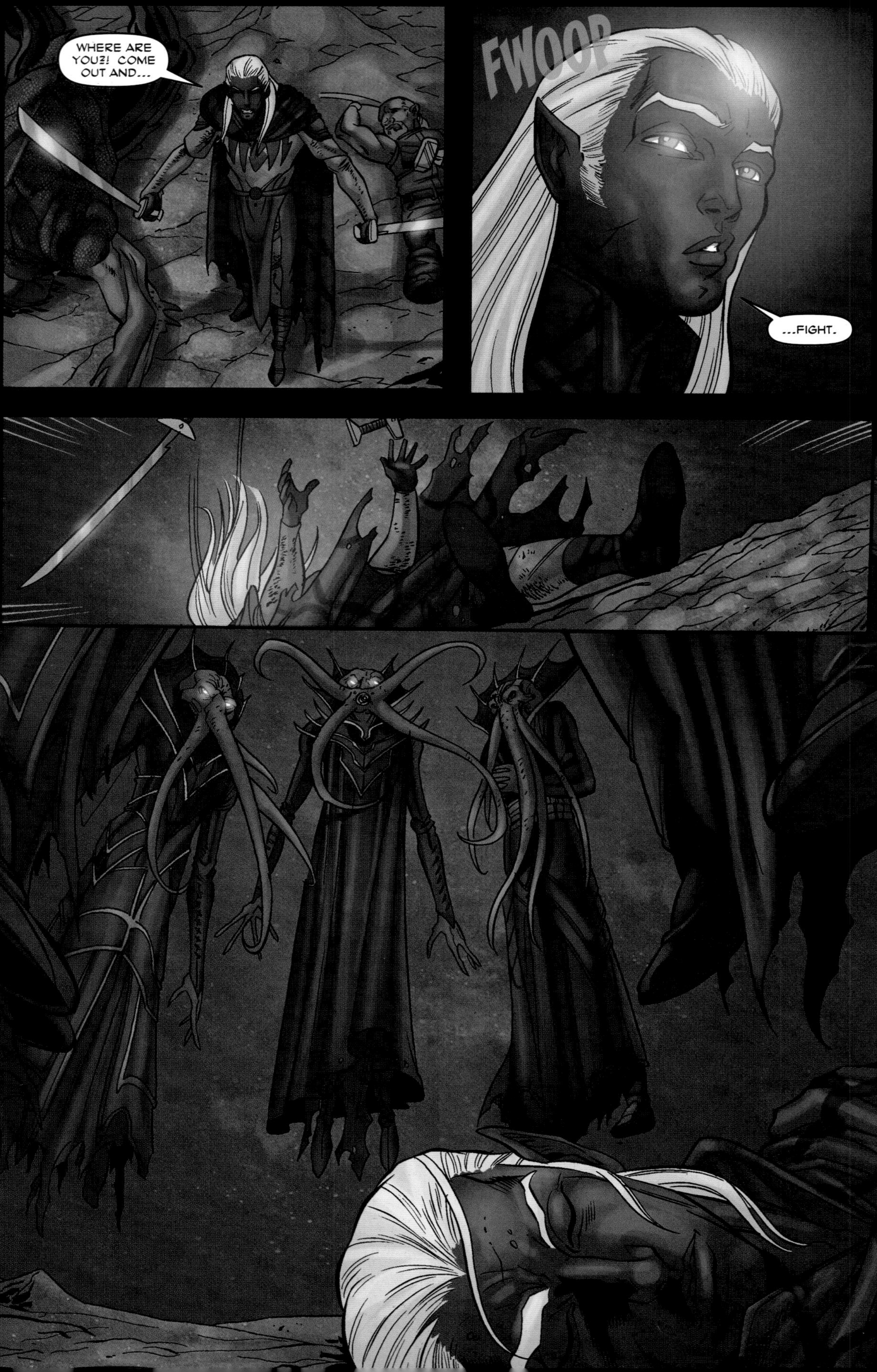
WHERE ARE YOU?! COME OUT AND...
FWOOP
...FIGHT.

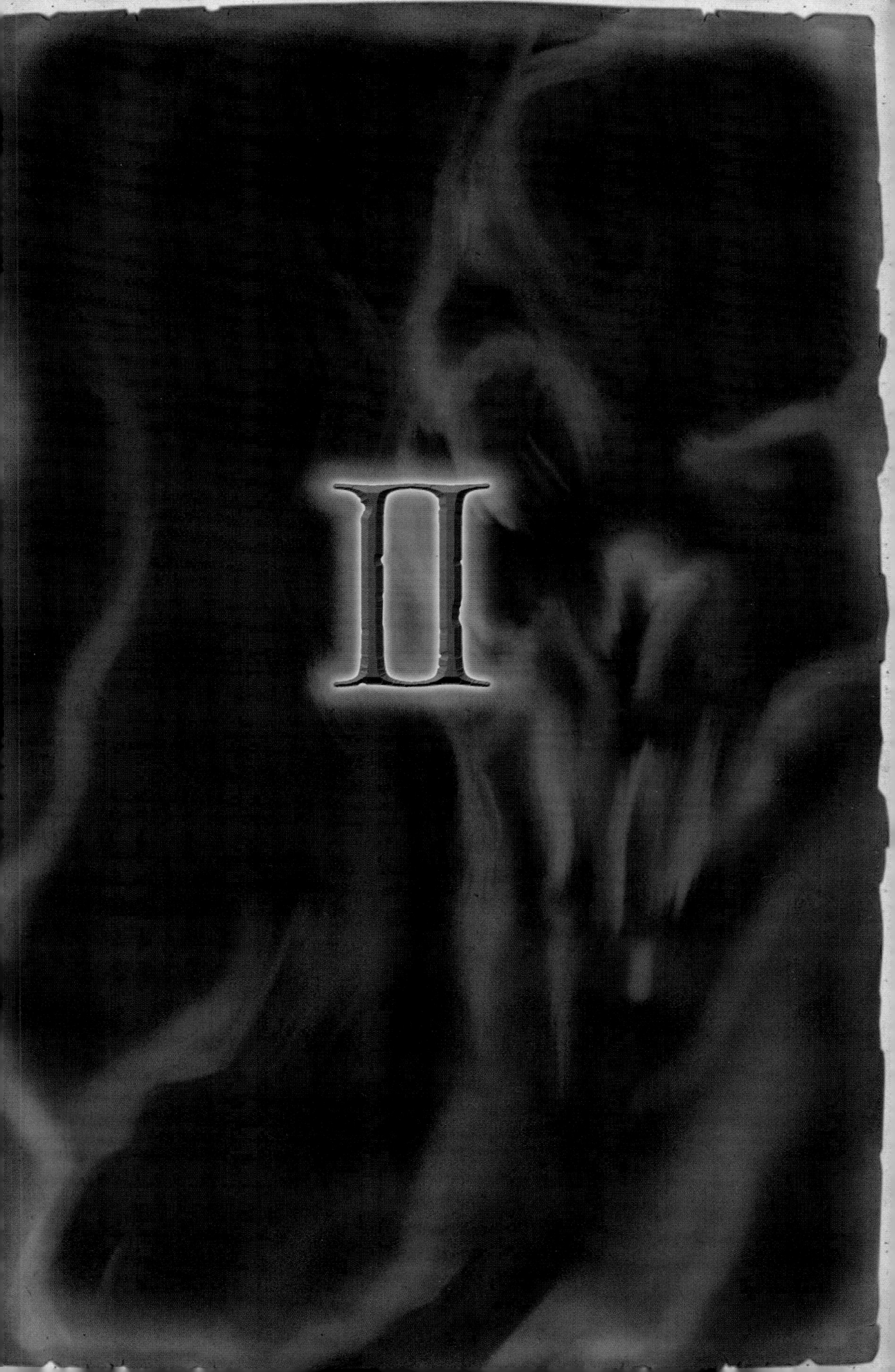
II

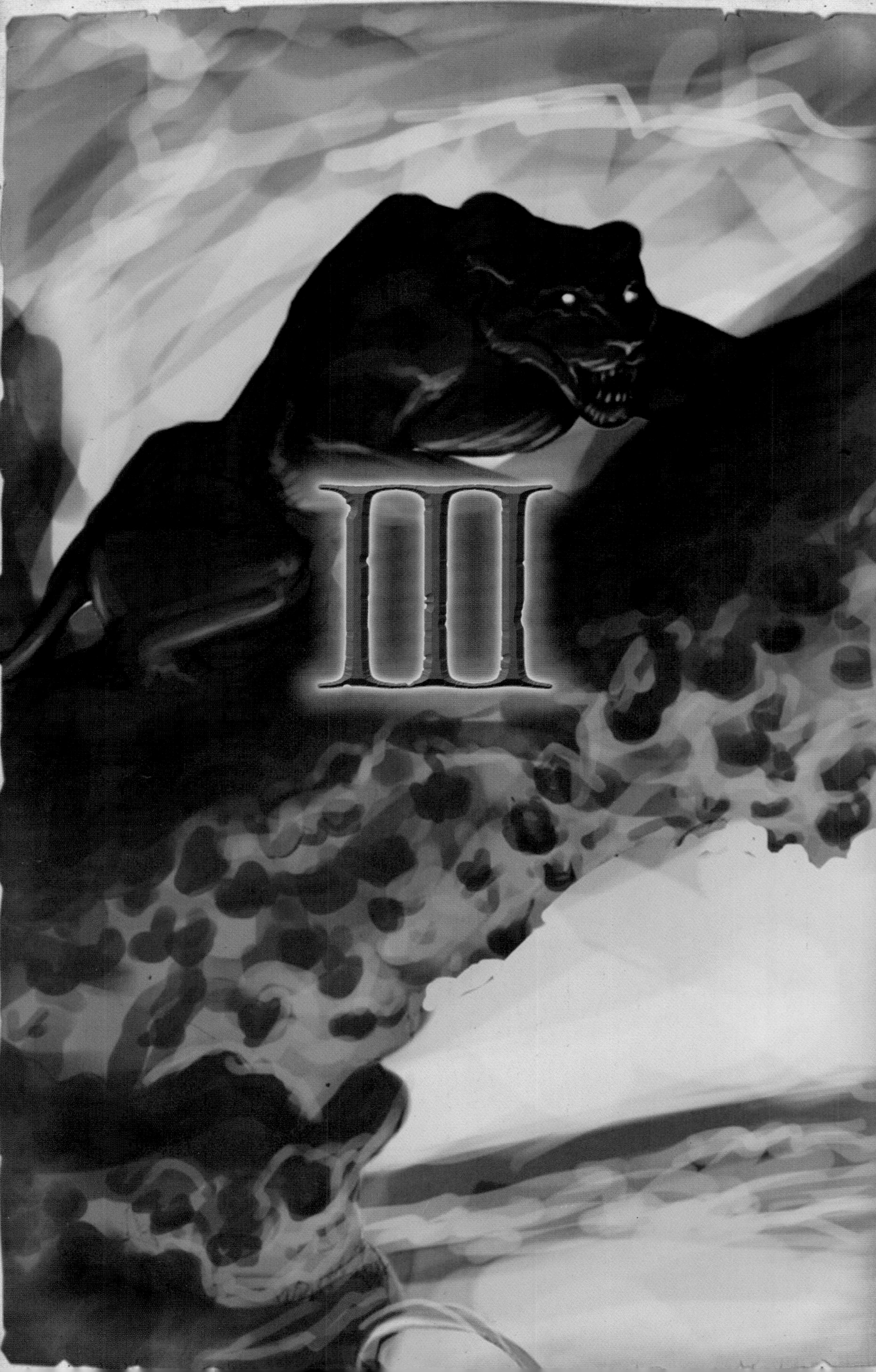
III

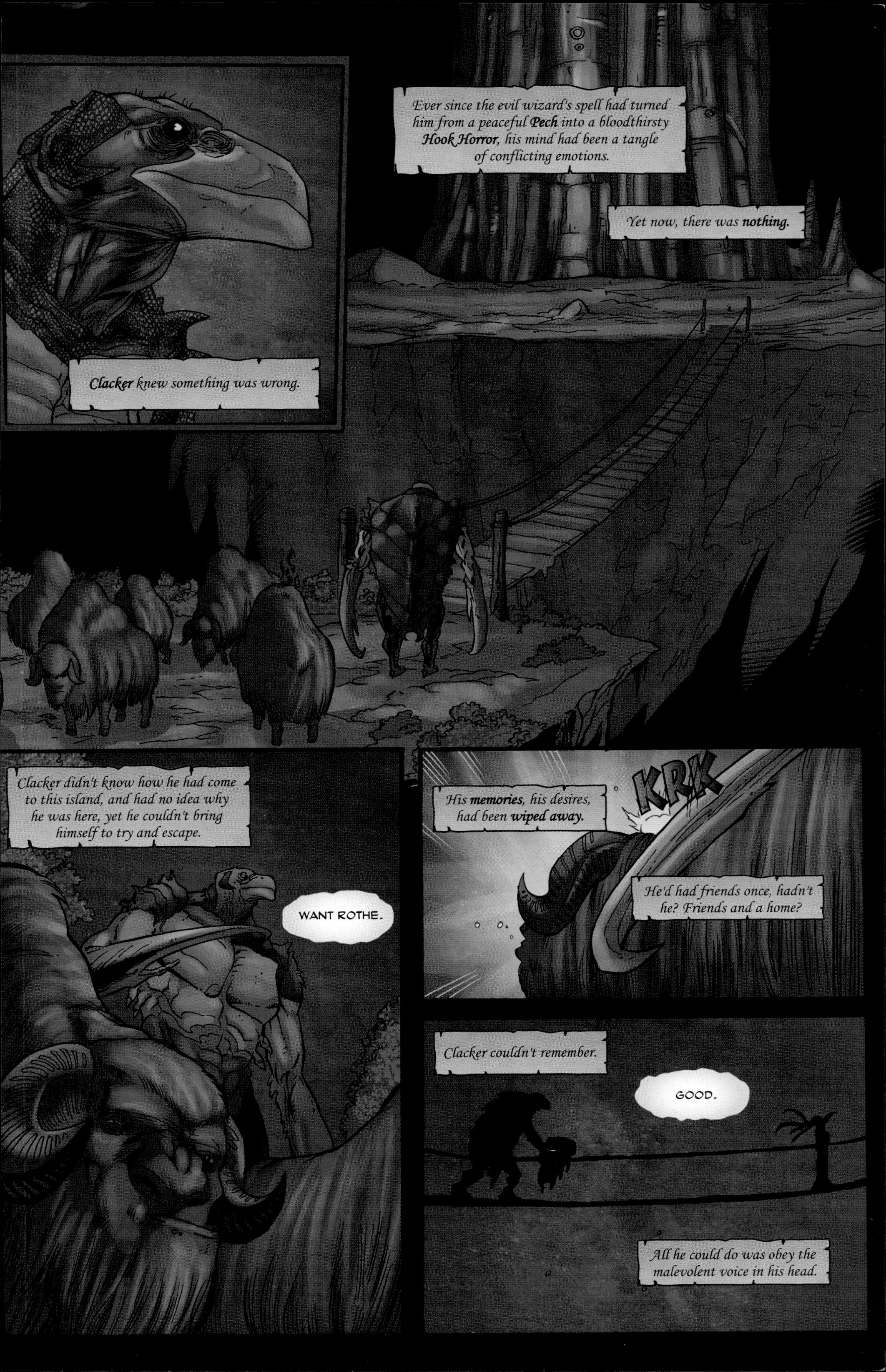
Clacker knew something was wrong.
Ever since the evil wizard's spell had turned him from a peaceful Pech into a bloodthirsty Hook Horror, his mind had been a tangle of conflicting emotions.
Yet now, there was nothing.
Clacker didn't know how he had come to this island, and had no idea why he was here, yet he couldn't bring himself to try and escape.
WANT ROTHE.
His memories, his desires, had been wiped away.
KRK
He'd had friends once, hadn't he? Friends and a home?
Clacker couldn't remember.
GOOD.
All he could do was obey the malevolent voice in his head.

Lying deep in a remote cavern of the Underdark, the **Illithid castle** housed a hundred **Mind Flayers,** and twice that many **slaves.**

Using their **telepathic powers,** Mind Flayers could twist the thoughts and desires of any creature to their own **needs...**

...turning even the most violent monster into a **docile slave** willing to follow any command.

Those with some skill were put to work in the **mines,** digging precious metal from the unforgiving stone...

...while the more bestial were sent to **the arena,** where they fought and died for the Illithids' amusement.

There was no escape from a Mind Flayer's psionic grasp--no freedom granted for a job well done.

And in the end, after they'd become too old to work, or had their minds warped beyond repair, every slave went to the same destination:

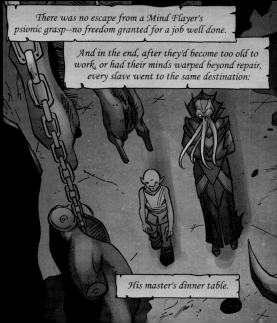

His master's dinner table.

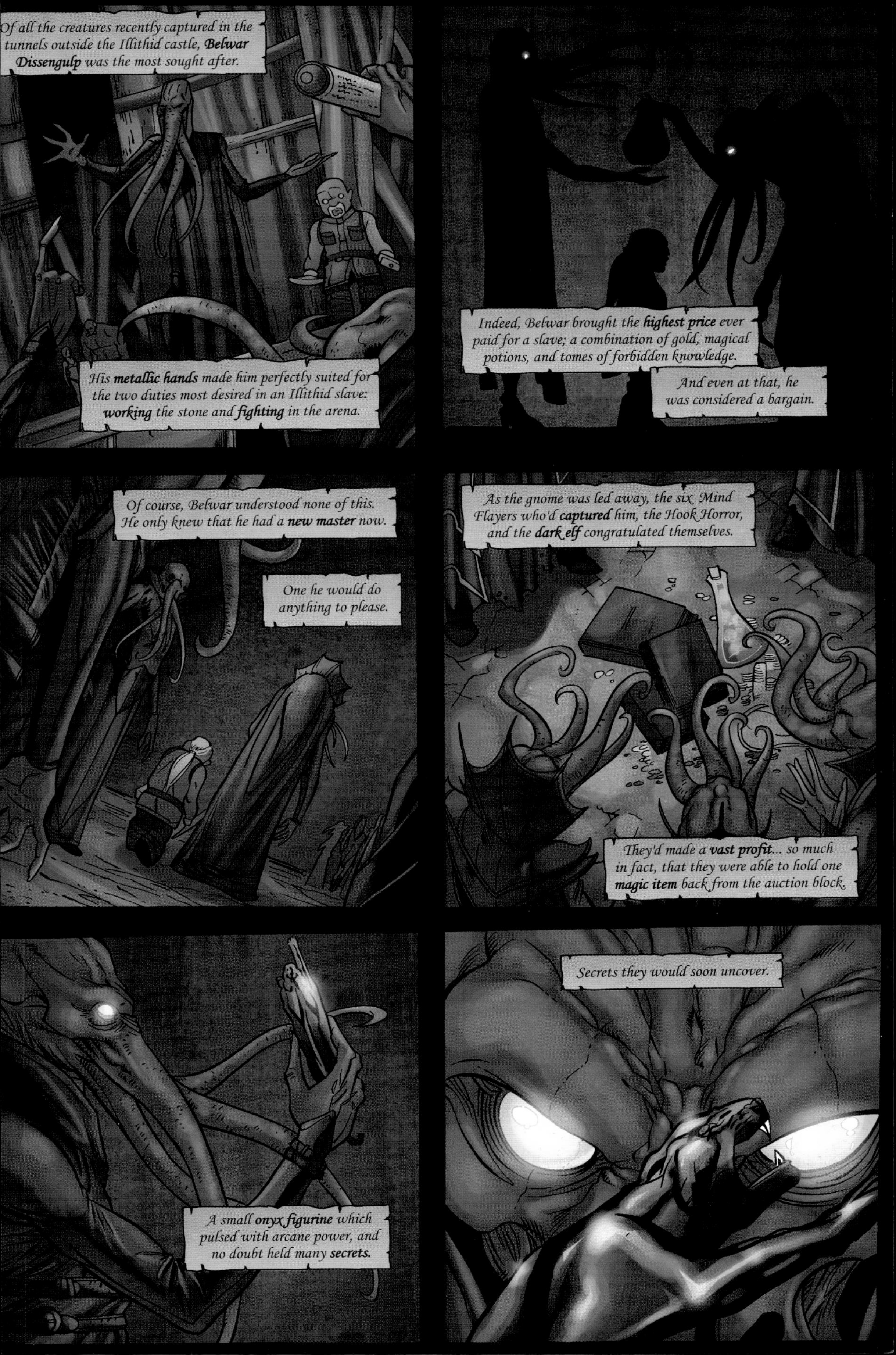
Of all the creatures recently captured in the tunnels outside the Illithid castle, Belwar Dissengulp was the most sought after.
His metallic hands made him perfectly suited for the two duties most desired in an Illithid slave: working the stone and fighting in the arena.
Indeed, Belwar brought the highest price ever paid for a slave; a combination of gold, magical potions, and tomes of forbidden knowledge.
And even at that, he was considered a bargain.
Of course, Belwar understood none of this. He only knew that he had a new master now.
One he would do anything to please.
As the gnome was led away, the six Mind Flayers who'd captured him, the Hook Horror, and the dark elf congratulated themselves.
They'd made a vast profit... so much in fact, that they were able to hold one magic item back from the auction block.
A small onyx figurine which pulsed with arcane power, and no doubt held many secrets.
Secrets they would soon uncover.

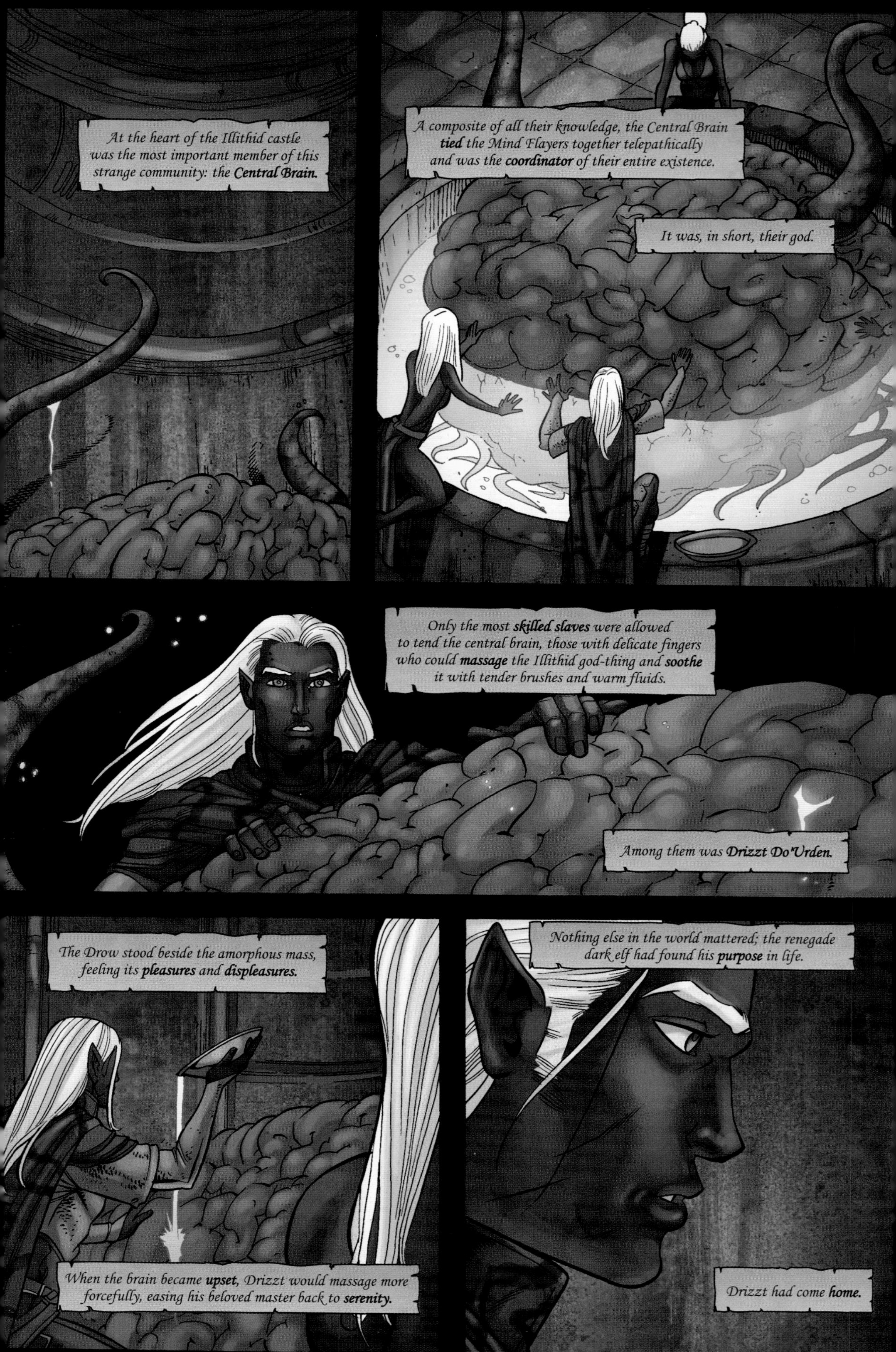
At the heart of the Illithid castle was the most important member of this strange community: the Central Brain.
A composite of all their knowledge, the Central Brain tied the Mind Flayers together telepathically and was the coordinator of their entire existence.
It was, in short, their god.
Only the most skilled slaves were allowed to tend the central brain, those with delicate fingers who could massage the Illithid god-thing and soothe it with tender brushes and warm fluids.
Among them was Drizzt Do'Urden.
The Drow stood beside the amorphous mass, feeling its pleasures and displeasures.
When the brain became upset, Drizzt would massage more forcefully, easing his beloved master back to serenity.
Nothing else in the world mattered; the renegade dark elf had found his purpose in life.
Drizzt had come home.

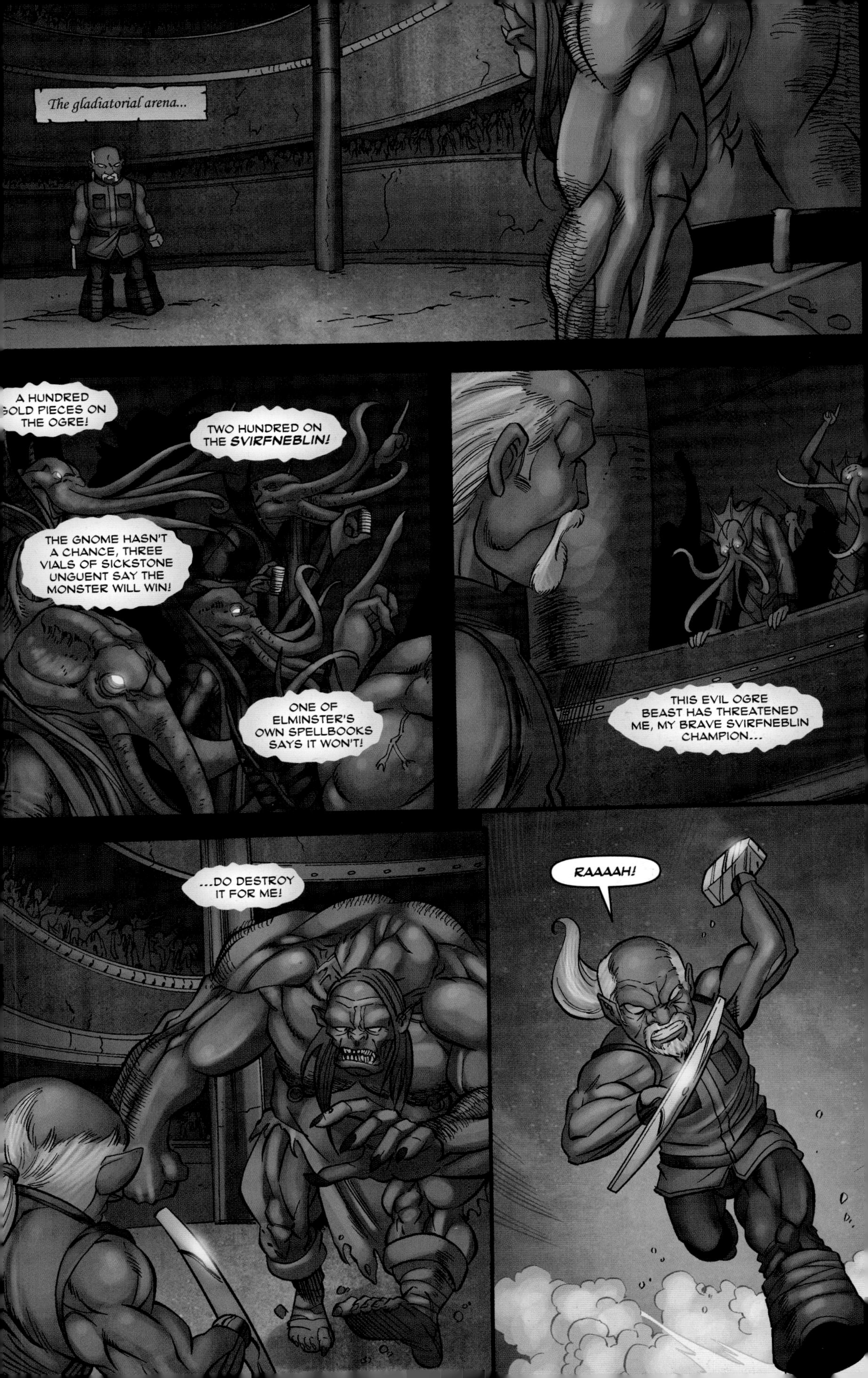
The gladiatorial arena...
A HUNDRED GOLD PIECES ON THE OGRE!
TWO HUNDRED ON THE SVIRFNEBLIN!
THE GNOME HASN'T A CHANCE, THREE VIALS OF SICKSTONE UNGUENT SAY THE MONSTER WILL WIN!
ONE OF ELMINSTER'S OWN SPELLBOOKS SAYS IT WON'T!
THIS EVIL OGRE BEAST HAS THREATENED ME, MY BRAVE SVIRFNEBLIN CHAMPION...
...DO DESTROY IT FOR ME!
RAAAAH!

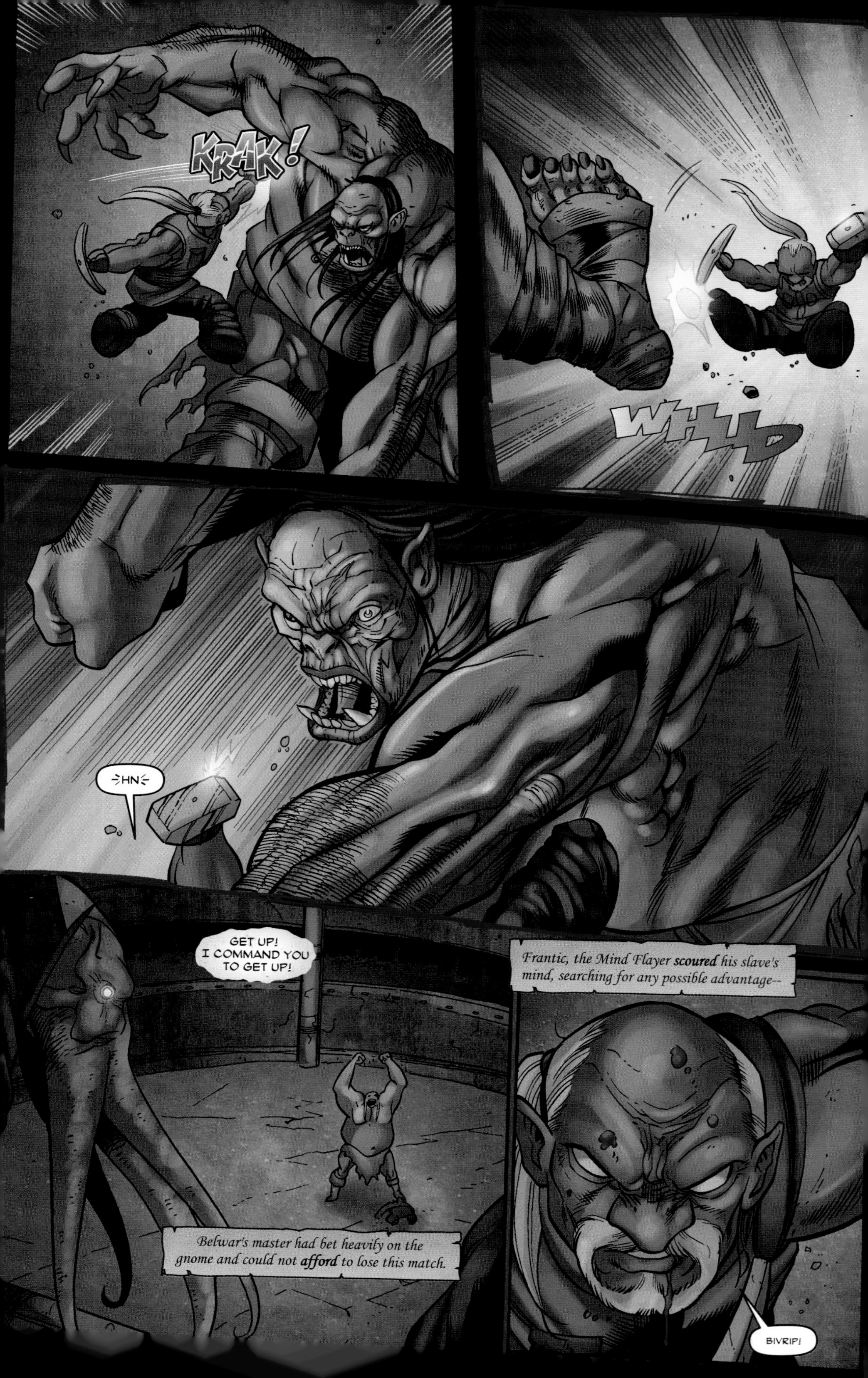
KRAK!
WHUD
HN
GET UP! I COMMAND YOU TO GET UP!
Belwar's master had bet heavily on the gnome and could not **afford** to lose this match.
Frantic, the Mind Flayer **scoured** his slave's mind, searching for any possible advantage--
BIVRIP!

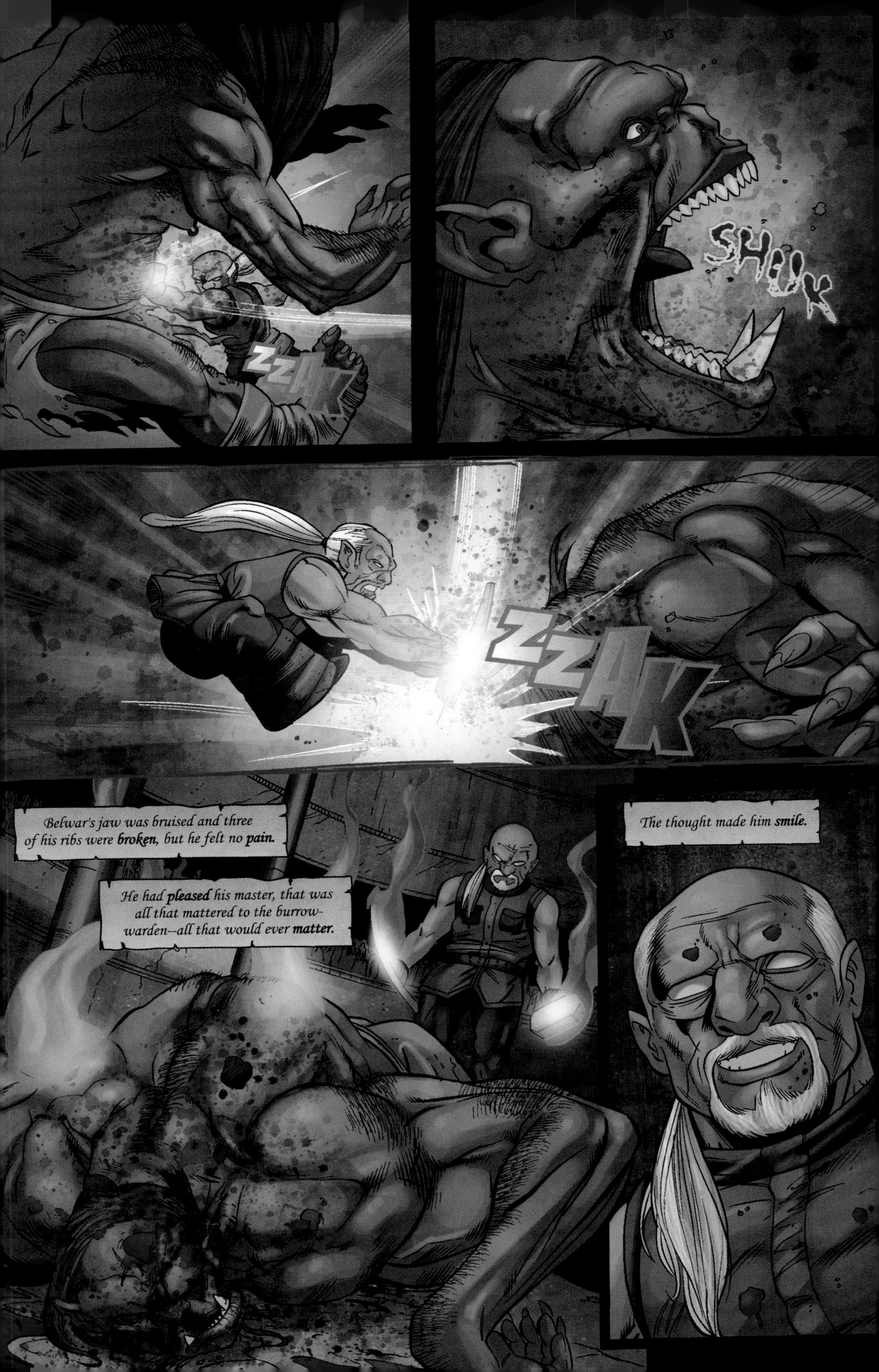
ZZAK
SHUK
ZZAK
Belwar's jaw was bruised and three of his ribs were **broken**, but he felt no **pain**.
He had **pleased** his master, that was all that mattered to the burrow-warden--all that would ever **matter**.
The thought made him **smile**.

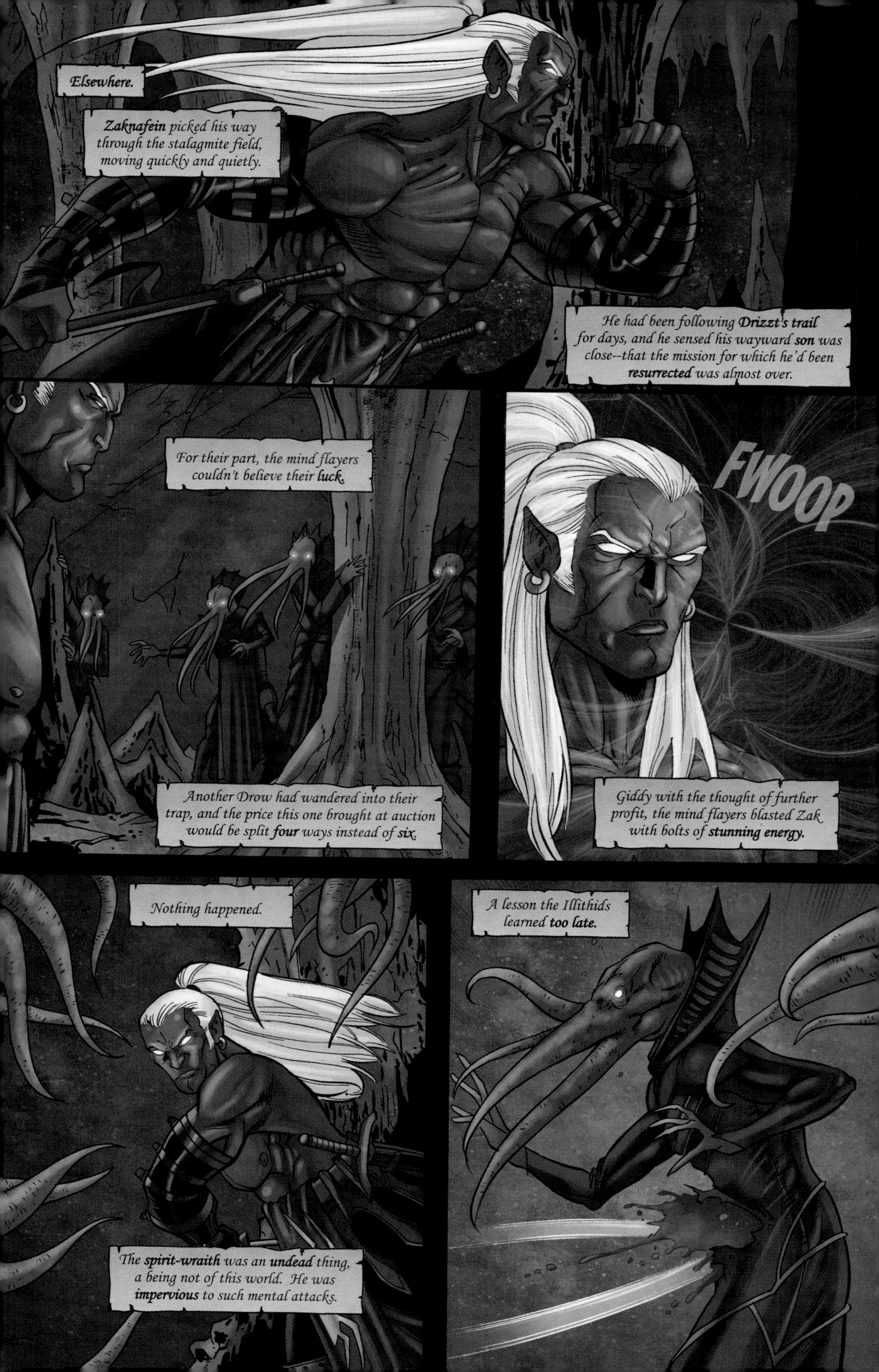
Elsewhere.
Zaknafein picked his way through the stalagmite field, moving quickly and quietly.
He had been following Drizzt's trail for days, and he sensed his wayward son was close--that the mission for which he'd been resurrected was almost over.
For their part, the mind flayers couldn't believe their luck.
Another Drow had wandered into their trap, and the price this one brought at auction would be split four ways instead of six.
FWOOP
Giddy with the thought of further profit, the mind flayers blasted Zak with bolts of stunning energy.
Nothing happened.
The spirit-wraith was an undead thing, a being not of this world. He was impervious to such mental attacks.
A lesson the Illithids learned too late.

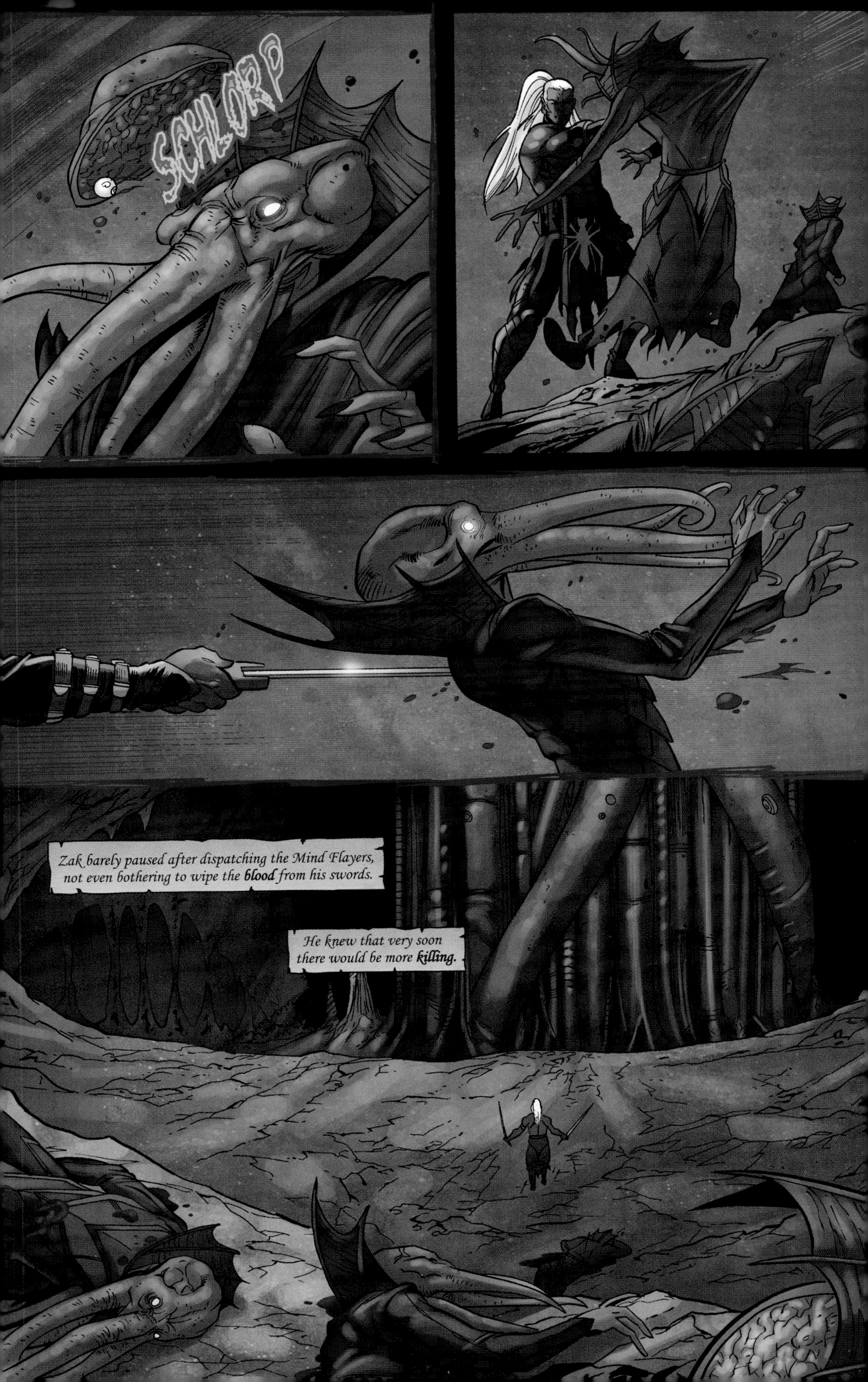
SCHLORP
Zak barely paused after dispatching the Mind Flayers, not even bothering to wipe the blood from his swords.
He knew that very soon there would be more killing.

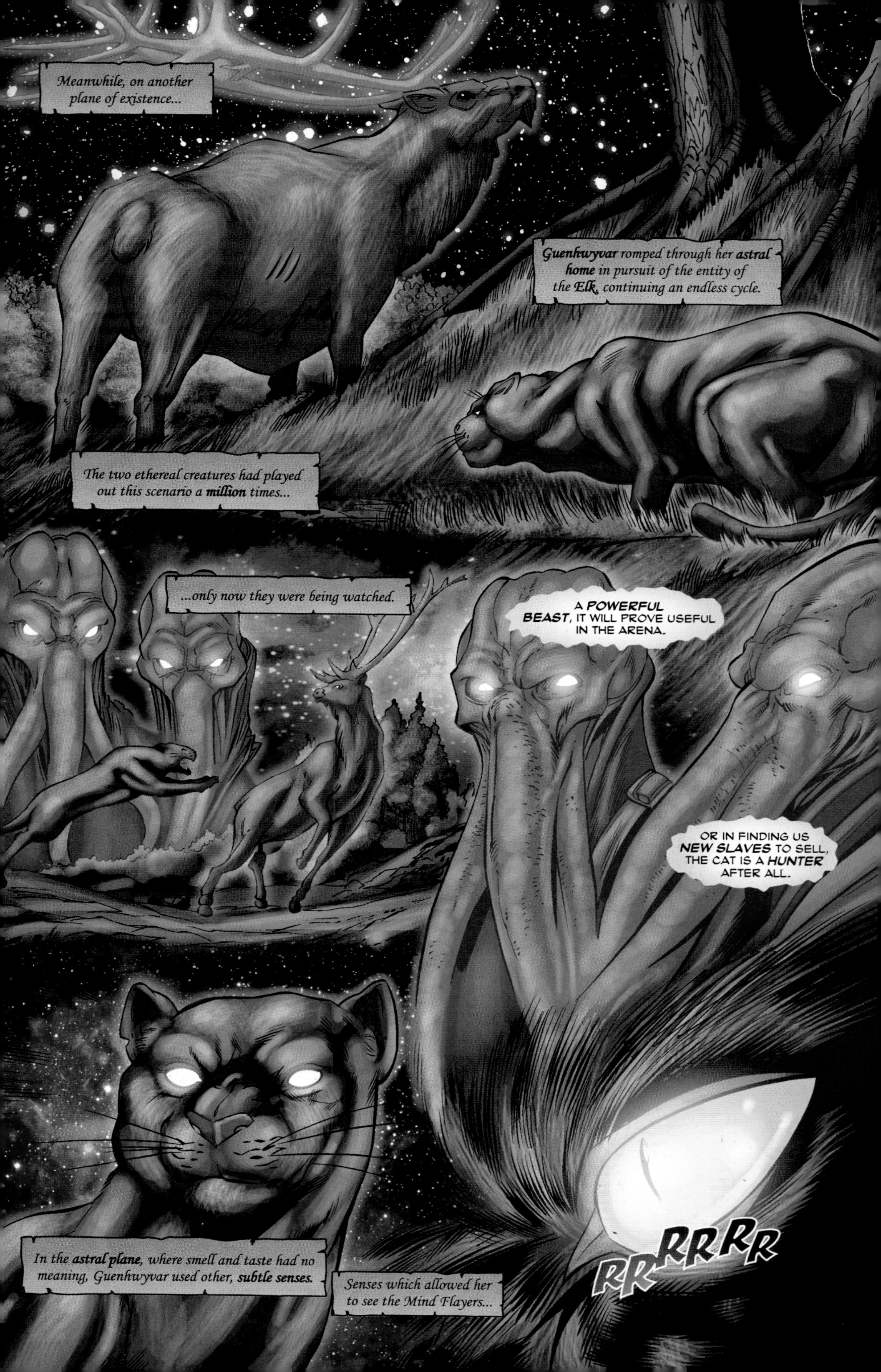
Meanwhile, on another plane of existence...
Guenhwyvar romped through her astral home in pursuit of the entity of the Elk, continuing an endless cycle.
The two ethereal creatures had played out this scenario a million times...
...only now they were being watched.
A POWERFUL BEAST, IT WILL PROVE USEFUL IN THE ARENA.
OR IN FINDING US NEW SLAVES TO SELL, THE CAT IS A HUNTER AFTER ALL.
In the astral plane, where smell and taste had no meaning, Guenhwyvar used other, subtle senses.
Senses which allowed her to see the Mind Flayers...
RRRRRRR

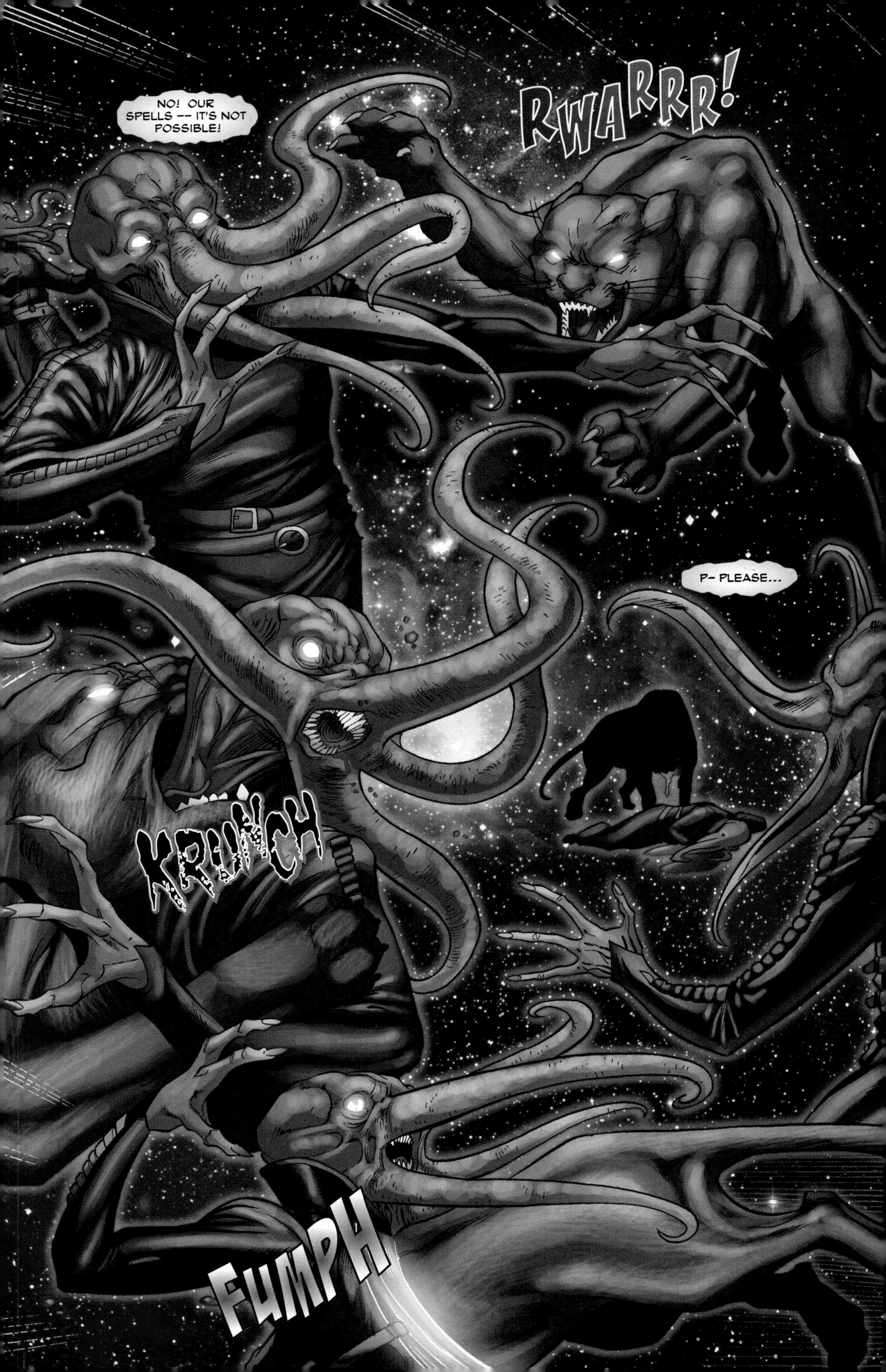
NO! OUR SPELLS -- IT'S NOT POSSIBLE!
RWARRR!
P- PLEASE...
KRUNCH
FUMPH

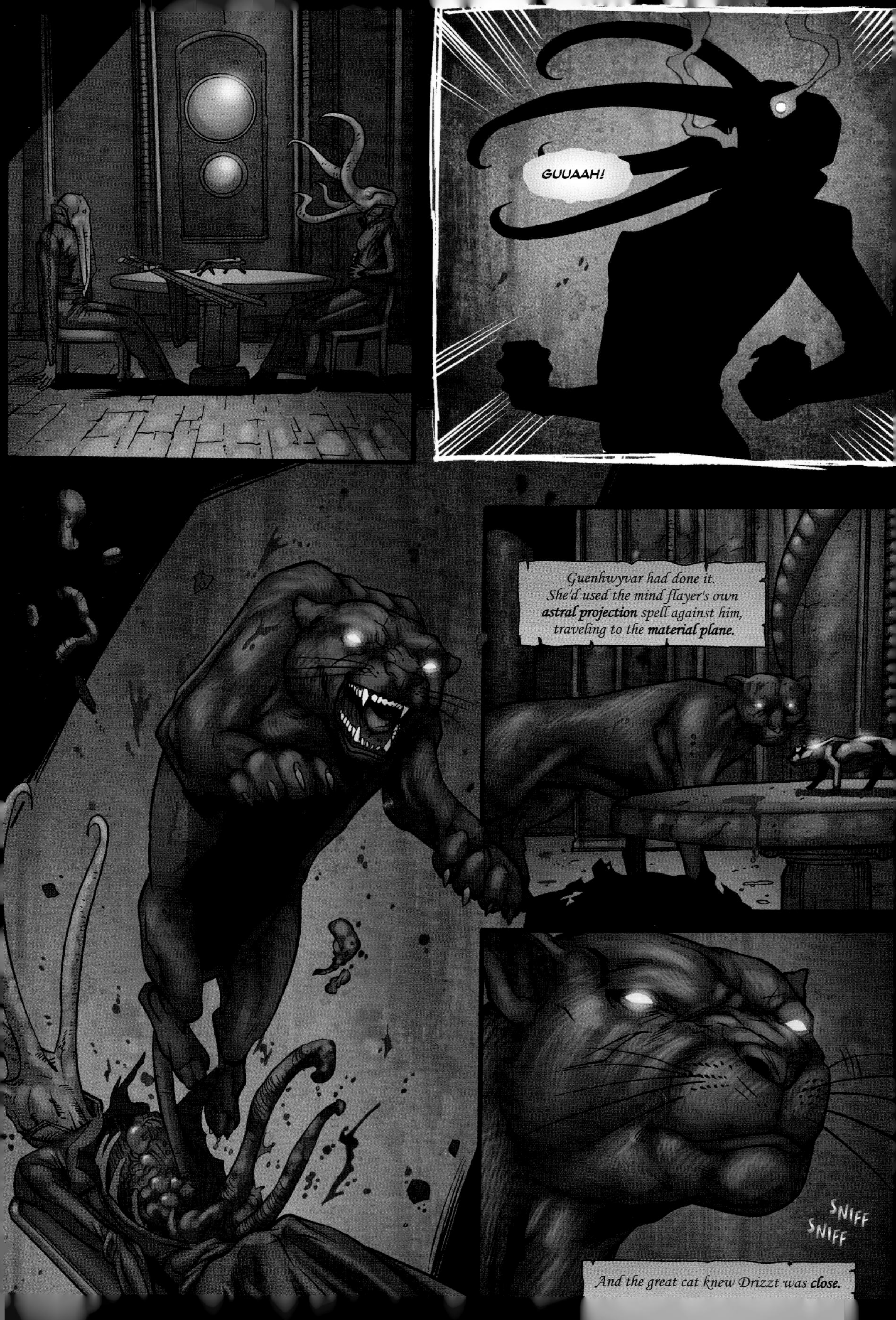
GUUAAH!
Guenhwyvar had done it. She'd used the mind flayer's own **astral projection** spell against him, traveling to the **material plane.**
SNIFF SNIFF
And the great cat knew Drizzt was **close.**

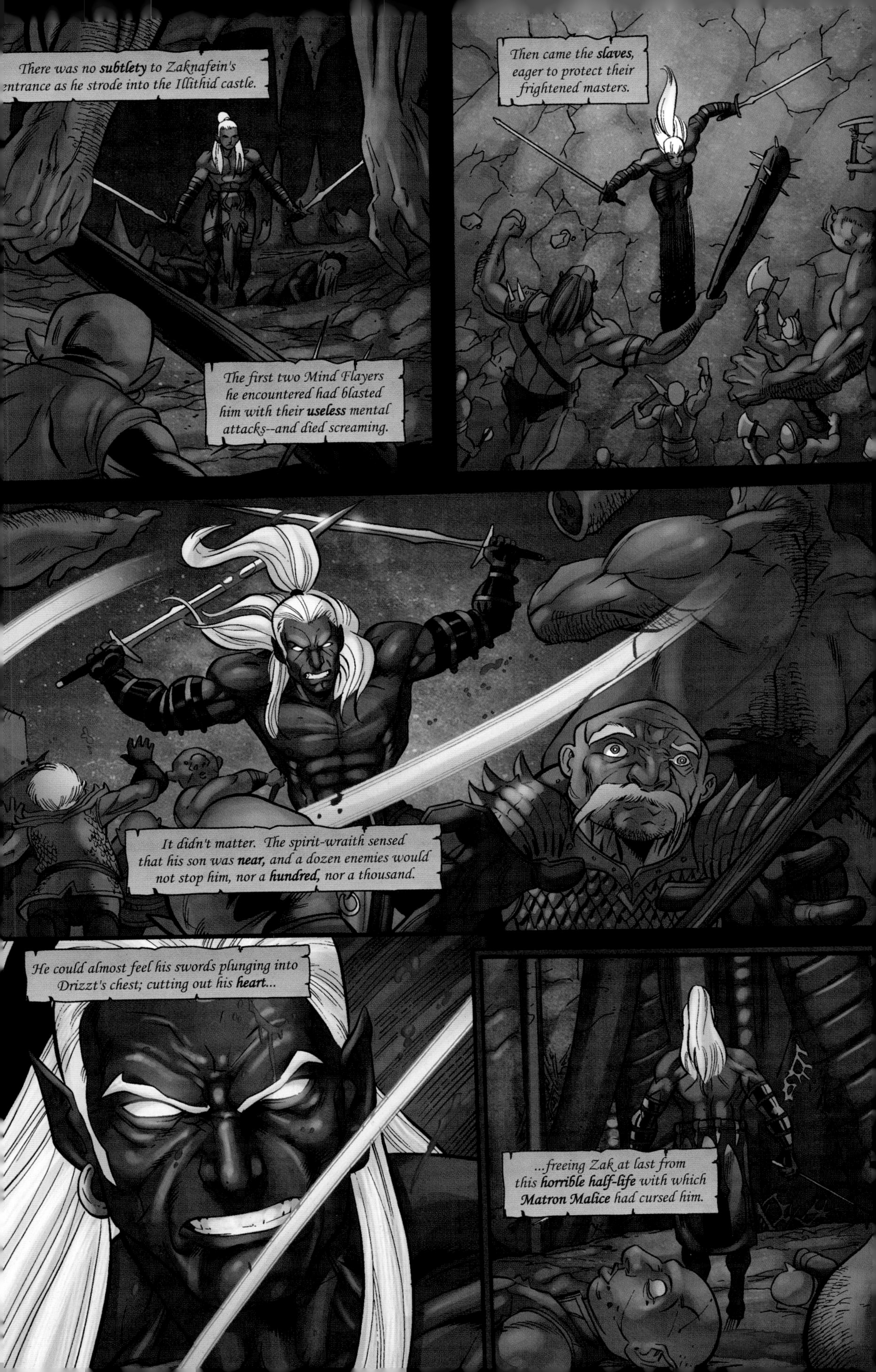
There was no subtlety to Zaknafein's entrance as he strode into the Illithid castle.
The first two Mind Flayers he encountered had blasted him with their useless mental attacks--and died screaming.
Then came the slaves, eager to protect their frightened masters.
It didn't matter. The spirit-wraith sensed that his son was near, and a dozen enemies would not stop him, nor a hundred, nor a thousand.
He could almost feel his swords plunging into Drizzt's chest; cutting out his heart...
...freeing Zak at last from this horrible half-life with which Matron Malice had cursed him.

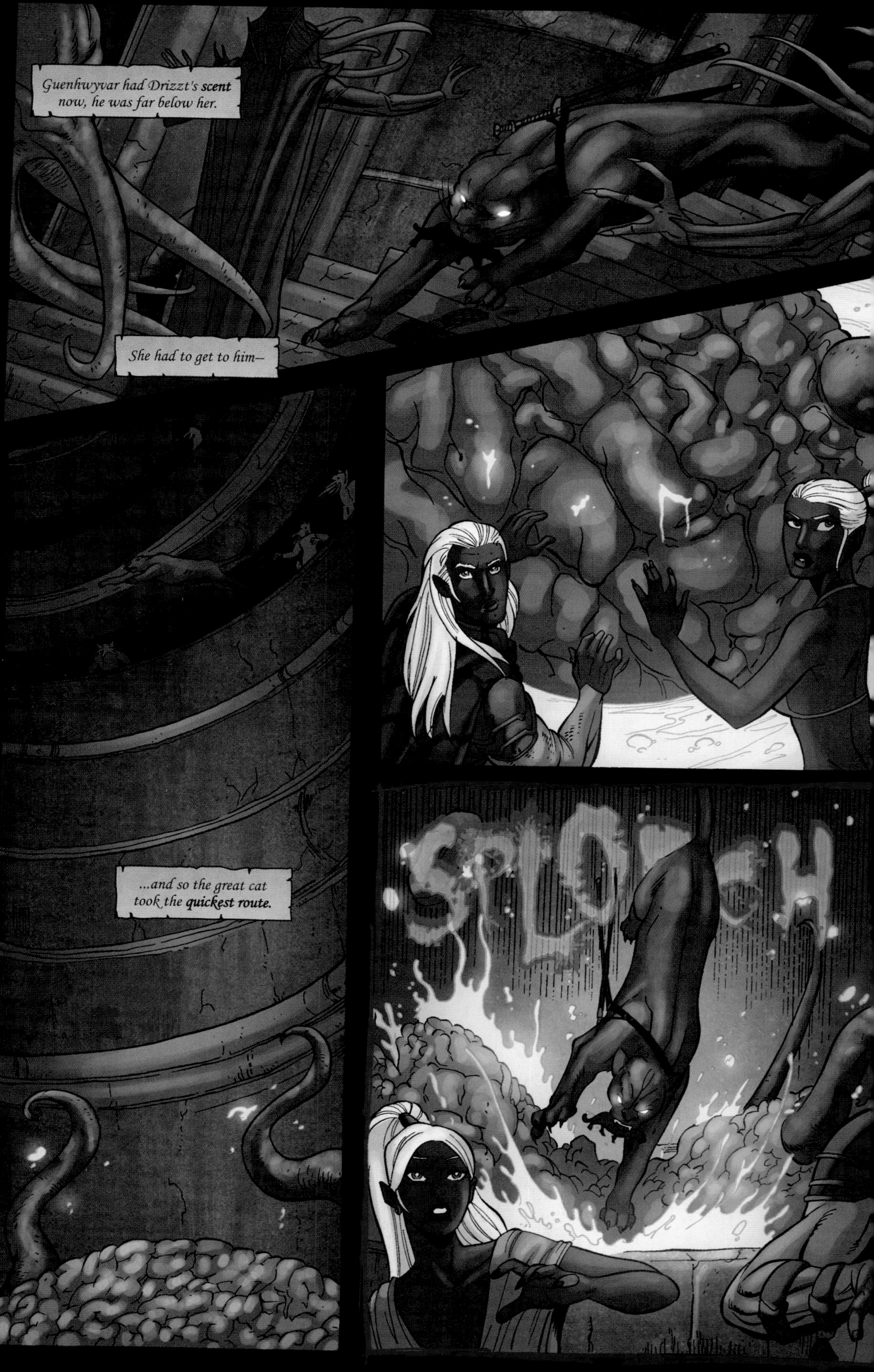
Guenhwyvar had Drizzt's **scent** now, he was far below her.
She had to get to him--
...and so the great cat took the **quickest route.**
SPLOOSH

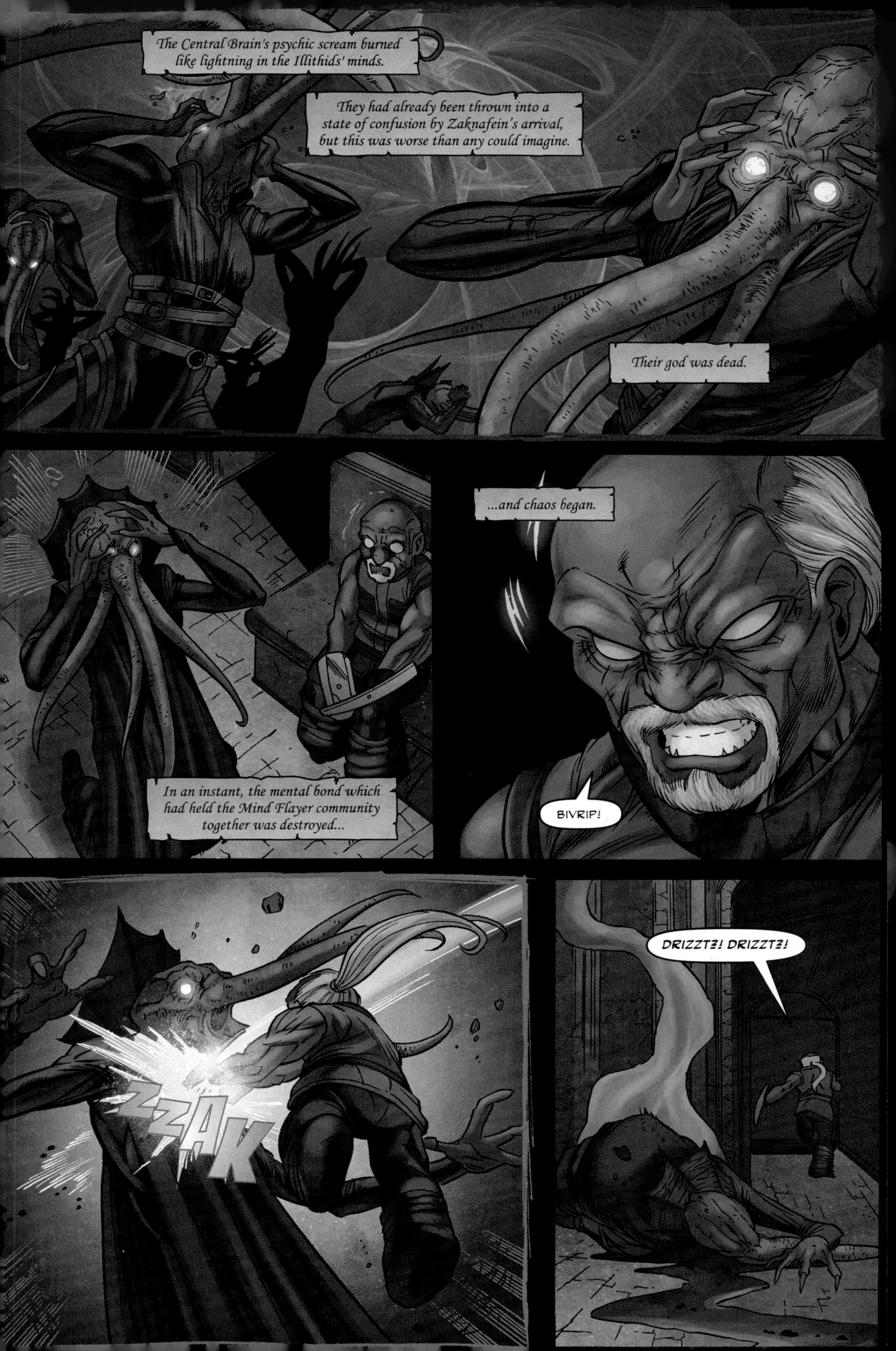
The Central Brain's psychic scream burned like lightning in the Illithids' minds.
They had already been thrown into a state of confusion by Zaknafein's arrival, but this was worse than any could imagine.
Their god was dead.
In an instant, the mental bond which had held the Mind Flayer community together was destroyed...
...and chaos began.
BIVRIP!
ZZAK
DRIZZT?! DRIZZT?!

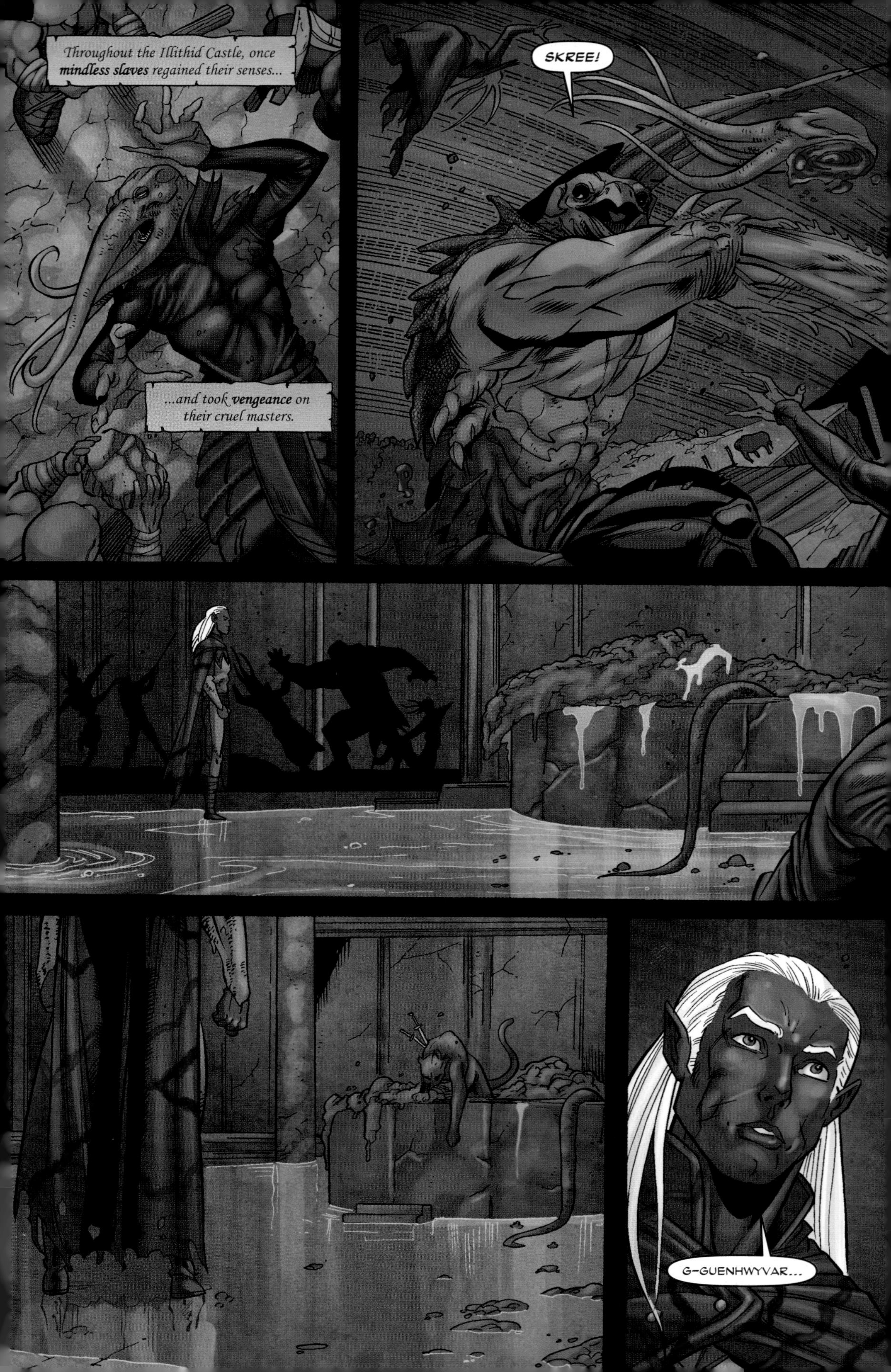
Throughout the Illithid Castle, once **mindless slaves** regained their senses...
...and took **vengeance** on their cruel masters.
SKREE!
G-GUENHWYVAR...

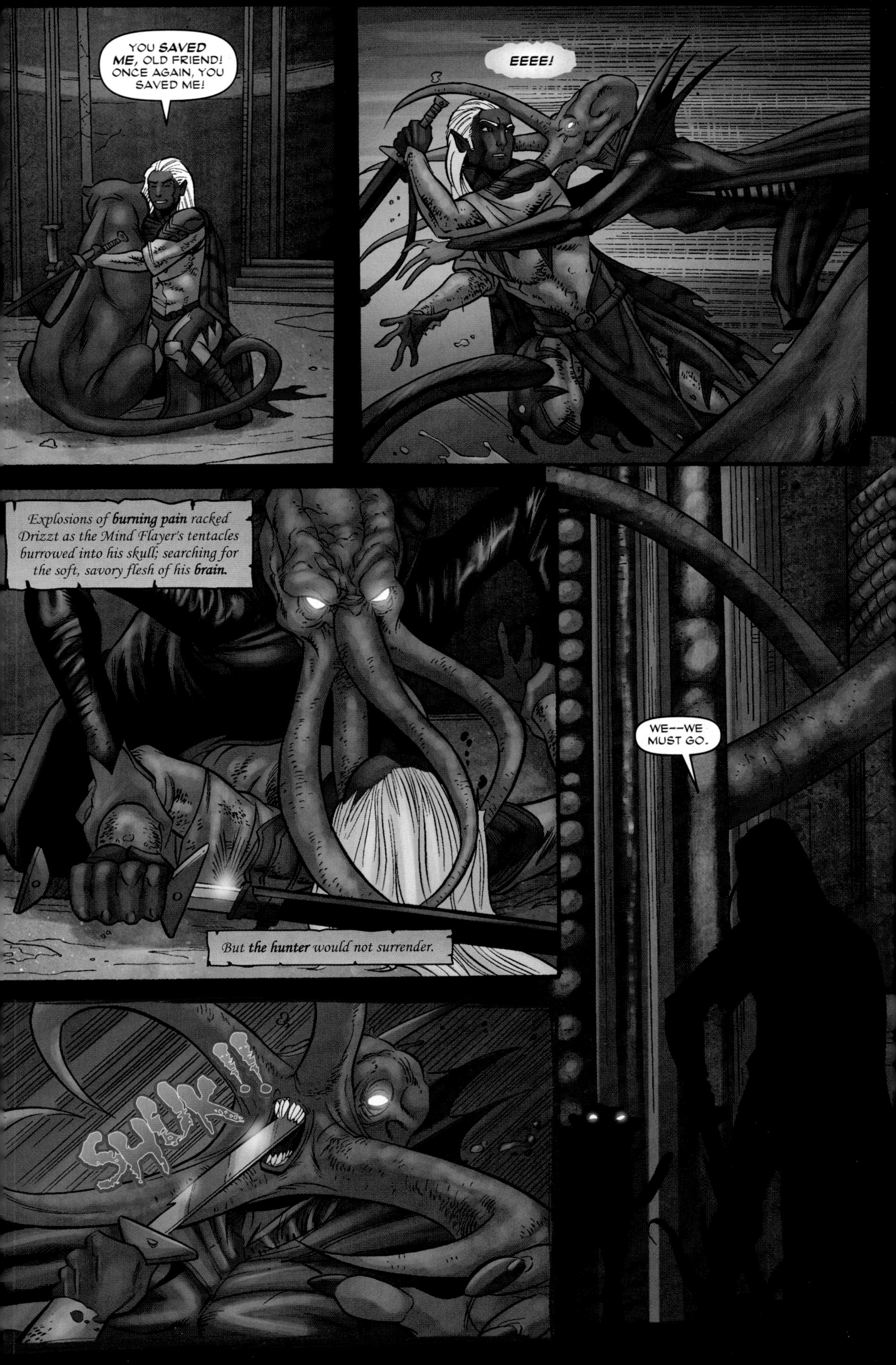

YOU **SAVED ME,** OLD FRIEND! ONCE AGAIN, YOU SAVED ME!
EEEE!
*Explosions of **burning pain** racked Drizzt as the Mind Flayer's tentacles burrowed into his skull; searching for the soft, savory flesh of his **brain.***
*But **the hunter** would not surrender.*
WE--WE MUST GO.
SHUK!!

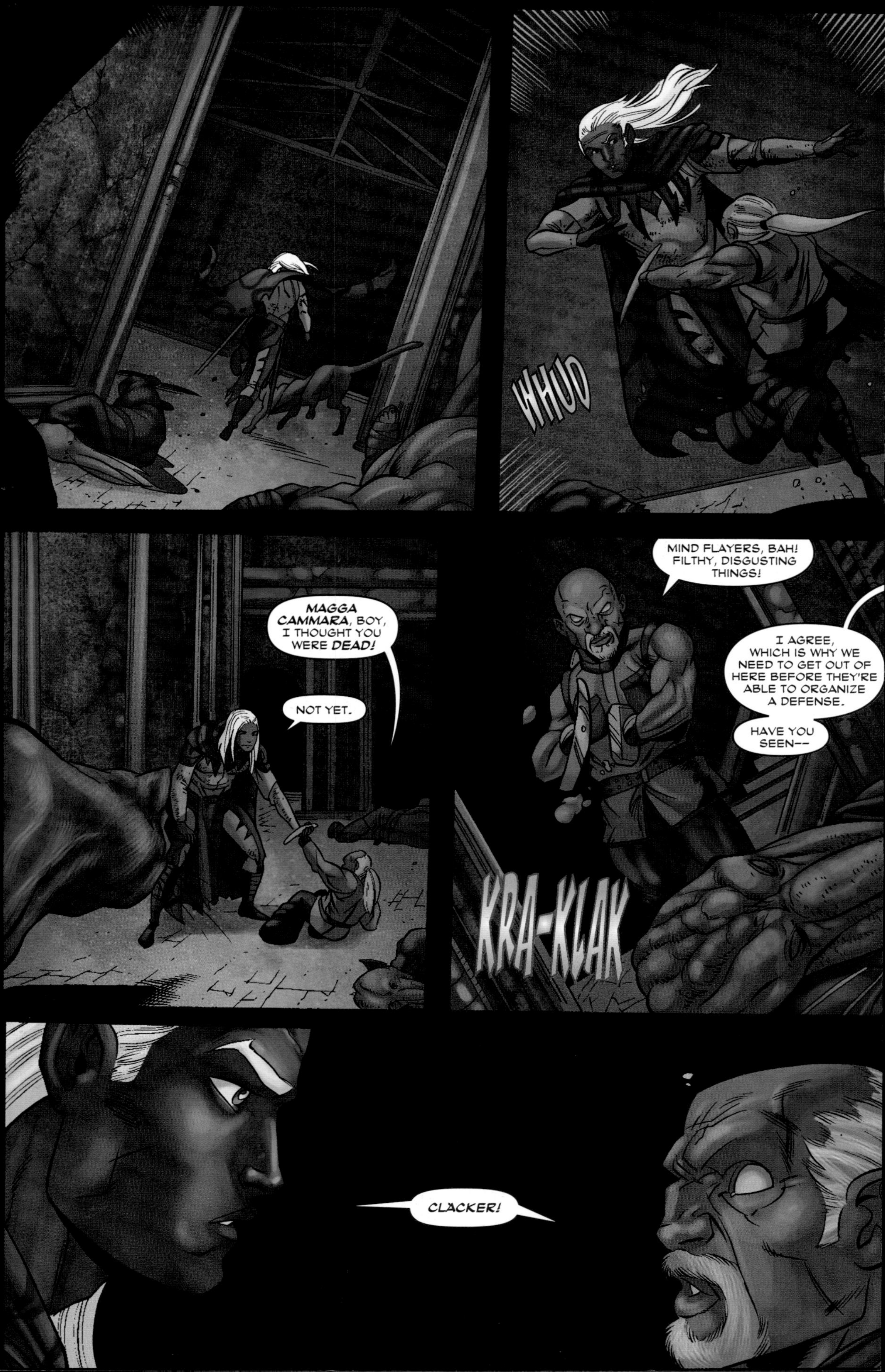
WHUD
MAGGA CAMMARA, BOY, I THOUGHT YOU WERE DEAD!
NOT YET.
MIND FLAYERS, BAH! FILTHY, DISGUSTING THINGS!
I AGREE, WHICH IS WHY WE NEED TO GET OUT OF HERE BEFORE THEY'RE ABLE TO ORGANIZE A DEFENSE.
HAVE YOU SEEN--
KRA-KLAK
CLACKER!

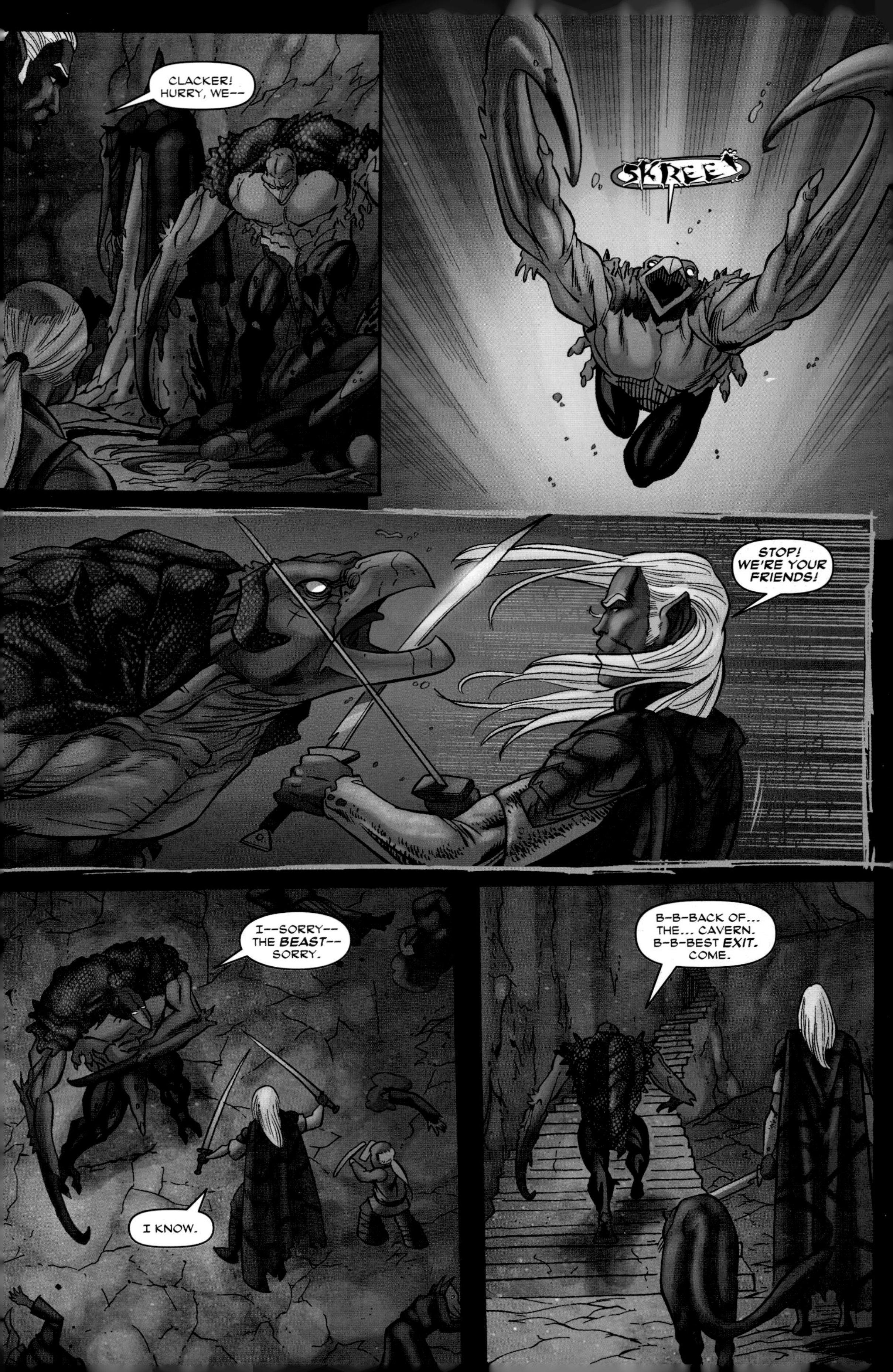
CLACKER! HURRY, WE--
SKREE!
STOP! WE'RE YOUR FRIENDS!
I--SORRY-- THE BEAST-- SORRY.
I KNOW.
B-B-BACK OF... THE... CAVERN. B-B-BEST EXIT. COME.

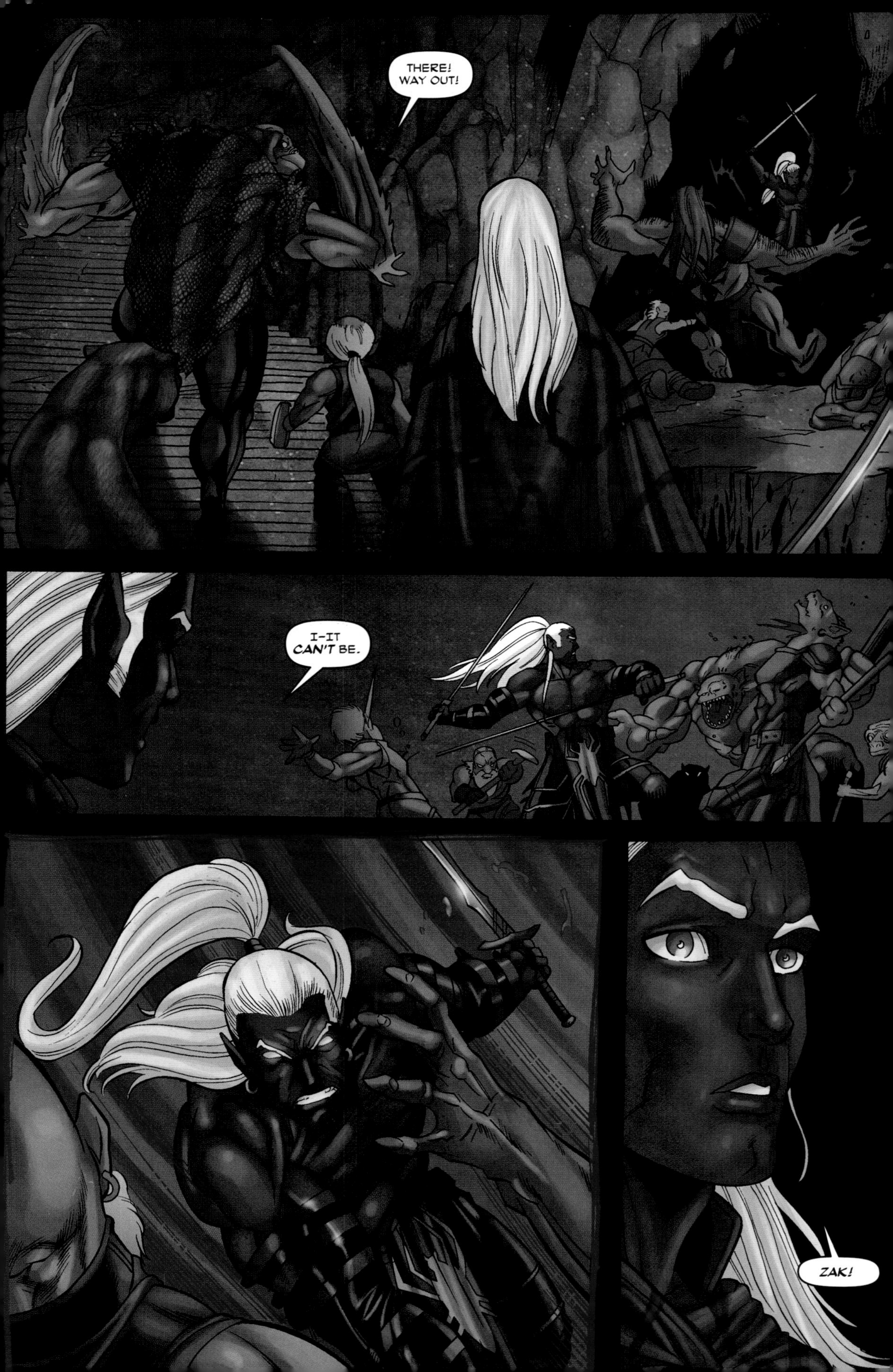
THERE!
WAY OUT!
I-IT
CAN'T BE.
ZAK!

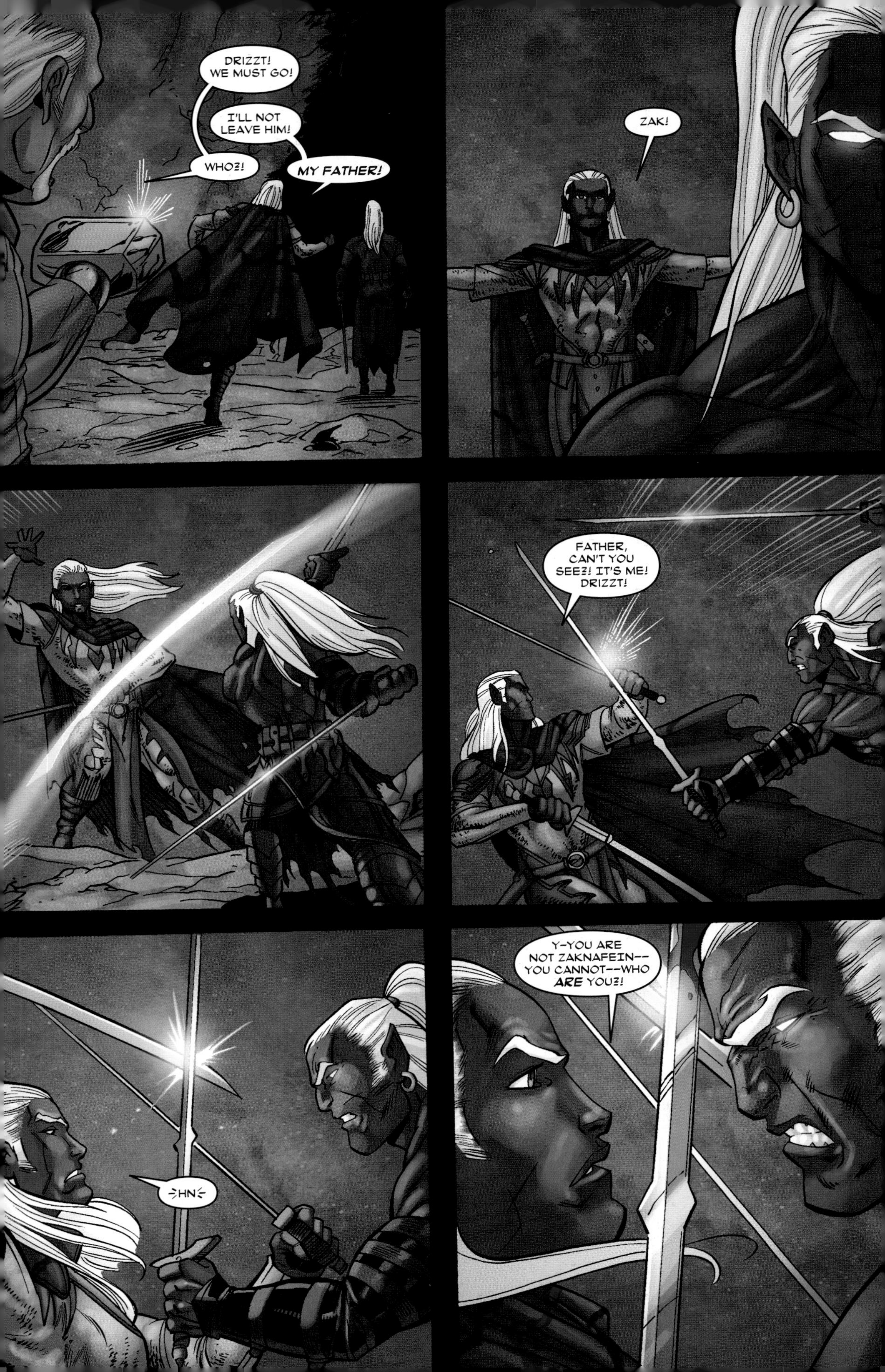
DRIZZT! WE MUST GO!
I'LL NOT LEAVE HIM!
WHO?!
MY FATHER!
ZAK!
FATHER, CAN'T YOU SEE?! IT'S ME! DRIZZT!
HN
Y-YOU ARE NOT ZAKNAFEIN-- YOU CANNOT--WHO ARE YOU?!

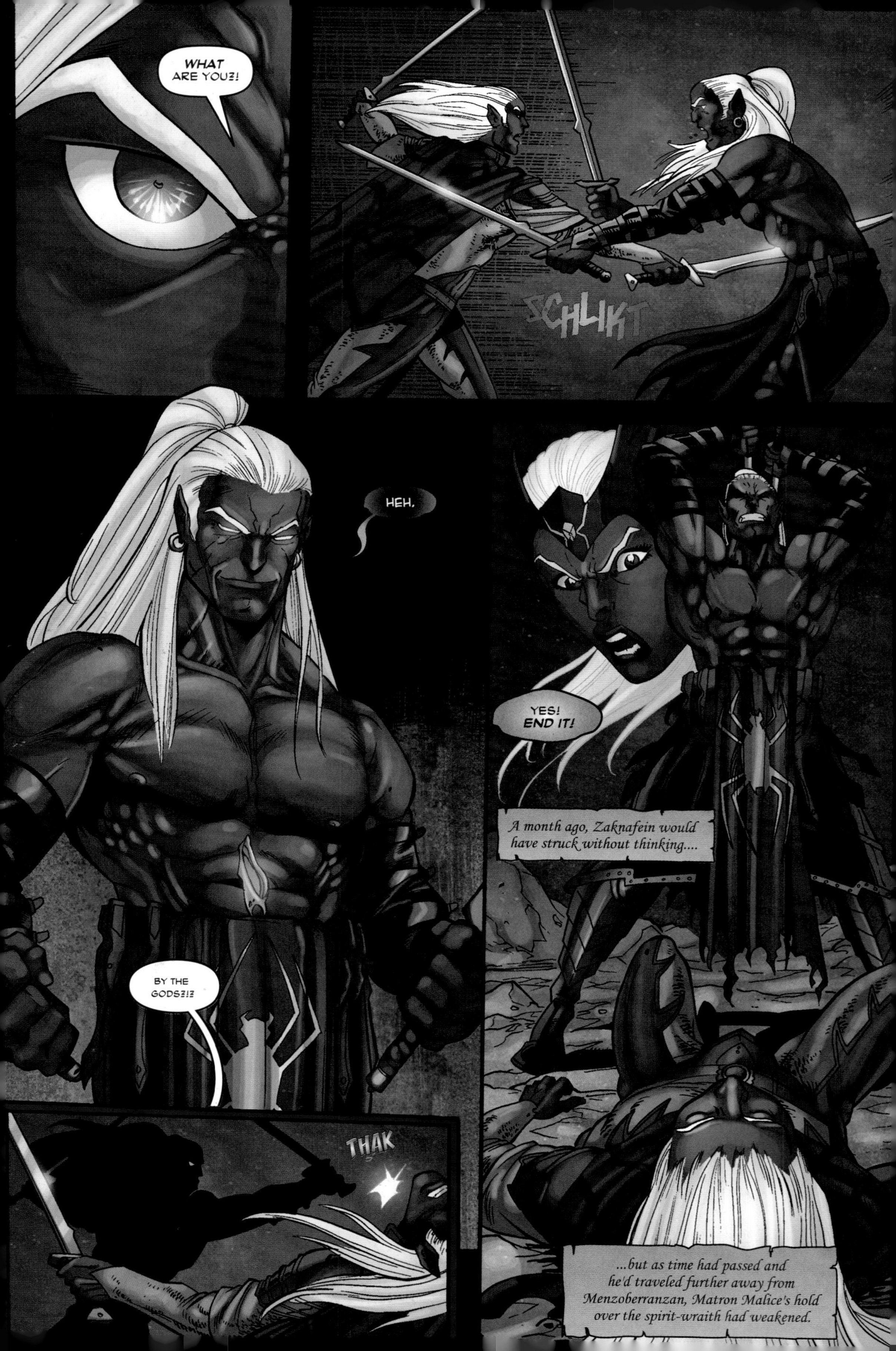
WHAT ARE YOU?!
SCHLIKT
HEH.
BY THE GODS?!?
THAK
YES! END IT!
A month ago, Zaknafein would have struck without thinking....
...but as time had passed and he'd traveled further away from Menzoberranzan, Matron Malice's hold over the spirit-wraith had weakened.

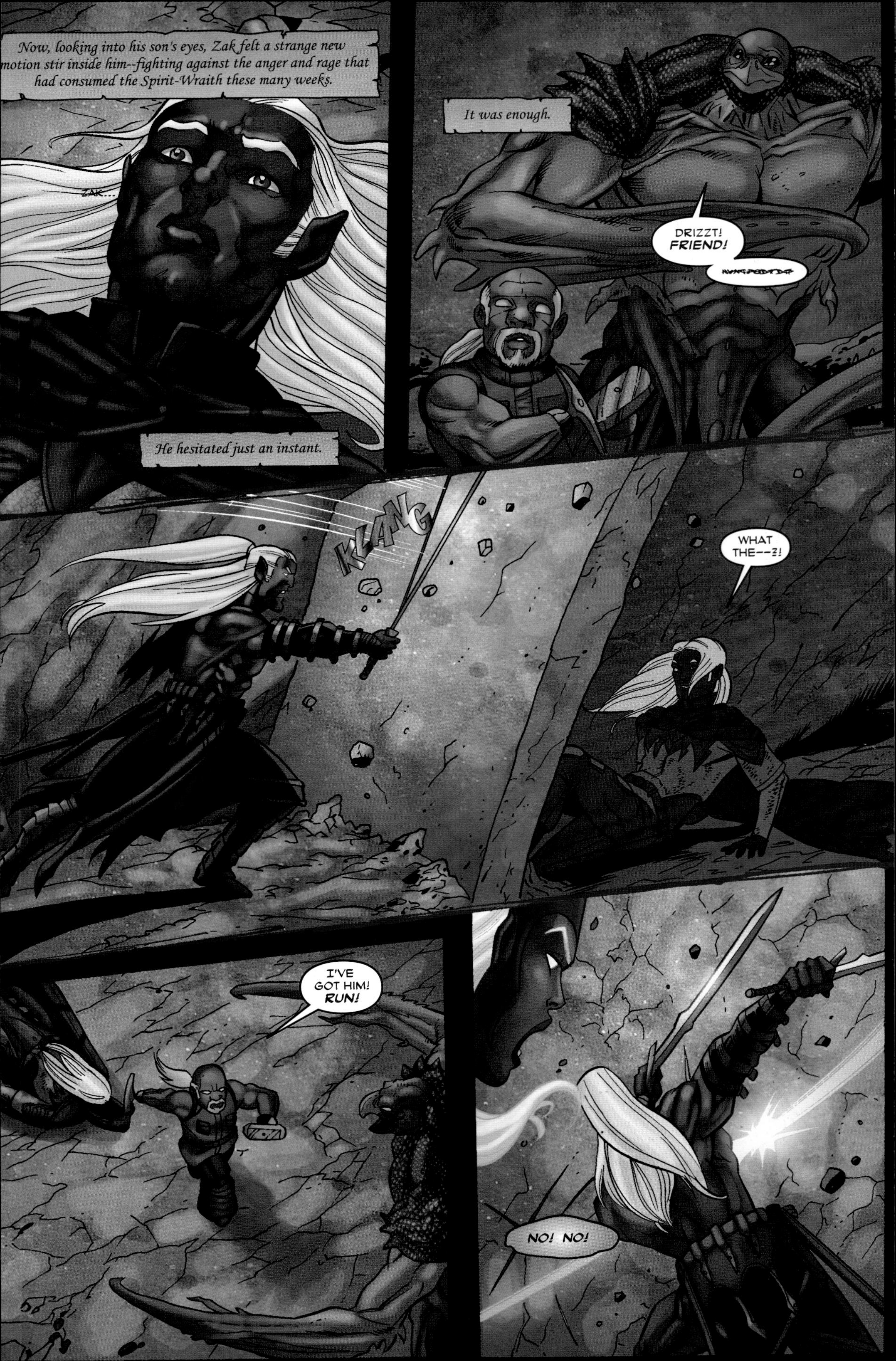

Now, looking into his son's eyes, Zak felt a strange new
motion stir inside him--fighting against the anger and rage that
had consumed the Spirit-Wraith these many weeks.
ZAK...
He hesitated just an instant.
It was enough.
DRIZZT! FRIEND!
KLANG
WHAT THE--?!
I'VE GOT HIM! RUN!
NO! NO!

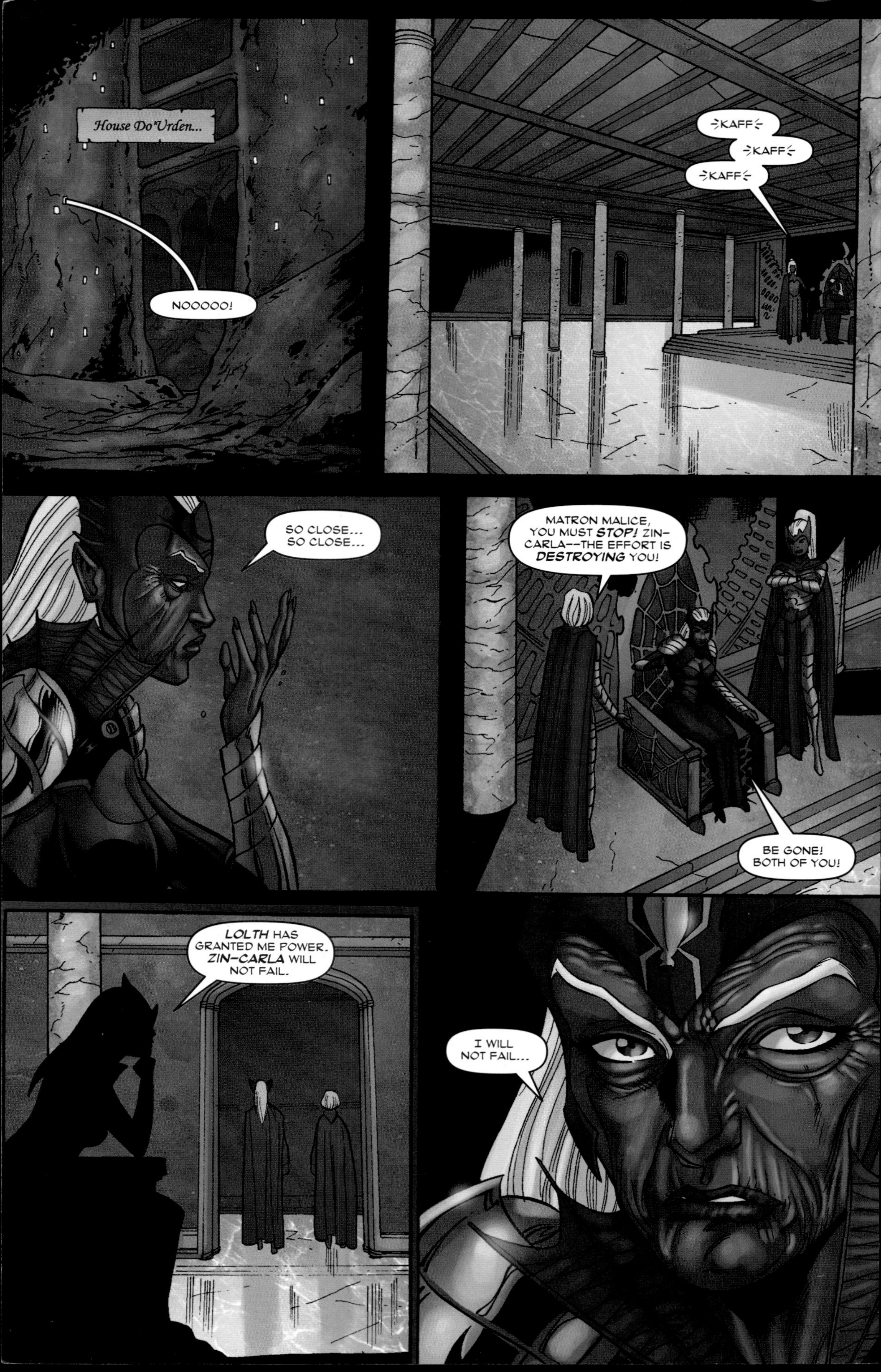
House Do'Urden...
NOOOOO!
KAFF
KAFF
KAFF
SO CLOSE... SO CLOSE...
MATRON MALICE, YOU MUST STOP! ZIN-CARLA--THE EFFORT IS DESTROYING YOU!
BE GONE! BOTH OF YOU!
LOLTH HAS GRANTED ME POWER. ZIN-CARLA WILL NOT FAIL.
I WILL NOT FAIL...

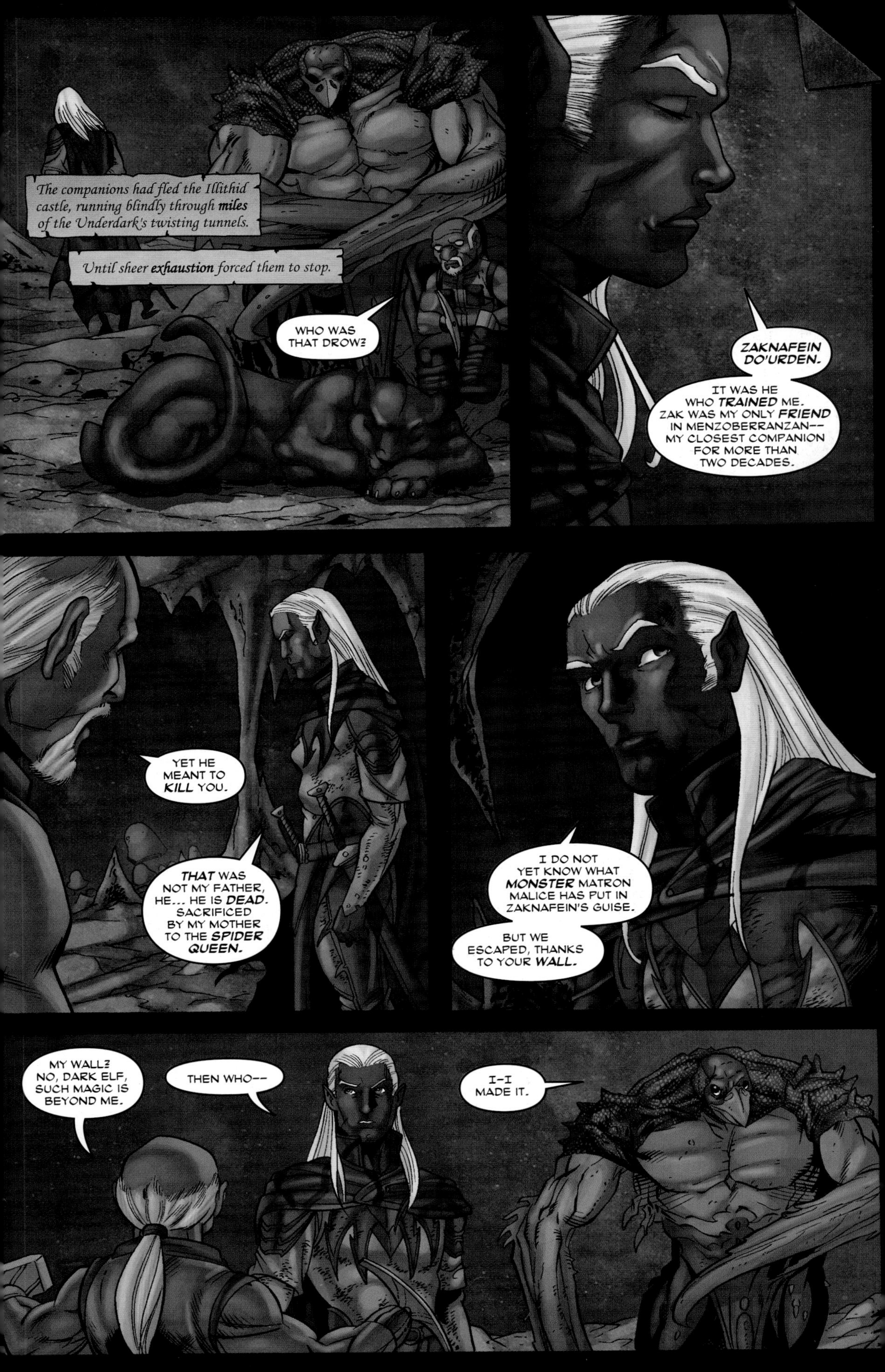
The companions had fled the Illithid castle, running blindly through **miles** of the Underdark's twisting tunnels.
Until sheer **exhaustion** forced them to stop.
WHO WAS THAT DROW?
ZAKNAFEIN DO'URDEN.
IT WAS HE WHO TRAINED ME. ZAK WAS MY ONLY FRIEND IN MENZOBERRANZAN-- MY CLOSEST COMPANION FOR MORE THAN TWO DECADES.
YET HE MEANT TO KILL YOU.
THAT WAS NOT MY FATHER, HE... HE IS DEAD. SACRIFICED BY MY MOTHER TO THE SPIDER QUEEN.
I DO NOT YET KNOW WHAT MONSTER MATRON MALICE HAS PUT IN ZAKNAFEIN'S GUISE.
BUT WE ESCAPED, THANKS TO YOUR WALL.
MY WALL? NO, DARK ELF, SUCH MAGIC IS BEYOND ME.
THEN WHO--
I-I MADE IT.

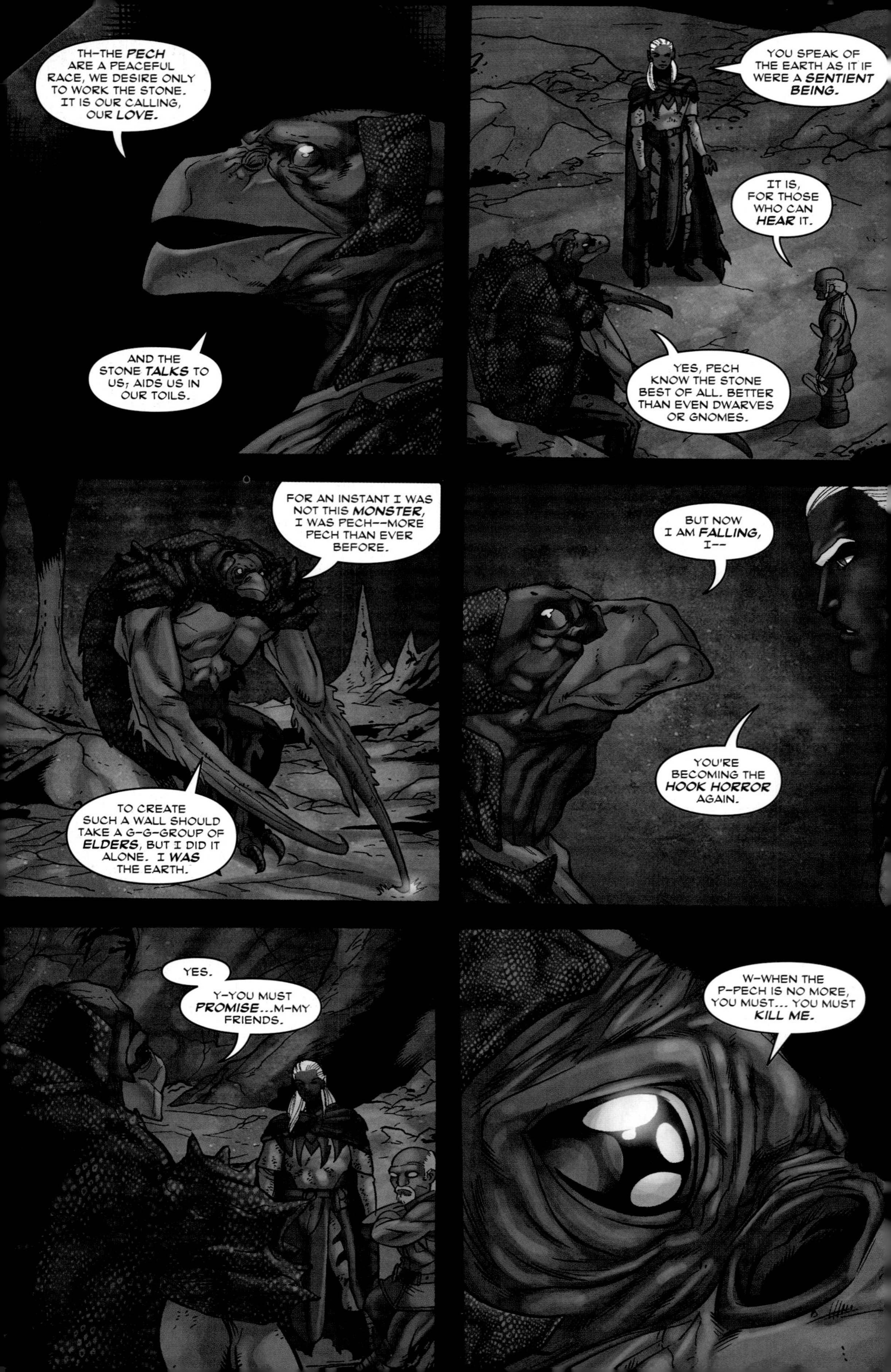
TH-THE PECH ARE A PEACEFUL RACE, WE DESIRE ONLY TO WORK THE STONE. IT IS OUR CALLING, OUR LOVE.
AND THE STONE TALKS TO US; AIDS US IN OUR TOILS.
YOU SPEAK OF THE EARTH AS IT IF WERE A SENTIENT BEING.
IT IS, FOR THOSE WHO CAN HEAR IT.
YES, PECH KNOW THE STONE BEST OF ALL. BETTER THAN EVEN DWARVES OR GNOMES.
FOR AN INSTANT I WAS NOT THIS MONSTER, I WAS PECH--MORE PECH THAN EVER BEFORE.
TO CREATE SUCH A WALL SHOULD TAKE A G-G-GROUP OF ELDERS, BUT I DID IT ALONE. I WAS THE EARTH.
BUT NOW I AM FALLING, I--
YOU'RE BECOMING THE HOOK HORROR AGAIN.
YES.
Y-YOU MUST PROMISE...M-MY FRIENDS.
W-WHEN THE P-PECH IS NO MORE, YOU MUST... YOU MUST KILL ME.

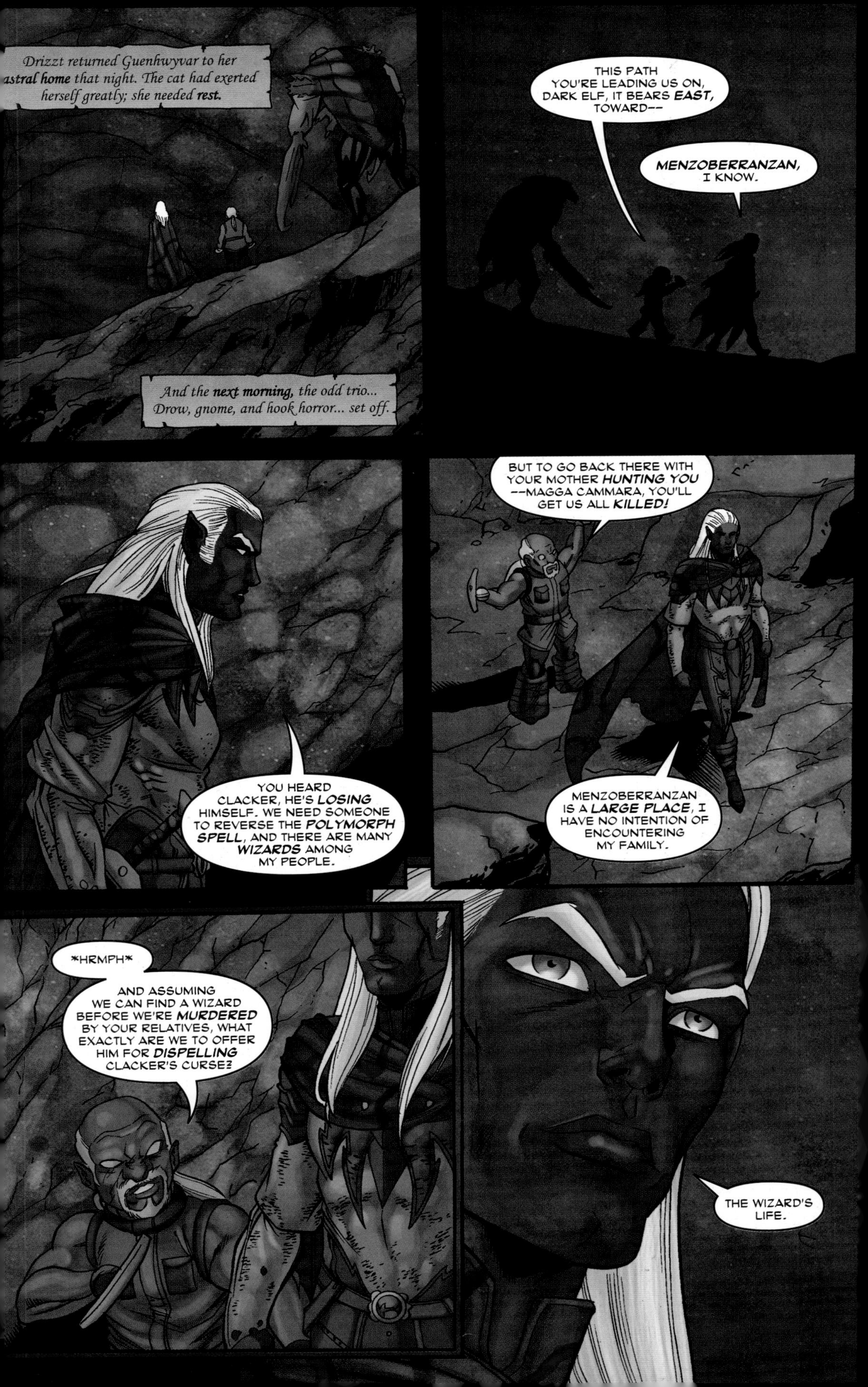
Drizzt returned Guenhwyvar to her astral home that night. The cat had exerted herself greatly; she needed rest.
And the next morning, the odd trio... Drow, gnome, and hook horror... set off.
THIS PATH YOU'RE LEADING US ON, DARK ELF, IT BEARS EAST, TOWARD--
MENZOBERRANZAN, I KNOW.
YOU HEARD CLACKER, HE'S LOSING HIMSELF. WE NEED SOMEONE TO REVERSE THE POLYMORPH SPELL, AND THERE ARE MANY WIZARDS AMONG MY PEOPLE.
BUT TO GO BACK THERE WITH YOUR MOTHER HUNTING YOU --MAGGA CAMMARA, YOU'LL GET US ALL KILLED!
MENZOBERRANZAN IS A LARGE PLACE, I HAVE NO INTENTION OF ENCOUNTERING MY FAMILY.
HRMPH
AND ASSUMING WE CAN FIND A WIZARD BEFORE WE'RE MURDERED BY YOUR RELATIVES, WHAT EXACTLY ARE WE TO OFFER HIM FOR DISPELLING CLACKER'S CURSE?
THE WIZARD'S LIFE.

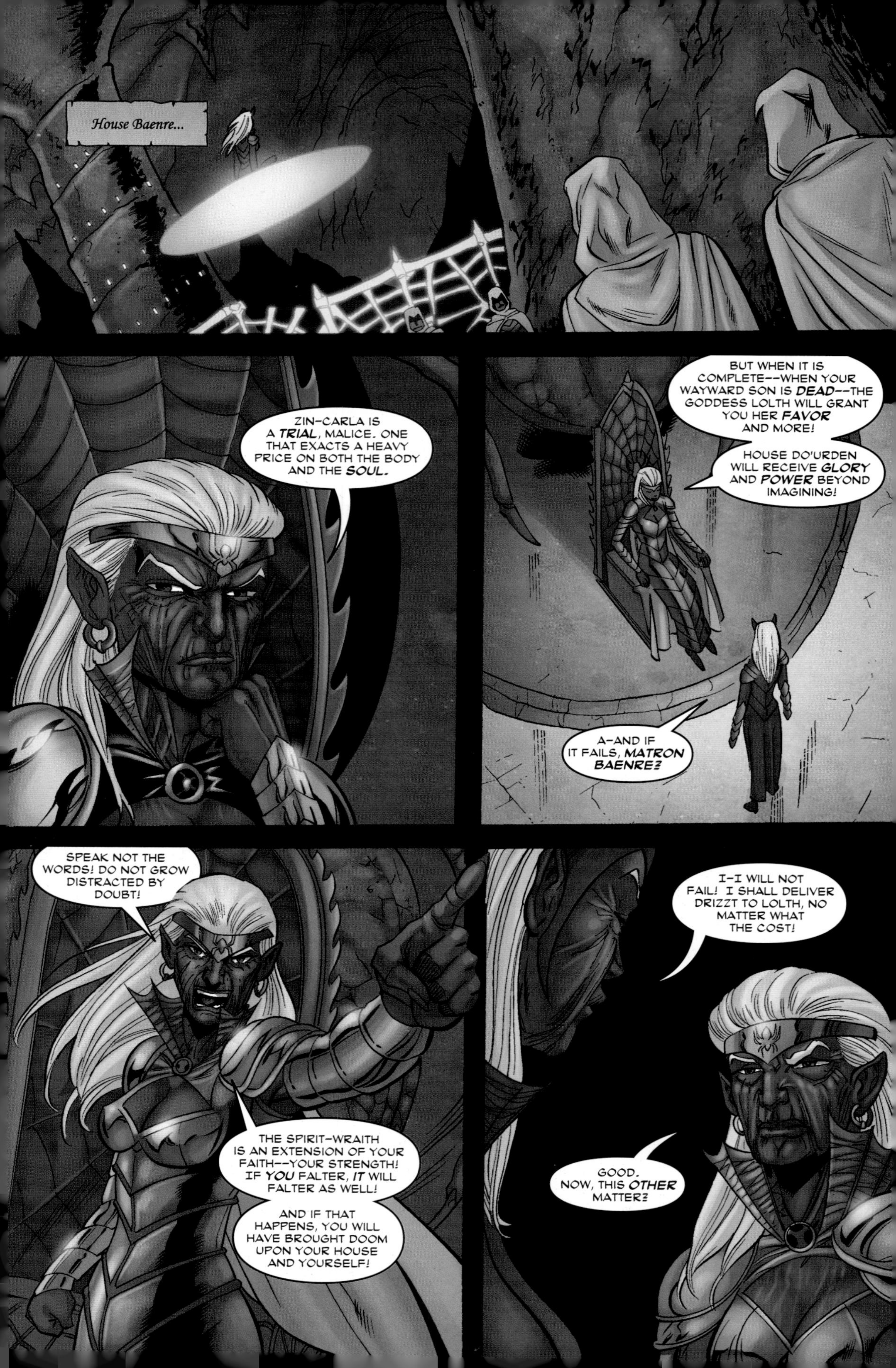
House Baenre...
ZIN-CARLA IS A TRIAL, MALICE. ONE THAT EXACTS A HEAVY PRICE ON BOTH THE BODY AND THE SOUL.
BUT WHEN IT IS COMPLETE--WHEN YOUR WAYWARD SON IS DEAD--THE GODDESS LOLTH WILL GRANT YOU HER FAVOR AND MORE!
HOUSE DO'URDEN WILL RECEIVE GLORY AND POWER BEYOND IMAGINING!
A-AND IF IT FAILS, MATRON BAENRE?
SPEAK NOT THE WORDS! DO NOT GROW DISTRACTED BY DOUBT!
THE SPIRIT-WRAITH IS AN EXTENSION OF YOUR FAITH--YOUR STRENGTH! IF YOU FALTER, IT WILL FALTER AS WELL!
AND IF THAT HAPPENS, YOU WILL HAVE BROUGHT DOOM UPON YOUR HOUSE AND YOURSELF!
I-I WILL NOT FAIL! I SHALL DELIVER DRIZZT TO LOLTH, NO MATTER WHAT THE COST!
GOOD. NOW, THIS OTHER MATTER?

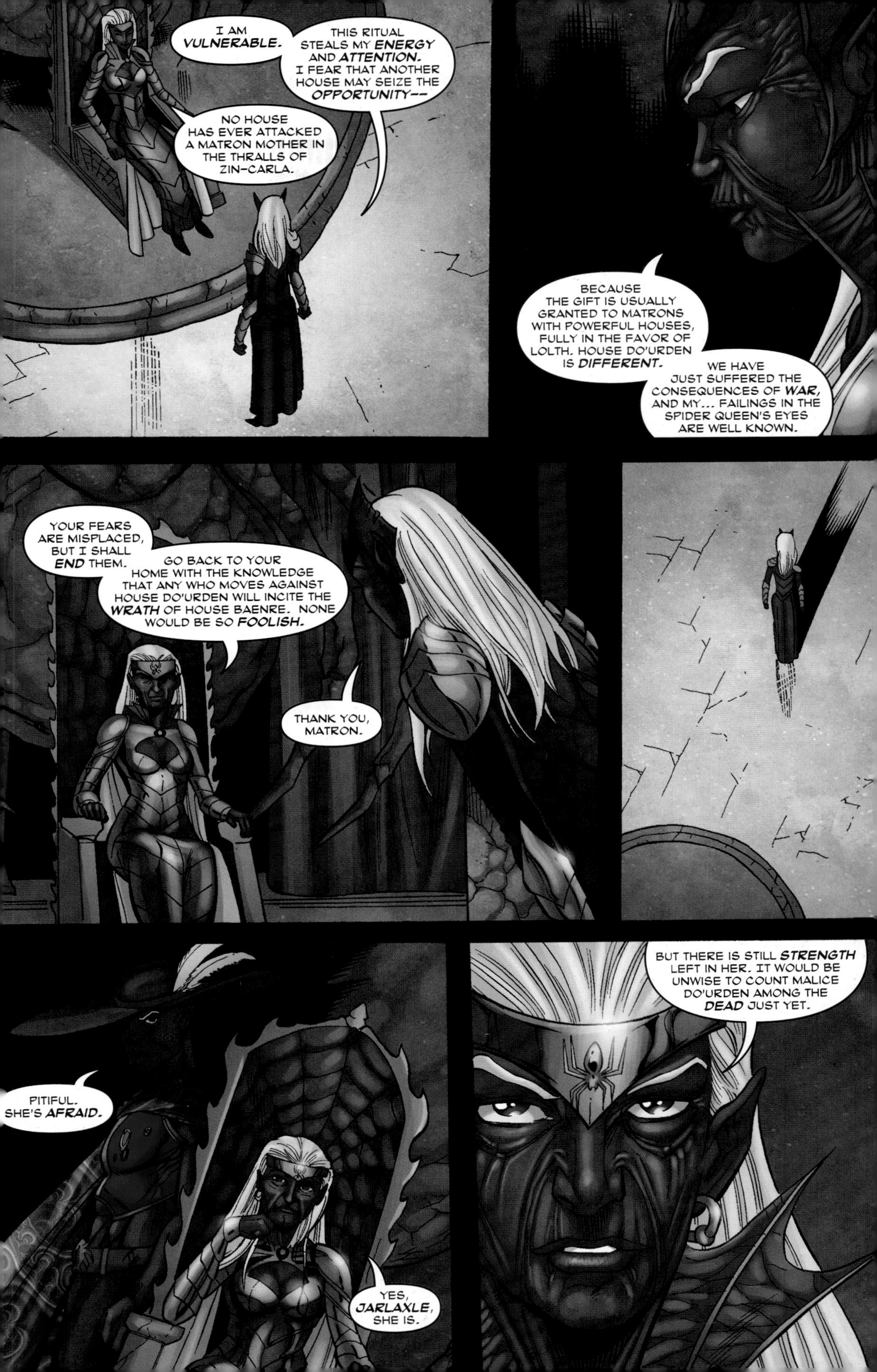
I AM VULNERABLE.
THIS RITUAL STEALS MY ENERGY AND ATTENTION. I FEAR THAT ANOTHER HOUSE MAY SEIZE THE OPPORTUNITY--
NO HOUSE HAS EVER ATTACKED A MATRON MOTHER IN THE THRALLS OF ZIN-CARLA.
BECAUSE THE GIFT IS USUALLY GRANTED TO MATRONS WITH POWERFUL HOUSES, FULLY IN THE FAVOR OF LOLTH. HOUSE DO'URDEN IS DIFFERENT.
WE HAVE JUST SUFFERED THE CONSEQUENCES OF WAR, AND MY... FAILINGS IN THE SPIDER QUEEN'S EYES ARE WELL KNOWN.
YOUR FEARS ARE MISPLACED, BUT I SHALL END THEM.
GO BACK TO YOUR HOME WITH THE KNOWLEDGE THAT ANY WHO MOVES AGAINST HOUSE DO'URDEN WILL INCITE THE WRATH OF HOUSE BAENRE. NONE WOULD BE SO FOOLISH.
THANK YOU, MATRON.
PITIFUL. SHE'S AFRAID.
YES, JARLAXLE, SHE IS.
BUT THERE IS STILL STRENGTH LEFT IN HER. IT WOULD BE UNWISE TO COUNT MALICE DO'URDEN AMONG THE DEAD JUST YET.

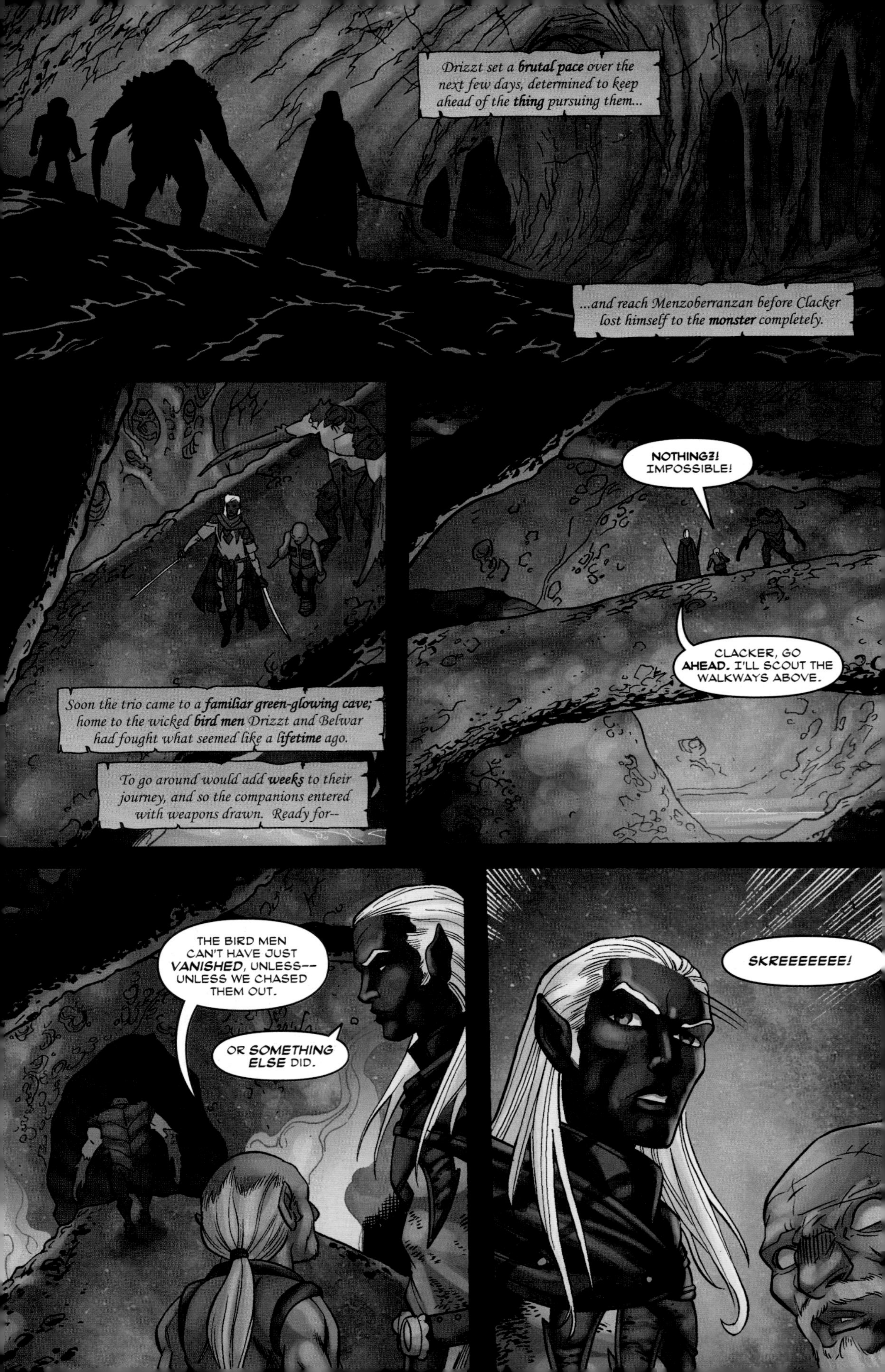
Drizzt set a brutal pace over the next few days, determined to keep ahead of the thing pursuing them...
...and reach Menzoberranzan before Clacker lost himself to the monster completely.
Soon the trio came to a familiar green-glowing cave; home to the wicked bird men Drizzt and Belwar had fought what seemed like a lifetime ago.
To go around would add weeks to their journey, and so the companions entered with weapons drawn. Ready for--
NOTHING?! IMPOSSIBLE!
CLACKER, GO AHEAD. I'LL SCOUT THE WALKWAYS ABOVE.
THE BIRD MEN CAN'T HAVE JUST VANISHED, UNLESS-- UNLESS WE CHASED THEM OUT.
OR SOMETHING ELSE DID.
SKREEEEEEE!

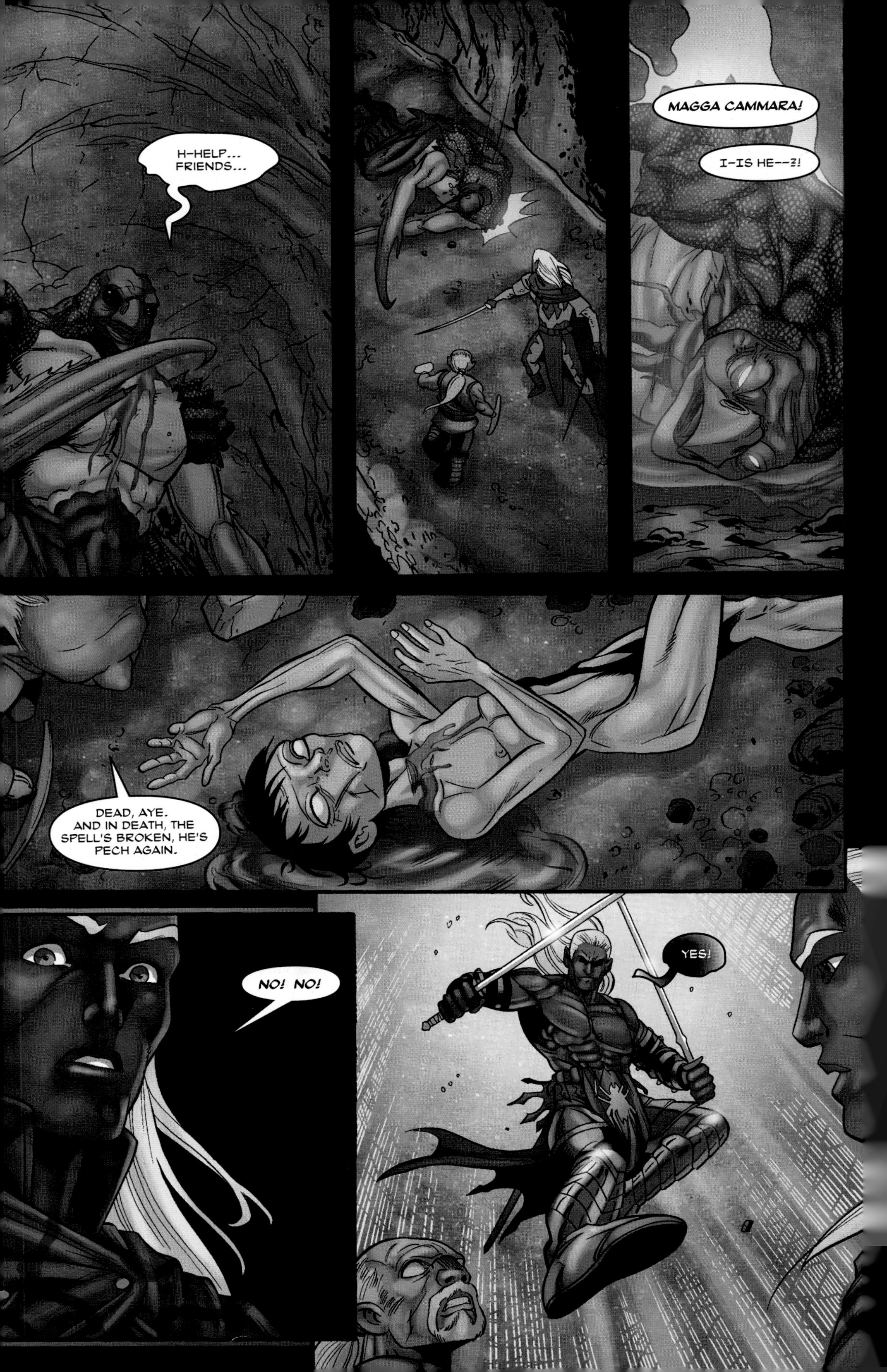
H-HELP... FRIENDS...
MAGGA CAMMARA!
I-IS HE--?!
DEAD, AYE. AND IN DEATH, THE SPELL'S BROKEN, HE'S PECH AGAIN.
NO! NO!
YES!

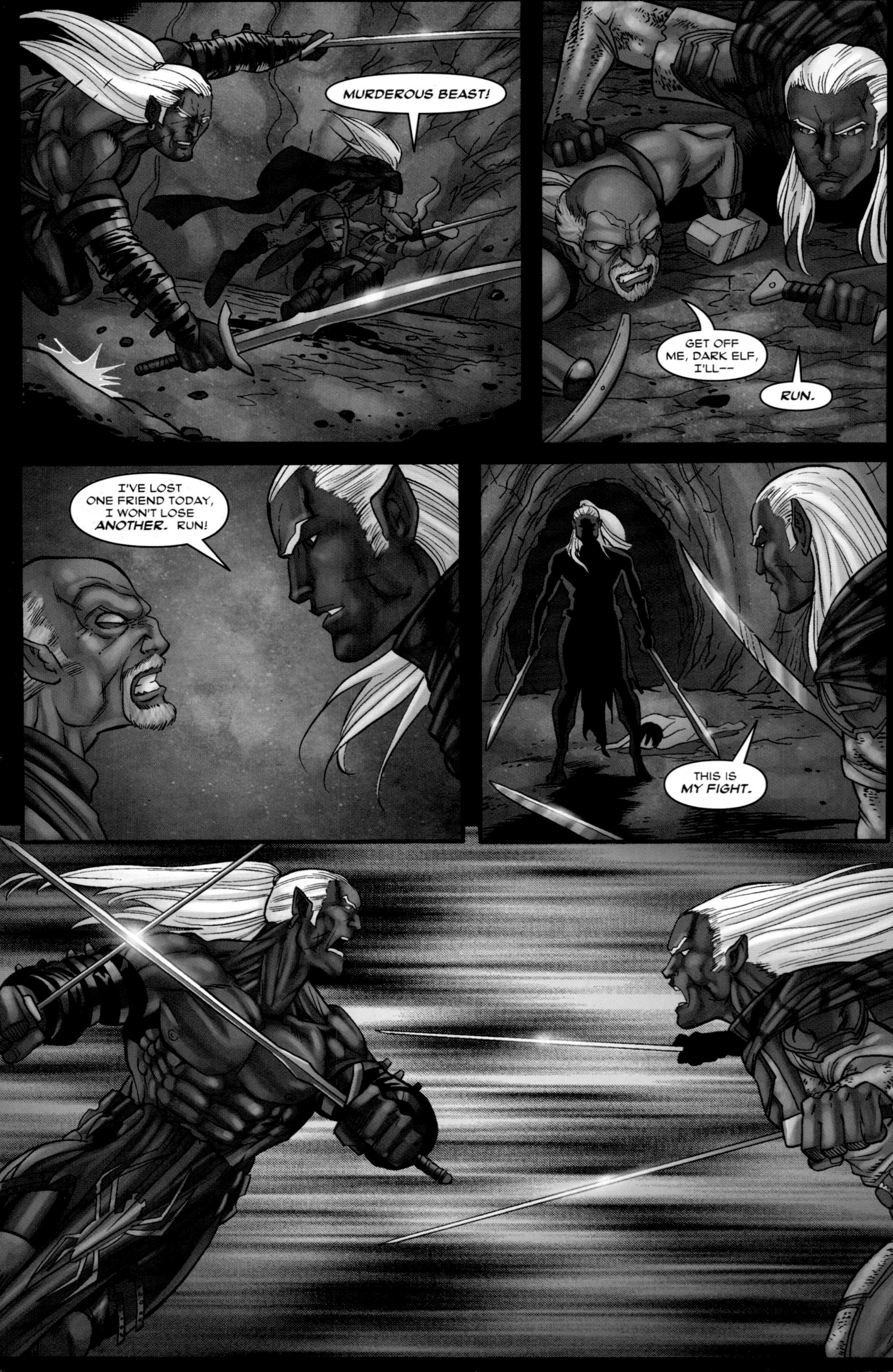
MURDEROUS BEAST!
GET OFF ME, DARK ELF, I'LL--
RUN.
I'VE LOST ONE FRIEND TODAY, I WON'T LOSE ANOTHER. RUN!
THIS IS MY FIGHT.

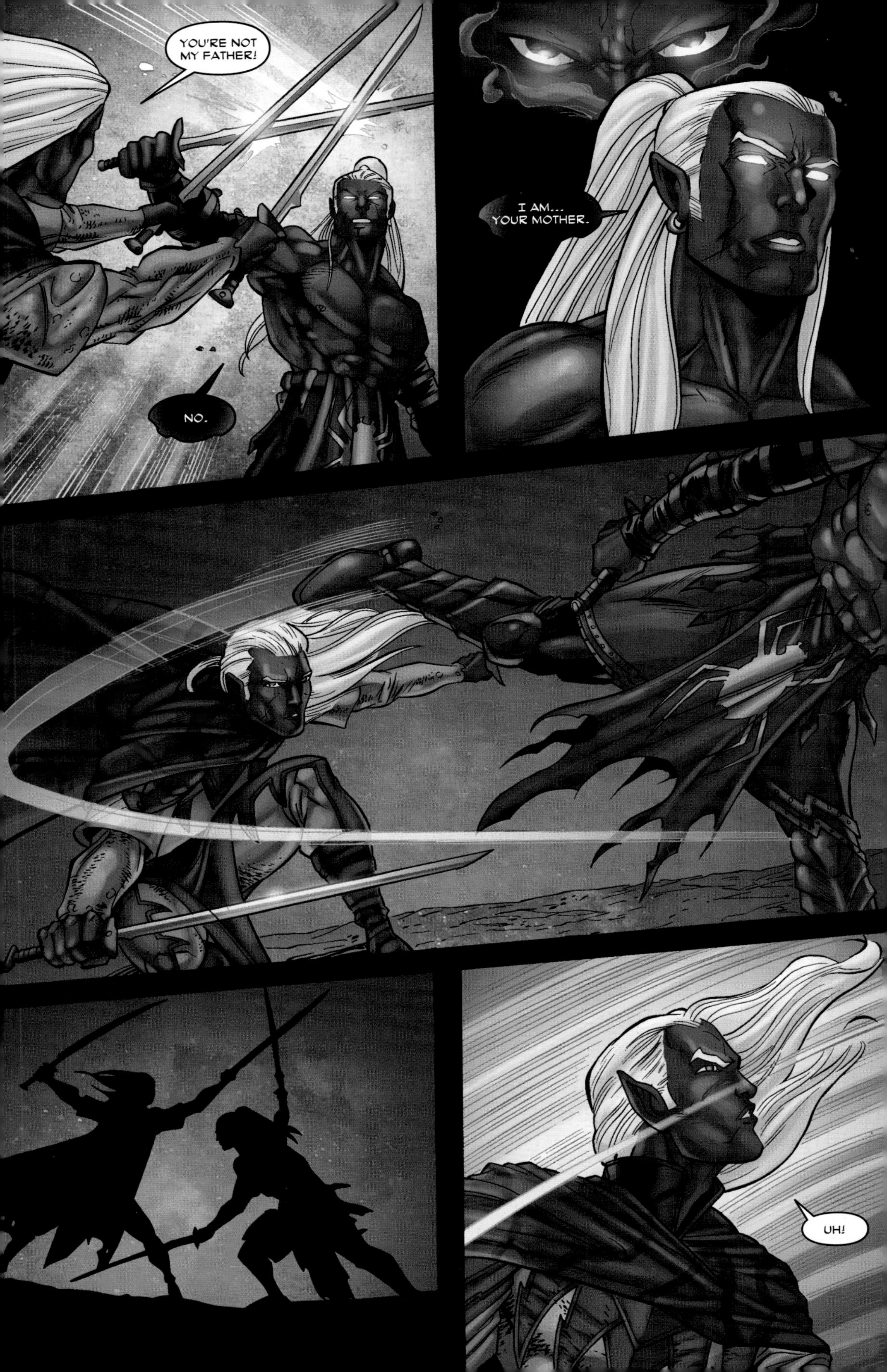
YOU'RE NOT MY FATHER!
NO.
I AM... YOUR MOTHER.
UH!

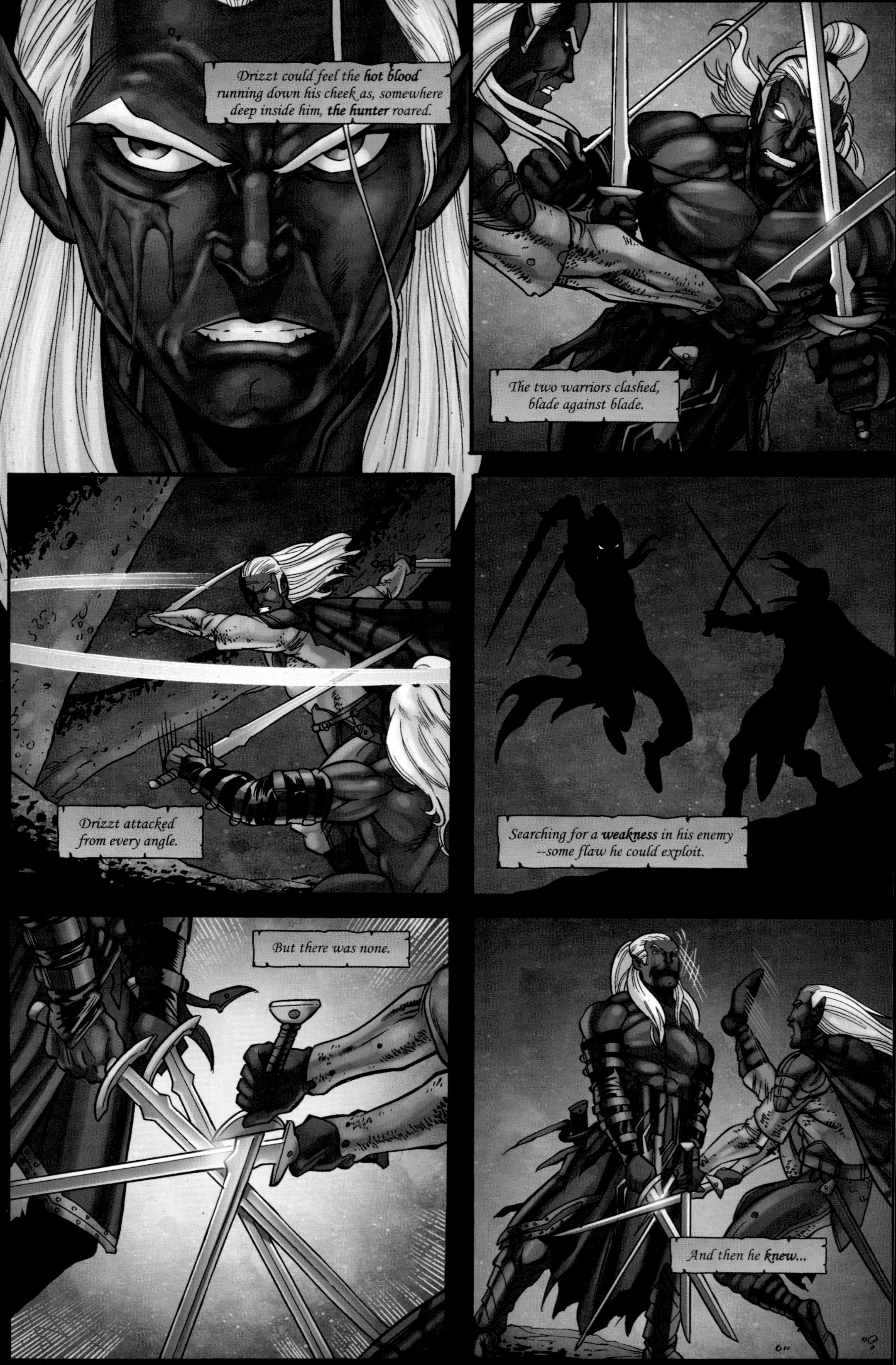
Drizzt could feel the hot blood running down his cheek as, somewhere deep inside him, the hunter roared.
The two warriors clashed, blade against blade.
Drizzt attacked from every angle.
Searching for a weakness in his enemy --some flaw he could exploit.
But there was none.
And then he knew...

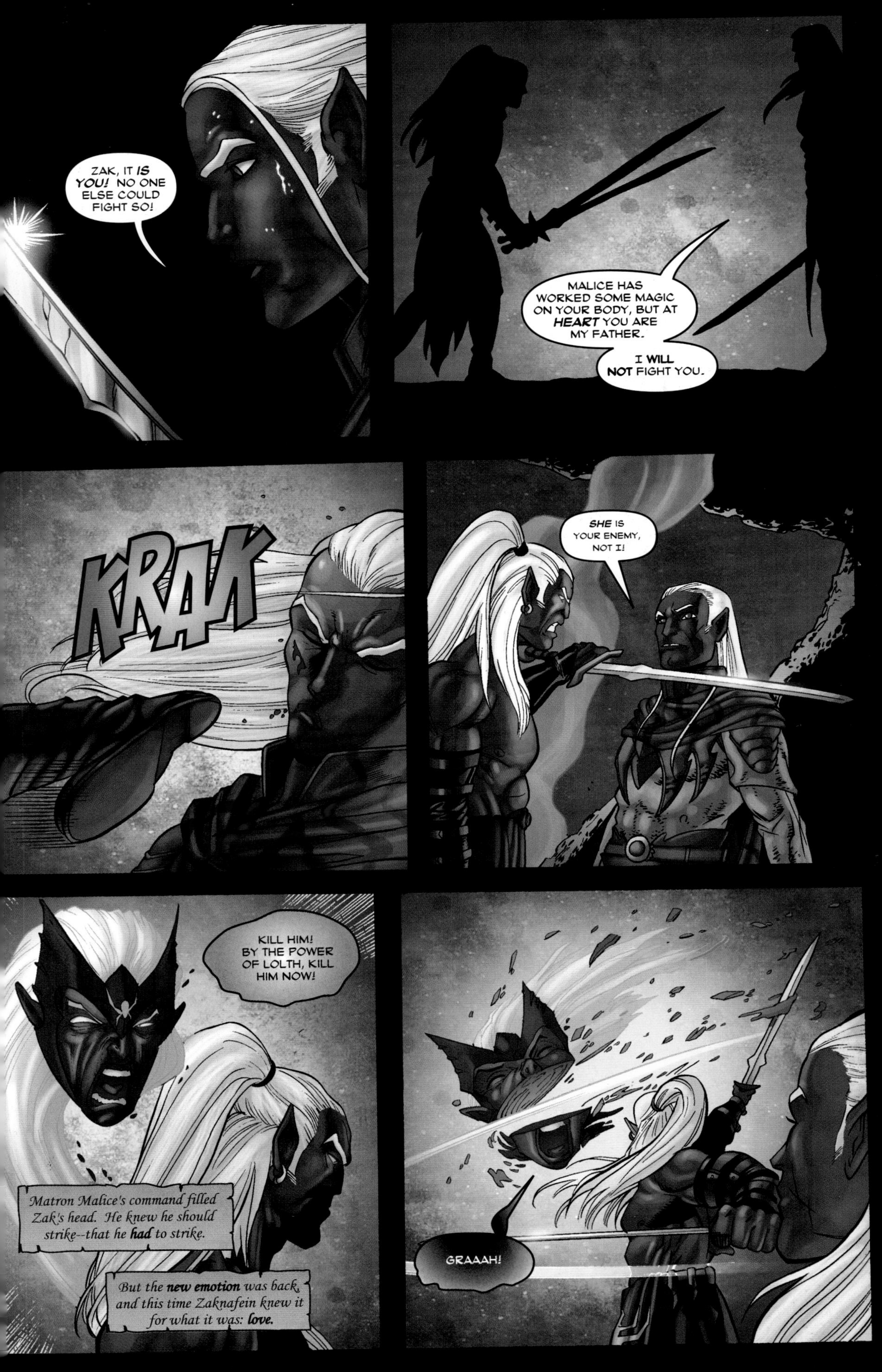
ZAK, IT **IS** **YOU!** NO ONE ELSE COULD FIGHT SO!
MALICE HAS WORKED SOME MAGIC ON YOUR BODY, BUT AT **HEART** YOU ARE MY FATHER.
I **WILL** **NOT** FIGHT YOU.
KRAK
SHE IS YOUR ENEMY, NOT I!
KILL HIM! BY THE POWER OF LOLTH, KILL HIM NOW!
*Matron Malice's command filled Zak's head. He knew he should strike--that he **had** to strike.*
*But the **new emotion** was back, and this time Zaknafein knew it for what it was: **love.***
GRAAAH!

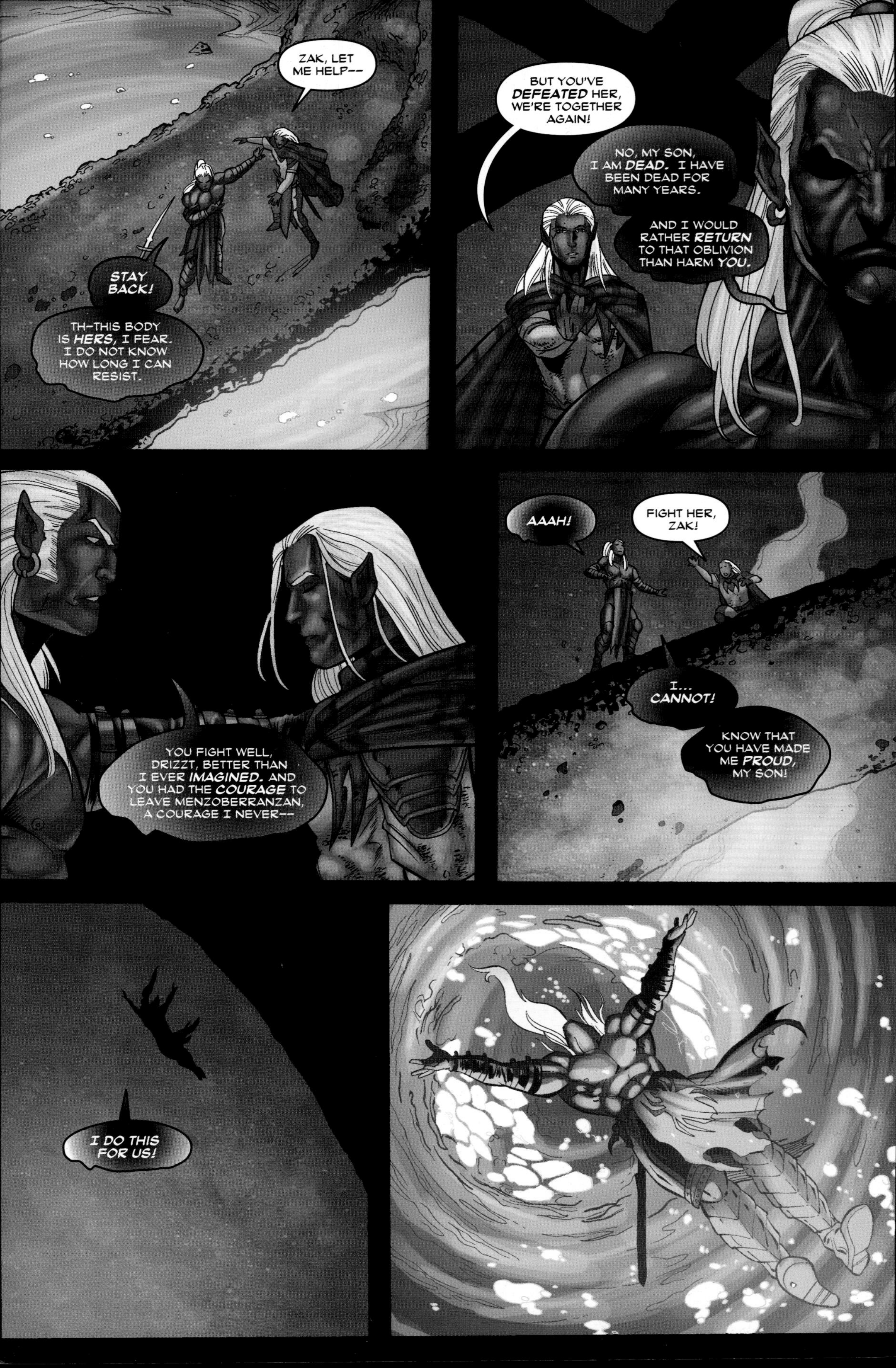
ZAK, LET ME HELP--
STAY BACK!
TH-THIS BODY IS HERS, I FEAR. I DO NOT KNOW HOW LONG I CAN RESIST.
BUT YOU'VE DEFEATED HER, WE'RE TOGETHER AGAIN!
NO, MY SON, I AM DEAD. I HAVE BEEN DEAD FOR MANY YEARS.
AND I WOULD RATHER RETURN TO THAT OBLIVION THAN HARM YOU.
YOU FIGHT WELL, DRIZZT, BETTER THAN I EVER IMAGINED. AND YOU HAD THE COURAGE TO LEAVE MENZOBERRANZAN, A COURAGE I NEVER--
AAAH!
FIGHT HER, ZAK!
I... CANNOT!
KNOW THAT YOU HAVE MADE ME PROUD, MY SON!
I DO THIS FOR US!

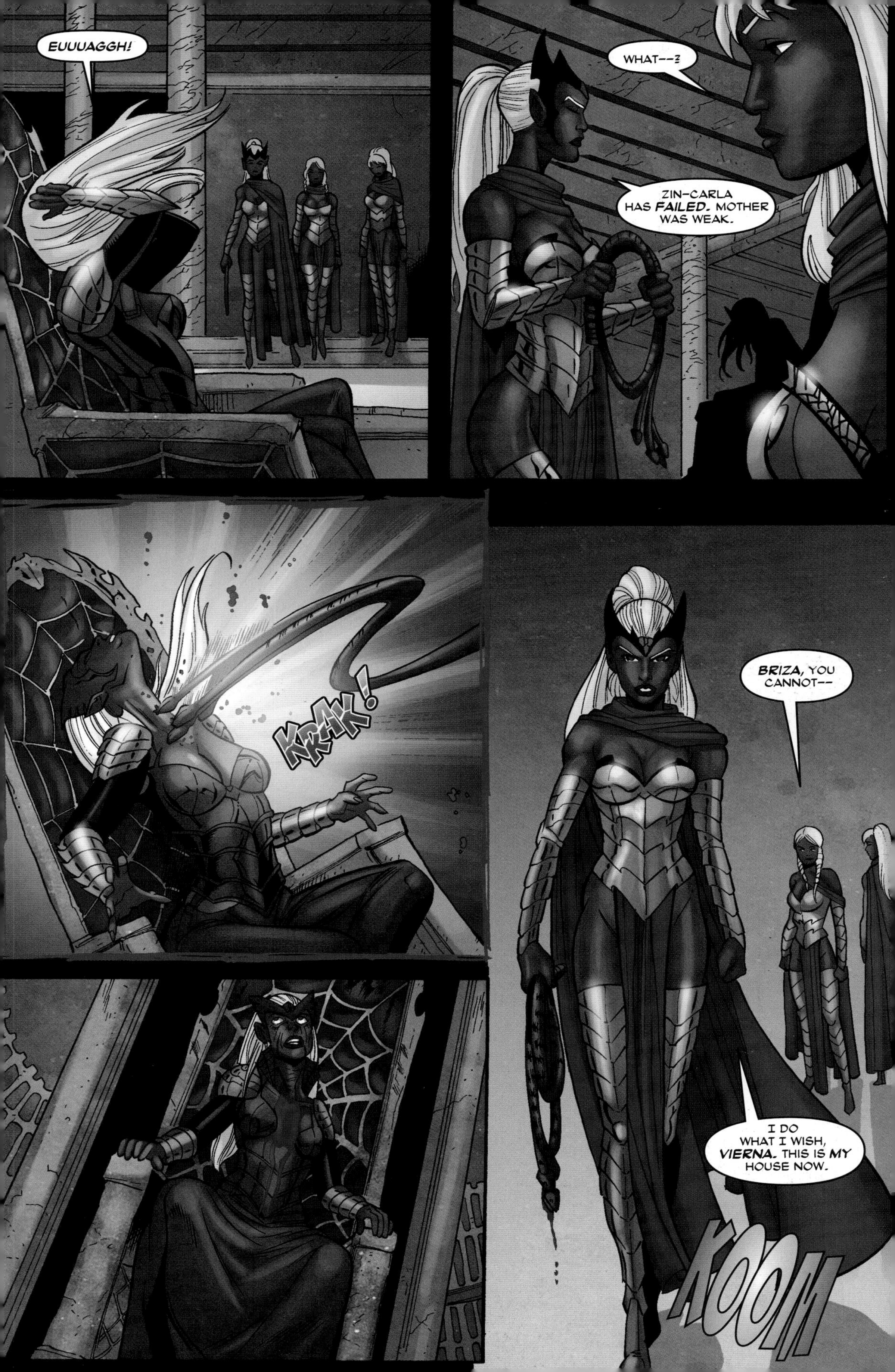
EUUUAGGH!
WHAT--?
ZIN-CARLA HAS FAILED. MOTHER WAS WEAK.
KRAK!
BRIZA, YOU CANNOT--
I DO WHAT I WISH, VIERNA. THIS IS MY HOUSE NOW.
KOOM

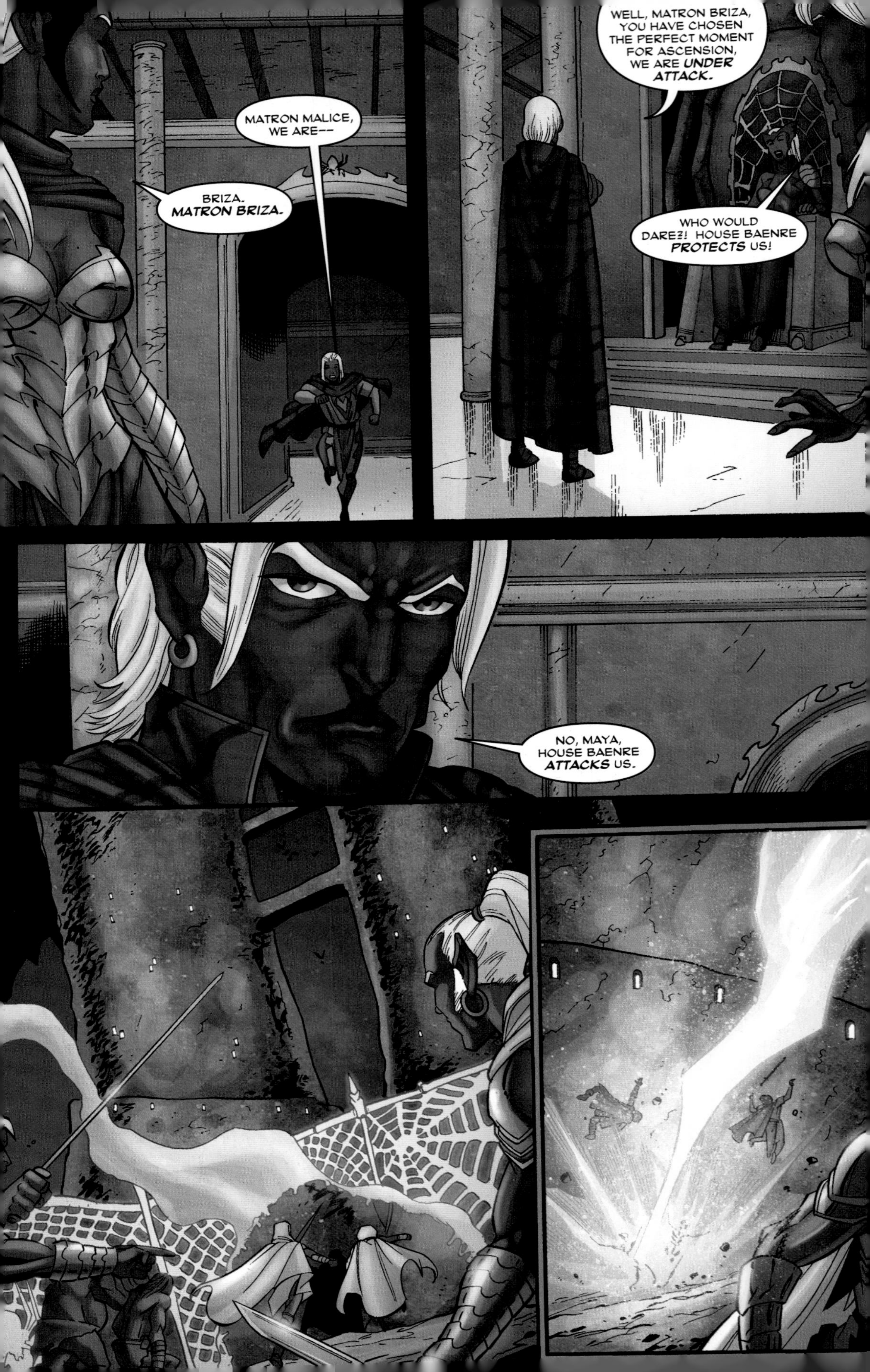
MATRON MALICE, WE ARE--
BRIZA. MATRON BRIZA.
WELL, MATRON BRIZA, YOU HAVE CHOSEN THE PERFECT MOMENT FOR ASCENSION. WE ARE UNDER ATTACK.
WHO WOULD DARE?! HOUSE BAENRE PROTECTS US!
NO, MAYA, HOUSE BAENRE ATTACKS US.

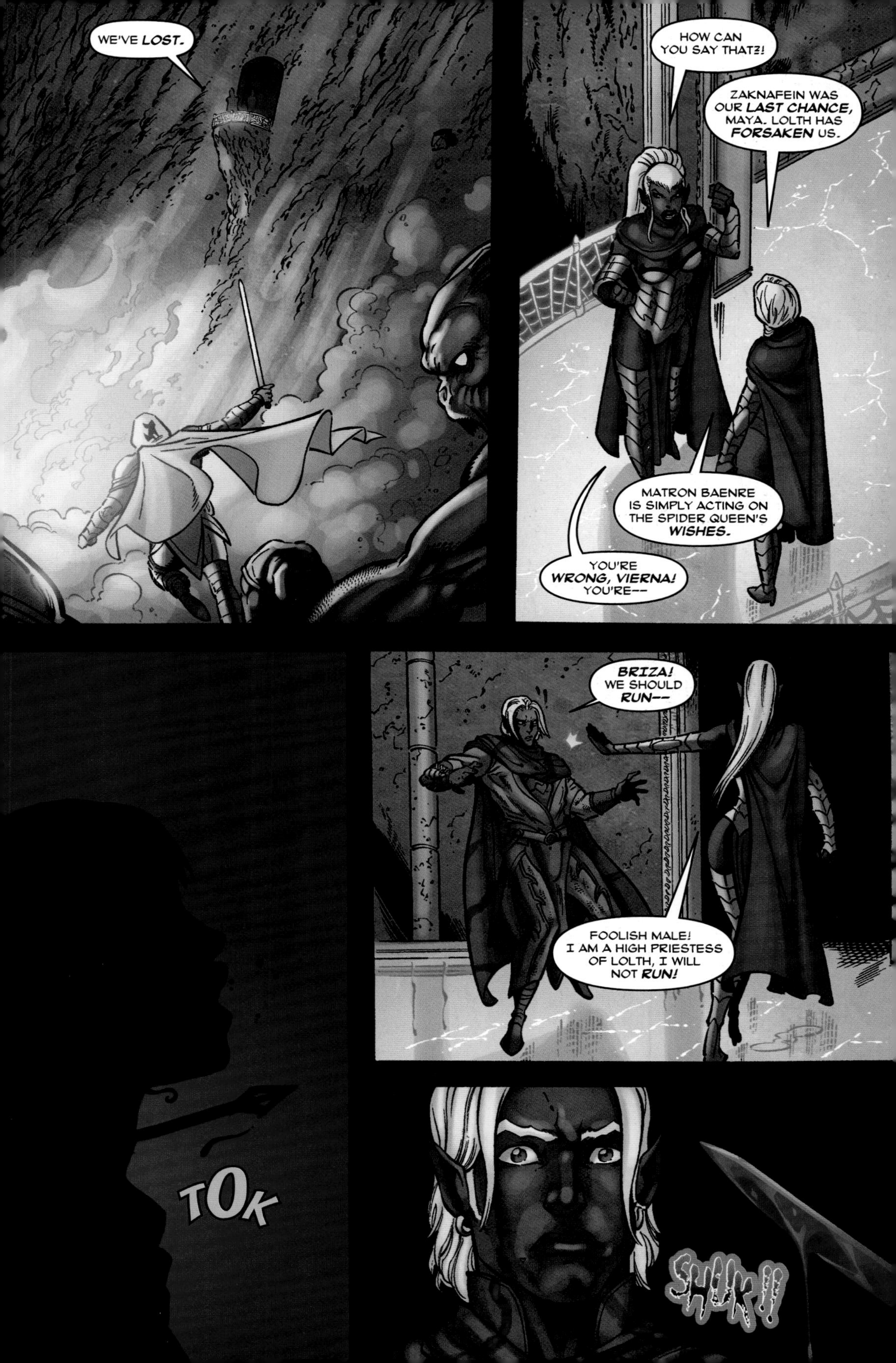
WE'VE LOST.
HOW CAN YOU SAY THAT?!
ZAKNAFEIN WAS OUR LAST CHANCE, MAYA. LOLTH HAS FORSAKEN US.
MATRON BAENRE IS SIMPLY ACTING ON THE SPIDER QUEEN'S WISHES.
YOU'RE WRONG, VIERNA! YOU'RE--
BRIZA! WE SHOULD RUN--
FOOLISH MALE! I AM A HIGH PRIESTESS OF LOLTH, I WILL NOT RUN!
TOK
SHUK!!

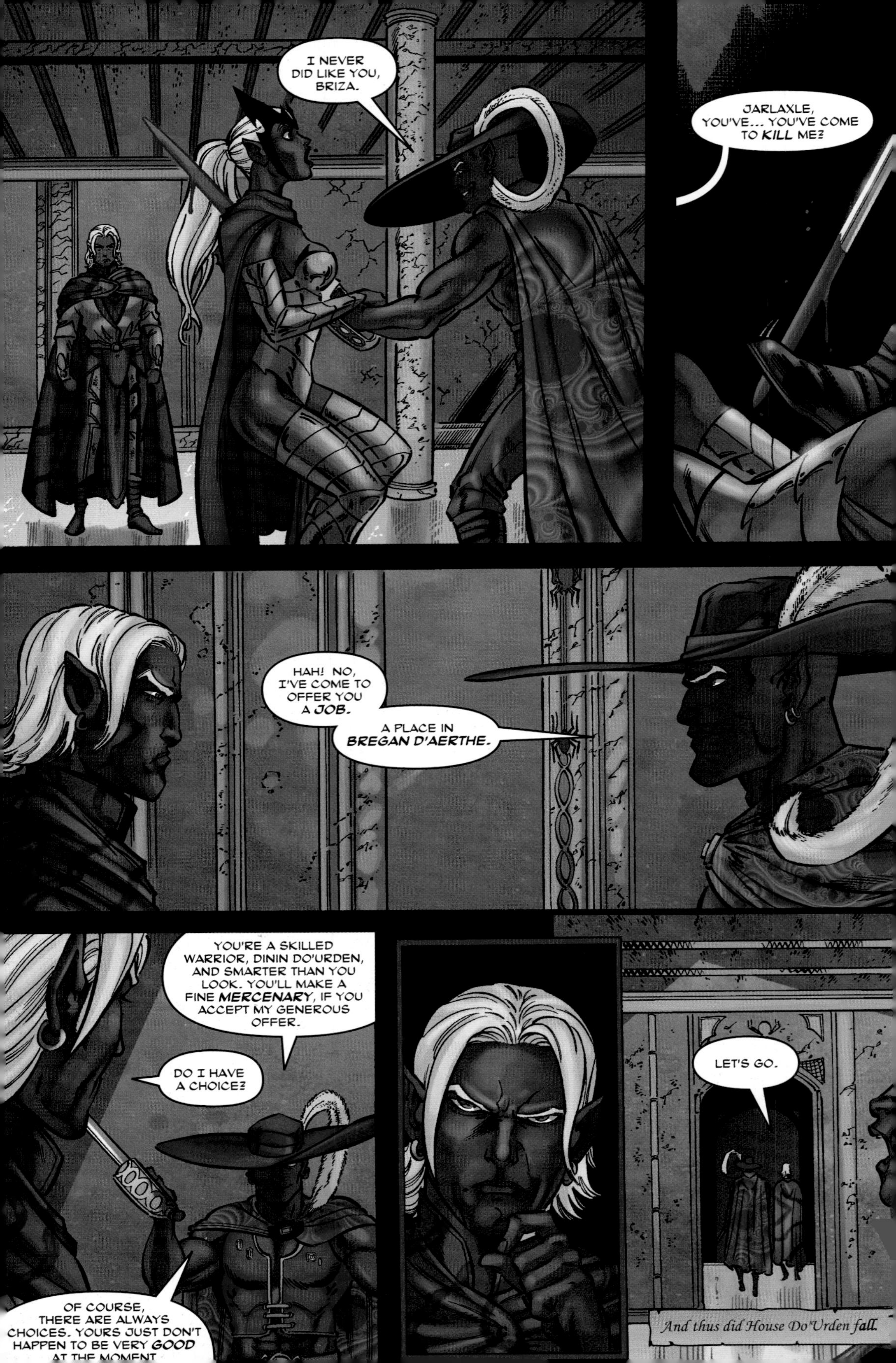
I NEVER DID LIKE YOU, BRIZA.
JARLAXLE, YOU'VE... YOU'VE COME TO **KILL** ME?
HAH! NO, I'VE COME TO OFFER YOU A **JOB.**
A PLACE IN **BREGAN D'AERTHE.**
YOU'RE A SKILLED WARRIOR, DININ DO'URDEN, AND SMARTER THAN YOU LOOK. YOU'LL MAKE A FINE **MERCENARY**, IF YOU ACCEPT MY GENEROUS OFFER.
DO I HAVE A CHOICE?
OF COURSE, THERE ARE ALWAYS CHOICES. YOURS JUST DON'T HAPPEN TO BE VERY **GOOD** AT THE MOMENT.
LET'S GO.
*And thus did House Do'Urden **fall.***

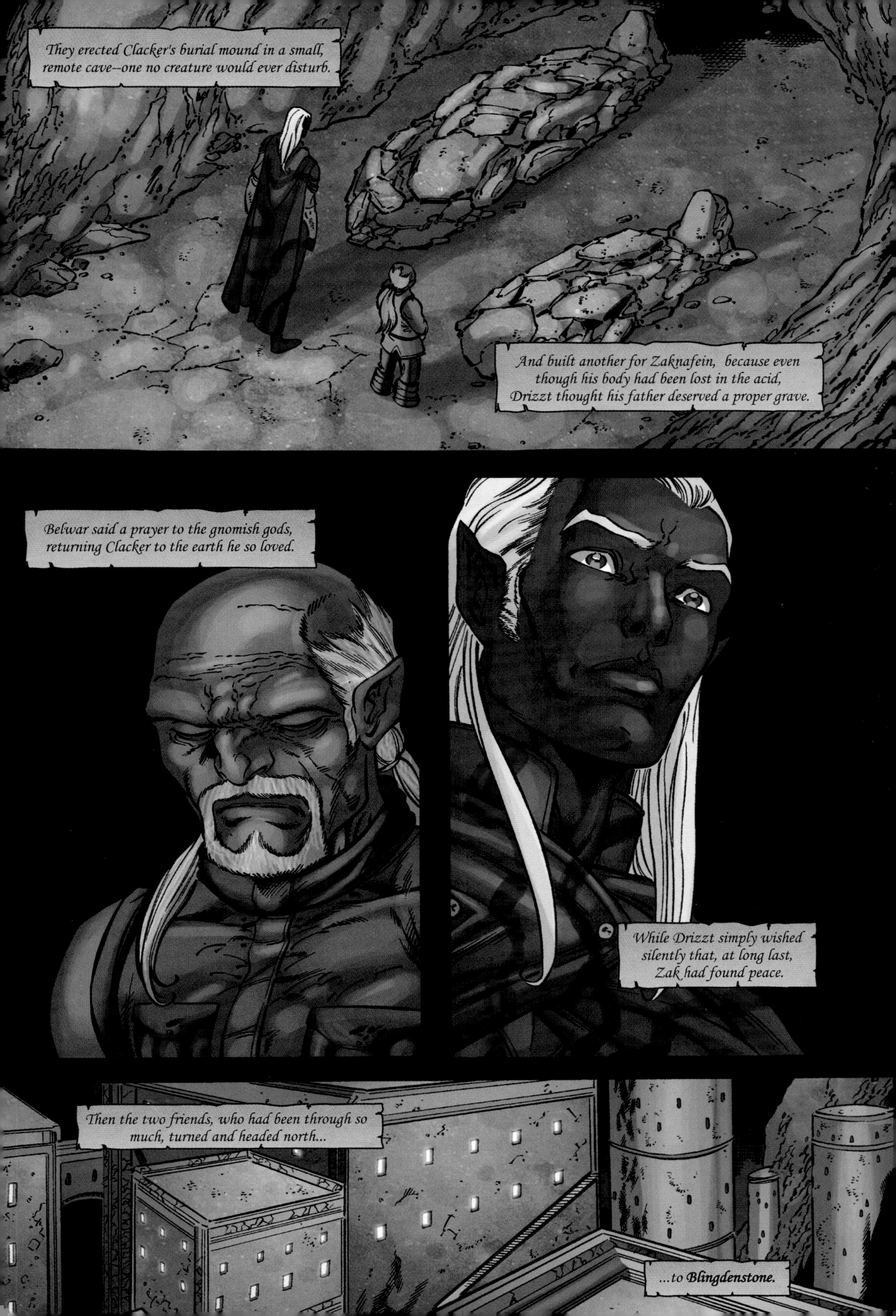
They erected Clacker's burial mound in a small, remote cave--one no creature would ever disturb.
And built another for Zaknafein, because even though his body had been lost in the acid, Drizzt thought his father deserved a proper grave.
Belwar said a prayer to the gnomish gods, returning Clacker to the earth he so loved.
While Drizzt simply wished silently that, at long last, Zak had found peace.
Then the two friends, who had been through so much, turned and headed north...
...to **Blingdenstone.**

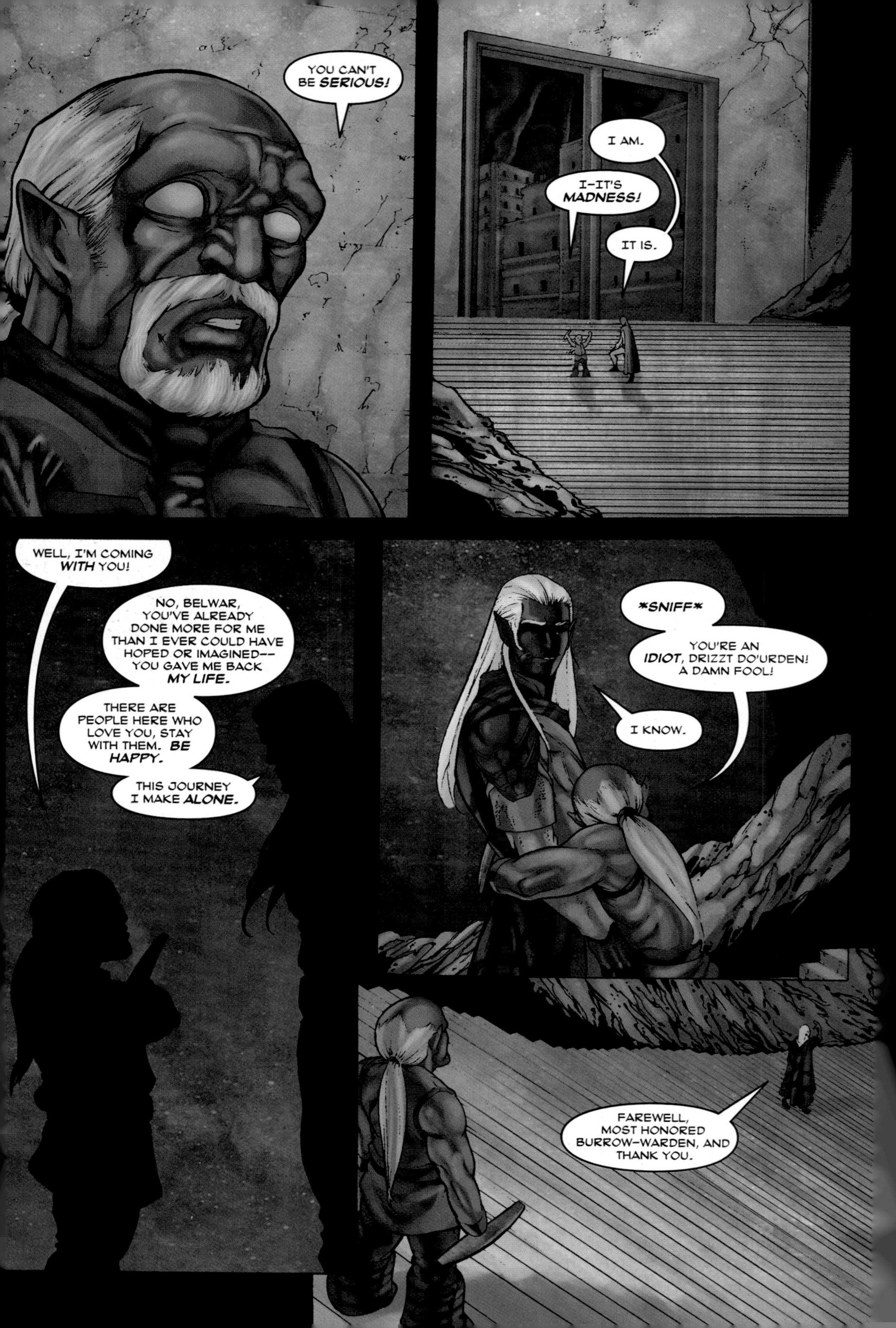
YOU CAN'T BE SERIOUS!
I AM.
I-IT'S MADNESS!
IT IS.
WELL, I'M COMING WITH YOU!
NO, BELWAR, YOU'VE ALREADY DONE MORE FOR ME THAN I EVER COULD HAVE HOPED OR IMAGINED-- YOU GAVE ME BACK MY LIFE.
THERE ARE PEOPLE HERE WHO LOVE YOU, STAY WITH THEM. BE HAPPY.
THIS JOURNEY I MAKE ALONE.
SNIFF
YOU'RE AN IDIOT, DRIZZT DO'URDEN! A DAMN FOOL!
I KNOW.
FAREWELL, MOST HONORED BURROW-WARDEN, AND THANK YOU.

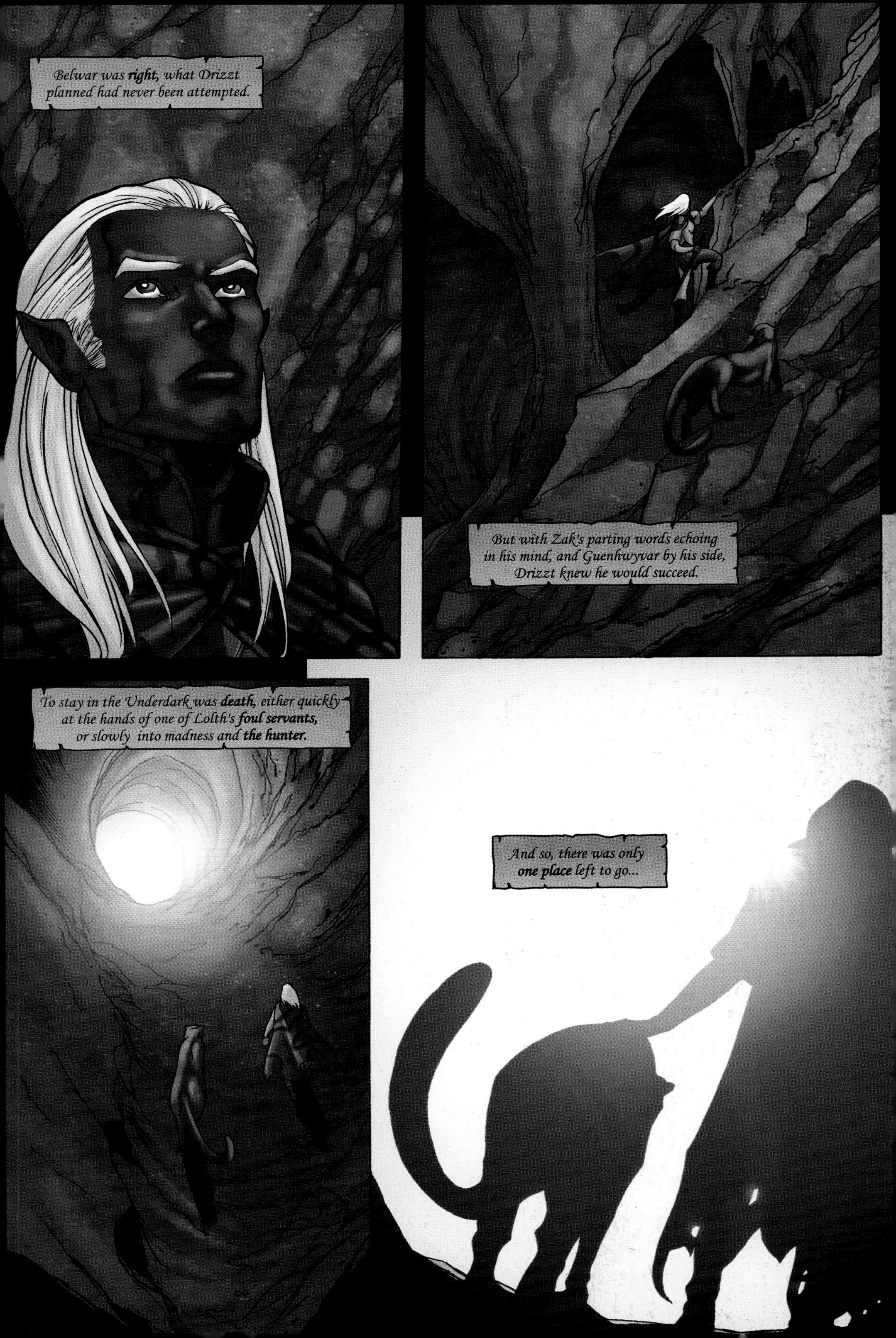
Belwar was **right**, what Drizzt planned had never been attempted.
But with Zak's parting words echoing in his mind, and Guenhwyvar by his side, Drizzt knew he would succeed.
To stay in the Underdark was **death**, either quickly at the hands of one of Lolth's **foul servants**, or slowly into madness and **the hunter**.
And so, there was only **one place** left to go...

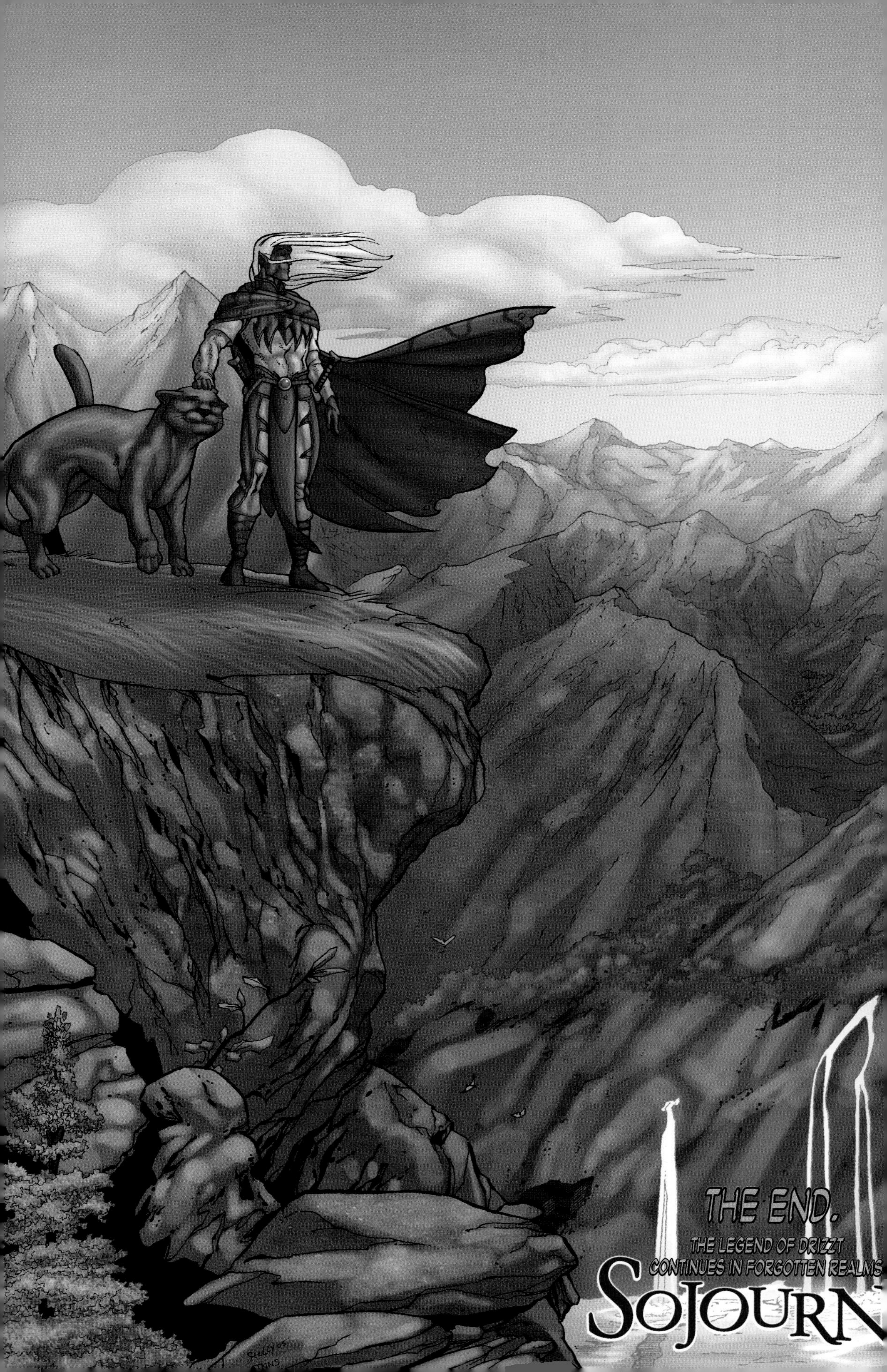
THE END.
THE LEGEND OF DRIZZT
CONTINUES IN FORGOTTEN REALMS
SOJOURN

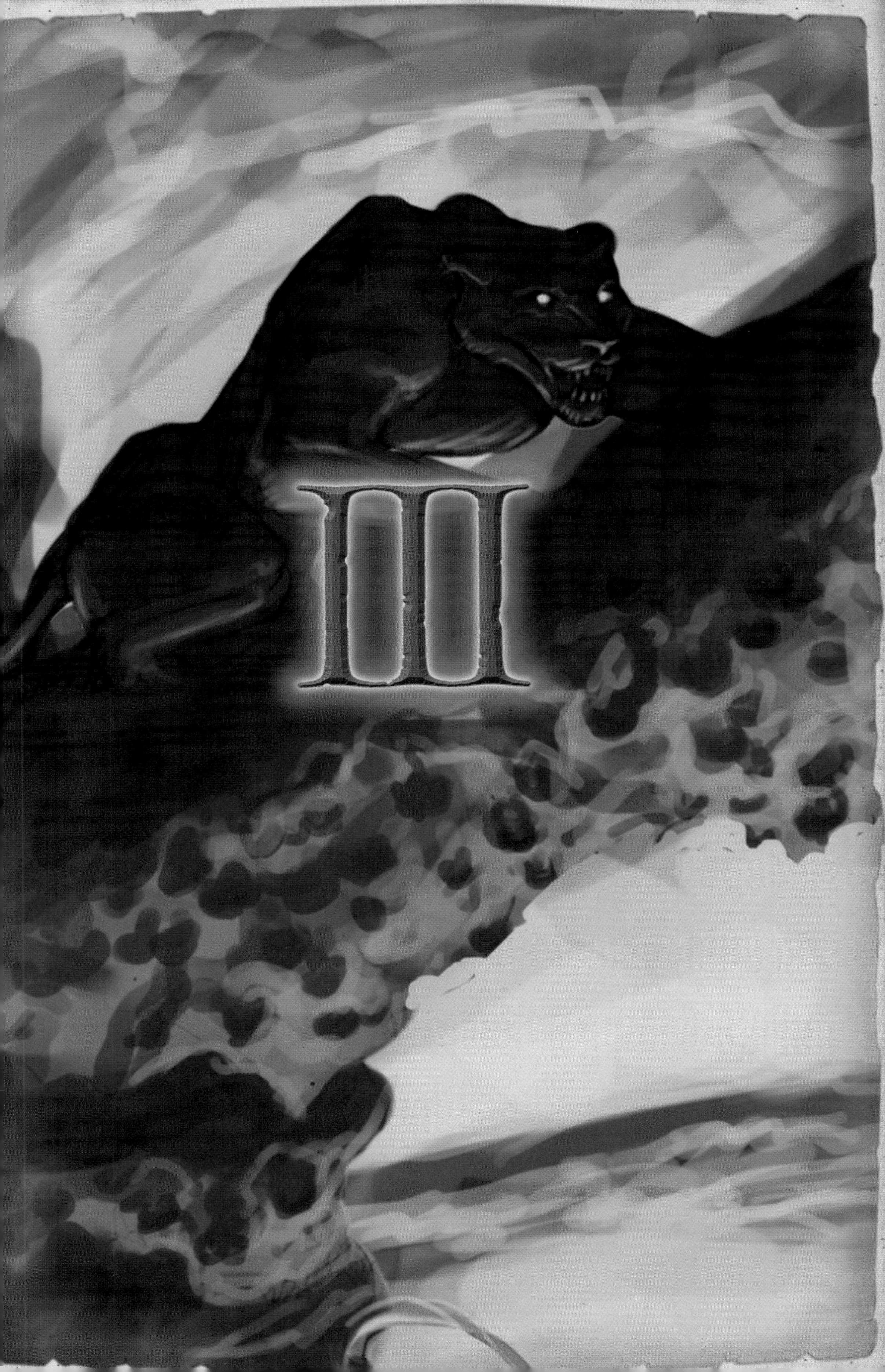
III

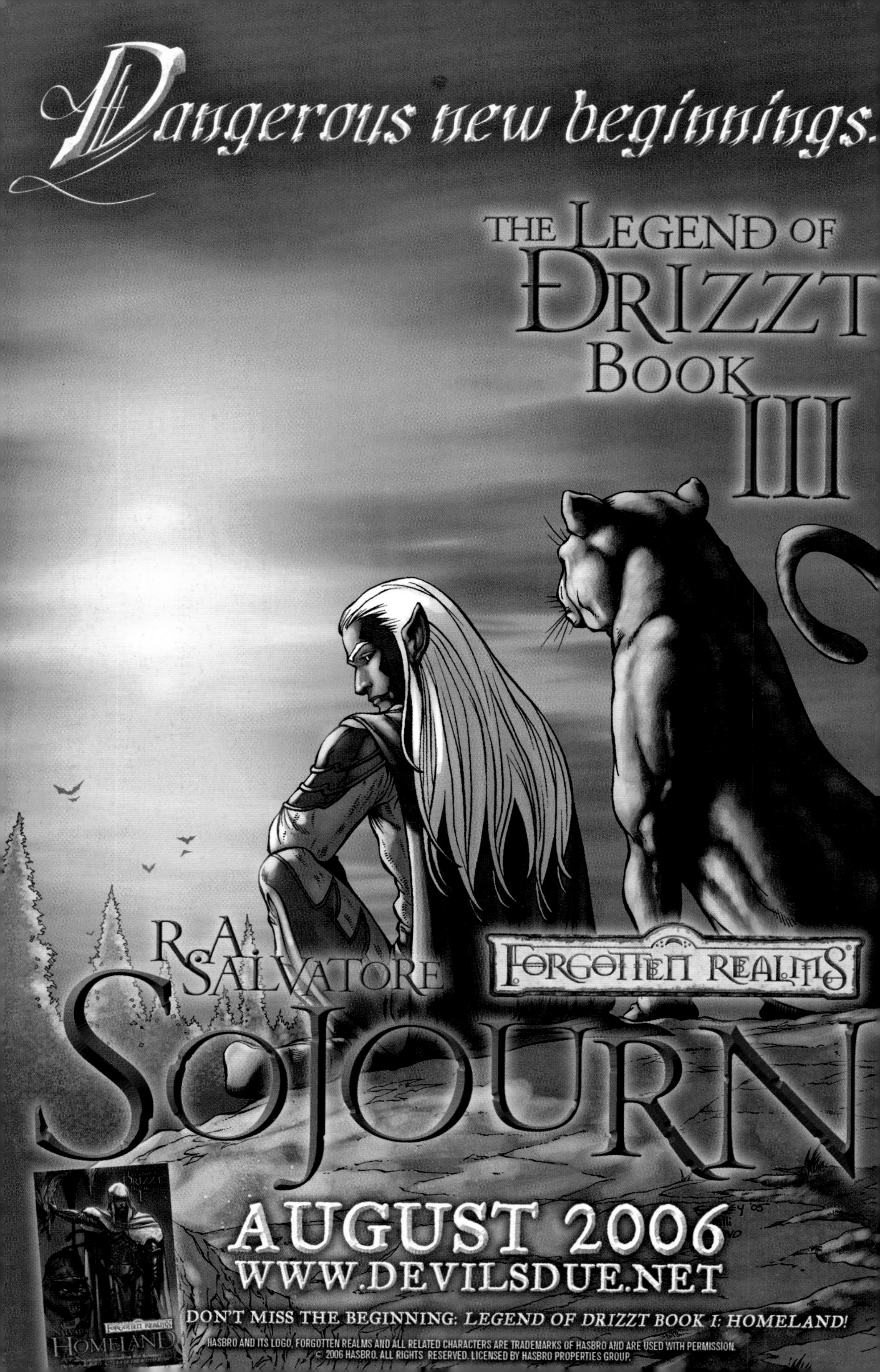
Dangerous new beginnings.
THE LEGEND OF DRIZZT BOOK III
R.A. SALVATORE
FORGOTTEN REALMS
SOJOURN
AUGUST 2006
WWW.DEVILSDUE.NET
DON'T MISS THE BEGINNING: LEGEND OF DRIZZT BOOK I: HOMELAND!
HASBRO AND ITS LOGO, FORGOTTEN REALMS AND ALL RELATED CHARACTERS ARE TRADEMARKS OF HASBRO AND ARE USED WITH PERMISSION.
© 2006 HASBRO. ALL RIGHTS RESERVED. LICENSED BY HASBRO PROPERTIES GROUP.

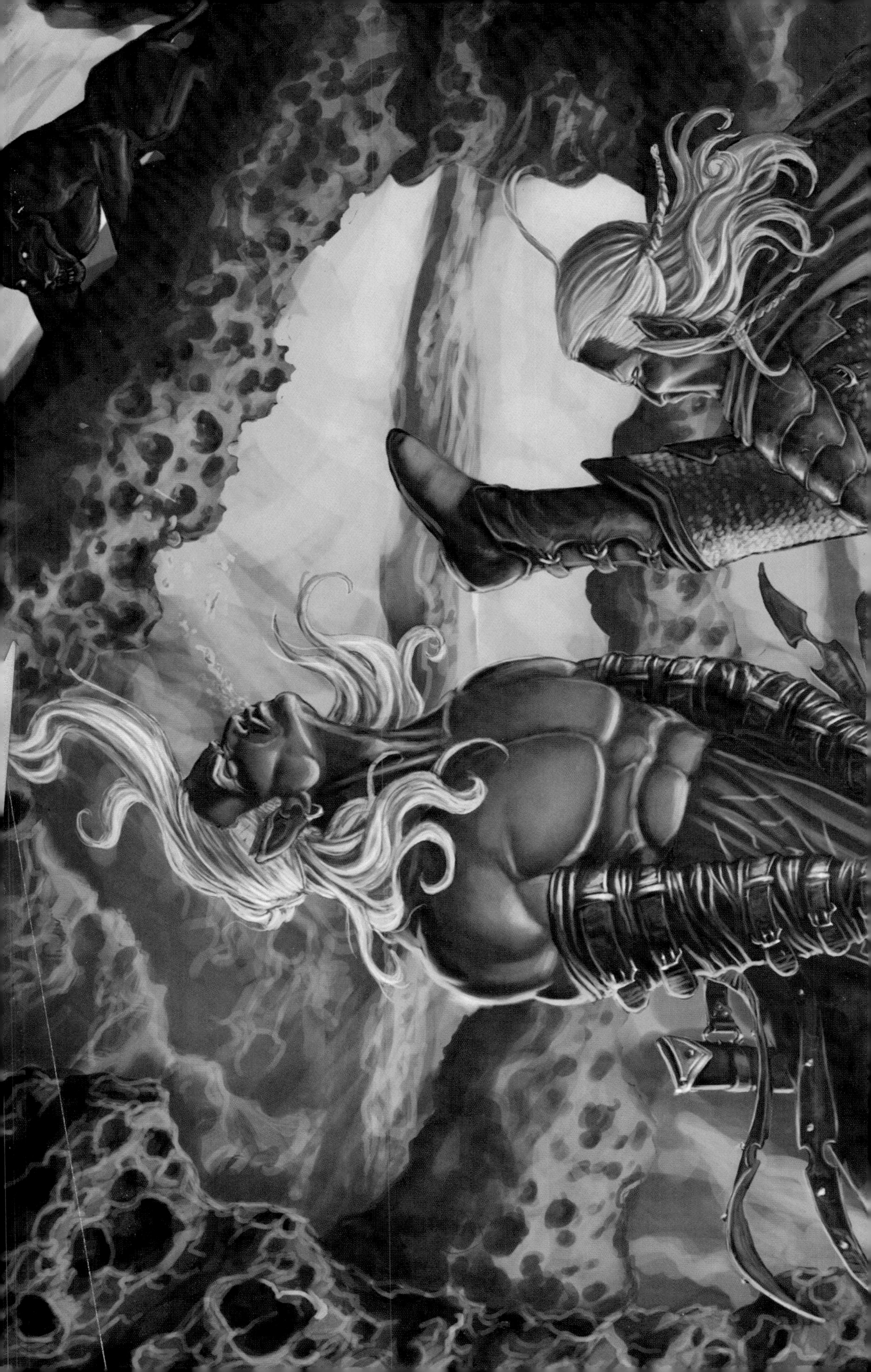

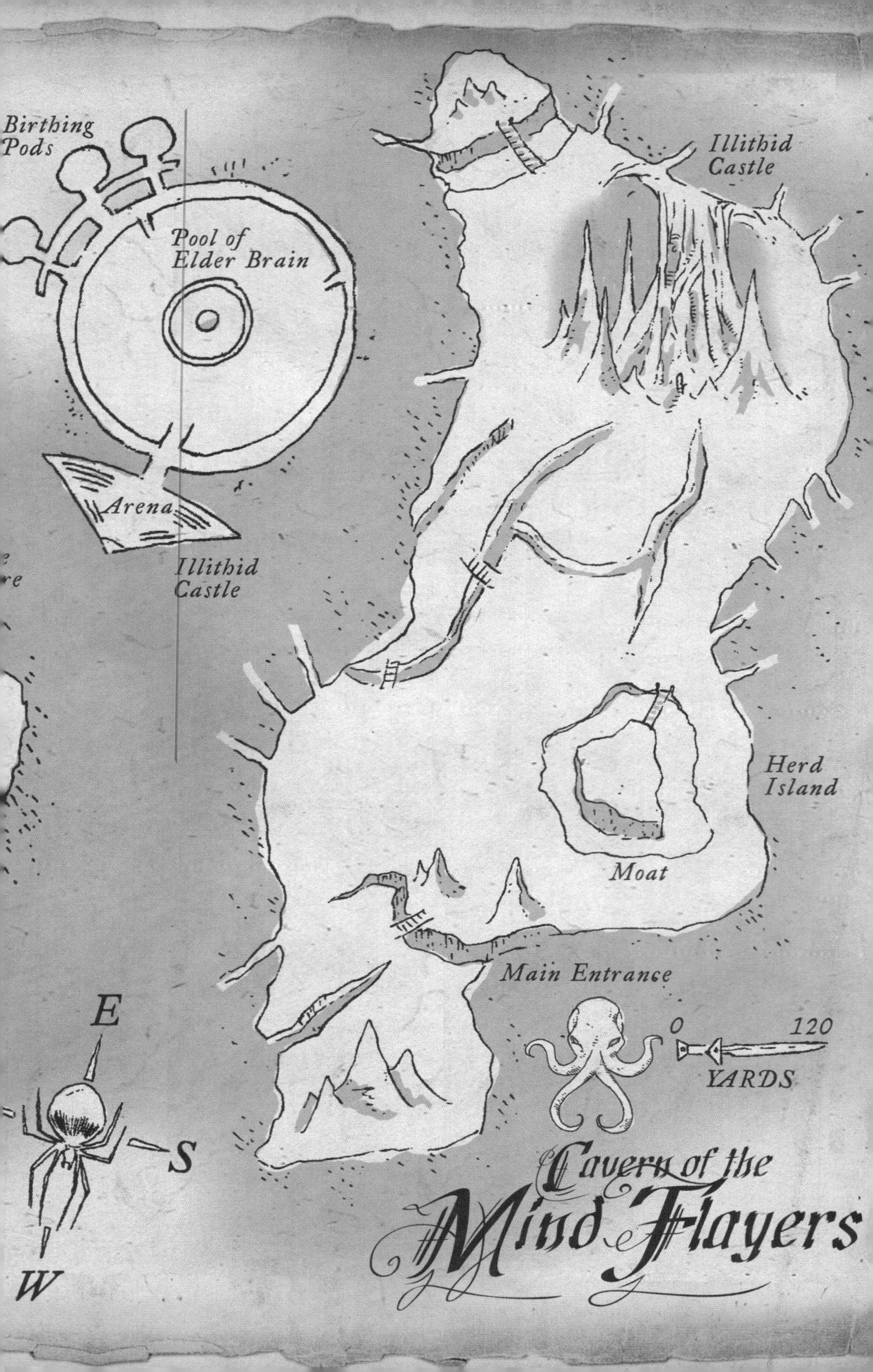
Birthing Pods
Pool of Elder Brain
Arena
Illithid Castle
Illithid Castle
Herd Island
Moat
Main Entrance
0
120
YARDS
E
S
W
Cavern of the Mind Flayers

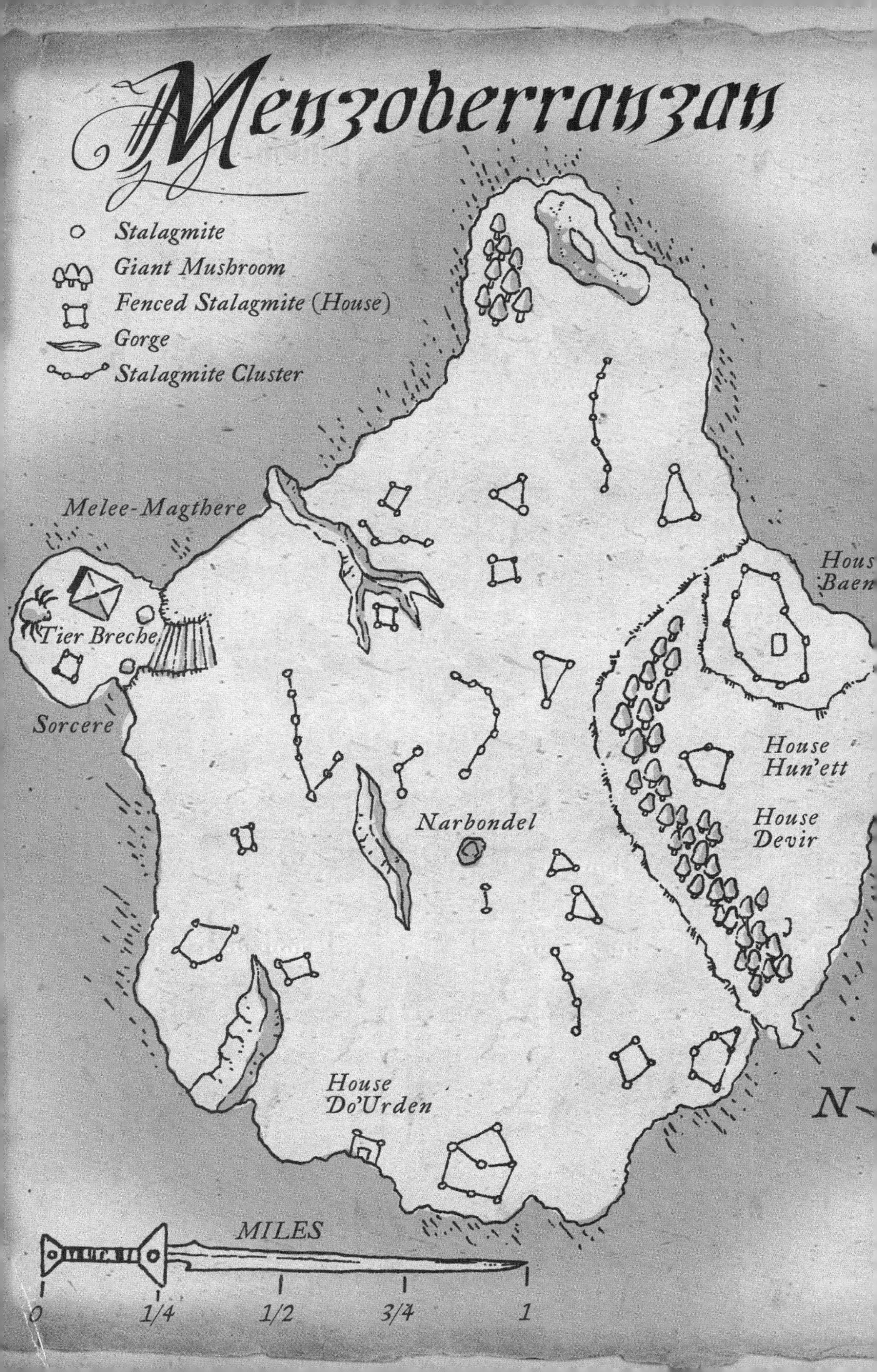
Menzoberranzan
Stalagmite
Giant Mushroom
Fenced Stalagmite (House)
Gorge
Stalagmite Cluster
Melee-Magthere
Tier Breche
Sorcere
Hous
Baen
House
Hun'ett
House
Devir
Narbondel
House
Do'Urden
N
MILES
0
1/4
1/2
3/4
1

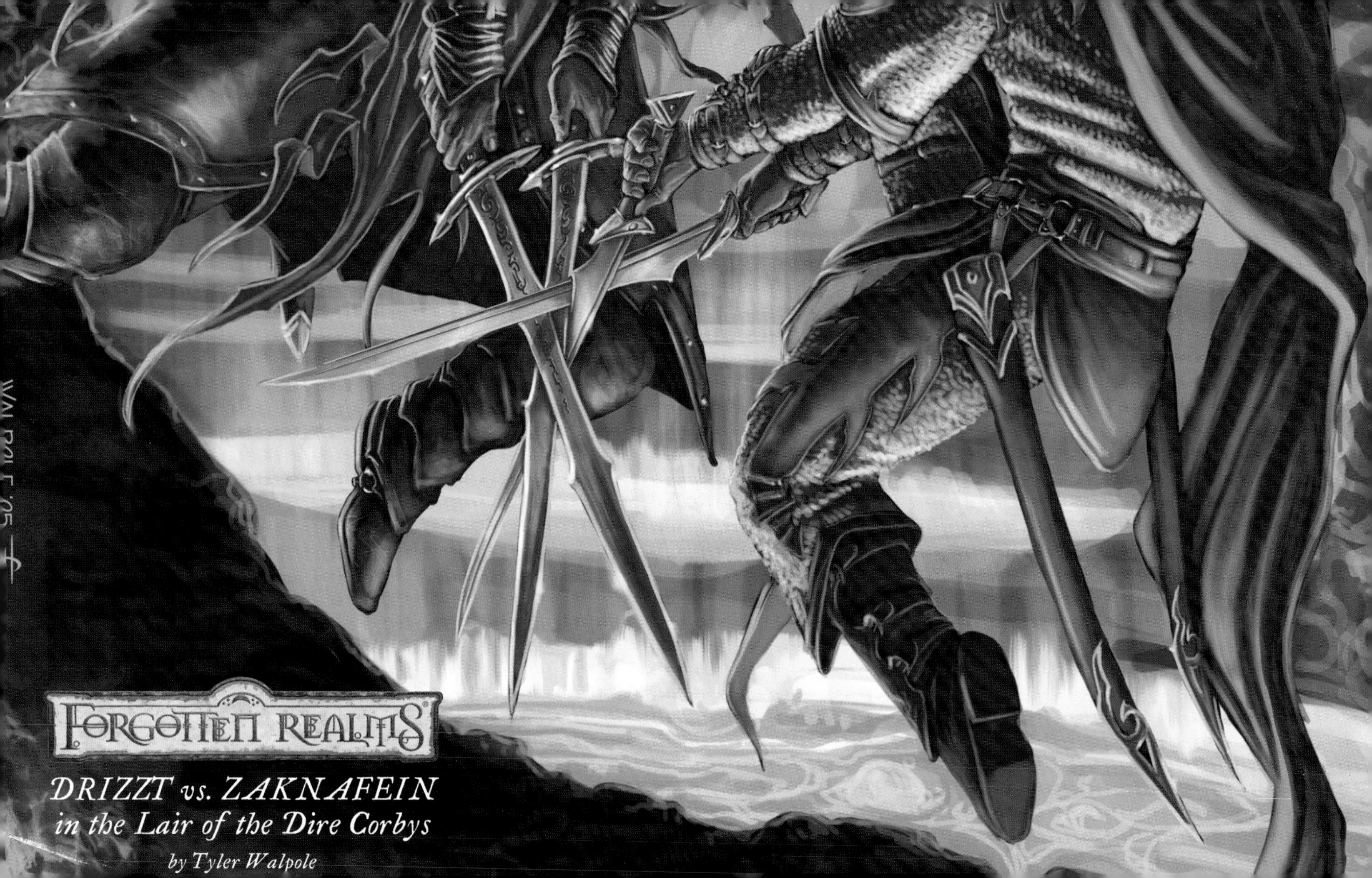
FORGOTTEN REALMS®
DRIZZT vs. ZAKNAFEIN
in the Lair of the Dire Corbys
by Tyler Walpole
WALPOLE '05

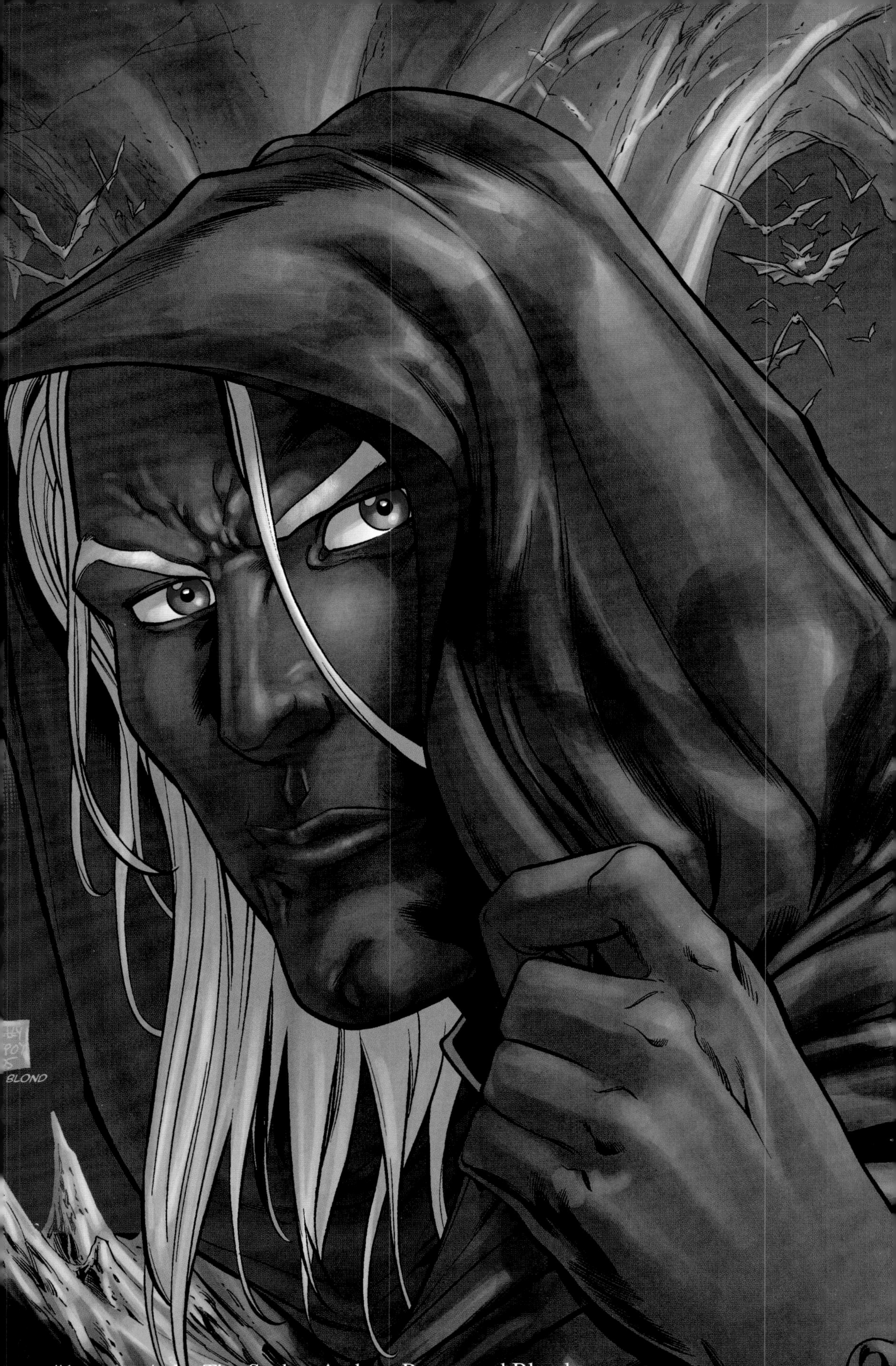
BLOND
ssue #1, cover A, by Tim Seeley, Andrew Pepoy, and Blond.

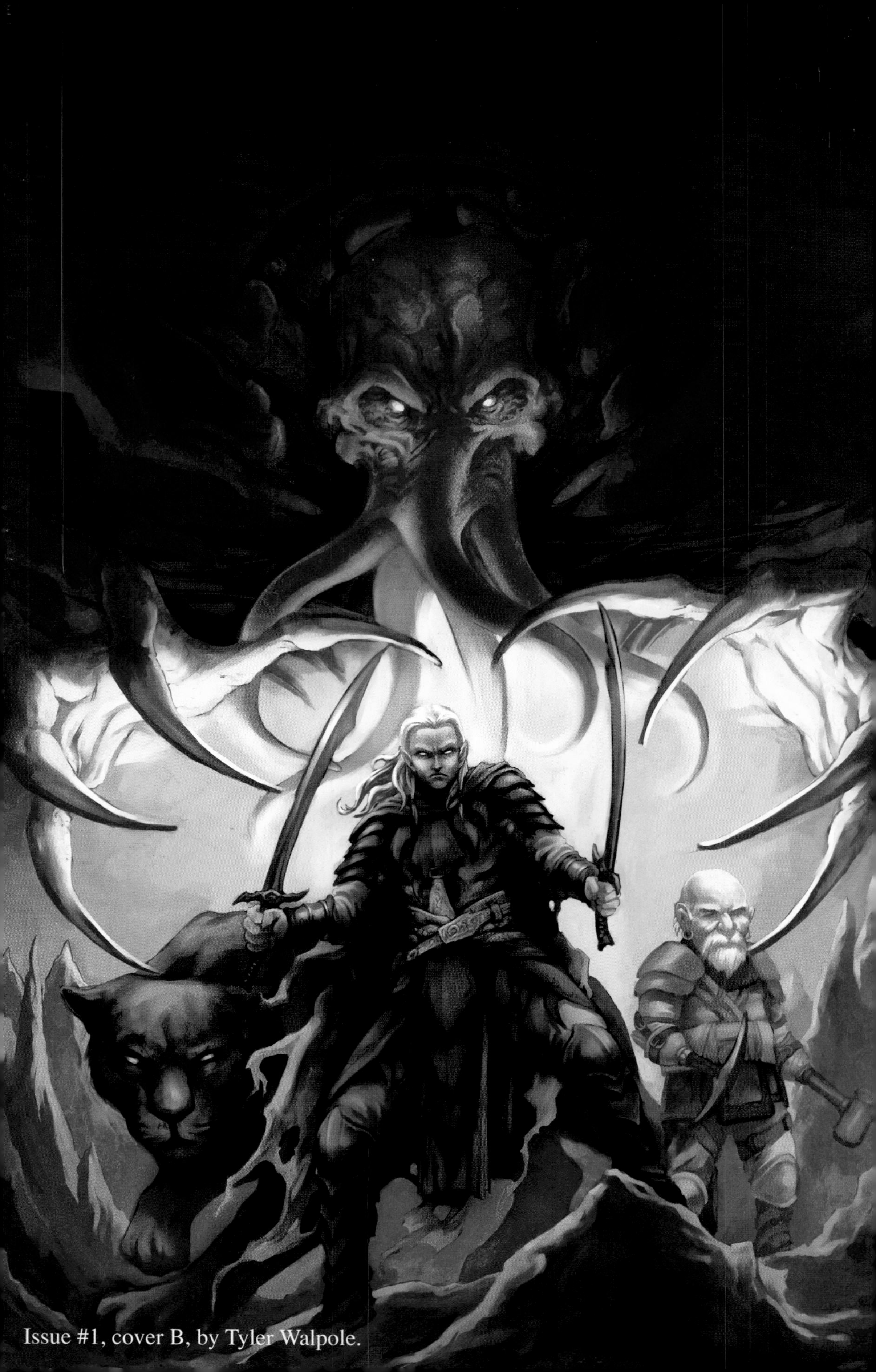

Issue #1, cover B, by Tyler Walpole.

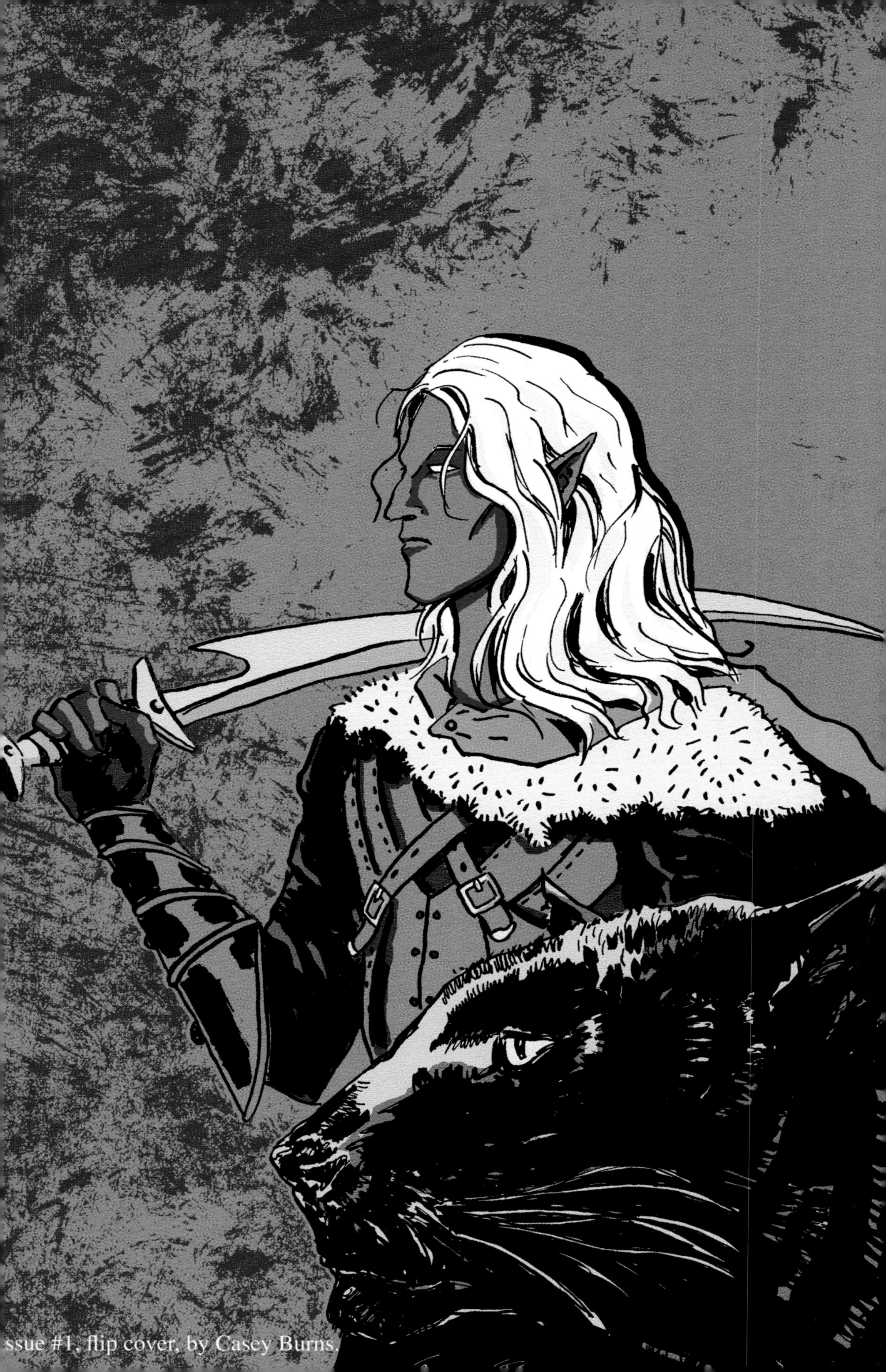

ssue #1, flip cover, by Casey Burns.

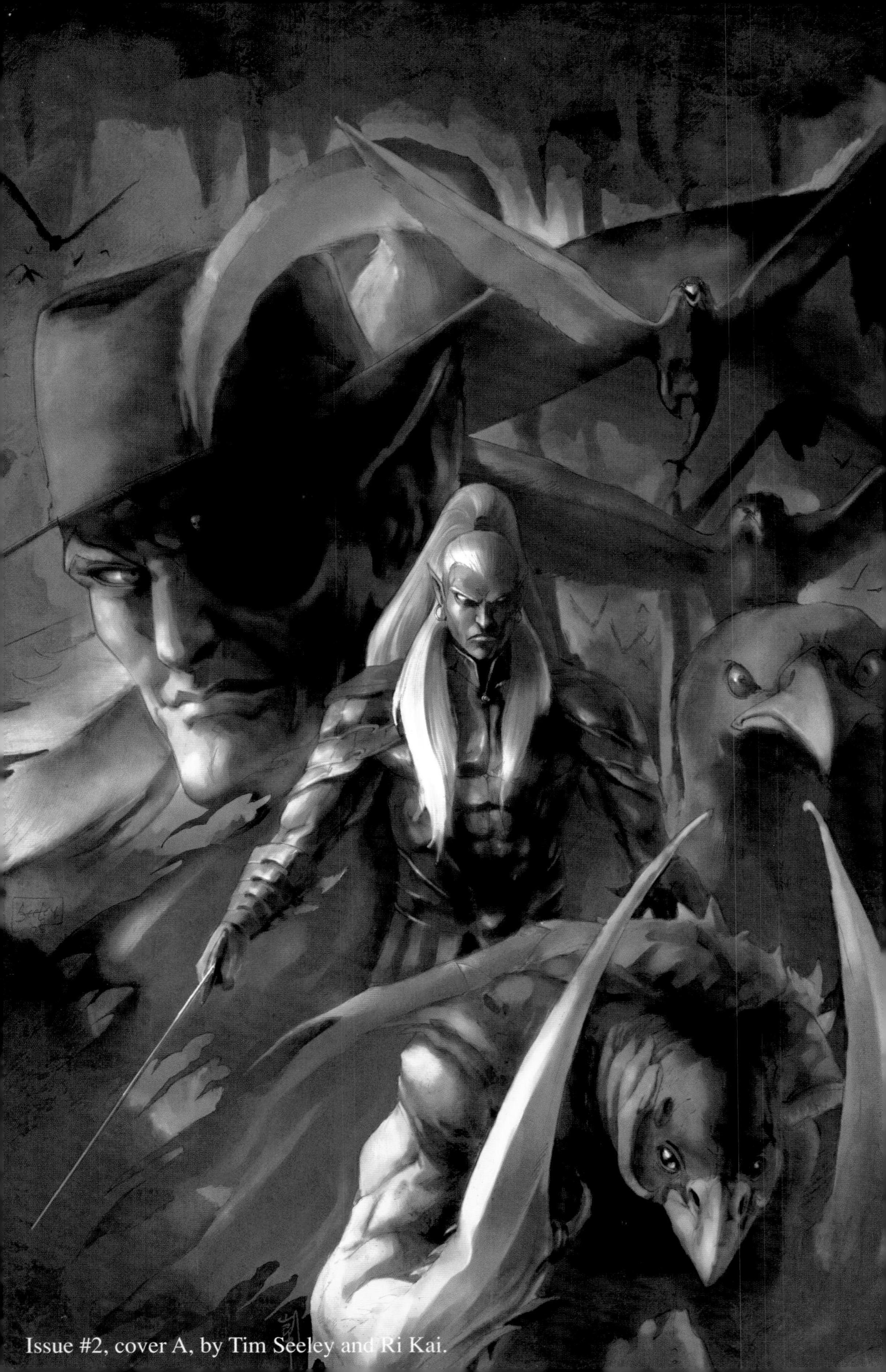
Issue #2, cover A, by Tim Seeley and Ri Kai.

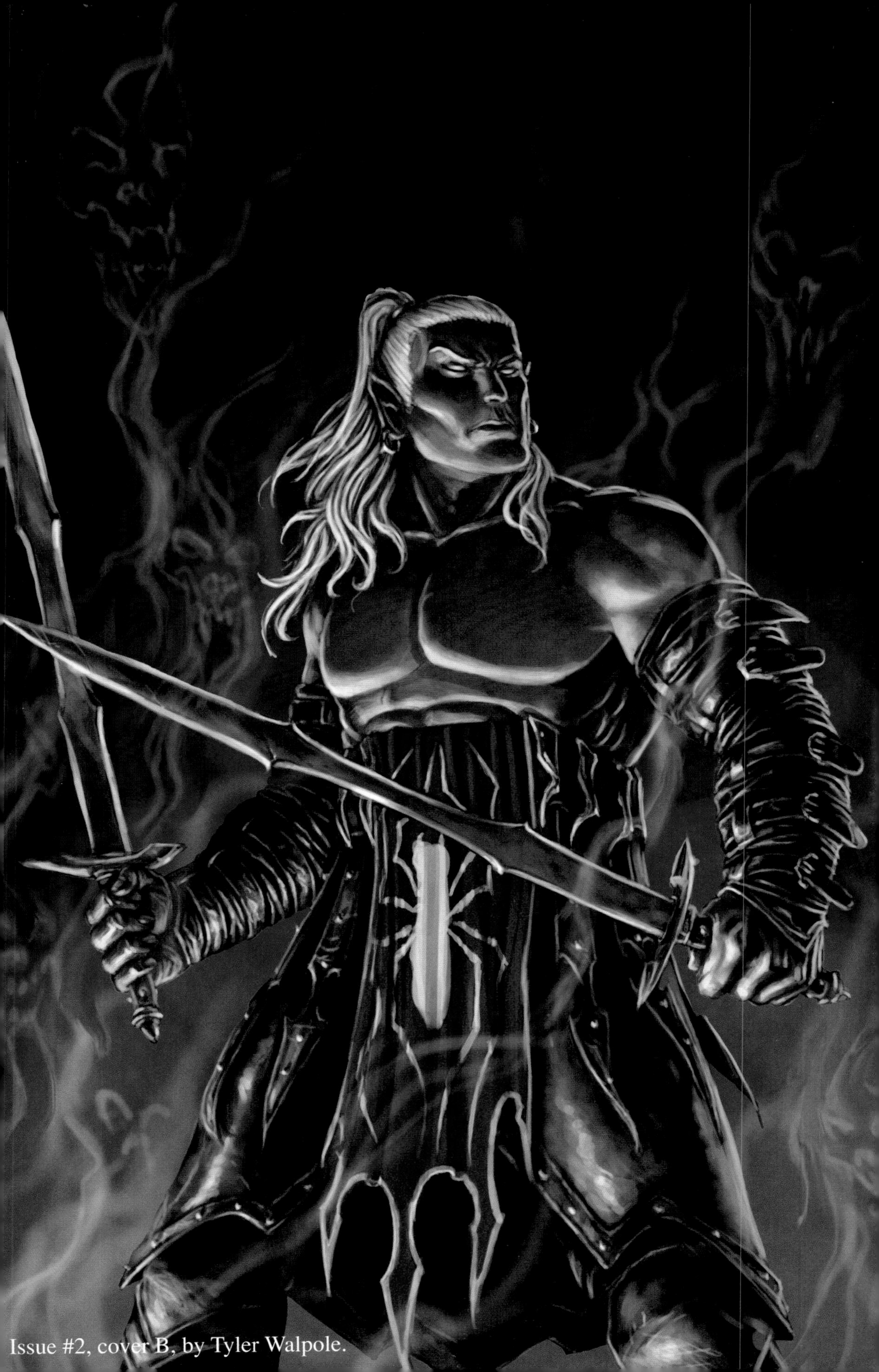

Issue #2, cover B, by Tyler Walpole.

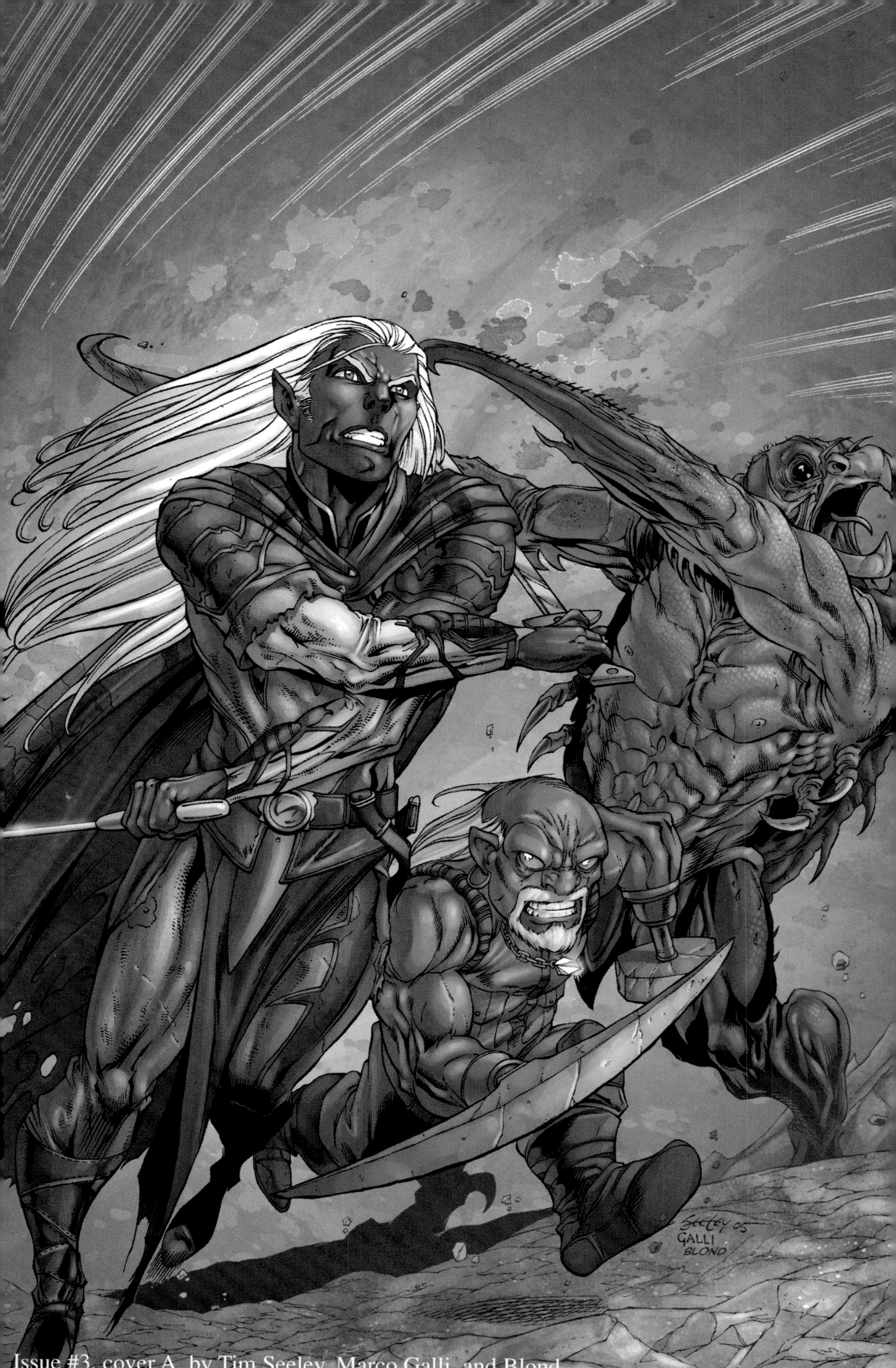
SEELEY 05
GALLI
BLOND

Issue #3, cover A, by Tim Seeley, Marco Galli, and Blond.

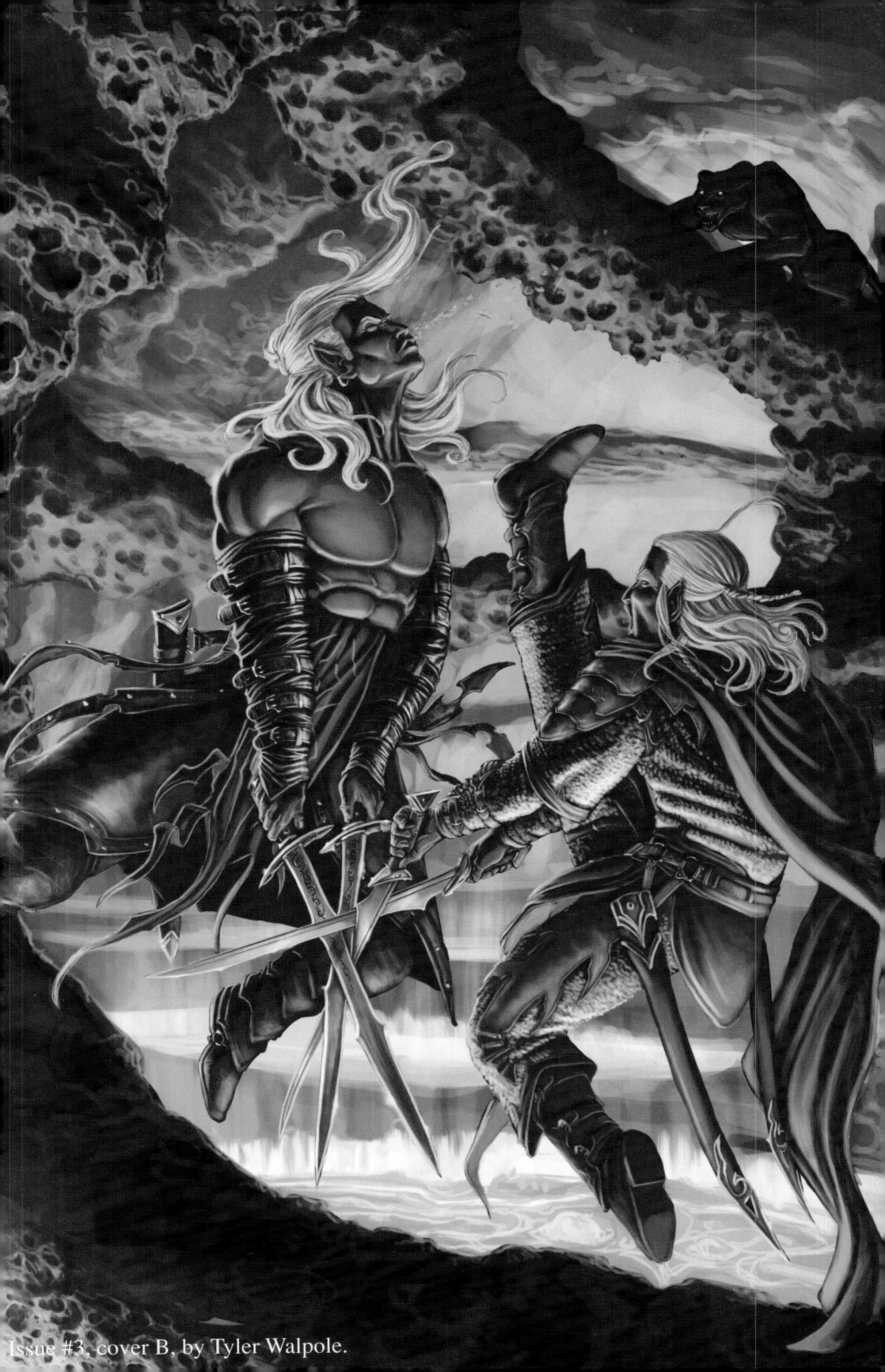

Issue #3, cover B, by Tyler Walpole.

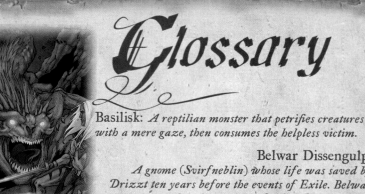

Glossary

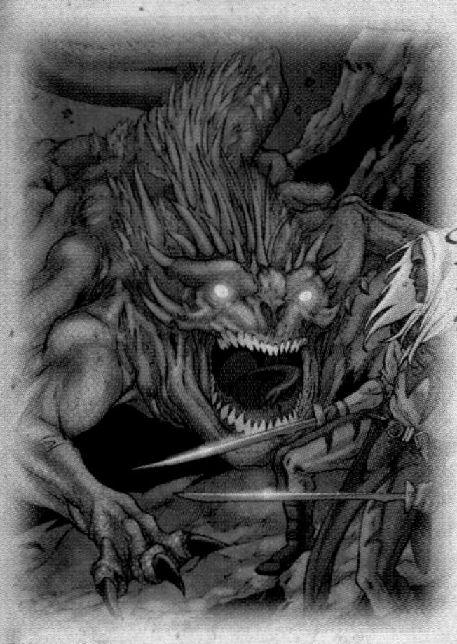

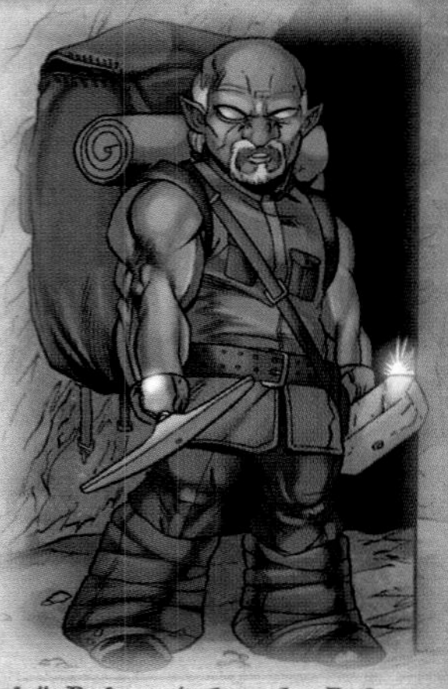

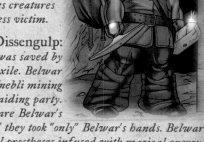

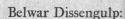

Basilisk: *A reptilian monster that petrifies creatures with a mere gaze, then consumes the helpless victim.*

Belwar Dissengulp: *A gnome (Svirfneblin) whose life was saved by Drizzt ten years before the events of Exile. Belwar was the sole survivor of a Svirfnebli mining expedition attacked by a Drow raiding party. Drizzt convinced his comrades to spare Belwar's life. In an act of cruel Drow "mercy," they took "only" Belwar's hands. Belwar now has mithral prostheses infused with magical energy.*

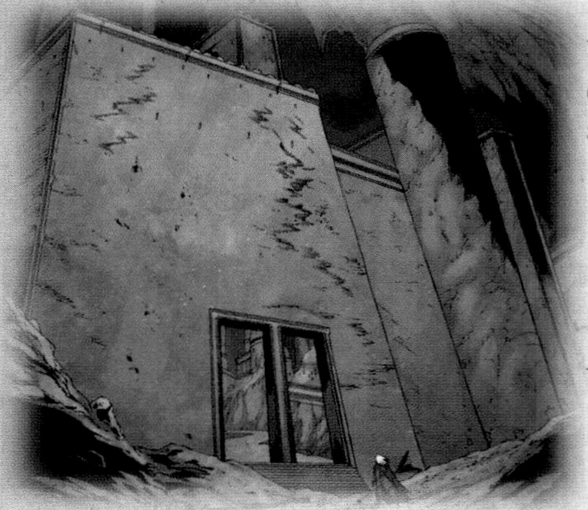

Blingdenstone: *The fortress-like city of the deep gnomes (Svirfneblin). Hewn from the living rock itself, this vast metropolis is home to thousands of gnomes.*

Bregan D'Aerthe: *A Drow mercenary cadre comprised of rogue males and led by the infamous Jarlaxle. Bregan D'Aerthe is rightfully feared and respected throughout Menzoberranzan.*

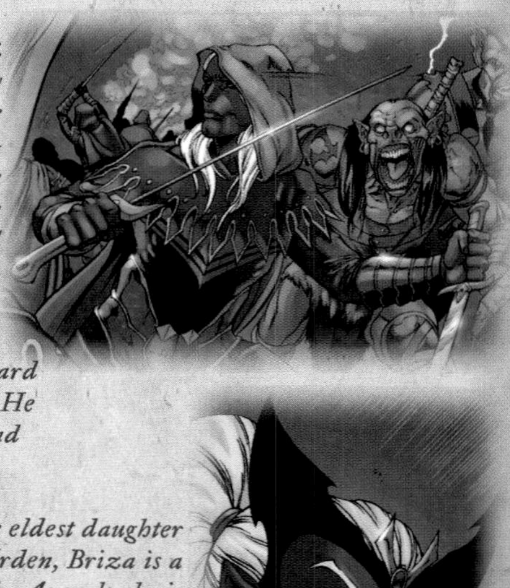

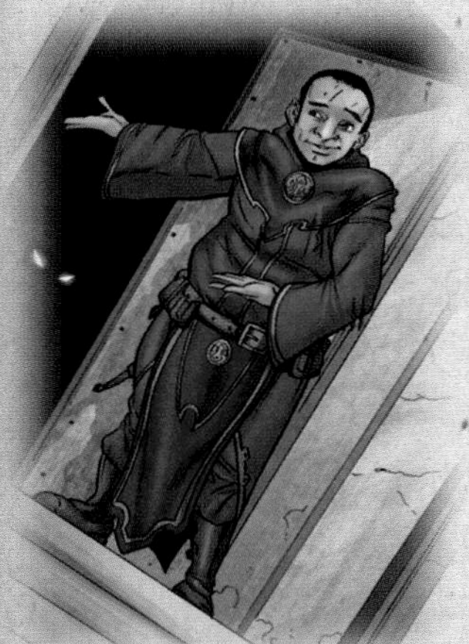

Brister Fendlestick: *A human wizard who makes his home in the Underdark. He lives in a tower made of adamantite and rarely ventures from it.*

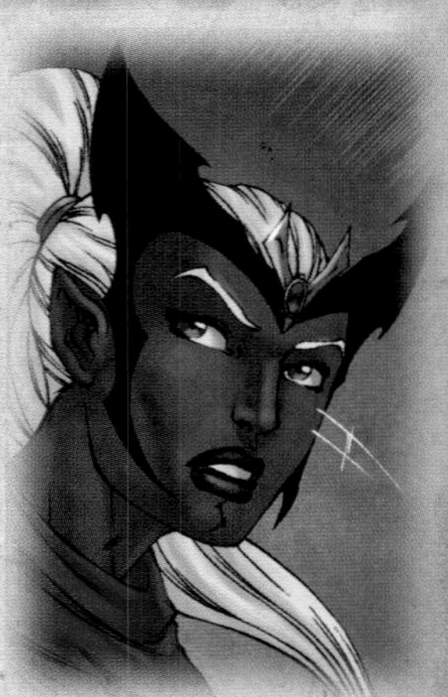

Briza Do'Urden: *The eldest daughter of Matron Malice Do'Urden, Briza is a High Priestess of Lolth. As such, she is extremely powerful, but hungers for her mother's seat of power. She is the archetypal Drow female: arrogant, selfish, beautiful, and distrustful of everyone.*

Central Brain: *The brain-like mass that comprises all the combined knowledge of the Mind Flayer (Illithid) society; telepathically connects every individual Mind Flayer, and coordinates their entire existence.*

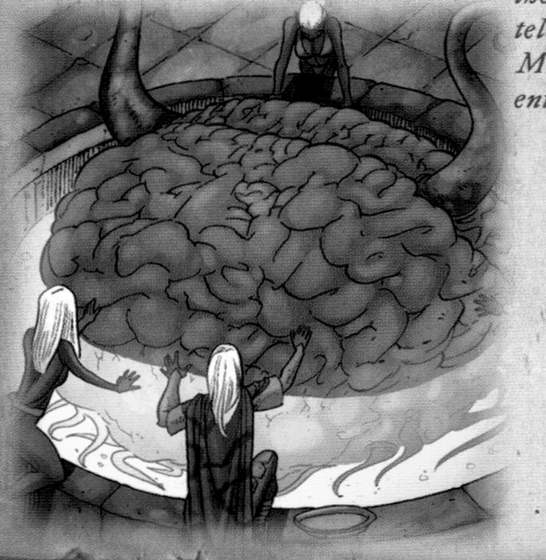

Clacker: *An innocent Pech trapped in the monstrous body of a Hook Horror, because of the spells of the human wizard Brister Fendlestick. He loses a little more of his Pech personality with every passing day.*

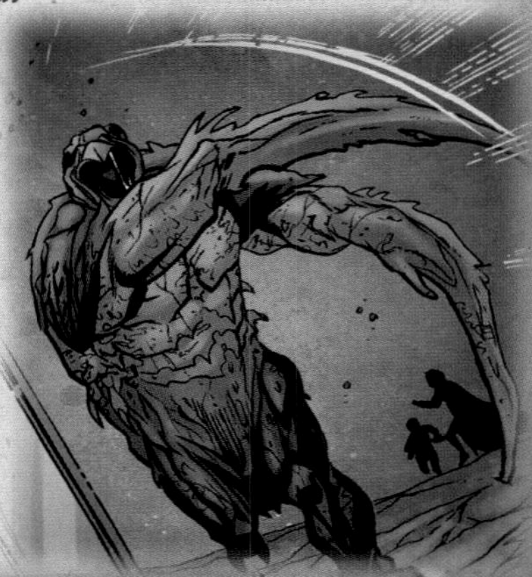

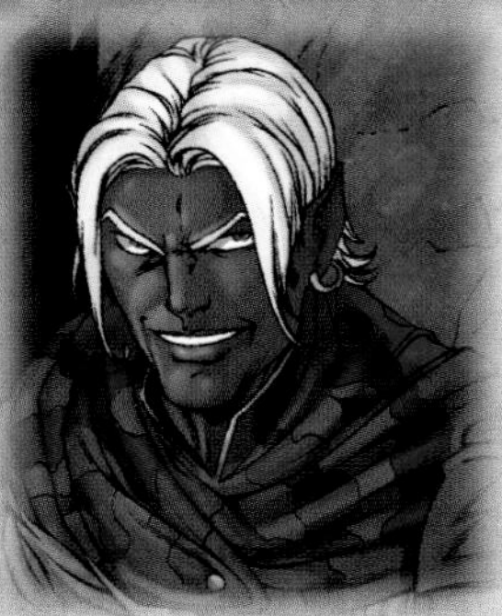

Dinin Do'Urden: *Elderboy of House Do'Urden, and older brother of Drizzt.*

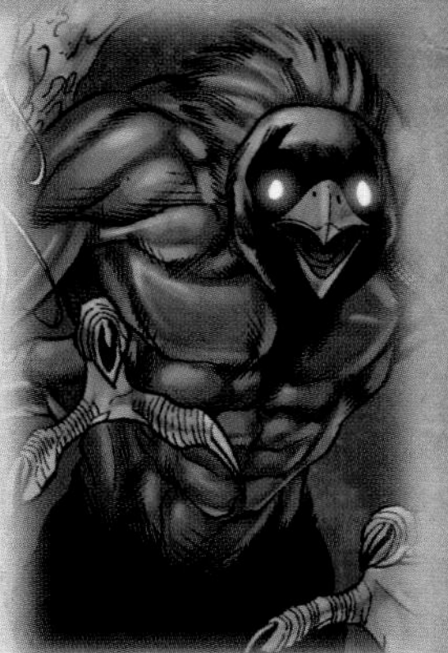

Dire Corby: *A predatory race of avian creatures who inhabit a cavernous lair filled with pools of glowing green acid.*

Drizzt Do'Urden: *A Drow warrior of exceptional ability, possessed of rare purple eyes and a noble heart—a trait almost unknown among the Drow. Son of Matron Mother Malice. Rejecting the violence and debauchery of Drow society, Drizzt underwent self-imposed exile in order to escape the bloody machinations of his mother.*

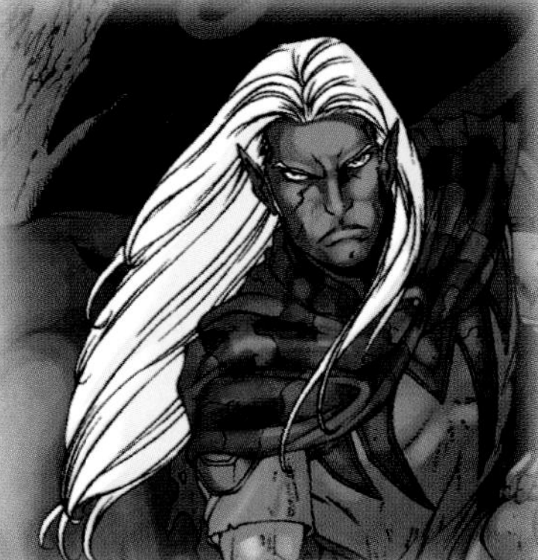

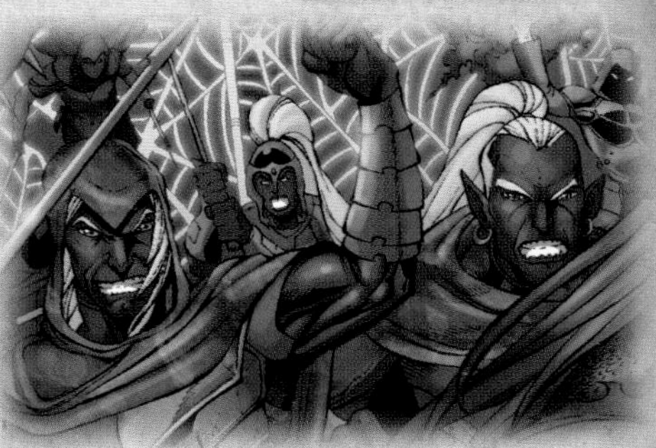

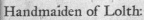

Drow: *An ebony-skinned race of elves, also known as "dark elves," who make their home in the subterranean world of the Underdark. Their violent society is ordered along matriarchal lines and is dominated by its Matron Mothers. The Drow are motivated by a hunger for individual power and wealth, and will employ any means, no matter how sadistic or treacherous, in pursuit of these goals.*

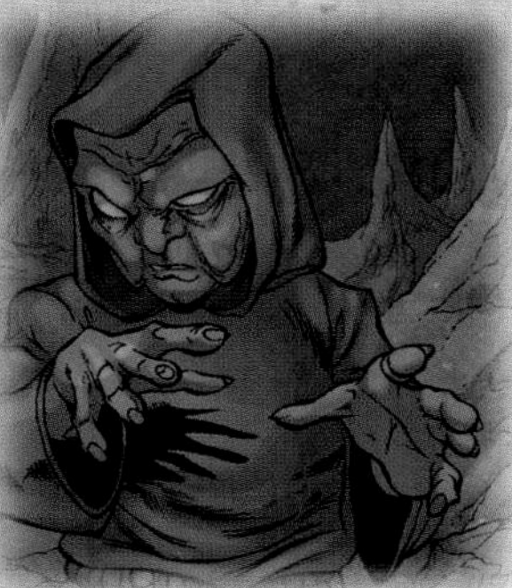

Firble: *Chief of security for the Svirfneblin city of Blingdenstone.*

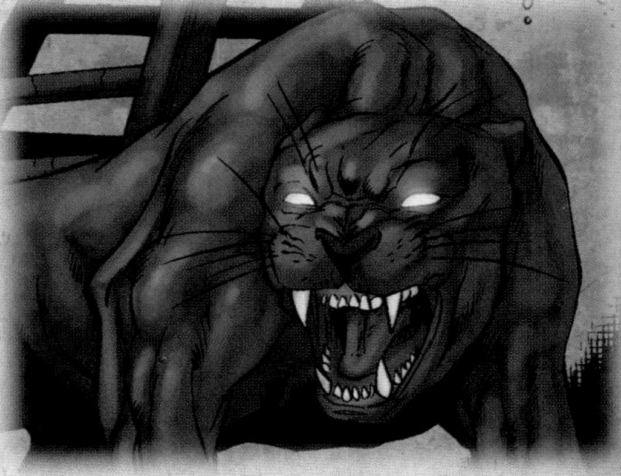

Guenhwyvar: *A black panther conjured through an onyx figurine, and the constant companion of Drizzt.*

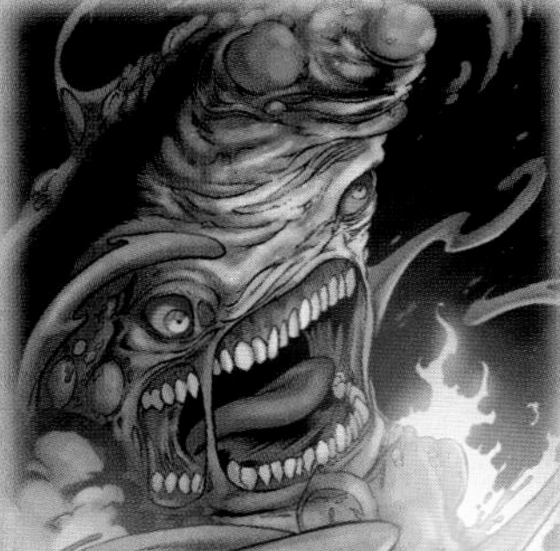

Handmaiden of Lolth: *A Yochlol, the tentacled, otherwordly entity who speaks for the evil goddess Lolth.*

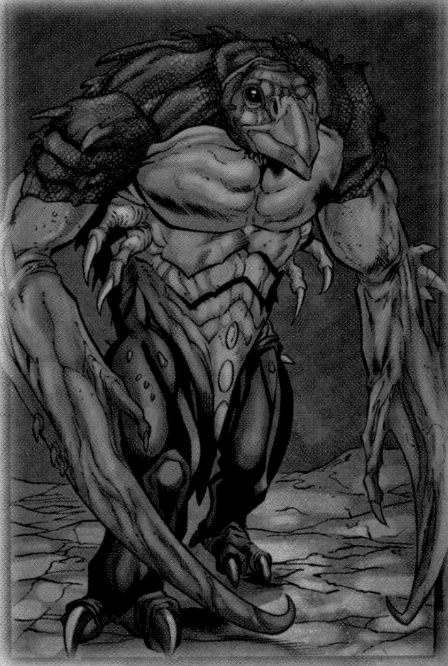

Hook Horrors: *Predators of the Underdark, these huge, armor-plated beasts utilize razor-sharp, hooklike appendages to attack their prey.*

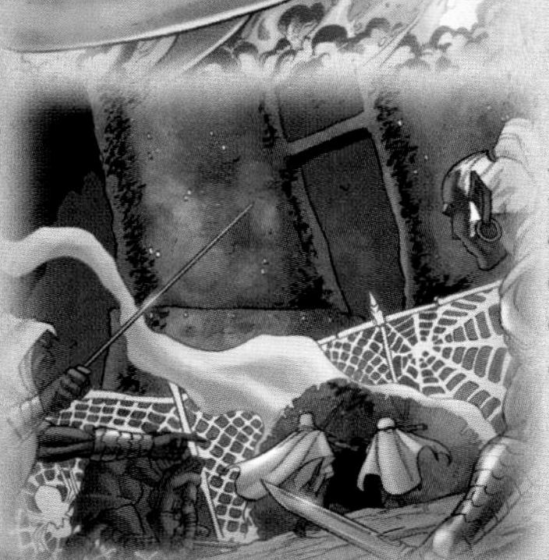

House Do'Urden: *The eighth house, or family, in the Drow city of Menzoberranzan. Ruled by the conniving Matron Malice, their quest for power has been hampered by the actions of the house's rogue son Drizzt.*

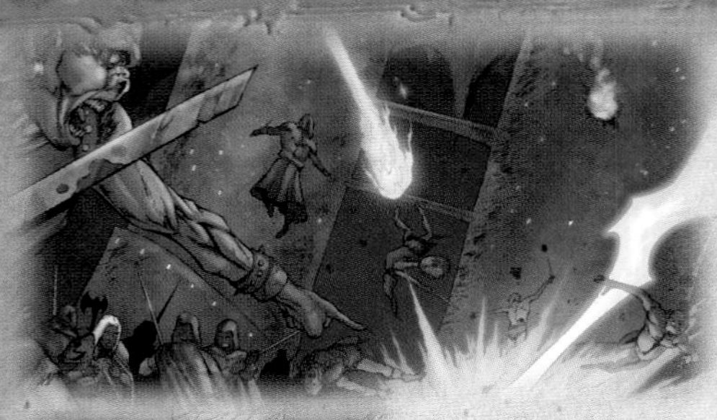

House System: *The system of government employed by the Drow of Menzoberranzan. The city's eight most powerful families (or Houses) are prepresented on the Ruling Council. Every House is constantly plotting against its rivals, either in an effort to maintain position, or to ascend to the ruling eight. Warfare is the most common result of this race for ascendancy.*

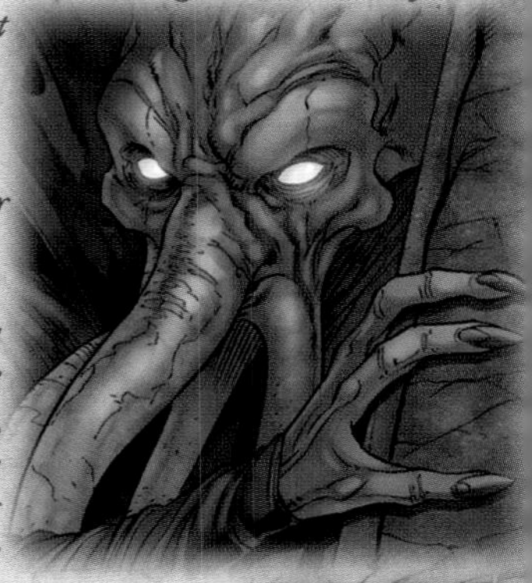

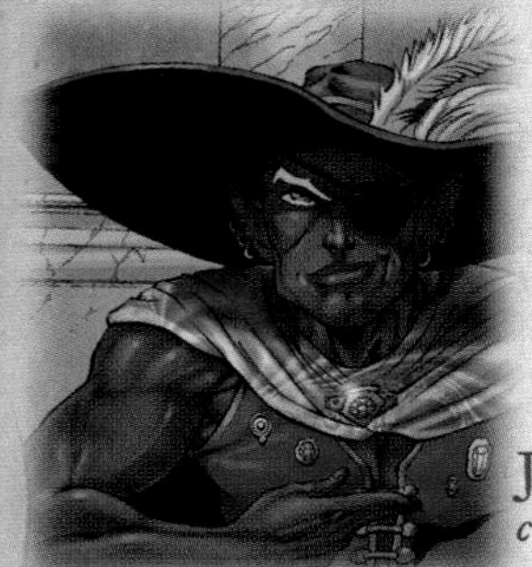

Illithids: *Telepathic creatures (also known as Mind Flayers) who mentally enslave unsuspecting pilgrims in the Underdark, forcing them to compete as gladiators in their arena of sport. When their usefulness is finished, slaves are generally consumed by their Illithid captors.*

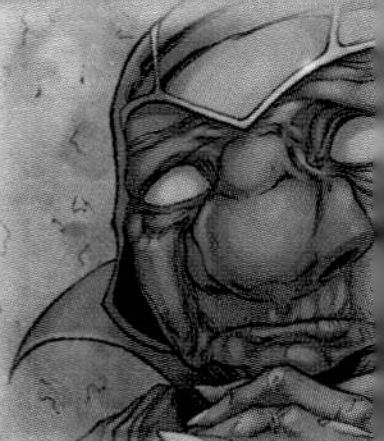

Jarlaxle: *Leader of Bregan D'Aerthe, a drow mercenary company. With his unique combination of charm and cleverness, this houseless rogue has managed to carve out a position of independence for himself and his elves.*

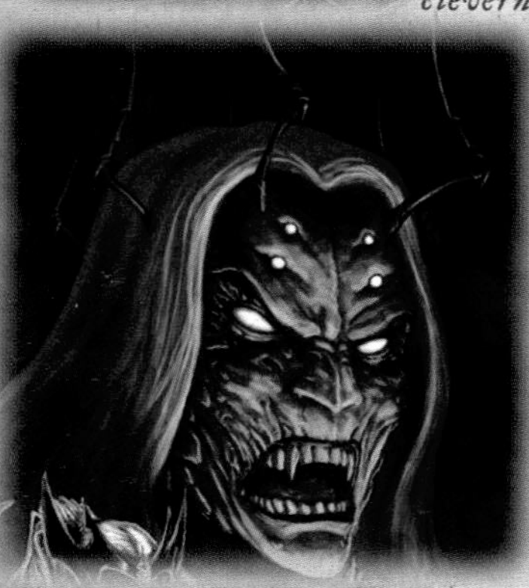

King Schnicktick: *The Svirfneblin king of Blingdenstone.*

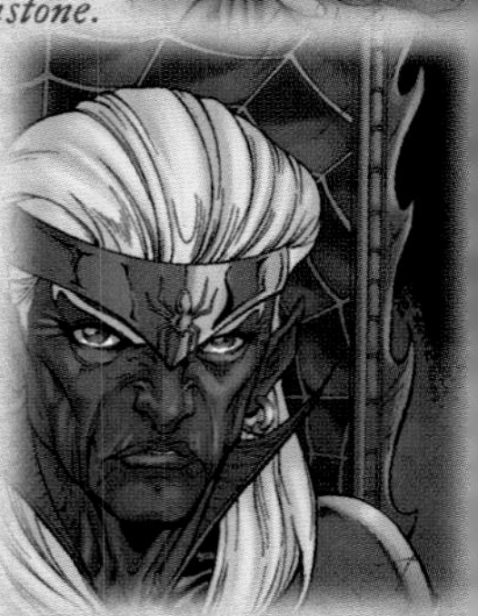

Lolth: *The queen of the Demonweb Pits, and the principle deity of the dark elves.*

Matron Baenre: *Matriarch of the House Baenre. So long as her House remains at the top of the House System, she is the most powerful figure in Menzoberranzan.*

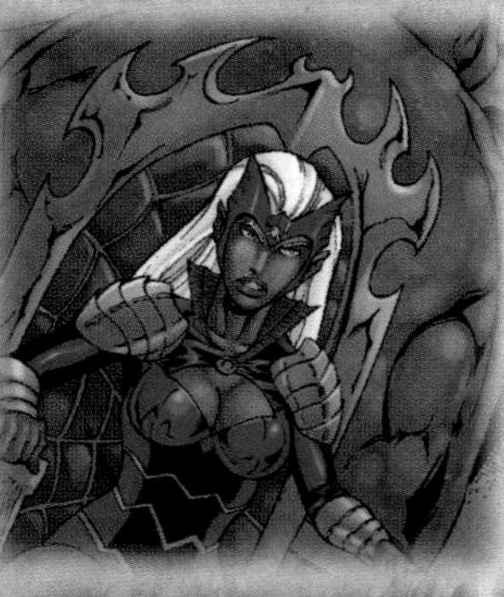

Matron Mother Malice: *Matriarch of the House Do'Urden, and the mother of Drizzt. Considered one of the most fearsone leaders in all of Menzoberranzan.*

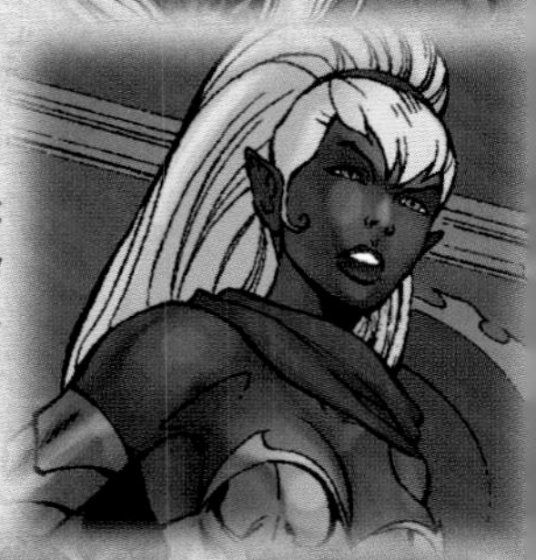

Maya: *Youngest daughter of Matron Malice, also a high priestess of Lolth.*

Menzoberranzan: *The largest and most powerful Drow city in the Underdark.*

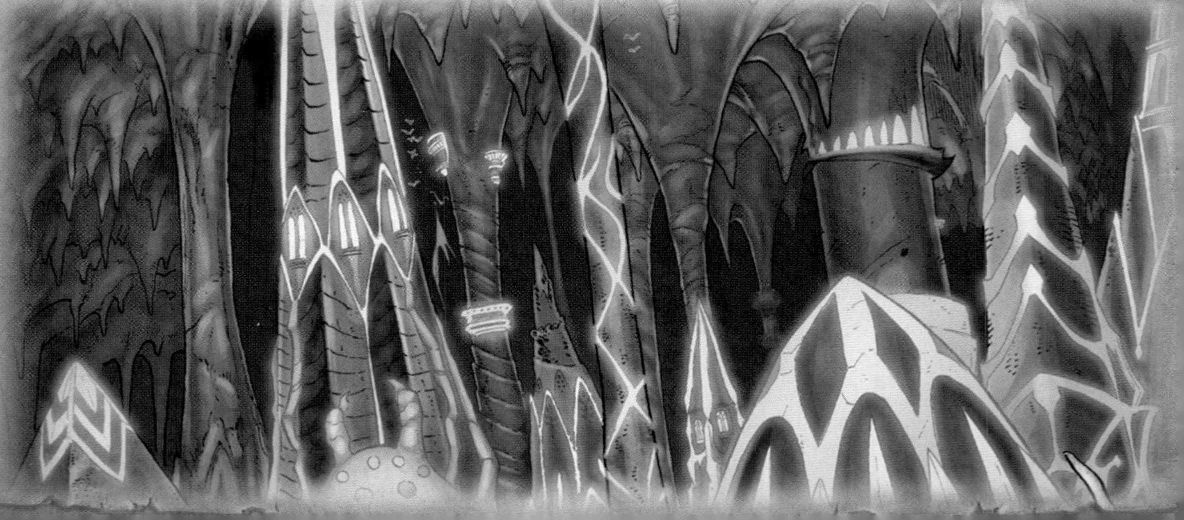

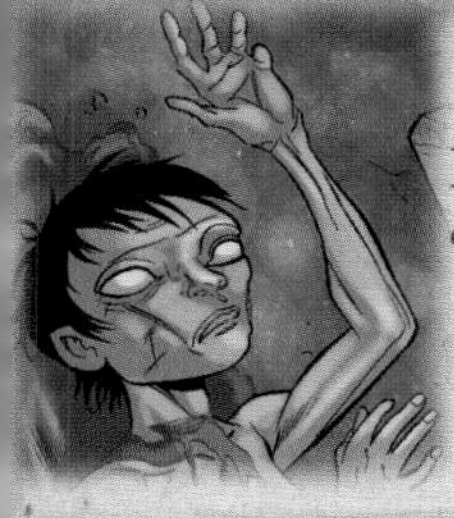

Pech: *Small, peaceful creatures who desire only to commune with the living rock of the Underdark.*

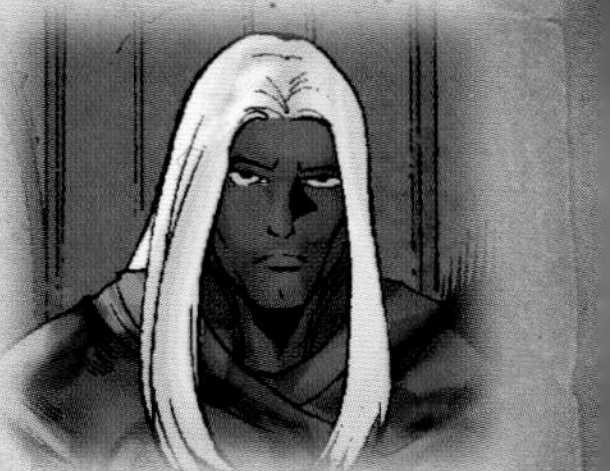

Rizzen: *Current Patriarch of House Do'Urden, and one in a long line of Matron Mother Malice's companions.*

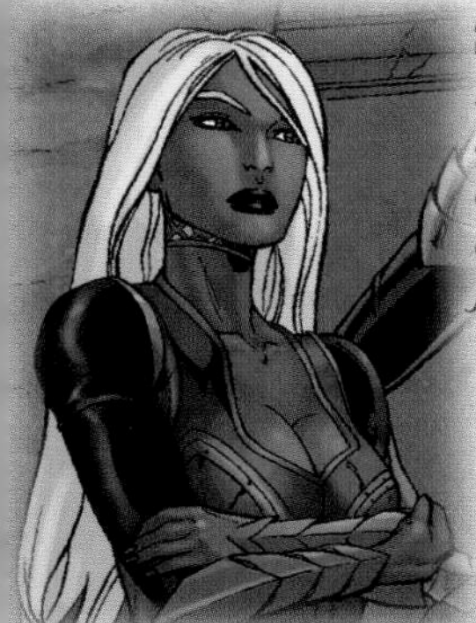

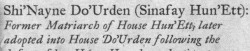

Shi'Nayne Do'Urden (Sinafay Hun'Ett): *Former Matriarch of House Hun'Ett, later adopted into House Do'Urden following the defeat of her House. Upon her adoption, to disguise her identity, her name was changed from Sinafay to Shi'Nayne.*

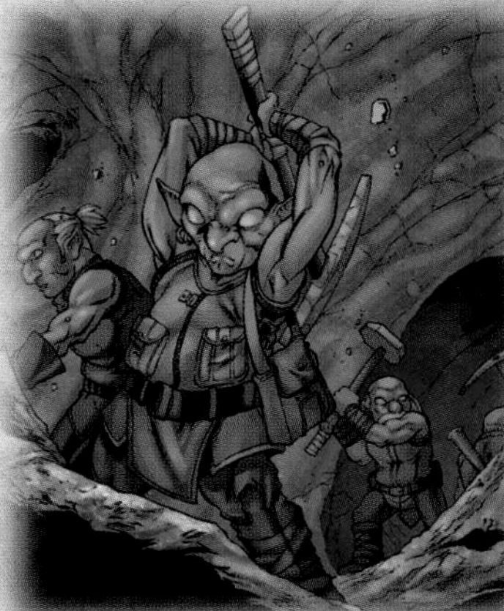

Svirfnebli: *Also known as Deep Gnomes. Neither kind nor evil, the Svirfnebli are content to live peacefully while mining the rich ore of the Underdark.*

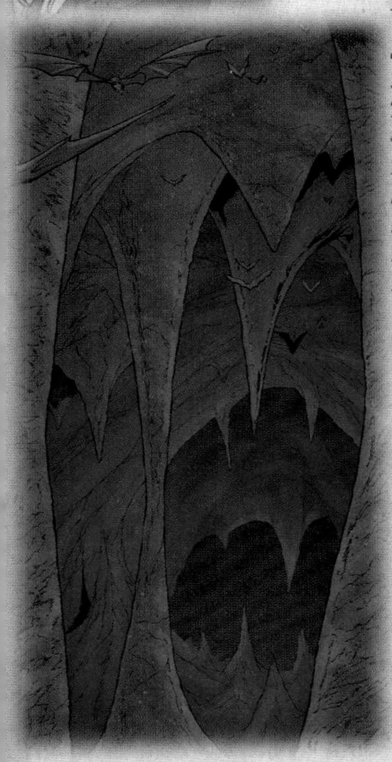

Underdark: *An extremely dangerous and expansive subterranean wilderness. Populated by races of many varieties, including the Drow, Illithids, Dire Corbys, Svirfnebli, Hook Horrors, and untold others. Central Cities include Menzoberranzan and Blingdenston.*

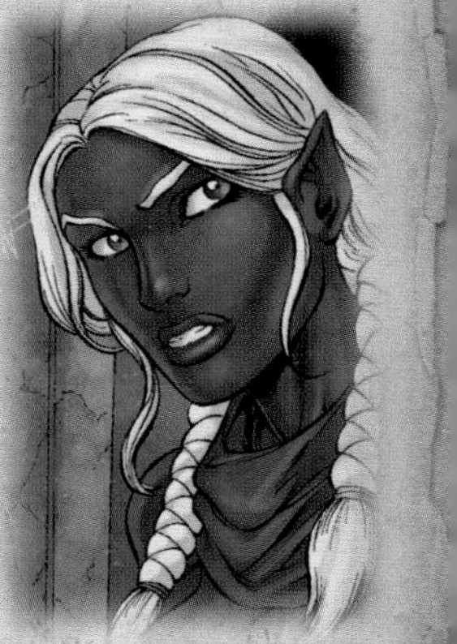

Vierna: *Second daughter of Matron Mother Malice. Responsible for the rearing of her younger brother, Drizzt, in his earliest years.*

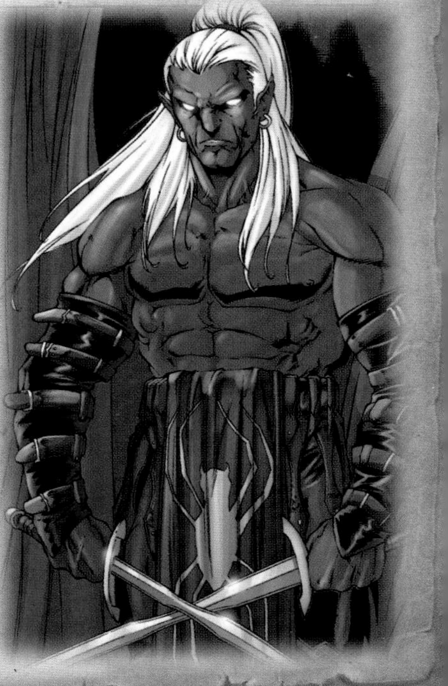

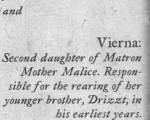

Zaknafein: *Father and confidante of Drizzt. Former Weapons-Master of House Do'Urden, once considered the most fearsome Drow warrior in all the Underdark. Allowed Malice to sacrifice him to Lolth in order to save his son. Resurrected as a mindless slave by Matron Mother Malice through the arcane Zin-Carla ritual in order to huntdown and destroy Drizzt.*

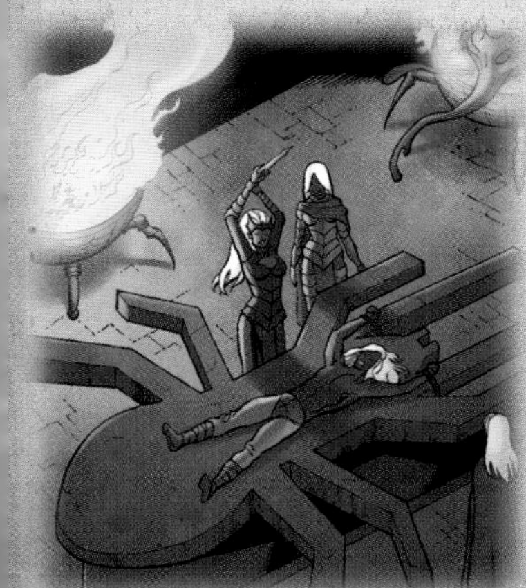

Zin-Carla: *An arcane ritual in which the goddess Lolth grants the power to raise the dead as slaves. The power of the spell derives from the power of the priestess who casts it, slowly draining her life force away. Very powerful and very dangerous, Zin-Carla occurs very rarely, even in fractious Menzoberranzan.*

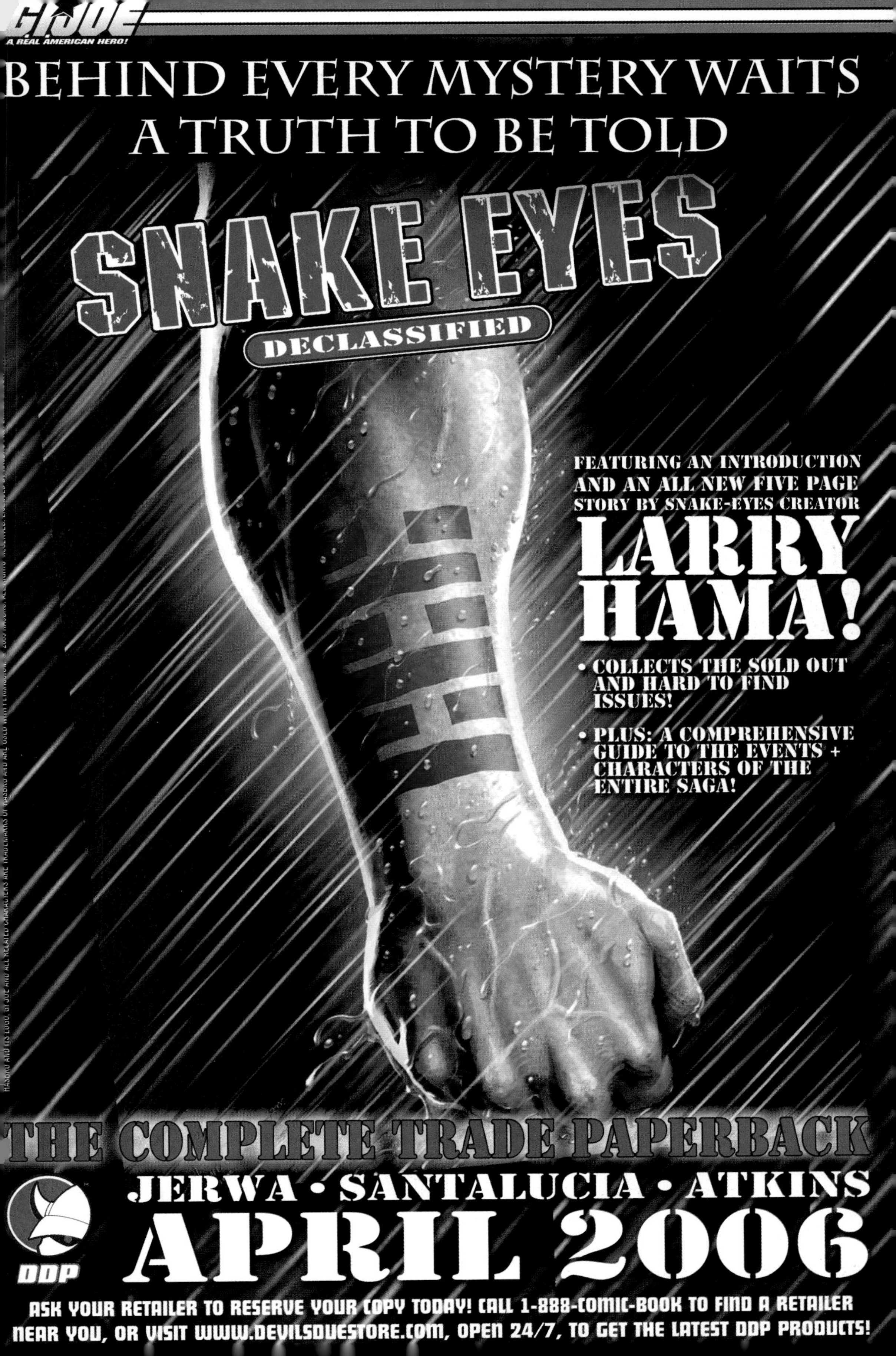
G.I. JOE
A REAL AMERICAN HERO!
BEHIND EVERY MYSTERY WAITS A TRUTH TO BE TOLD
SNAKE EYES
DECLASSIFIED
FEATURING AN INTRODUCTION AND AN ALL NEW FIVE PAGE STORY BY SNAKE-EYES CREATOR
LARRY HAMA!
• COLLECTS THE SOLD OUT AND HARD TO FIND ISSUES!
• PLUS: A COMPREHENSIVE GUIDE TO THE EVENTS + CHARACTERS OF THE ENTIRE SAGA!
THE COMPLETE TRADE PAPERBACK
JERWA • SANTALUCIA • ATKINS
APRIL 2006
DDP
ASK YOUR RETAILER TO RESERVE YOUR COPY TODAY! CALL 1-888-COMIC-BOOK TO FIND A RETAILER NEAR YOU, OR VISIT WWW.DEVILSDUESTORE.COM, OPEN 24/7, TO GET THE LATEST DDP PRODUCTS!

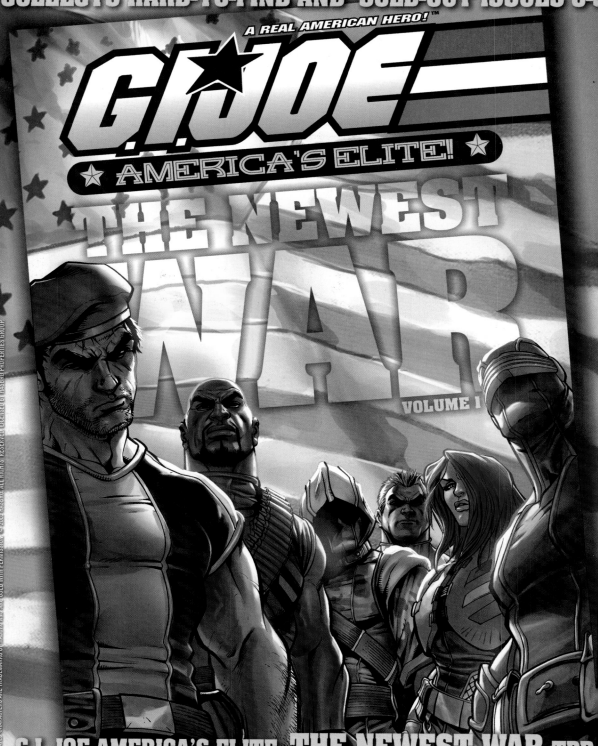